WITHDRAWN

Developmental Reading

Developmental Reading:
A Psycholinguistic Perspective

DANIEL R. HITTLEMAN

Rand McNally College Publishing Company   Chicago

Rand McNally Education Series
B. Othanel Smith, Advisory Editor

Passages on pp. 370 and 371 are from *Misty of Chincoteague* by Marguerite Henry. Copyright 1947 by Rand McNally & Company.

Passages on p. 371 are from "The Thing from Ennis Rock" by Thomas F. Monteleone, in *More Science Fiction Tales,* edited by Roger Elwood. Copyright 1974 by Rand McNally & Company.

Passage on p. 371 is from *Tonka, The Cave Boy* by Ross Hutchins. Copyright 1973 by Rand McNally & Company.

Passage on p. 370 is from *A Spy in Old West Point* by Anne Emery. Copyright 1965 by Rand McNally & Company.

Passage on p. 370 is from *Noise in the Night* by Anne Alexander. Copyright 1960 by Rand McNally & Company.

Passage on p. 77 is from *Choosing Materials to Teach Reading* by Kenneth S. Goodman, et al. Copyright 1966 by Wayne State University Press.

The "Basic Framework of a Language Experience Approach" on pp. 191–192 is from *Teacher's Resource Book, Language Experiences in Reading* by Roach Van Allen and Claryce Allen. Copyright 1970, 1966 by Encyclopaedia Britannica Press.

The passage on pp. 375–377 is from Children's Literature in the Elementary School, Second Edition, by Charlotte S. Huck and Doris Young Kuhn. Copyright 1968, 1961 by Holt, Rinehart and Winston.

Photo credits:
Rohn Engh, 68, 84, 108, 309, 314, 372, 405; Stuart Huck, 142; Dan Miller, 29, 54, 111, 344, 383; Barbara Van Cleve, 283. From Stock, Boston: Elizabeth Hamlin, 24, 50, 182, 209, 224, 265, 276; Cary Wolinsky, 392; Frank Siteman, 360; Bohdan Hrynewych, 419; Jean-Claude Lejeune, 133; Daniel S. Brody, 147; Owen Franken, 89; Anna Kaufman Moon, 190; D. Dietz, 229. From Van Cleve: Carol Ann Bales, 12, 100, 169, 320. From Jeroboam: Russell Abraham, cover, xiv; Elizabeth Crews, 41. From Rapho-Photo Researchers, Don Getsug, 7.

79 80 10 9 8 7 6 5 4 3 2

Copyright © 1978 by Rand McNally College Publishing Company
All Rights Reserved
Printed in U.S.A.
Library of Congress Catalog Card Number 76-17177

To Carol, Margo, and Jill

Preface

Developmental Reading: A Psycholinguistic Perspective is intended for use in introductory courses for teachers-in-training. My aim has been to provide a theoretical framework for creating instructional strategies that is firmly supported by recent research. The text that follows gives the teacher-in-training information about the reading process and suggestions as to how this knowledge can be applied in the classroom. I have tried not to treat topics peremptorily, since I am convinced it is wise that teachers develop an independence for making instructional decisions. The suggestions herein are only suggestions, and readers are given ample room to find their own solutions.

I view reading as a cognitive process. When readers read, they use all of their language learnings and past experiences in order to search for and reconstruct the meanings intended by writers.

The chapters in the text provide a broad overview of the nature and extent of a reading program in the elementary school. In Chapter 1, I examine the needs and functions of reading in our society and how a reading program may be established to meet those demands. In Chapters 2 and 3, I examine the psycholinguistic insights that allow for understanding how spoken and written language convey meaning, how thinking and memory develop, and what the nature of the reading process is. In Chapters 4 and 5, I examine the principles of a total school assessment program. Chapter 6 gives attention to how the teacher can develop the readiness to read any type of material at any stage of development. In Chapters 7 and 8, I trace the development of strategies that can lead pupils to understand how sentence patterns and structure words within sentences can be used to determine the author's meaning in sentences, paragraphs, and extended discourse. In Chapter 9, I examine strategies for extending vocabularies and recognizing words in context. In Chapter 10, I look at the strategies needed for reading the various content areas. In Chapter 11, I deal with the literary techniques used by authors, and in Chapter 12, I examine instructional programs for pupils who have special needs.

It is always difficult to determine where one's own ideas originate and those of others end. Throughout this text I have tried to acknowledge the influence of many colleagues, students, and friends who have responded to my ideas or whose ideas have provided me with some additional insights about the reading process. Yet, the responsibility for the form these ideas have finally taken remains mine.

One individual must be singled out for his profound influence. H. Alan Robinson, as teacher, as colleague, and most importantly, as friend, has contributed immeasurably to my professional growth and development. This acknowledgment of my esteem for him is only a token. Any repayment I can make will come through whatever positive influence my text may have on the thinking and teaching of others.

For their reviews and comments on various portions of the preliminary outline and the manuscript of this book, I wish to acknowledge the efforts of Kenneth S. Goodman, Esther Schatz, Walter J. Moore, and P. David Pearson. Their contributions were helpful and most appreciated. I would like especially to thank Charles H. Heinle, of Rand McNally, for his confidence that this text should be written and for his constant encouragement throughout its preparation. I am grateful to Geoffrey Huck, also of Rand McNally, for his discerning comments and suggestions as editor of the manuscript.

The creation of this text has been in some ways a family affair. Although the actual writing was solely my effort, everyone in the family has shared in the joys and frustrations of its creation. I dedicate this book to my wife and daughters because they have endured with patience, understanding, encouragement, and love.

Contents

Preface   vii

1   Reading Programs in Today's Society   1

Reading in a Changing World   2
Relevant Reading Programs   4
   Reading Defined   5
   Assumptions About Reading Programs   5
Organizing for Reading Instruction   6
   Philosophical assumptions   8   □   Teacher roles   9   □   Facilities   10   □   The learner's needs   10   □   Subject matter   11   □   Organizational patterns   11
The Informed Teacter   16
Discussion Questions and Activities   17
Further Readings   18

2   Understanding the Nature of Verbal Communication   25

Definition of Human Communication   25
Barriers to Communication   28
Signaling Meaning   31
   Structure of Language   33
   The Structure of English   35
   History of the English language   35   □   Phonological features   36   □   Syntactic features   40   □   Semantic features   44   □   Graphic features   46
Discussion Questions and Activities   48

3   Understanding the Thinking and Reading Processes   51

Human Thinking   51
   Human Cognition   52
   Developmental Stages of Human Thinking   53
   The Structure of Human Intellect   56
   The Structure of Human Memory   59
   Conclusion   63
The Development of Language in Children   64

Implications for Education   67
The Reading Process   69
    Significance of a Psycholinguistic Model of Reading   69
    A Psycholinguistic Model of the Reading Process   71
        Definition of reading   72   ☐   Research into the reading process   72
        ☐   Description of the reading process   73
Selecting Appropriate Instructional Materials   77
Discussion Questions and Activities   79
Further Readings   80

4 Principles of Analytical Teaching Through Standardized Tests   85

Analytic Teaching   85
Objectives of Assessment   86
Standardized Tests   88
    Characteristics of Standardized Tests   88
    Standardized Reading Tests   94
    Limitations of Standardized Tests   97
    Effective Use of Standardized Reading Test Results   101
Obtaining Information About Academic Potential   102
Discussion Questions and Activities   105
Further Readings   106

5 Strategies for Analytical Teaching Through Informal Tests   109

Useful Background Information   110
    Information About Academic Potential   111
Obtaining Information About Reading Performance   112
    Assessing Oral Reading Performance   113
        Obtaining the miscues   113   ☐   Tabulating the miscues   115   ☐   Tabulating the retelling   117
        ☐   Analyzing the miscues   124   ☐   Evaluating the Pupil Profiles   127
    Assessing Silent Reading Performance   132
        Oral retelling   132   ☐   Cloze procedure   135
Discussion Questions and Activities   138
Further Readings   139

6 Strategies for Developing Readiness for Reading Instruction   143

Readiness for All Reading   144
Development of Reading Readiness   145
Readiness for Formal Reading Instruction   148
    Strategies for Developing Readiness to Read   150
        Cognitive factors   151   ☐   Affective factors   157   ☐   Psychomotor factors   159   ☐   Linguistic factors   161
Determining Pupil Readiness to Read   168
Developing Readiness for Participating in Group Activities   171
    Group Functions   172
    Forming Groups in a Classroom   174
Resources for the Teacher   175
Discussion Questions and Activities   177
Further Readings   178

7 Strategies for Guided Reading Development   183

Using Instructional Objectives   184
The Language Experience Approach   187
    Implementing the Language Experience Approach   189
    Implementing a Thematic Unit   196
Resources for the Teacher   198
Strategies for Guiding Pupils' Reading   200
Strategies for Questioning   207
Discussion Questions and Activities   210
Further Readings   211
Appendix   213

8 Strategies for Reconstructing Meaning   225

The Reader Reconstructs the Author's Message   227
    Prediction Strategies   227
    Strategies for Understanding Textual Material   235
        Sentence reading strategies   237   ☐   Paragraph reading strategies   241   ☐   Reading longer discourse   247
Developing Strategy Learning Lessons   254
Activities to Develop Use of Reading Strategies   256
Resources for The Teacher   268
Discussion Questions and Activities   271
Further Readings   272

9 Strategies for Vocabulary Development and Word Recognition 277

Strategies for Developing and Extending Word Knowledge 278
    Increasing General Vocabularies 279
    Activities for Developing General Vocabularies 281
Using Context to Determine Unknown Words 286
    Contextual Signals to Word Meanings 287
    Activities for Using Context Signals 289
Strategies For Using Grapho-Phonological Information 292
    Clarification of Misunderstandings about Grapho-Phonological Information 293
    Effective Instruction in Grapho-Phonological Information 295
    Immediate Word Recognition 296
    Mediated Word Recognition 297
        Letter clusters 297 □ Morphological units 299
Dictionary Usage Strategies 301
    Activities for Developing Dictionary Strategies 305
Resources for the Teacher 307
Discussion Questions and Activities 310
Further Readings 311

10 Developing Strategies for Content Area Reading 315

The Structure of Content Area Materials 316
Writing Patterns in Content Area Texts 317
    Vocabulary 317
    Paragraph Structures 320
    Graphics 325
Guiding Reading in the Content Areas 328
Strategies for Independent Reading in the Content Areas 330
Activities for Developing Content Area Reading Strategies 335
Strategies for Locating Information and Using Reference Materials 339
    Locating Information in Books 340
    Locating Information in Libraries 340
    Strategies for Using the Encyclopedia 342
    Strategies for Locating Information on Maps 344
Strategies for Reading the Newspaper 345
    Activities for Developing Newspaper Reading Strategies 346
Strategies for Organizing Information 349
    Strategies for Using Outlines 350
    Activities for Developing Outlining Strategies 353
Resources for the Teacher 354
Discussion Questions and Activities 356
Further Readings 357

11 Developing Strategies for Literature Reading 361

Reading in a Pluralistic Society 362
Current Trends in Children's Literature 363
Strategies for Developing a Literature Program 365
    Recognizing the Categories of Literature 365
    Recognizing Literary Forms 366
        Fiction 366 □ Nonfiction 367 □ Poetry 367 □ Plays 368
    Recognizing Elements of Style 369
        Characterization 369
        Plot development 369
        Figurative language 370
        Theme development 371
Uses of Literature 372
Strategies for Bringing Children and Literature Together 373
    Using Library Resources 373
    Selecting Children's Literature 374
Resources for the Teacher 378
    Professional Texts 378
    Book Lists 378
    Professional Journals 379
    Instructional Materials 380
Activities for Developing an Understanding and Appreciation of Literature 381
Strategies for Using Bibliotherapy 383
Discussion Questions and Activities 385
Further Readings 386

12 Strategies for Pupils with Special Needs 393

Understanding the Needs of Divergent Dialect Speakers 394
    Black American Dialects 394
    Barriers To Comprehension 395
    Developing Comprehension Across Dialects 397
Understanding The Needs of Speakers of English As A Second Language 399
    Strategies for Teaching 402
        Assessment 402 □ Instructional strategies 404 □ Resources 406
Understanding the Needs of Pupils Who Have Difficulty In Learning To Read 406
    Identification of the Reading Disabled 408
    A Developmental Concept of Disability 410
    Assessment of Disability 411
Discussion Questions and Activities 413
Further Readings 414

Name Index 421
Subject Index 425

Developmental Reading

1
Reading Programs in Today's Society

Focus Questions:

1. How does reading fit into a world in which ideas are to a greater extent than ever being transmitted via multimedia devices?
2. What kind of school instructional program seems appropriate for the teaching and learning of reading in today's society?
3. What knowledge should a teacher possess in order to implement an effective reading program in today's society?
4. How can the classroom teacher maintain an up-to-date knowledge of reading theory and practice?

During the past decade, the teaching of reading has come under severe attack. Reading has been characterized as being "irrelevant" and even "antisocial." It has been contended that print is no longer the dominant medium of communication in our culture even though the schools are acting as if it is (Postman, 1973). This polemic is reminiscent of that of McLuhan (1964), who explained how our information about the world is being obtained more and more through multimedia devices than through print alone. (But note the following line from an advertisement: "Marshall McLuhan says the printed word is 'obsolete' and to prove it, he wrote fifteen books.")

Obviously, there are many people who do not think that reading is going to become an "art form" limited to an elitist group. There can be no denying that "reading instruction" has become a very volatile political issue. However, part of the explosive nature of the polemics results from misconceptions about the nature of reading as well as confusion over the differences between "reading" and "the instruction of reading."

Reading instruction has become a political issue

The purpose of this chapter is to examine (1) some of the functions of reading in our society today and in the future, (2) how a reading instructional program might be formulated to meet the demands of society, (3) what the components are of an instructional program which attempts to meet the demands placed upon readers in that evolving society, and (4) how teachers can maintain for themselves a current knowledge of reading theory and practice in relation to the changing demands of society.

The remaining chapters will attempt to explain the nature of the reading process, distinguish the "process" from instruction developing that process, and provide models and suggestions for implementing an instructional program that is consistent with the nature of human growth and development and the character of our society.

READING IN A CHANGING WORLD

We seem to be standing on the "edge of history" (Thompson, 1971). It is possible to look back and see what has already transpired in our society and in other societies of the world. We can look forward, although we cannot "see" the society that will be coming. But we can predict, and these predictions will shape our lives.

Where does reading fit in a changing world? There is, of course, McLuhan's point of view: changes that have occurred have made the printed word obsolete—therefore eliminating the necessity of reading—and instruction in the schools should focus on developing "literacy" in the other modes of communication.

Yet, reading is an act of communication, and as such, it shares many characteristics with other modes of communication. Now and in the future, we will have various alternatives for gaining information and communicating with other people. The educational process should provide for the development of enlightened selection of the means of communication.

Those who attempt to play down the importance of reading fail to realize that literacy, in a sense more appropriate to a changing world, means not only being able to read print, but being able to read language in all its forms. To be denied the opportunity to read is in effect to be made a "slave," as when one is "forced" to learn to read. The entire focus of education should be "to strengthen the individual's practical ability to anticipate and adapt to change" (Toffler, 1974). We must be aware that "since reading is a distinctive, human enterprise embedded in the larger contexts of communication and language, its importance emanates from its usefulness to the person doing it" (Jacobs, 1971).

Reading will never be totally replaced in our society by other media

It is hardly conceivable that reading will ever be totally replaced in our society by other communication media. Unless all books, magazines, newspapers, and other printed material are converted to other forms of media, the function of reading in our society is going to remain extremely important. Even if we accept the premise that new information does not need to be recorded in print, there will remain a need to read in order to maintain some sort of contact with our cultural heritage.

Reading has a vital role in our complex society for the development of understanding citizens. It is important for improving one's understanding of government, expanding one's understanding of contemporary conditions in conflict with the rights and responsibilities of a free people, and accepting one's obligation to participate in social and political discussions.

Reading, moreover, is the one means of communication in which the receiver of the message is in almost full control of the communicative situation. The author's intended sequence can be followed or the information can be ordered differently from that proposed by the author. Communication can begin and terminate at the reader's will. The reader can find other sources to verify meanings or find sources with differing ideas. The rate at which the ideas will be processed and also how many of the ideas will be processed can be adjusted. No other medium allows an individual this much flexibility. Even the use of pictures does not provide for total control by the viewer, for pictures have one basic shortcoming in relation to printed ideas—"you cannot make a picture of the concept of a statement" and all "statements cannot be transcribed into images" (Gombrich, 1974).

There are surely limitations in the use of the printed word for conveying ideas, and surely many ideas can be conveyed in ways other than in print. But that is not the question. That alternative modes of communicating exist does not obviate the need for reading in our society.

The idea is not to fault print as a technology. We cannot stop or retard the explosion of knowledge, nor can we usurp the freedom of the press nor the freedom of authors to write and publish. The responsibility lies in teaching pupils to discriminate between what is worthy and what is not. We have, then, a situation where we must be concerned with educating pupils to become efficient and discriminating processors of all language. The more important political and social issue is not whether individuals should be taught to read but *what* they are taught about communicating. Are they taught to question and analyze the information they receive regardless of its source? Are they literate with language in whatever form?

The important issue is *what* people are taught about communicating

The educational discussion should perhaps center around the theoretical analysis of what kinds of learning experiences can be transmitted best by books and other printed materials. ("Best" is a consideration of the efficiency and economy of the learner's achievement.) Discussion might also consider the kinds of learning experiences we want to give to the learner.

As teachers, our concern is not to be caught up on the polemic of whether reading is outmoded, irrelevant, or politically stultifying. Our concern is with developing full citizens who possess the capabilities of selecting the most advantageous means for learning at a particular time, at a particular place, and for a particular subject. Our values and knowledge of the world will be in constant flux. No one can ever be sure what the world over the "edge of history" will be like. The pupils, though, will be shortchanged if educational practices are not adjusted so that pupils can "learn what to want" and so that they can explore the "range and quality of experiences" available to them (Bell, 1974). If pupils are not provided the opportunity to learn to read, they will be forever limited in their range of choices and in the fullness and satisfaction they will be able to obtain from life.

RELEVANT READING PROGRAMS

When McLuhan stated that the "medium is the message," he was merely restating an old saying with which many are familiar: "It isn't what you say (do), it's how you say (do) it!" Various activities, meetings, or curriculum programs often have "hidden agendas." The idea that there can be two levels of purpose for an activity disturbs some people. For example, children are a captive audience, and as such, they quite often rebel when the purpose they suppose for school is not quite the same as the purpose they encounter.

This book is concerned with putting forth some ideas about the nature of an elementary school reading program. These ideas should be relevant for the world in which today's pupils must function and at the same time, prepare them for a world that may be quite different by the time they are adults. As such, the "program is part of the message." Not that *what* is done, the substance of the program, is unimportant, but *how* the program is implemented has a great impact on pupil learning. The acquisition of the reading process is an interaction among the learner, the teacher, the instructional material, and the environment in which the learning occurs. "The ways in which the child is taught to read have direct bearings on both his productivity as a reader and his aspirations about being a reader" (Jacobs, 1971).

At this point, it seems fitting to set forth a general statement of the nature of the reading process and how the *process of reading* is different from the *teaching/learning situation* in which the process develops. Much more attention will be devoted in chapters 2 and 3 to the theoretical suppositions underlying the definition of the reading process.

Reading is acquired through interaction with the teacher, the material, the environment

Reading Defined

Reading is a verbal process interrelated with thinking and with all other communication abilities—listening, speaking, and writing. Specifically, reading is the process of reconstructing from the printed patterns on the page the ideas and information intended by the author. It is somewhat equivalent to the process of listening to someone talk and reconstructing his or her ideas from sound patterns. Learning to read develops from learning to use and understand language. An ability to use a secondary language system (a written representation of language) has to be preceded by an ability to communicate in a primary language system (oral language for normal individuals). Learning to read adequately is the application of existing thinking strategies to written ideas; therefore, the cultivation and nurturing of the cognitive learning processes are integral parts of any program to develop the reading process. "Reading," Gephart says,

Reading is the process of reconstructing an author's ideas

> is a term used to refer to an interaction by which meaning encoded in visual stimuli by an author becomes meaning in the mind of the reader. The interaction always includes three facets: (1) the material to be read; (2) the knowledge possessed by the reader; and (3) physiological and intellectual activities. The variability apparent when the interaction is viewed at different points in time is a result of the variability possible in each of the several facets (Gephart, 1970).

One should not assume that the meaning intended by the author automatically becomes the meaning assumed by the reader. Errors in both the encoding and decoding of the message militate against the possibility of this one for one correspondence.

What constitutes the process of reading will affect the instructional program. However, the *teaching of reading* and *reading* must be kept conceptually apart. The environment of the classroom, the methodology of the teacher, the materials used, the strategies presented, the amount and effectiveness of practice all interrelate to aid or inhibit the development of the reading process by children. The instructional question teachers should address themselves to is not "How can I teach reading?" but "How can I best promote the learning of reading?"

Assumptions about Reading Programs

A few basic assumptions about reading programs are made in this book. Much of what ensues is an elaboration of these assumptions to illustrate how teachers might provide situations for the efficient and productive development of the reading process in children. These assumptions are:

1. All language activities have as their prime purpose communication. Reading is only learned through the attempt to "communicate" via written language.
2. There are benefits to possessing the ability to read and these benefits will aid an individual in coping with the demands of society.
3. Instruction directed toward developing the reading process is planned and purposeful, involves children in direct experiences in using reading strategies in meaningful situations, and allows children to assume some of the responsibilities for their learning.

ORGANIZING FOR READING INSTRUCTION

Reading curriculums should be based upon the premise that reading is "using language" and that the function of language is the communication of thoughts. It should be recognized that "reading is not reading without some level of comprehension, and reading materials, however simple, must have something to say; there must be some thought to be comprehended" (Goodman, 1969).

An instructional program in reading should be educationally sound

An instructional program in reading should be educationally sound in terms of general curriculum principles. The program should have a theoretical foundation and relate the means of instruction to what has been confirmed about human potential and human development. Bruner (1966) has given some general characteristics of instruction. His ideas are summarized in the following paragraph.

Learning and problem solving should depend upon the exploration of alternatives, and instruction should aid and guide these explorations. The teacher should activate the exploration of alternatives, maintain the learner's interest and constantly direct the learner's search for solutions to problems. Any idea, problem, or fact can be presented to pupils in a form simple enough so that any learner can understand it in some recognizable form. The efficacy with which the information is understood and recognized will depend upon the interaction of certain variables. Instructional techniques should be selected with consideration for (1) the age of the learners, (2) the style of learning evidenced by the learners, (3) the subject matter, (4) the mode of presentation, (5) the concepts to be learned, and (6) the conceptual capacity of the learners. The learners should be led through sequences of statements and restatements that increase their ability to grasp, transform, and transfer what is learned. Essential to learning is

Reading is "using language"

a knowledge of results at a time when the knowledge can be used for corrections. Learners should be aided in developing self-sufficiency in problem solving. This should be accomplished by always translating the information to be learned into the learners' way of solving problems.

The organized procedures for the teaching of reading strategies should provide for multiple and varied learning situations. There should be specific guidance in the development of the thinking strategies, of the pupils. The instructional activities should include teaching and learning that allows the teacher and pupils to mutually assess the pupils' needs. Instructional activities and experiences should be created to allow the development of those strategies relevant to an individual's learning needs and capabilities.

The structure given to the reading program is commonly thought of as the school or classroom organizational pattern. Many beginning teachers have been faced with the following question: "Do you group, or do you individualize, your teaching of reading?"

This question—whether posed by the principal or superintendent, by a parent, or by a colleague—often causes defensive responses by the teacher. Yet the question shows a lack of understanding of the purposes and manner of providing a flexible learning environment that fosters rather than retards the acquisition of the reading process.

In selecting school or classroom organizational patterns for learning, one does not make an either/or decision. The type of organizational pattern implemented within a whole school or within a single classroom should be selected because it "fits" the learning environment. The selection of a school or class organizational pattern should be made after consideration of various factors. These factors include (1) the concepts about learning and reading held by the school administration and the classroom teacher, (2) the recognized role(s) of the teacher, (3) the facilities available for instruction and the daily classroom interpersonal interactions desired, (4) the perceived needs of the learners, and (5) the subject matter and the format in which the subject matter is presented.

The organizational pattern should be picked because it "fits."

Philosophical Assumptions.   Different philosophical assumptions about learning are held depending upon whether one works within a Behavior-Control Model, a Rational Model, or a Discovery-Learning Model (Nuthall & Snook, 1973). With the Behavior-Control Model, teaching is conceived of as a method of controlling both the students and the conditions of learning. Sometimes the term *behavior modification* is applied to this type of teaching. The teacher working under this model considers teaching to be an application of general behavioral learning principles. A learning situation created by a teacher working under this model is one in which the learner is manipulated and instructed to follow a course of study prescribed by the teacher. An underlying assumption is that the learner will arrive at the desired outcome by successfully following and completing certain procedures. Programmed instruction is one type of instructional program that is built upon this model.

In the Rational Model, the aim of teaching is the transmission of knowledge. A student has learned when he can demonstrate that he knows, but "knowing" cannot be identified with giving answers. Knowing is an activity that is performed through the way one lives his life and functions within society. An instructional program created within this model would encourage the "search for knowledge" as an end in itself. Through "knowing," one acquires the tools for creating the "good life."

Although the Discovery-Learning Model has various descriptions, and alternate points of view about it are held, in the main it calls for (1) the creation of attractive alternatives, (2) the encouragement and the development of divergent as well as convergent thinking, (3) the rearranging and transforming of evidence, (4) the learning of the process of "discovery" through various kinds of learning, and (5) the encouragement and development of creative thinking. The psychological theory supporting the Discovery-Learning Model is not as "precise" as that supporting the Behavior-Control Model. There exists, however, very strong evidence to support it in the research of cognitive psychology, child development, and the study of creativity.

A reading program consistent with the ideas in this book would need to be developed along the guidelines of a Discovery-Learning Model. Within such a model, the instructional program would aim at (1) developing learning environments in which the pupils develop and accept some responsibility for educational decisions, rather than just follow directives, (2) tying learning not just to performing some task, but to conscious decision making as to what is appropriate at any given time, and (3) encouraging the generation of many answers rather than just accepting a "right" answer.

An appropriate reading program would use the Discovery-Learning Model

Teacher Roles. The roles teachers can play in an instructional setting are dependent upon their perceptions of the expectations of others in the immediate social and educational system, the self-concepts they have, and the value systems to which they adhere (Morine & Morine, 1973). Among the roles the teacher could decide to play are those of reporter, model, problem-poser, counselor, diagnostician, systems manager, policeman, experimenter, and consumer.

Each of these roles is valid in a classroom. Each has its valid assumptions about the teacher's expectations and about the teacher's functions in acting out that role in an instructional situation. The various roles can be used in a complementary and supportive manner. The integration of several roles can provide more options for pupils as well as for teachers. The kind and number of roles a teacher will select and perform ought to reflect the instructional situation that is served, and hence each of these roles may or may not be necessarily appropriate at all times with all children.

The kind of roles a teacher plays should reflect the instructional situation

An instructional program should always have options for diversity in order to use and develop the special talents of all individuals concerned—teachers and learners—in a manner which will be self-rewarding, educationally sound, and socially effective. The question is not, "Which role should I perform?" but rather, "Which role is appropriate for a particular instructional purpose, with a particular child or group of children, and with a particular subject matter?"

Facilities. The physical environment most assuredly places some limitations on the type of instructional organization that can be implemented. Quite often, however, the size and arrangement of rooms, as well as the age and construction of the school building, is used as an excuse for adhering to one particular organizational pattern. The facilities of a school should not be a hindrance to the creative teacher who wishes to implement a particular organizational structure or a variety of organizational structures. The decision as to what pattern or patterns to use should be in only a small way influenced by the physical conditions of the school.

The Learner's Needs. There is evidence (Havighurst, 1964) that children have a "drive" to learn. What is not fully known is whether this drive is innate or acquired, but most children display this drive. Some evidence also points to the possibility that there may be crucial periods of life in which certain learnings are more easily undertaken. The crucial periods for learning language and communicative tasks seem to be within the first twelve years of life. What does seem to be most evident, though, is that children need a curriculum that

1. Provides experiences in exploring and explaining the unfamiliar in both the social and physical worlds;
2. Offers experiences in a variety of sensory modalities and experiences while talking about these sensory impressions;
3. Develops experiences with increasingly complex social relationships;
4. Gives practice in the fundamentals of reading that are tied to relevant discussion and explanations of these fundamentals; and
5. Allows for experiences in expanding one's control of language and meanings as expressed in speech.

Learning does not seem to occur rapidly—at least not those learnings needed for long-term decision making and control over one's life. Facts are learned rather quickly, but the processes of thought and communication are acquired slowly and in a cumulative fashion. These processes require practice, and are undertaken in some sort of anticipation of reward. Factors that influence the extent to which learnings are acquired are such things as intelligence, the mode or modes of learning, motivation, and the expectations developed through family relationships (Havighurst, 1964). (See chapters 2, 3, and 4 .)

The school organizational pattern should be responsive to the needs of the children

The school organizational pattern should reflect a responsiveness to the various and varying needs of the children in any learning situation. The teacher cannot be tied to one specific organizational pattern if it does not meet the needs and purposes of all of the learners.

Subject Matter. Every subject area has some features of organization that are unique. Some subjects are more efficiently presented in certain formats and require certain strategies for their effective processing by the reader. Subsequent chapters will deal with developing strategies for reading specific subject areas in greater detail.

Organizational Patterns. The modern concept of school organization is that of providing "flexibility" (Congreve & Rinehart, 1972), that is, providing options and alternative patterns which provide for learning and teaching opportunities which would not otherwise be available. Following is a discussion of a number of school-wide and intraclass organizational patterns for reading instruction that are commonly implemented in the elementary schools.

Flexibility is providing options

School-wide plans:
Grade level classes. Classes are arranged by grade level, and all children of a particular age are grouped into one or more classes at that grade level.
Nongraded units. Groups of children are formed, usually randomly selected and representing a number of different age levels. This is sometimes referred to as a "multi-age" grouping.
Cross-class or cross-grade groupings. These are arrangements whereby children from different classrooms are regrouped for instruction in a particular content area. The cross-grade groups are usually composed of children from the same grade level. Their purpose is to reduce the range of achievement of the children; sometimes called the "Joplin" plan.
Team teaching. Two or more teachers cooperatively plan an instructional program; each is responsible for teaching a particular subject area or a particular group of children. This plan usually fits with other organizational plans, such as cross-class grouping, open classrooms, and nongraded units.
Learning laboratory. This is a special room, usually with a supervising teacher, to which children go (either as a whole class or as part of a class) for instruction in particular areas; sometimes called reading laboratory, skills center, or learning center.
Differentiated staffing. A situation in which teachers are hired because they possess unique or particular skills; also included within this type of organization are different levels of staff: master teacher, teacher, assistant teacher, paraprofessional, teacher interns (student teachers), and volunteers. The features of cooperative planning found in team teaching are part of this plan.
Scheduling or departmentalization. This is a situation in which the day is divided into periods with the children moving about much as stu-

Children have a "drive to learn"

dents do in junior or senior high school; variations of this plan include "semidepartmentalization," in which the pupils remain in a "home room" for language arts/reading instruction or language arts/reading/social studies instruction and then move to different classrooms for other instruction.

Intraclass plans:

Homogeneous grouping. A situation in which children are placed in a classroom based upon some characteristic, usually a reading or intelligence achievement test score, for the purpose of reducing the range of achievement within any one classroom.

Heterogeneous grouping. A situation in which children are placed in a classroom on a random basis without any attention given to reducing the range of pupil achievement.

Individualized reading. Usually a reference to a situation in which the pupils are allowed to select their own reading material and read as much or as little as they are capable of or wish to. Other features include (a) pupil-teacher conferences for checking progress, (b) comprehension or the answering of questions, (c) the forming of temporary groups for specific skills instruction, and (d) the sharing of the children's reading experiences with others in the class.

Needs grouping or activities grouping. Situations in which small groups of children are brought together for short-term purposes. The reason for forming the group may be that the children have some instructional need in common or that they are interested in developing an activity or a project together. No achievement level limitations are imposed in the formation of these groups.

Independent or contract learning. A situation in which the individualizing of learning is developed through specific assignments for each pupil in the class. The children's contracts, or learning assignments, are cooperatively planned by the pupil and the teacher, but the pupil has certain options depending upon the pupil's level of independence. The contract usually covers such things as the subject(s) to be covered, the material(s) to be used, the location for completing various parts of the assignment (classroom, library, skills center, etc.), the time limits, the manner of learning (self-instruction, teacher, pupil-teaming, etc.), and the manner in which the assignment will be evaluated (pupil or teacher checking); sometimes referred to as differentiated learning.

Pupil pairs. A situation in which pupils are paired for learning. One pupil sometimes possesses certain knowledge or strategies, and it is his responsibility to teach them to the other child. At other times the pair searches for certain information or processes, sharing their ideas until the assignment is completed.

Diagnostic/prescriptive instruction. A situation in which the pupils are given some pretesting to determine their status with regard to a set of criteria or sequence of learning strategies. Individual assignments and learning situations—sometimes in the form of contracts—are created to fit the diagnosed needs of the children. Follow-up testing or diagnosis is done to determine the pupils' progress or need for additional assignments in a particular area. Usually this approach is used when the curriculum is based upon a specific hierarchy of learnings.

Open classroom. This is more a concept than a specific organizational pattern. It is a classroom organization that departs from the traditional in the goals, attitudes toward children, grouping patterns, and philosophy of the teachers involved (Weiner, 1974). It is especially difficult to define and is usually described in terms of some observable characteristics. Whatever its outward form, the essential philosophy behind the open classroom is "that children are unique individuals whose learning needs can be met only in a free, active atmosphere where each child can pursue his particular interests and learning needs as they arise" (Blitz, 1973).

The patterns are not mutually exclusive

It should be quite evident that none of the above patterns of schoolwide or intraclass organization can be considered as mutually exclusive. A number of these "plans" actually rely upon other plans for their implementation. Returning to the question posed earlier, "Do you group, or do you individualize, your teaching of reading?" it can now be seen that there is reason to believe the questioner might be naive about the considerations that should be given to the organization of an instructional program for the learning of reading.

Research into the effective use of classroom organization for meeting individual differences of pupils seems to substantiate the belief that all of the above forms of organization have at least some potential. A comparison of research between intraclass and interclass organization, heterogeneous and homogeneous groupings, and divided day and whole-day instruction (Oliver, 1970) has some implications for teaching. What the research seems to indicate is that the best organizational plan for reading instruction is the one that permits the most appropriate teaching for the teacher, the pupils, and the reading lesson. Also, homogeneous groups composed of children who are selected on one criterion will be composed of children with different instructional needs. And, teachers tend *not* to move pupils from group to group to the extent that individual differences would suggest is necessary.

The research did not make it possible to state conclusively whether the advantages of the ungraded school outweigh the disadvantages. It seems that the claims of the proponents are excessive and that many advantages claimed for those who favor the ungraded structure can be achieved by excellent teachers working in a "traditional" school organization. The literature shows there are many different types of ungraded organizations in schools and that it is hard to determine whether a cause and effect relationship exists between many of the advantages and disadvantages of these patterns (Kingston, 1969). The main advantage of the ungraded structure seems to be that it accelerates the awakening to the essential inflexibility and impracticality of the self-contained classroom as a form of horizontal organization.

A summary of the issues and principal findings of homogeneous and heterogeneous ability grouping research (Esposito, 1973) shows, in part,

1. No consistent positive value for students in general or for a particular group of students to achieve more academically or to experience efficient learning conditions within a homogeneous ability grouping.
2. Evidence of an unfavorable effect on the affective development of students due to homogeneous ability grouping.

3. No improvement of achievement under either homogeneous or heterogeneous grouping patterns seems to be a factor unique to the organization and could be considered as a factor separate and apart from curriculum modifications.
4. Teaching methods, materials and other variables that can be considered intrinsic to the learning process could be conceived more readily as having a cause and effect relationship with achievement than could the type of grouping pattern.

Research concerned with the sociological conditions for effective student/teacher interactions and the effect of classroom environmental variables on learning seems to verify the conclusions found in the above research. Pupil growth and learning seem to be directly related to the kind of teaching done in the classroom. It appears that certain personal characteristics of a teacher may be as important in determining success in teaching as any particular knowledge or set of skills. Effective teaching seems to occur in those situations where there is some kind of conscious rationale for the relationship between what the teacher does and what the pupils do. Good teachers seem to be asking the question, "Do instructional activities take place as planned and are they producing the outcomes intended?" Also, the relationship between the teacher's activities and the pupils' learning will depend upon the state of the social system in the classroom. In school, the teacher has the right and the obligation to control and evaluate the pupils. Learning appears to be dependent upon how this authority is used (Cohen, 1972).

Another conclusion reached about learning in the classroom is that it is dependent upon a number of interacting variables. In any determination of the success of a learning situation, consideration should therefore be given to the developmental history of each member of the group, including background conditions, personality variables, cognitive variables, socio-economic status, and sex. These variables, in fact, seem to interact with the behavior of the participants in a certain environment (Randhawa and Fu, 1973).

From the above research, the inference can be drawn that there is no one organizational pattern which can be construed as ideal for all instructional situations. The question ceases to be one of selecting an "open" or "individualized" approach in contrast to a "self-contained" or "grouped" approach, but rather how best to integrate the various kinds of instructional organization patterns and procedures into an efficient and effective learning climate. As such, organizational patterns will be viewed primarily as an administrative device that never eliminates the individual differences existing between and among all children. "Openness" and "individualization"

No one pattern is ideal for all situations

seem to be as much attitudes as they are organizational procedures. Since there can never be a true homogeneous or heterogeneous group, organizing the classroom should not become an end in itself, but must always be a means for realizing the goals and objectives of a relevant reading program.

The degree to which children undertake directed and independent study should vary with different circumstances. In individualized instruction, each child does not need to work independently (which can sometimes be a very lonely undertaking), nor does each child need to do something completely different from all others, nor do all children need to work simultaneously. Individualized instruction means providing for the growing needs of every pupil by giving each the type of organizational structure that pupil needs to learn.

Reading is reconstructing an author's ideas

An educator needs to be a scholar in the field of education

THE INFORMED TEACHER

In order to develop lifelong learners among their pupils, teachers themselves must be lifelong learners. A continuously growing body of knowledge exists in almost every subject area. Teachers should, of course, be knowledgeable about the world in which they live. They should as well be familiar with the body of information that constitutes the field of education. The purpose of this book is not to inform teachers about their world. This they must do on their own. Suffice it to say, teachers should not only live their lives "as a teacher." To be complete human beings they must have interests that go beyond the vocational training they are or have been receiving. Thompson (1971) put it very succinctly when he stated that if an individual "could not survive the subtraction of his job from his identity, then there wasn't really much to him in the first place."

Yet as an educator, one needs to develop scholarship in the field of education by keeping abreast of current research, publications, theoretical positions, and instructional practices. Reading, since it is a communicative process, is the concern of many people and not just of educators. Many allied fields of study have both their own specialized knowledge of and their own techniques for approaching the study of reading. From the study of sociology, mass media and social class structure, social psychology, child development, cognitive and language development, linguistics, psycholinguistics, educational psychology, the media of instruction and behavior analysis, optometry and ophthalmology, and perception have come and will continue to come contributions to the development of techniques for learning the reading process (Spache, 1968). The classroom teacher must develop discriminatory tastes as to which information appears valid and insightful for the guiding of learning in a relevant reading program. Just as children should cultivate the art of critical and questioning acceptance of written communication, so must the classroom teacher. We must be wise consumers in the scholastic market.

As a teacher who is concerned with providing an educational program to foster the growth and development of the reading process, you must be a reader yourself. To develop readers who are independent and self-reliant, who are comfortable and proficient in the handling of reading matter from many sources and disciplines, who search for alternatives to problems without dogmatically accepting the "printed word" just because it is printed, who realize that education does not occur just within the walls of the classroom, to develop readers who can do all these things, you must be able to do them yourself. Schools that are going to develop the complete human potential of their pupils must be staffed with teachers who recognize their own human and humane qualities and are continually searching to fulfill their potential as informed teachers and citizens of our society. As Jacobs (1971) puts it:

> The essence of being human is to be in charge of one's life—to assume responsibility for oneself, to be willing to renew and remake oneself on the basis of evidence that renewal and remaking are essential to one's well-being as an individual.

DISCUSSION QUESTIONS AND ACTIVITIES

1. How would you explain to a group of parents why their children should learn to read? What factors or characteristics of the school population would you have to take into consideration when formulating your answer? After considering the manner in which you would explain this issue, what would be the thrust of your presentation?

2. Explain how proponents of two different school or classroom organizational patterns might react to the following statement by William Armentrout (1970):

> School has the obligation to provide flexibility and diversity for the vast differences and rates of growth children come to school with.

3. Explain what the following statement by John Goodlad (1969) means to you:

> Take the educational environment beyond school and classroom and learning can be humanized.

4. What is your reaction to the following statement by H. Alan Robinson (1969)?

> The saddest scene is to observe those teachers who work in the midst of a changed environment but don't recognize it—who go on trying to do what they have learned and, in the face of failure, blame their failure on the learners.

5. What has appeared in the professional literature about classroom organizational procedures—grouping, individualizing instruction, "open" classroom—in the last year?

For students who are currently teaching:

6. Keep a record for one week of the different grouping procedures you have used in your classroom. What kind of activities did you undertake in each grouping? Might any particular instructional lesson have been made more effective if done with a different grouping procedure? What kind of activities and groupings seem to go together best?

7. Keep a record for one week of the different roles you have used as a classroom teacher. Did you use the same type of role in all instructional situations? Did you use a different role for the teaching of arithmetic or social studies? Did you ever start out to function in one role and find that you had to change roles? If so, what was it that made you change?

FURTHER READINGS

The national Right to Read movement has made the teaching of reading a political issue, and the critics of the "reading establishment" have not gone unanswered. The following book contains Postman's original article and reactions to it from leaders in professional organizations, reading specialists, a teacher, and a publisher.

> Winkeljohann, Sr. Rosemary, ed. 1973. *The Politics of Reading: Point-Counterpoint.* Newark, Del.: International Reading Association/ERIC-RCS.

In his book, *Future Shock,* Toffler explains how rapid change in technology and values affect our daily lives. In the following book he has drawn together new writings of leaders in education, psychology, psychiatry, sociology, and the humanities which should be of special interest to teachers.

 Toffler, Alvin, ed. 1974. *Learning for Tomorrow: The Role of
   Future in Education.* New York: Random House.

Many teachers are concerned about what exactly is an "open classroom." Barth has spelled out twenty-nine assumptions about learning and knowledge that a teacher should consider before undertaking to "open" a classroom.

 Barth, Roland S. 1971. "So You Want To Change To An Open
   Classroom?" *Phi Delta Kappan,* October, pp. 97-99.

To help the teacher solve some of the dilemma about classroom organizational patterns, the following short but highly informative book deals with such topics as the nature of individual differences and various ways a school and classroom can be organized to meet the demands of pupil differences.

 Ramsey, Wallace Z. 1967. *Organizing for Individual Differences.*
   Newark, Del.: International Reading Association.

The teacher who wishes to be informed about resources related to the study and teaching of reading quite often is at a loss as to what information is available and where it can be found. The following guide should prove helpful in finding many of these information sources.

 Davis, Bonnie M. 1972. *A Guide to Information Sources for
   Reading.* Newark, Del.: International Reading Association and
   ERIC/CRIER.

There are two professional organizations dedicated to dispensing information about the teaching and learning of the verbal communication processes: The International Reading Association (800 Barksdale Road, Newark, Delaware 19711) and the National Council of Teachers of English (111 Kenyon Road, Urbana, Illinois 61801). Both publish journals (provided for all members) geared to the elementary school teacher. The International Reading Association publishes the *Reading Teacher*, which usually includes articles on all aspects of reading and language arts. Each issue (about eight per school year) contains five to ten articles, comments from readers, news of recent materials or instructional and professional literature, brief summaries of recent research, and information about the Association. The National Council of Teachers of English publishes *Lan-

guage Arts (formerly *Elementary English*), which includes articles and information about all aspects and phases of instruction in the language arts. Each issue (about eight per school year) contains about thirty major articles and is usually devoted to one or two major themes. Book reviews and information about Council activities are included in each issue. Both the *Reading Teacher* and *Language Arts* have advertisements about educational products.

Other magazines that devote all or a part of their editorial space to areas of reading and language arts are:

Reading Newsreport. Multi Media Education, Inc., 11 West 42nd Street, New York, NY 10036

Instructor. The Instructor Publications, Inc., P.O. Box 6099, Duluth, MN 55806

Teacher. CGM Professional Magazines, Inc., 22 West Putnam Avenue, Greenwich, CT 06830

The Elementary School Journal. The Elementary School Journal, 5835 Kimbark Avenue, Chicago, IL 60637

Reading World. The College Reading Association. Publications Business Manager. Shippensburg State College, Box 356, Shippenburg, PA 17257.

Two basic reference sources for finding general articles as well as research articles about the area of reading and its related topics are the *Education Index* and the *Current Index to Journals in Education.* These are monthly publications, with semiannual and annual cumulations, indexes to periodicals, book reviews, government documents, conference proceedings and yearbooks. *The Education Index,* which has subheadings arranged by author and subject, and the *Current Index to Journals in Education,* which has only subject subheadings, have some duplication of articles, but not enough to warrant the use of one index over the other.

As an aid to educators in locating and using information about the American educational system, a national network of information clearinghouses was established and is supported by the U.S. Office of Education/Department of Health, Education and Welfare. The purpose of the Educational Resources Information Center (ERIC) is to provide ready access to current research results and related information to the people who need it—teachers, administrators, researchers, educational policy-makers, and interested members of the general public. The ERIC Clearinghouse on Reading and Communication Skills (ERIC/RCS) is one center in the nationwide network whose task is to organize, analyze, and make available documents and products that will serve as basic information resources for people interested in the field of reading. There has been a wide variety of resources produced, including the Guides to Information Sources in Reading, state-of-the-art monographs (produced in conjunction with the International Reading Association and/or the National Council of Teachers of English), interpretive monographs directed to special audiences, special bibliographies and reviews, broad subject bibliographies, basic references on reading, and bibliographies related to special ERIC collections. Many of the above documents are reproduced in hard copy, but all of them are available in microfiche. The ERIC materials are found in the educational/periodicals section of most college and university libraries and in the periodicals section of many public libraries. All resources of the ERIC system are cataloged in the monthly journal, *Resources in Education* (RIE).

Teachers whose interest is in children's literature and its related aspects will be interested in *The Calendar,* a semiannual newsletter provided by the Children's Book Council, 175 Fifth Avenue, New York 10010, for a nominal, one time, handling fee. *The Calendar* reports on new publications, dates of interest for stimulating the use of books in the schools and libraries, information about authors and illustrators, free or inexpensive materials provided by commercial publishers, and suggestions for fostering the "reading habit."

Teachers wishing to be placed on mailing lists so they can receive catalogs and brochures about products can contact the publishers of instructional materials advertised in the professional journals. Quite often, publishers are willing to send teachers examination copies of instructional materials appropriate for their teaching situations. Names and addresses of the major educational publishing houses are easily obtained from the advertisements in any of the journals and magazines mentioned previously.

Of course, the teacher, seeking to maintain a current view on how the educational scene is viewed by the general public, should be aware of the many reports, articles, and critiques that are published in the mass media. Newspapers and popular magazines often carry articles pertaining to the teaching and/or learning of the reading process.

References

Armentrout, William A., ed. 1970. *What Should the Purpose(s) of American Education Be? A Collection of Notable Responses on the Subject.* Dubuque, Iowa: Kendall/Hunt.

Bell, Wendell. 1974. "Social Science: The Future as a Missing Variable" In Alvin Toffler, ed. *Learning for Tomorrow: The Role of Future in Education,* New York: Random House, pp. 97–104.

Blitz, Barbara. 1973. *The Open Classroom: Making it Work.* Boston: Allyn and Bacon.

Cohen, Elizabeth G. 1972. "Sociology and the Classroom: Setting the Conditions for Teacher-Student Interaction," *Review of Educational Research* 42:441-52.

Congreve, Willard J., and Rinehart, George J., eds. 1972. *Flexibility in School Programs.* Worthington, Ohio: Charles A. Jones.

Esposito, Dominick. 1973. "Homogeneous and Heterogeneous Ability Grouping: Principal Findings and Implications for Evaluating and Diagnosing More Effective Educational Environments." *Review of Educational Research* 43: 163-79.

Gephart, William J., et al. 1970. Application of The Convergence Technique to Basic Studies of the Reading Process. Final Report, Project No. 8-0737, Grant No. 0EG-0-8-080737-4335. Washington, D.C.: U.S. Office of Education/DHEW.

Goodman, Kenneth S. 1969. "A Communicative Theory of the Reading Curriculum." *Elementary English* 46:290-98.

Gombrich, E. H. 1974. "The Visual Image." In David R. Olsen, ed. *Media and Symbols: The Forms of Expression, Communication, and Education.* Chicago: University of Chicago Press, pp.: 241-270.

Goodland, John I. 1969. "The Schools vs. Education." *Saturday Review.* April 19, pp. 59ff.

Havighurst, Robert J. 1964. "Characteristics and Needs of Students That Affect Learning." In H. Alan Robinson, ed. *Meeting Individual Differences in Reading.* Chicago: University of Chicago Press, pp. 6-20.

Jacobs, Leland B. 1971. "Humanism in Teaching Reading." *Phi Delta Kappan,* April, 1958. Pp. 464-67.

Kennedy, John M. 1974. "Icons and Information." In David R. Olsen, ed. *Media and Symbols: The Forms of Expression, Communication, and Education.* Chicago: University of Chicago Press, pp. 211-240.

Kingston, Albert J. 1969. "So the Advantages of the Ungraded Schools Outweigh the Disadvantages?" In Nila Banton Smith, ed. *Current Issues in Reading.* Newark, Del.: International Reading Association, pp. 308-16.

McLuhan, Marshall. 1964. *Understanding Media.* New York: Signet Books.

Morine, Greta, and Morine, Harold. 1973. "Teaching." In John L. Goodlad and Harold G. Shane, eds. *The Elementary School in the U.S.* 72nd Yearbook of the National Society for the Study of Education. Chicago: University of Chicago Press, pp. 243-71.

Nuthall, Grahan, and Snook, Ivan. 1973. "Contemporary Models of Teaching." In Robert M. W. Travers, ed. *Second Handbook of Research on Teaching.* Chicago: Rand McNally, pp. 47-76.

Oliver, Marvin E. 1970. "Organizing for Reading Instruction." *Elementary School Journal* 71:97–104.

Postman, Neil. 1973. "The Politics of Reading." In Sr. Rosemary Winkeljohan, ed. *The Politics of Reading: Point-Counterpoint.* Newark, Del.: International Reading Association/ERIC-RCS, pp. 1–11.

Randhawa, Bikkar S., and Fu, Lewis L. W. 1973. "Assessment and Effect of Some Classroom Environmental Variables." *Review of Education Research* 43:303-21.

Robinson, H. Alan. 1969. "Reading in the Total School Curriculum." In J. Allen Figurel, ed. *Reading and Realism.* Newark, Del.: International Reading Association.

Toffler, Alvin. 1974. "The Psychology of the Future." In Alvin Toffler, ed. *Learning for Tomorrow: The Role of Future in Education.* New York: Random House, pp. 1–19.

Thompson, William Irwin. 1971. *At the Edge of History: Speculations on the Transformation of Culture.* New York: Harper and Row Colophon Books.

Wattenberg, Ben. J. 1965. *This U.S.A.* New York: Simon & Schuster.

Weiner, Roberta. 1974. "A Look at Reading Practices in the Open Classroom." *The Reading Teacher* 27:438–442.

2

Understanding the Nature of Verbal Communication

Focus Questions:

1. What do verbal and nonverbal communication systems have in common? How do they differ?
2. What can cause a breakdown in the communication process?
3. What are the basic structures of human language?
4. How is meaning signaled in present-day American English?

DEFINITION OF HUMAN COMMUNICATION

In the broadest sense, communication is all of the procedures by which one mind may affect another. Human communication is the process by means of which people relate to each other.

Language is the vehicle of verbal communication. It is an arbitrarily agreed upon pattern consisting primarily of human vocal sounds that retain their significance in different situations. The next section of this chapter contains a more detailed discussion of the structures and patterns of language and how they represent meaning.

Communication is the means by which information is transmitted from one human to another or from one group of humans to another group. It generally entails three stages: transmission, perception, and evaluation.

A message may be transmitted via means that are either verbal (language) or nonverbal (previously agreed upon or accepted patterns of

Communication is the transmission of information from one person to another

FIGURE 2-1: The Communication Process

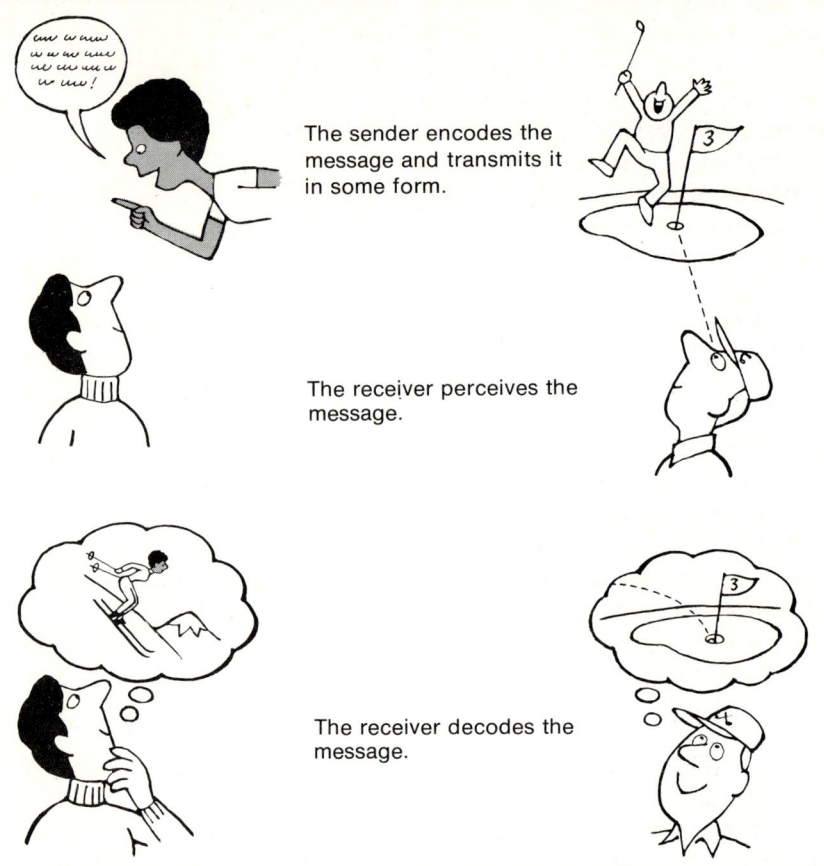

meaningful silent signals). The message, once received, may be retained or remembered for future reference or may necessitate a decision on the part of the receiver. In the latter case, the receiver may become the transmitter.

Human communication must be examined within the context in which it is used, that is, the cultural situation. "Every cultural pattern and every single act of social behavior involve communication in either an explicit or an implicit sense" (Sapir, 1967). Competence in using cultural patterns or codes is reflected in a person's ability to participate in social activities. This means that no manner of communication, either verbal or nonverbal, is learned outside of a social setting. Human communication is only learned in contact with and in relation to other humans. How well an individual learns to communicate with others determines how well he or

Human communication is learned only in contact with other humans

she will function within that social setting. Therefore, it may not be possible to take on the cultural practices of another group except through participation in that other group (Byers and Byers, 1972).

Nonverbal communication is sometimes referred to as *metacommunication* or as a *paralinguistic system*. It is the way individuals convey information, feelings, and attitudes without the use of words. These are referred to as languages because, like verbal means of communication, they are codified patterns of cues and signals to the members of a cultural group or social organization. They are usually learned intuitively by the group's members.

Sign languages, which constitute one form of nonverbal communication, generally consist of pictures. These may be stylized representations of actual things, places, or events, or they may be symbols of these situations. (For example, the international motoring pictures and symbols are examples of pictorial language.) Sign language, in addition, includes the body movements and gestures used by individuals as they perform various social acts. The individual who uses hand motions a great deal while speaking and who gesticulates differently because of attitude changes is easily recognized. These gestures do not necessarily represent what is being said. How often, for instance, can boredom be recognized by the body posture of someone regardless of that individual's spoken words?

Another form of nonverbal communication includes various kinds of intentional movements, like pantomime and dance, to convey a meaning. The intentional display of material things is also nonverbal communication. What is worn, the car that is driven, the house that is lived in, the manner in which an office is decorated, all are communications about feelings, beliefs and attitudes.

There is a strong relationship between the verbal and nonverbal communication systems of a culture. So much so, that many verbal messages really come across on two levels: (1) the statement itself, and (2) the factors pertaining to its interpretation. The receiver of a message quite unconsciously uses the nonverbal signals that accompany the verbal message in the interpretation of a message. The transmitter of the message may, also quite unconsciously, but sometimes very consciously, use paralinguistic signals. These signals are used to enlighten the receiver of the message or to obscure the true meaning of the message. The role of gesture in daily communications is so important that "one may intuitively interpret the relatively unconscious symbolisms of gesture as psychologically more significant in a given context than the words actually used" (Sapir, 1967).

The verbal and nonverbal systems work closely together

Other nonverbal communication signal systems to which all humans respond are the intonational patterns of speech and the use of space. The volume of a verbal message many times conveys meanings that reinforce or contradict the message delivered verbally. In addition, the pitch of one's voice portrays attitudes and feelings. Often there is a response to the openness of a speaker's voice, that is, the hollow or resounding effect of the voice, rather than to the message itself. Listeners are often affected by the softness or sharpness of speech (drawls or tight-lipped staccato speech). Also, the tempo of speech does much to influence the way a message is received.

In summary, human communication consists of an arbitrary, systematic set of symbols that are associated with ideas, feelings, and attitudes. The verbal signals—commonly spoken or written language—transmit meaning among individuals or groups on a conscious level. Nonverbal signals—signs, actions, gestures, vocal features—transmit meaning usually on an unconscious level. The verbal and nonverbal signaling systems are learned intuitively within a cultural setting in interaction with other humans.

Human communication consists of an arbitrary, systematic set of symbols associated with ideas, feelings, attitudes

BARRIERS TO COMMUNICATION

Some breakdown in the communication process may occur if an individual is unaware of any or all features of a communication code. The most immediately striking and apparent situation is when two individuals speak different languages. However, there are more subtle barriers to effective communication. These, because they are not consciously realized, can be confusing to the sender and the receiver of the message. The subtler aspects of communication are very important. In fact, one who is not familiar with the subtleties is likely to be baffled by the significance of certain kinds of behavior, even though there is thorough awareness of the general external forms and the verbal symbols that accompany them (Sapir, 1967).

Communication breaks down when one does not know the code

Although all communication is dependent upon some accord between the sender and the recipient of the message, it is impossible to know ahead of time the degree to which the agreement exists. Only after the message has been sent and attempts have been made to receive and evaluate it are breakdowns evident.

Failures in the communication of significant messages may occur when:

1. The receiver has a limited capacity. In humans, this would be any physical or cognitive inability of the receiver to effectively receive and evaluate a message.

Language is the vehicle of human communication

2. Unwanted noise is interjected. Static is easily recognized when it interferes with the reception of clear radio signals. Yet many times emotional noise blocks effective communication as easily as does environmental noise. Emotional noise may take the form of unstated assumptions by the receiver about the intended message. These assumptions, or prior expectations, are realized through the connotations given to certain words. When the receiver's connotations differ from those of the speaker, the intended communication does not occur.
3. The message is transmitted in a confounding manner. The speaker might make ambiguous statements or deliver it with nonverbal signals that contradict the verbal ones.

Language is marked by all sorts of variability that often remains just below the surface of awareness. Effective communication does not occur unless the individuals can participate in the life activities of a social group.

They are deemed competent in that group if they can use the group's communication system. An individual's skill in using verbal language is usually judged by looking at the message itself. That is, the verbal message is examined to see if it matches up to what was expected. When there is a high degree of correlation, the person is considered competent in using language skills. An individual's nonverbal communication competence is judged by examining what is occurring among communicators. When there seems to be reciprocal understanding among the communicators, efficient communication is considered to have occurred.

These insights have ramifications for the classroom. "When we teach children how to participate in communication with others, we are teaching them how to learn" (Byers and Byers, 1972). Quite often, an individual's failure to learn is due to the presence of a barrier to effective communica-

Failure to learn is often due to the presence of a communication barrier.

FIGURE 2-2

SOURCE: From *Amelia Bedelia* by Peggy Parish, illustrated by Fritz Siebel. Text copyright 1963 by Margaret Parish. Pictures copyright 1963 by Fritz Siebel. Reprinted by permission of Harper & Row.

tion. Simple translation of a verbal message will not overcome the lack of communication between a teacher who speaks English and a child for whom English is a second language. Also, dialogues between speakers of divergent dialects are not always successful because of felt, but not consciously realized, linguistic or emotional static. More about this will be discussed in Chapter 12.

Effective classroom communication between the teacher and the pupils, and among the pupils as well, is the result of a classroom environment that grows out of a sharing of knowledge by all within that classroom. Teachers have the responsibility for detecting the presence of differing social or cultural viewpoints that might impede communication. Once these have been identified, a shared system of communication can be developed. The result might well be the elimination of misunderstandings and conflicts that occur in many classrooms.

SIGNALING MEANING

Certain generalizations about language are accepted by linguists, as follows:

1. Language, any language, is a system of arbitrary vocal symbols used for human communication. The key to understanding languages in general is that they are systematic. The structure of any language can be described and predicted.

    Languages are systematic

2. All languages allow their speakers to deal with the world. In fact, no known natural language is any more advanced than any other. Each language can express any experience understood by its users.
3. The arbitrary vocal symbols are associated with objects and actions by convention. The users of a language agree (usually implicitly) to a relationship between the sounds uttered and the concepts to which the sounds refer.
4. Every language is unique and can be described only in terms of its own structure. It might be possible to compare languages, but only their similarities and differences can be noted. The structure of another language or the rules of how one language signals meaning cannot usually be used to explain these procedures in another language. For example, a knowledge of the rules of

how Latin conveys meaning will not necessarily help in the understanding of the way in which English conveys meaning.
5. All languages presently being used by some group or society in the entire world are constantly undergoing change. Examples of changes in present-day American English are most evident in the new words entering the language and the new meanings being assigned to already existing words. More subtle changes are evident in the dropping of the adverbial *ly* in a statement such as "Go slow!" Other changes include the use of alternative pronunciations of words (*add VER tiz ment* and *add ver TIZE ment*), variant spellings of the same word (programmed and programed), and the different ways for constructing what become accepted, grammatical statements ("I think I should go" and "I think that I should go").
6. The details of a language system must be learned within a social setting.
7. A spoken language generally varies from place to place, with social or occupational status, and in differing social situations.
8. Every language has built into its structure a factor of redundancy, that is, a feature in which meaning is signaled in more than one way. For example, in English, in the sentence "The boys are here," the information regarding plurality is signaled not only by the "s," but also by the form of the verb *to be* (Wardhaugh, 1972; Marquardt, 1965).

A distinction is usually made between the *structure* of language and the *function* of language. Structure refers to the form of the language. Function refers to what language is used for. Aside from its role as a means of expressing and recording thoughts, language functions as the tool with which we think. In a subtle way, it may play a part in shaping our thought processes.

> **Psycholinguistics is the science that investigates the mental processes that underlie language use**

The meaning of the term *psycholinguistics* may now become clearer. Psycholinguistics is the science that investigates the mental processes that underlie language use. The individuals engaged in this study make a distinction between language as a communication system and cognition as the thought processes of the language user. Because of the increasing evidence that thought and language are mutually inclusive, some researchers are led to the conclusion that "thinking is always thinking in some language" (Schaff, 1973). Language is conceived as a template or screen through which the world is codified. The language of a society or group provides the categories into which the events of the world are placed. When a language does not have a specific category for an event, a

FIGURE 2-3: Chomsky's Transformational Theory of Grammar (1965)

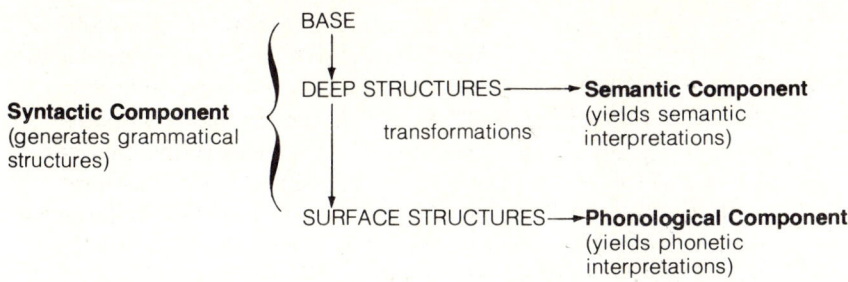

Note: Chomsky has recently modified his theory so that the Semantic Component interprets *Surface Structures* rather than *Deep Structures*. For our purposes, it will be worthwhile to ignore this refinement.

distinction, or some aspect of reality, then one of two things seems to happen: (1) the event or distinction is totally ignored, or (2) it is placed into another category and the two events, although observed by members of another group as different, are conceived to be the same thing. This is another way of saying that unless two individuals share similar social and linguistic contexts, then communication is impossible.

Structure of Language

Many of the psycholinguistic insights discussed here emanate from the theory of language developed by Noam Chomsky and called *generative* or *transformational grammar*. His theory is called generative because it tries to explain how speakers are able to produce, or generate, all of the sentences of their language. A generative grammar of a language is a "system of rules that can . . . generate an indefinitely large number of structures" (Chomsky, 1965). Figure 2-3 is a representation of the components of a natural language grammar.

Chomsky's theory postulates that language is a system of three components: (1) the syntactic, (2) the semantic, and (3) the phonological. The syntactic component is that which deals with the formation of sentences. The study of syntax is the study of how sentences are formed in a language. Semantics is the study of the meaning of linguistic units. The semantic component is that which deals with how meanings are assigned

Chomsky's generative or transformational theory of grammar tries to explain how speakers produce all the sentences of their language

The system has three components: the syntactic, the semantic, and the phonological

to strings of words. The phonological component is that which deals with how strings of words are put into sounds and transmitted. As we are concerned with written language, we can, without damage to Chomsky's model, call this component the grapho-phonological and specify that it determines how words are written as well.

The theory holds that for every generated, or produced, sentence there is a *deep structure* that determines the semantic interpretation given to the sentence. This deep structure specifies the basic syntactic relations that hold among the elements of the sentence, and is considered to be close to the basic underlying meaning of the sentence. The *surface structure* is arrived at by repeated application of certain formal operations called grammatical transformations. The surface structure is the form of the sentence that is either spoken or written. It is the only form of a language that we can truly observe and describe.

The syntactic component is said to contain two subcomponents, the base and the transformation rules. The base contains a definition of the system of grammatical relationships, and determines the ordering of the parts of a sentence. It also contains a denotative lexicon. This is a dictionary of terms about which there is a fairly consistent symbol-referent relationship and in which there is the absence of any emotional or attitudinal overtones. The transformation subcomponent determines which of a number of alternative rules will be used to arrive at the surface structure. Two sentences having the same deep meaning but which have undergone different transformations and thus are represented by two different surface structures are:

The hungry cat ate the bird.

The bird was eaten by the cat that was hungry.

The rules about sentence production and transformations in all languages deal, to varying degrees, with such things as word order, inflectional endings, and structure words. Although not all languages consider the order of individual words in a sentence at all times as meaningful, we all are aware of differences that exist among languages in word placement. Languages differ in the placement of the subject and its modifiers and in the ways they may reorder words to change simple statements into questions. Inflectional endings are used in languages to indicate tense, parts of speech, plurals, mood, the status of the speaker or hearer, agreement between different parts of speech, and voice. Structure words do not usually have any direct meaning in themselves, but are words that indicate relationships among other words. They also assist other words in express-

---

The deep structure specifies the basic syntactic relations

ing meanings. Languages may employ rules in one or more of the above categories. The rules may parallel or be completely different from those of another language.

The semantic component pairs the deep structure of a sentence with its meaning. The semantic component gives interpretations to terms, "colors" the dual or multiple meanings of words, deals with certain aspects of specialized vocabulary, places limitations on the common parlance that may be used in various situations, and changes meanings within the context of a social situation.

The semantic component pairs the deep structure with its meaning

The grapho-phonological component determines what sounds or graphic representations will be given to the message. This component determines, in addition, such things as intonational patterns, stress, accent, and pitch, and the junctures, or pauses, used by speakers.

It should not be inferred that any part of this process actually goes on inside the head of a speaker. The base, transformations, deep structures, and surface structures are convenient linguistic notions that help explain numerous phenomena. It is postulated that these notions have biological correlates of some sort, though none have yet been identified.

The Structure of English

The structure of modern American English might be better understood through an understanding of its origin and the changes it has undergone. The brief description of the history of the English language will be followed by a discussion of the phonological, semantic, and syntactic structures of present day American English. This will then be followed by a description of the features of written English and some differences between the written and spoken forms of our language.

English has changed over time

History of the English Language. The known history of the English language begins sometime during the sixth or seventh centuries when the Germanic Angle, Saxon, and Jute tribes invaded Celtic Britain. The Germanic languages belonged to the large family of languages known as Indo-European from which almost all the languages of Europe and India are said to be descended. (At present, there is no known language ancestor for all of the spoken languages known to exist, or to have existed, in the world.)

In the eighth or ninth centuries, known historically as the Middle Ages, texts written by English writers began appearing. The English of this period is called Old English or Anglo-Saxon. The English spoken from about the year 1100 to the Renaissance (about 1450 to 1550) is generally called Middle English. The language of Shakespeare, called Early Modern English, was spoken until about the beginning of the eighteenth century. From that time to the present, the English that has been spoken is called Modern English. These classifications are entirely general, and tend to distinguish social history rather than language characteristics. However, the historians of language use these distinctions to try to account for the gross differences in language that existed between these periods.

In its early periods, the English language was influenced greatly in the form of its grammar and vocabulary by other languages. Old English was influenced by the language of the invaders from Scandinavia and by the Norman invaders and conquerors. During the late Middle Ages, changes were caused by the strong influence of the French language. Early Modern English, that spoken during the age of world exploration, was influenced as a result of the contact of English with many different cultures. American English from the 1700's on developed separately from British English through constant contact with Dutch, Spanish, French, the various Indian languages, German, the Scandinavian languages, Yiddish, and the speech of the Afro-American.

The sounds of English have undergone changes, too. Many of these changes are easier for us to follow for the Old English and Middle English periods because the spellings in these periods had a more direct relationship to the pronunciation of the words. After the Middle English period, spellings were more consistent and unified. No longer was it necessarily true that pronunciations were reflected in the spellings. To identify the different present-day American regional pronunciations and to classify changes in these sounds, special records must be kept. As we shall see below, consistent and fixed spelling patterns aid us today in written communications across regional speech patterns. On the other hand, they keep us completely unaware of changes in pronunciations that have occurred and are occurring.

Phonological Features. The human voice can make hundreds of different sounds. However, each language uses no more than a few dozen of them. Even though there is considerable overlap among languages in the sounds used, no two languages share exactly the same sounds.

The particular sounds of a language are called *phonemes*. The individual phonemes do not carry any meaning in themselves. It is only to sequences of phonemes that meaning is assigned. Within a speech community, there is an implicit agreement to group speech sounds into a few dozen classes. These are the particular sounds that constitute the phonemes of a language. When speakers of a language recognize two

Each language uses only a few dozen of the hundreds of possible vocal sounds

sounds as being significantly different, then two distinct phonemes exist. But if the differences in pronunciation are not considered to change the word, then the two sounds are considered to be variations of the same sound. For example, the English sounds /t/[1] and /d/ are recognized as being distinct sounds. The words /tad/ and /dad/ are different words. Yet the /p/ heard when *pit* and *sap* are pronounced, although physically and acoustically different, are not considered by English speakers to be different. Therefore, they are considered as one phoneme.

All English speech sounds are made by the muscular movement of the speech organs as breath is expelled. Traditionally, the phonemes of a language are divided into two groups, consonants and vowels. A consonant is a speech sound in which the breath is stopped, hindered, or diverted while being emitted. A vowel is a speech sound in which the vocal tract is open and the tone is selectively changed as it passes through the resonating chambers of the throat and head. Differences in the vowel sounds depend upon the position of the tongue and changes in the shape of the mouth opening and cavity.

Some disagreement exists as to the exact number of phonemes that are used in English. There is more consensus of opinion as to the number of consonant phonemes than there is as to the number of vowel phonemes. Generally, it is felt that twenty-four consonant sounds are used. Depending upon the source and method of categorizing, the number may be higher or lower (Fairbanks, 1940; Friend, 1967; Meyers, 1966). Table 2-1 contains one listing of the phonemes of present-day American English.

The categories of consonants are: (1) stops, (2) fricatives, (3) affricates, (4) nasals, (5) liquids, and (6) glides. The stops are produced by impeding the flow of breath by either the lips or some part of the tongue. The fricatives are produced by forcing air through an opening restricted by the lower lip or the tongue. Affricates are produced in a manner similar to the fricatives except that the tongue comes in contact with the roof of the mouth just behind the front upper teeth. The stops and the fricatives, can be either voiced or unvoiced, that is, together with the flow of air the vocal cords can be made to vibrate. The only difference between /f/ and /v/, for example, is that the latter is voiced. The nasals, all of which are voiced sounds, are produced by emitting the sound through the nasal passage rather than through the mouth. The liquids are produced by emitting air

Languages allow their speakers to deal with the world

---

1. A letter within slash marks, such as /t/, represents the spoken sound usually associated with that letter or group of letters. When there is possibility of confusion, examples will be used. An italicized letter or word represents the written form.

TABLE 2-1: The Phonemes of Present Day American English

Consonants
  Stops
    /p/   pig, nipple, speak, rap
    /b/   big, tumble, stab
    /t/   take, stop, little, fat
    /d/   dog, middle, mad
    /k/   kite, skate, tickle, back
    /g/   got, bigger, rag
  Fricatives
    /f/   fat, rifle, fluff
    /v/   vote, savor, save
    /th/ them, either, clothe
    /th/ think, ether, cloth
    /s/   sink, hassle, pass
    /z/   zone, fuzzy, quiz
    /sh/ shell, fashion, fish
    /zh/ vision, mirage
  Affricates
    /ch/ chin, kitchen, such
    /dj/ fudge
  Nasals
    /n/   name, manner, fin
    /m/   miss, hammer, ram
    /ng/ ring
  Liquids
    /l/   long, follow, fill
    /r/   rabbit, barrel, tear

Vowels

	Front		Center		Back	
High	/ee/	feet			/oo/	pool
	/i/	it			/oo̱/	look
Mid	/ay/	table	/u/	up	/oh/	nose
	/e/	bed				
Low	/a/	act	/o/	ox	/aw/	saw
			/ah/	Amen		

  Diphthongs
    /ie/ pie, final
    /ow/ cow, found
    /oy/ boy, soil
  Glides
    /w/   win, away
    /y/   yes
    /h/   have

over or around the tongue. Glides are like vowels in that the stream of air is relatively unimpeded in the oral cavity, but nevertheless act like consonants in the flow of speech.

There is much less agreement among speech and language researchers as to the exact number of vowel phonemes that are used in present-day

American English. Since the production of a vowel depends upon the position of the tongue, a very large number of different sounds can be produced. All could conceivably be considered as vowel sounds. It is only through ear training during the speech acquisition process that individuals learn how to distinguish a few of these sounds as the usable vowels for any language. There is general agreement about the nine relative positions of the tongue during the production of English vowel sounds. In Table 2-1, "front," "center," and "back" refer to the placement of the tongue in relation to the teeth (front) or the throat opening (back). The labels "high," "mid," and "low" refer to the height of the tongue in relation to the roof of the mouth. The low vowels are generally produced with a wider mouth opening than are the mid or high vowels.

In addition to the basic vowels, there are a number of vowel combinations called *diphthongs*. These are produced by combining two of the basic vowels. The "basic difference between a diphthong and a vowel is that in a diphthong two vowel elements are blended in rapid succession" (Fairbanks, 1940).

It is no wonder that confusion exists among reading teachers over the teaching of the "vowel sounds" since there is a lack of agreement among the linguistic experts who study the phonology of American English. It should be evident that all speakers of American English *know* the vowel sounds. The confusion among educators arises because they try to teach these sounds to pupils who already know them. Where the emphasis should be placed is in helping pupils make the association between the sounds of the language and the printed symbols used to represent these sounds. A great deal of frustration on the part of teachers and pupils can be avoided if variant forms of the phonemes are recognized. No value judgment should be placed upon the various pronunciations themselves. Many of us probably do not pronounce the words *idea, father, dog,* and *merry* the same, and the main differences in the way they will be pronounced will be in the vowel sounds. We have learned to consider the variations caused by regional and individual speech patterns as normal, and to treat variations in vowel sounds most of the time as not significant in terms of meaning.

Other features of spoken English are the phonemic elements of stress, pitch, and juncture. Stress refers to the relative loudness of a syllable or word. Four levels of stress are usually indicated: primary, secondary, tertiary, and weak. They are signals to differences of meaning. For example, one way we know the difference between the noun *record* and verb *record* is by the shift in stress. Also, /GROWING corn/ is not the same as /growing CORN/.

Pitch is the relative level of a speaker's voice in speaking. English is considered to have four pitch levels. We can see by the example below that a change in pitch level can signal a change in meaning:

```
                       ing
                    go
   /we are all
                              home/
```

```
                              home/
                       going
   /we are all
```

The first follows the normal intonational pattern for a declarative statement, the second follows the normal intonational pattern for a question.

Juncture is a phonemic element closely related to pitch. Juncture refers to the pauses made between syllables, words, phrases, and sentences. Most of these pauses are so slight that they are almost imperceptible. Together with stress and pitch they combine to convey various meanings. The feature of juncture is what helps us, together with other syntactic and semantic features, to distinguish between *Seymour* and *see more, night rates* and *nitrates, scenic* and *see Nick,* and *syntax* and *sin tax.*

Word order in English is important

Syntactic Features.   The normal English sentence contains a subject and a predicate. In English, the order of words in a sentence is very important. In fact, the order of certain classes of words is quite often how meaning is signaled.

The main English word classes are nouns, verbs, adjectives, adverbs, and structure words. How a word should be classified is determined more by how it is used in the sentence than by any dictionary designation it might be given. The first four classes of words are considered *content words.* These words have basic referents in the world and usually carry the content or subject of a message. The fifth class of words are considered *structure* or *function words* because they do not generally have any meaning in themselves. Their purpose is to act as markers of the content words and to establish relationships between the classes of words, or between groups of these classes of words.

You will remember that the base of the syntactic component of a grammar generates deep structures to which transformations apply. A transformation is some sort of change that has been made to the basic sentence so that its surface features are not exactly those of its deep structure. There is general agreement among linguists as to the five common patterns of deep structure sentences. When considering the basic sentence patterns, the structure words are not considered to be important since the meaning of the sentence is predominately carried by the word order of the four content word classes. To illustrate these classes we will use surface structure sentences that have undergone a minimum of transformations and are thus very similar to their deep structures. We will call such sentences "kernel sentences."

The deep structure sentence patterns are:

1. *Noun-verb* or *subject-verb* structures.

   Birds fly.
   He works happily hour after hour.

2. *Noun-verb-noun* or *subject-verb-direct object* structures.

   Freddy threw the stick.
   The gerbil ate the sunflower seed quickly.

3. *Noun-verb-noun-noun* or *subject-verb-indirect object-object* structures.

   John gave Harry a watch.
   Father gave me a new bat.

The following patterns are often considered as *noun-verb-noun-noun* patterns, especially at the elementary school level. It should be remembered our purpose is not to set forth a definitive description of sentence patterns, but to explain the general patterns of classifying English sentences. These sentence patterns are included here for the sake of simplicity and clarity.

Subject-verb-direct object-object of preposition structures.

Billy took a letter to school.

Subject-verb-direct object-object complement structures.

The class voted Jim door monitor.

4. *Noun-linking verb-noun* or *subject-linking verb-predicate noun*. A linking verb is the verb *to be*.

   Walter is a monitor.

5. *Noun-linking verb-adjective* or *subject-linking verb-predicate adjective structures*.

   Sheila is pretty.

Five common kinds of transformations that deep structure sentences can undergo are:

1. Passive voice.
   Kernel: John gave Harry a watch.
   Transform: A watch was given to Harry by John.

2. Questions.
   Kernel: Freddy threw the stick.
   Transform: Did Freddy throw the stick?
3. Negative.
   Kernel: Walter is a monitor.
   Transform: Walter is not a monitor.
4. Imperative.
   Kernel: George gives Alice a new book.
   Transform: George, give Alice a new book!
5. Beginning with *it* and *there*.
   Kernel: Answering a teacher is wise.
   Transform: It is wise to answer a teacher.
   Kernel: Birds are flying.
   Transform: There are birds flying.

Not all English sentence patterns can be accounted for by the above categories. However, for our purposes, the vast majority of them can be. From these basic patterns, an unlimited number of other sentences can be formed. These new sentences are created through the application of rules governing the expansion and combination of whole sentences or parts of sentences. Another term for this phenomenon is *embedding*. Embedding occurs when one sentence is put into another sentence through the application of various rules of transformation.

Five common patterns of expansion and combination are:

1. Compounding. Words, phrases and independent clauses are combined to form compound subjects, compound predicates, compound objects, and compound sentences.

   Kernel: Carol sat.
                 Carol waited.
                 Betty sat.
                 Betty waited.
   Transform: Carol and Betty sat and waited.

2. Modification. Adjectives, adverbs, qualifiers, adjective and adverbial phrases, and adjective and adverbial clauses are added.

   Kernel: The man gave away chickens.
   Transform: The little man who wore a red hat gave away three chickens.

3. Apposition. Words, phrases, or clauses are used in apposition with nouns.

    Kernel: Gerald Ford was President of the United States.
                     Gerald Ford nominated Nelson Rockefeller for Vice-president.
    Transform: Gerald Ford, President of the United States, nominated Nelson Rockefeller for Vice-president.

4. Subordination. Words, phrases, and clauses that are closely associated with the main idea are added.

    Kernel: John bought an ice cream cone.
                     John was not really hungry.
    Transform: Although John was not really hungry, he bought an ice cream cone.

5. Parallel structure. A series of ideas in the form of equally important phrases or clauses are added.

    Kernel: The children had to read a story.
                     The children had to draw a picture.
                     The children had to write three sentences.
    Transform: The children had to read a story, draw a picture, and write three sentences.

Reading comprehension means being able to reconstruct the meaning intended by an author. Subsequent chapters will deal with various strategies for guiding pupils to maturity in this reconstruction process.

Semantic Features. Upon hearing the word semantics, one usually thinks first of word meanings. Semantics as a language study, however, is concerned with the ability of speakers to interpret sentences. Thus semantics deals with both the meanings or concepts attached to words, singly and in strings, and the relationship of meaning to syntactic and phonological structure.

In English, words have various functions as parts of a sentence. When words are discussed as parts of a sentence, they are referred to as *parts of speech,* and this signifies the positions certain words have in sentences and the meaning that usage signals. When words are discussed from a structural point of view, it is those features—either sound or graphic—that are partial signals to their meanings that are being discussed.

> **Semantics is concerned with the ability of speakers to interpret sentences**

The discussion that follows is not one of semantics in its strict sense. Rather, it is a discussion of syntactic features that allow the reader to determine certain meaningful relationships between and among words and sentences. The syntactic roles and functions of words are important to understand because they provide signals to the meaning of other words, and phrases and sentences. (The reader's use of these signals for understanding an author's message is discussed in Chapter 8, and strategies for developing and expanding pupils' understanding of words are discussed in Chapter 9.)

The content words can often be recognized by certain structural features and by the changes that occur in these words according to the part of speech they take in a sentence. For example, the word *know* becomes *knowledge* or *knowledgeable,* the word *nation* becomes *national* or *nationalize* as they function as different parts of speech. In these cases, a signal to the meaning of the word can be found within the word itself.

Linguists refer to the smallest meaningful unit in the language as a morpheme. The smallest sound unit is the phoneme. But a sound by itself usually does not convey any meaning. It is only combinations of these sounds that convey meaning. These combinations are considered as morphemes. A morpheme is the minimal meaningful form in the language.

The English language has two forms of morphemes; free and bound. A free morpheme is a group of sounds that by themselves signal meaning. For example, *walk, tooth,* and *pretty* are free morphemes because they can be combined with other free morphemes to create sentences. A bound morpheme is a sound or group of sounds that only signals meaning when it is combined with other free or bound morphemes. For example, *s* is a bound morpheme that signals meaning when it is combined with *coat* to form *coats.*

Sometimes a morpheme can be both a free and a bound morpheme. For instance, *ball* and *meter* are considered free morphemes, yet they are bound morphemes in *football* and *thermometer.* The bound forms of the morphemes are spelled identically, but they don't always retain their original meanings or pronunciations.

Structure words are classified by the role they play in sentences. The various categories of structure words are:

1. Noun markers. Included in this category are words such as *a, an, the, their, this, my, some.* Their purpose is to signal the appearance of a noun or noun phrase.
2. Verb markers. Included in this category are words such as: (a) forms of *to be, to have,* and *to do* used as auxiliary verbs; (b) other auxiliaries such as: *well, shall, ought, may, can.* They

signal the oncoming of a verb or verb phrase.
3. Qualifiers. Included in this category are words such as: *very, too,* and *much.* They signal the relative strength of an oncoming adjective or adverb.
4. Prepositions. Included in this category are words such as: *up, down, in, out, out of, above,* and *below.* They combine with noun forms to create phrases that modify other parts of speech.
5. Clause markers. Included in this category are words such as: (a) the relative pronouns: *who, whom, which, what, that,* and (*b*) the subordinating conjunctions: *if, because, although, even, while,* and *until.* They all signal the onset of a dependent clause.
6. Question markers. Included in this category are such words as: *who, why, how, where, when, what, did, are, is, have, do, has.* They often begin sentences and signal question transformations.
7. Negatives. Included in this category are words such as: *no, not, never, nor, none.*

Written English is not directly phonetic

Graphic Features. The spelling of words in English at one time directly reflected their pronunciation. Spelling conventions, however, outlast those of pronunciation. As spoken language changes, the writing system lags behind. With the invention of movable type that made mass distribution of books possible, there was a tendency to codify the spelling of words; and the advent of the dictionary only made this tendency stronger. This process of graphic fossilization has both beneficial and negative effects.

Written English at present is not directly phonetic. There is no longer a single, simple, one letter to one sound relationship. In some cases, one letter represents a sequence of sounds, as in /x/. In other cases, a sequence of letters represents a single sound, as in /th/. There has been a tendency to retain the same spelling a word had when it first entered the language or the spelling it had in the language from which it was borrowed. For example, the /sh/ pronounced in *ocean* reflects the spelling of its Greek origin; the same sound in *nation* reflects the spelling of its Latin origin.

It is commonly heard that writing is talk written down. In a way it is. However, there are a number of stylistic features of language found in one form that are not found in the other. Writing does not have the features of stress, juncture, or pitch—they are replaced with various graphic representations. (Pitch and juncture are partly indicated by punctuation marks. Stress can be indicated by bold print or italics.) Other differences between spoken language and written language become evident as spoken conversation and spoken prose are compared. To read an unedited transcript of a conversation, even of a discussion in which one was a participant, is not easy; indeed, it is extremely difficult to follow such speech "written down."

Spoken prose and conversation differ in the use of tempo, juncture, and redundancy. Juncture in spoken prose is related to the written message and follows the pattern of punctuation. In conversation, juncture can be quite unpredictable. In spoken prose, tempo will be rather uneven. In conversation, there is much use of redundancy, not only for emphasis, but for maintaining the continuity of one's ideas. Also, the pronunciation of words—especially articulation deviations—goes relatively unnoticed in conversation.

In conclusion, written English, according to Friend (1967),

> is more standardized than our speech, for it has been subject to the emendations of editors, the restrictive injunctions of style manuals and handbooks, and the standards imposed by teachers and other authorities. Scholars sometimes refer to the English that appears in reputable books and periodicals as Edited English; it may be regarded as another dialect of the language, generally more conservative than spoken dialects. There are, of course, varieties of written English; some writings are more literary than others, some are more scientific and technical, some are more scholarly and formal, etc. We may well think of these varieties as functional, for their characteristics are largely determined by the use to which the language is being put in them. An over-all survey of Present-Day English leads us to conclude . . . that it is divisable, whether spoken or written, into Standard and Nonstandard levels, and that within each of these levels there are, in both speech and writing, a number of functional varieties, ranging from very formal to highly informal. Standard English, written or spoken, is that characteristically used . . . in the conduct of public affairs of various sorts; it generally avoids provincial, local, and eccentric expressions and constructions. But it may be very colloquial—that is, conversational and hence informal. The degree of formality it shows will be appropriate to the use to which it is being put. Nonstandard English, written or spoken, includes every other kind of English. . . . But it, too, has its degrees of formality. Between Nonstandard and Standard English, we should note, there goes on constantly a kind of traffic: expressions that were at one time Nonstandard may rise in the social scale and become Standard. . . . The converse may also take place.
>
> One of our main jobs is obviously to master Standard Present-Day American English, both spoken and written. . . . [This] means that we need to know what Standard Present-Day American English really is. Blind adherence to outmoded, arbitrary prescriptivism will not do. . . . We must keep abreast of [standard usage] by constant reading, not merely in the classics of the past, but in what is being written and published today. And we must keep our ears open, too, so that we can know the patterns of living speech.

DISCUSSION QUESTIONS AND ACTIVITIES

1. What does the following statement by George Miller (1973) mean to you?

> Not all physical features of speech are significant for vocal communication, and not all significant features of speech have a physical representation.

2. Observe a group of people in different situations—waiting in a line, eating in a restaurant, etc. What are their attitudes and feelings? What gives you this impression?

3. Collect a series of advertisements for some product. For example, collect ads for a particular car or television set. What message is directly stated in the written copy of the ads? What messages are implied in both the physical appearance of the ad and in the copy?

4. Examine a series of elementary school reading or language arts texts. What information does the series contain about the history and structure of the English language? How is it presented and what should the pupil do with the information?

5. A parent comes to you and says she has heard about the "linguistic" method of teaching reading. From the discussion, you realize she means a program that emphasizes the one to one correspondence between letters and sounds. She wants her child taught by this method. How will you answer her?

FURTHER READINGS

Much that is presently being written about nonverbal communication you may already know intuitively. The following is a popular treatment of nonverbal communication and, unlike many other books on the subject, is not intended to be a "code" for you to use to "psyche out" someone's intentions through nonverbal behavior.

    Davis, Flora. 1973. *Inside Intuition: What We Know About Nonverbal Communication,* New York: McGraw-Hill.

The following two books, although slightly more scholarly, are still popular presentations of nonverbal communication. Their subjects are the unstated aspects of language.

    Hall, Edward T. 1959. *The Silent Language.* New York: Doubleday.
    Hall, Edward T. 1966. *The Hidden Dimension.* New York: Doubleday.

In the following popular presentation of the nature of language and its use by humans for communication, the author tries to answer basic questions about what happens when people talk.

Farb, Peter. 1974. *Word Play*. New York: Alfred A. Knopf.

Originally, Miller was asked to prepare a series of short broadcasts for the Voice of America about psychology and communication. He has edited the original scripts, written by outstanding figures in the fields of psychology, communication, sociology, and education, and collected them in the following volume.

Miller, George, ed. 1973. *Communication, Language, and Meaning: Psychological Perspectives*. New York: Basic Books.

Another book of readings about communication for the person who does not have a specialized knowledge of the subject is the following.

De Vito, Joseph A. 1973. *Language: Concepts and Processes*. Englewood Cliffs, N.J.: Prentice Hall.

References

Byers, Paul, and Byers, Happie. 1972. "Nonverbal Communication and the Education of Children." In Courtney B. Cazdin, Vera P. John, and Dell Hymes, eds. *Functions of Language in the Classroom*. New York: Teachers College Press, Columbia University, pp. 3–31.

Chomsky, N. 1965. *Aspects of the Theory of Syntax*. Cambridge: MIT.

Fairbanks, Grant. 1940. *Voice and Articulation Drillbook*. New York: Harper & Row.

Friend, J. 1967. *An Introduction to English Linguistics*. New York: World.

Marquardt, William F. 1965. "Linguistics and Reading Instruction: Contributions and Implications." In H. Alan Robinson, ed. *Recent Developments in Reading*. Chicago: University of Chicago Press, pp. 112–21.

Miller, George, ed. 1973. *Communication, Language, and Meaning: Psychological Perspectives*. New York: Basic Books.

Myers, L. M. 1966. *The Roots of Modern English*. Boston: Little, Brown.

Sapir, Edward. 1967. "Communication." In John P. de Cecco, ed. *The Psychology of Language, Thought, and Instruction*. New York: Holt, Rinehart & Winston, pp. 75–78.

Schaff, Adam. 1973. *Language and Cognition*. New York: McGraw-Hill.

Wardhaugh, R. 1972. *Introduction to Linguistics*. New York: McGraw-Hill.

Understanding the Thinking and Reading Processes

Focus Questions:

1. What are the developmental stages of growth in human thinking?
2. What are the traits of human intelligence?
3. What is the difference between the way long term memory and short term memory retain information?
4. What are the developmental stages of language acquisition?
5. In what way is the reading process really a thinking process?

HUMAN THINKING

Living entails thinking, and thinking entails resolving uncertainty. The term *problem solving* is applied to thinking that is aimed toward adjusting to a new situation or resolving some conflict. Problem solving can be thought of as the manipulation of concepts that arise out of a situation. According to Carroll (1964), a person will solve a problem when

1. Concepts relevant to the problem are mentally stored.
2. Concepts appropriate to the structure and nature of the problem are selected.
3. The skill to use the selected concepts is possessed.
4. A strategy of solution is devised.
5. Flexibility to change a mode of attack is maintained.
6. The relevance of a concept to the problem is seen.

Concepts are categories of mental experiences learned by individuals during the course of their lifetime (Carroll, 1966). These categories

Problem solving is thinking aimed toward adjusting to new situations or resolving conflicts

are created by humans for sorting out and responding to the world. The categories reflect the culture of the individual and serve as a means to reduce environmental complexity, to identify objects about us, to reduce the necessity of constant learning, to provide direction for basic life activities, and to order and relate different kinds of events (Bruner et al., 1956).

In order for a concept to be developed, an individual must have a series of experiences that are similar in one or more respects. The nature of the similarity of the aspects is what we consider a concept (Carroll, 1966). However, just experiencing the concept is not enough. The experiences must be interspersed with instances of the absence of the concept. In this way, an individual learns what properties of the concept are relevant. For example, a young child only learns what *dog* is by having experiences with other non-dog, but dog-like, animals while experiencing dogs.

The structure of the concepts we learn is reflected in the syntactic and semantic properties of the language we speak (Deese, 1971). Each culture selects various critical attributes that it uses to differentiate concepts. Certain values are applied by a culture to many of these attributes. The process of socialization is acquiring knowledge (concepts) through the reduction of uncertainty. Uncertainty is reduced as information is categorized and questions are answered. This is the process we call problem solving.

Children's thinking is basically different from adults'

Human Cognition

Presently, the most widely known name in the research of the development of human thinking and cognition is that of Piaget. Piaget has been concerned with explaining the developmental process by which we learn to think and to use language. Guilford, an American psychologist, is concerned with explaining how the mind is structured so that we can realize the kinds of thinking that can occur. Many researchers are involved with attempts to explain the nature of human memory as a cognitive function. Many of these researchers are using a computer analogy to assist them in their explanations. The following discussions of Piaget's developmental stages, of Guilford's structure-of-intellect model, and of the structure of human memory attempt to synthesize their ideas. These discussions provide the basis for understanding a psycholinguistic explanation of the reading process, which is presented in the last section of this chapter.

Developmental Stages of Human Thinking

According to Piaget, intelligence develops gradually over a long period. This growth shows itself in differences in the way an individual solves problems at different developmental stages (Furth, 1969, 1970). Acquiring knowledge is not just the adding on of information to already acquired information. Acquiring knowledge is an active process of incorporating new information. A thing in the world is not an object of knowledge until the individual relates it to something that has already been learned. The new information is then reorganized into a new, larger meaning or understanding. However, the manner in which an individual relates new information to prior learnings is dependent upon the psychological frame of reference, or cognitive structure, of the individual. Piaget's four developmental stages (see Table 3-1) are an attempt to explain how a child thinks as he progresses through the stages of increasing cognitive maturity.

Basically, Piaget considers humans as biological organisms. This means that we are responsive to our environment. Our reaction is not merely a response to an outside stimulation. It is a response in an attempt

Intelligence develops gradually over a long period

TABLE 3-1: Piaget's Stages of Intellectual Development

Approximate Age (years)	Characteristics
0-2	**SENSORIMOTOR DEVELOPMENT** Acquires skills and adaptations which are reflexive in nature. Coordinates and integrates information from senses; operates with a sense of object permanency; exhibits goal directed behavior.
2-7	**PREOPERATIONAL THOUGHT** Develops internal cognitive picture of external world. Begins language development; classifies on perceived attributes.
7-11	**CONCRETE OPERATIONS** Organizes through the logical structure of groups. Manipulates concrete ideas; develops concepts of reversibility and conservation.
11-15	**FORMAL OPERATIONS** Develops fundamentals of logical thought. Understands principles of causality and hypothesis testing.

to incorporate the environmental information into our own intellect. We then make some changes within our cognitive structure to meet the newly incorporated information. These are what Piaget calls *assimilation* and *accommodation*. As a biological organization, we have an innate tendency to preserve the status quo. But instead of our functioning state being a static one, it is a dynamic situation in which we try to maintain a balance between assimilation and accommodation. The process of maintaining this balance is, according to Piaget, *equilibration*. It results in developmentally successive changes that lead from the most elementary and basic knowledge (shown by adaptive reflex action) to abstract knowledge (shown by adult intelligent actions). Intelligence is considered as the "regulating force" of a living organism that "tends towards a stable equilibration between the organism and environment" (Furth, 1969).

The four stages of development are:

1. *Sensorimotor stage.* According to Piaget, the sensorimotor stage occurs during the first two years of a child's life. In it, the child develops the

Children learn best by activity and movement

practical knowledge of the world that will serve as a structure for all future knowledge of the world. The skills and adaptations that occur during this stage are of a reflex kind. The child organizes sensory information from the various sensory modalities and begins integrating this information in goal directed, deliberate actions. Discoveries are still primarily through manipulation. The child begins to understand the permanency of space. However, there is not yet an internalized representation of the world. During this period, language begins.

Piaget's four stages are the sensorimotor, the preoperational, concrete operations, and formal operations

2. *Preoperational stage.* The second stage is filled with experiments with objects in play. The child is beginning to establish relationships between experiences and actions. The child imitates adults and begins to internalize any observations of adult activities. The result is that these internalizations become the basis for imagery and for language development. At first, the child identifies words and symbols with the object and its characteristics. A cow is a cow because it has "cowness." By the end of the period of growth, the child begins to understand the arbitrariness of symbol to object associations. Different things and people may be called by different names. Thinking during this period is "transductive," which means that information can be related from particular to particular, but not from particular to general. The child's activity is limited to concrete actions. Relationships are made because objects have some features in common. For instance, associations may be made based upon environmental conditions rather than by some inherent quality of the object. Things are grouped together because "Mommy uses them in the kitchen" rather than because they are all round or made of metal. Finally, the child cannot distinguish between the motives of the external world and the internal world. Egocentricity will not allow the child to take another's point of view. Thinking during the period is irreversible as shown by the widely known experiments on conservation of mass.

3. *Concrete operations.* The concrete operations stage occurs approximately during the ages of seven to eleven and covers the largest portion of the elementary school years. During this stage the child develops concepts of time, space, number, and logic. These concepts control the child's understanding of events and objects. An understanding of the logical structure of groups and a sense of multiple classifications develops. The child realizes that objects have multiple characteristics. There is a realization that the significance of each characteristic can change with a change of purpose. Objects can be grouped because they are red or round, and then again because they are used for cooking or building. Although thought still remains tied to actual objects and events, that is, things that actually exist,

there is an internalization of the world. A need to manipulate objects physically no longer exists. By the end of this stage, the child can perform mental arrangements of objects.

4. *Formal operations.* The fourth stage, formal operations, occurs during the eleventh to fifteenth years. The child develops, in this period, an understanding of basic principles of causal thinking. The child can perform experiments and deduce implications. There is a fundamental grasp of logical thought and the occurrence of hypothetical reasoning. The child, by the end of the period, can think through a full set of alternatives for a problem.

Children and adults think differently

A very important distinction exists between the thinking of elementary school age children and that of adults. Quite often adults make assumptions about the way children think that are erroneous according to Piagetian principles (Elkind, 1974). One misconception is that children and adults are alike in the way they think and different in the way they feel about things. The opposite seems to be true. However, many adults treat children as if they do not have personal preferences or likes and dislikes and as if children's emotions are different from adults'. Another misunderstanding is that children learn by sitting and listening. From the description of Piaget's developmental stages, one should infer that children learn best by activity and movement. Children learn about the world through active manipulation of that world and by imitating the people they encounter in their lives. A third misunderstanding is that children learn best by learning rules. Again, the child learns by living and acting in the world, not by associating some abstract rule to a situation. A fourth misunderstanding concerns the matter of horizontal versus vertical acceleration. In general, the results of Piaget's work seem to indicate that children at each stage of development would benefit more from enriching activities than from an attempt to speed up their education.

The Structure of Human Intellect

Guilford's model cross classifies intellectual abilities

Guilford's structure-of-intellect model is unlike Piaget's in that it is not hierarchical in nature (see Figure 3-1). Guilford cross classifies the various intellectual abilities that seem to be possessed by adults. His model classifies the intellectual abilities in three different ways so that the subunits, or categories, of each ability intersect with those of the other abilities. The three major classifications are mental operations, content, and product (Guilford, 1967; 1971).

Operations are the major kinds of intellectual activities we undertake,

FIGURE 3–1: The Structure-of-Intellect Model

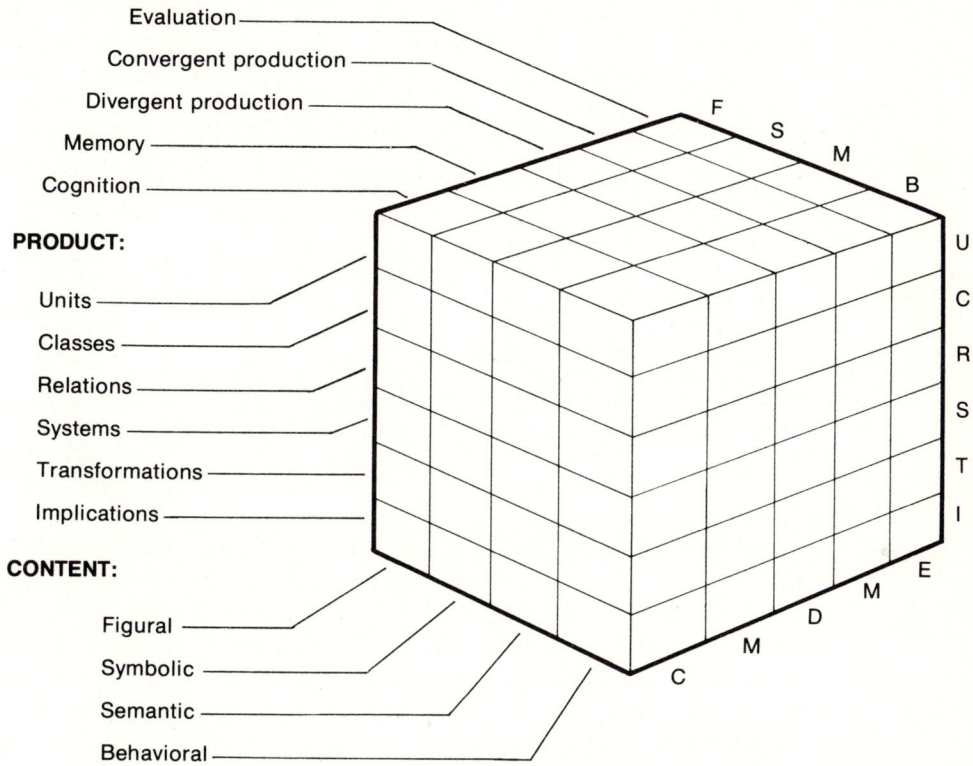

SOURCE: J. P. Guilford. 1967. *The Nature of Human Intelligence.* New York: McGraw-Hill. Used with permission of McGraw-Hill Book Company.

that is, the things we do in the processing of information. Five categories of operations are:

Cognition. The awareness or recognition of information in its various forms.
Memory. The process of storing information; not to be confused with the memory storage capacity of an individual.
Divergent production. The generating of logical conclusions from any given or known information with the emphasis on achieving variety, quantity, and relevance of outcomes.

"Operations" are the things we do in the processing of information

Convergent production. The generating of logical conclusions from any given or known information with the emphasis on achieving conventionally best outcomes.
Evaluation. The comparison of information and the making of judgments about information.

"Contents" are substantive kinds of information

Contents are the broad, substantive kinds of information as presented to or perceived by the individual. Four kinds of contents are:

Figural. Information in concrete form, that is, the actual object or a realistic picture of the object involving perception by visual, auditory, or kinesthetic sensory modalities.
Symbolic. Information in the form of denotative signs having no basic significance in and of themselves, such as letters, numerals, musical notes, codes, and words.
Semantic. Information in the form of conceptions or mental images.
Behaviors. Information, basically nonpictorial and nonverbal, that involves human interaction, that is, information representing attitudes, needs, desires, moods, and intentions.

"Products" are the forms information can take

Products are the forms that information can take. Six categories of products are:

Units. Sets of things, chunks of information, segregated wholes, or figures on grounds.
Classes. Sets of things having a common property or characteristic.
Relations. The connections between things, or groups of information, based on a definable relationship.
Systems. Organized or structured groupings of items of information, that is, complex structures of interrelated parts.
Transformations. Changes existing in information such as redefinitions, shifts, transitions, or modifications.
Implications. Circumstantial connections between different information; expectations, anticipations, or predictions; implications not usually verbalizable.

When the three classifications are combined in the cross classification model the result is a block of 120 cells, each representing a unique kind of ability. Each cell derives its uniqueness from the combination of one kind of operation with one kind of content and with one kind of product.

In his explanation of the model, Guilford (1967) advises us not to suppose that the 120 abilities represent all of the intellectual traits of human intelligence. There are reasons to suppose that the number might be much greater since many of the cells seem to represent two or three kinds of related abilities. For example, figural memory of units seems to be of two kinds, auditory and visual. Cognition seems to consist of auditory abilities, visual abilities, and kinesthetic abilities. It thus appears that within the cognition and memory operation categories there may be some general differentiation of abilities along sense-modality lines.

The Guilford structure-of-intellect model has parallels with Piaget's classifications of developmental stages. Although Guilford does not attempt to explain the developmental nature of his structures, he attempts to classify the kinds of thinking that can occur in adult humans. The basic implication of this construct is that there are different kinds of thinking that occur for different situations. In the classroom, a child might be able to perform certain types of mental functions, and yet not be able to perform others. For example, a child may understand individual things pictorially (represented by the intersection of the operation *cognition* with the product *units* and the content *figural*). Yet, the child may not be able to remember symbolic relations (represented by the intersection of the operation *memory* with the product *relations* and the content *symbolic*).

> Guilford's model has parallels with Piaget's stages

Another classroom implication comes from the realization that the concept of "product of information" is represented in different ways in our language (Guilford, 1967). The information in the form of units and classes are things or groups of things to which we normally apply nouns. Relations, the connections or bridges between two or more bits of information, are commonly expressed by prepositions. Systems are generally verbally stated arithmetic problems, outlines, mathematical equations, or plans. Transformations are generally expressed through participles, that is, a verb in noun form such as *thinking, running, reddening*. The ability to deal with these various parts of speech and to fully understand their use in our language may be dependent upon certain and separate mental abilities.

The Structure of Human Memory

There is a growing body of research indicating that human memory has the structure of a multiple storage system (Kumar, 1971; Lindsay and Norman, 1972). The components of the system are a sensory register, a short term memory, and a long term memory.

> Human memory has the structure of a multiple storage system

From the available evidence (Lindsay and Norman, 1972), we have some

> reasonably good agreement that permanent storage of information takes place either through chemical or structural changes in the brain. There is little

or no disagreement that the immediate, ongoing activities of thought, conscious processes, and the immediate memories—sensory information store and short term memory—are mediated through electrical activity.

One possibility in regard to the location of the various functions in the brain is that memories do not seem to be stored in specific locations. Rather they are found as patterns in different locations throughout the brain. Any specific memory, then, involves large sections of the brain. No one portion is absolutely necessary for memory processes, yet the more sections that function together, the clearer the recollection (Lindsay and Norman, 1972).

The amazing thing about the human brain is its vast complexity. The fact that its parts are interchangeable, or, at least, interdependent, has not allowed researchers to identify the specific sections functioning as memory systems. The complexity of the brain allows it, if it should encounter injury in one section, to have another of its sections perform certain life sustaining activities. What have been localized are the specific regions where certain sensory stimuli enter the brain, and the regions responsible for certain human activities. For example, motor areas, speech areas, and seeing areas have been identified. Still remaining a mystery is the precise manner in which information is transferred from one region to another and the exact process involved in problem solving and in storing, retrieving, and analyzing information. Although a precise description of the physical nature of the brain's activities has not yet been obtained, enough evidence is available to sustain a theory of a multiple storage system model of memory (see Figure 3-2).

Sensory images are deposited in the sensory register

The sensory register is the "place" where all sensory images are deposited by the sensory modalities. The five senses are constantly at work, and all the incoming information from them must be collected until it is determined what information is valuable and should be retained. That means that all information within one's fields of vision, hearing, touch, taste, and smell is stored. However, this information is stored only briefly and is subject to very rapid decay. Experiments show that the time limit for information stored in the sensory register must be measured in milliseconds. By half a second, a bit of registered information has disappeared. Information may also be eliminated, or forgotten, from the sensory register by the introduction of new information.

How does information, which will be quickly gone, get transferred to the other memory storage systems? Transfer is perhaps best thought of as a "copying" of information. What information is copied on one system from another depends to a great deal upon the individual. Each individual seems to employ procedures of selective attention. Information is selected

FIGURE 3-2: Structure of Human Memory

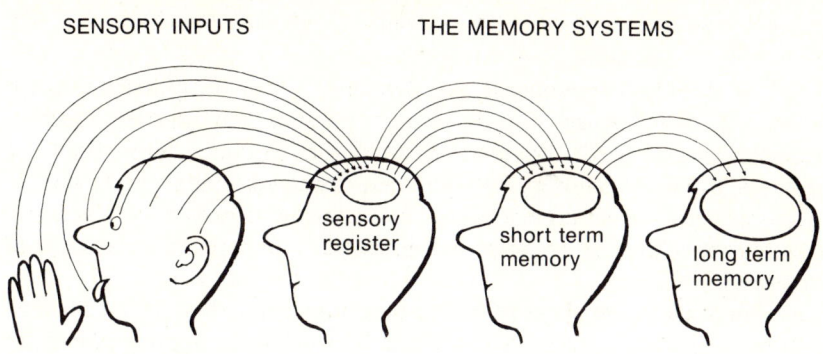

from the sensory register depending upon the importance of the information to the individual. The information is then retained in the short term memory storage. We are all aware of this phenomenon of "attenuating" as we direct our thinking to the heat in a room and do not listen to the lecturer, or as we are diverted by uncomfortable seats from the enjoyment of a theatrical performance.

The phenomenon of selective attention has both good and bad points. It is desirable because without it the collection of sensory inputs would be utterly chaotic. The world to us would be a jumble of sights, sounds, and smells. The procedure allows for the orderly selection of incoming sensory data based upon what seems important at the moment. A negative feature is that more than one thing cannot be given attention to in any one instant. Because of this we find it difficult to keep track of two conversations simultaneously, or to read a book and follow the progress of a sporting event on television without rereading many pages and relying on instant replay for continuity of action.

The information in the sensory register seems to undergo some sort of change as it is copied for transfer into the short term memory system. It seems the information is changed into a verbal code that retains the meaning of the information and not its original sensory image. An analogous situation exists with the computer. The symbolic language used for instructing the computer must undergo a translation into an internal machine language for the computer to carry on its functioning. The relationship between the symbolic language and the machine language is purely arbitrary, yet a computer must have the appropriate "program" before it can make the translation. In our brain, all information that is allowed to pass beyond the sensory register to the next storage system must be transformed into a basic meaning regardless of its sensory source. In terms of the hypothesized transformational grammar model, the information is transformed from its surface features to its deep structure features.

The short term memory is a working memory. In it information is retained for a slightly longer period than is possible in the sensory register. Information is generally retained for as long as fifteen seconds before it decays. The information in the short term memory is retained in what is called an "auditory-linguistic-verbal" store since it is extremely difficult to separate these aspects of short term memory. The capacity of short term memory is much more limited than that of the sensory register; however, this information is much more select than the information in the sensory register. The short term memory seems to be able to hold only about six units of information. The more meaningful the information is, or the more related to each other the bits of information are, the more likely is it that it will be retained as a single unit of information. For example, the letters x, y, l, n would probably be retained as four discrete units of information, whereas a rearrangement of those letters into a meaningful unit—*lynx*—would cause them to be retained as a single unit.

Information is eliminated from the short term memory by either decay or replacement. Information is lost, or forgotten, after about six seconds or when new information enters the short term memory to replace it. However, information may be retained for longer periods of time by a process of rehearsal. Rehearsal is a "silent, mental repetition of the material that is to be retained," and it seems to serve two primary functions: (1) the indefinite retention in short term memory of material, and (2) the aid in the transfer of material to a more permanent storage in long term memory (Lindsay and Norman, 1972).

The information that is transferred from short term memory to long term memory is, to a large extent, but unconsciously, under the control of the individual. The importance one places on information determines whether it is processed further (Kumar, 1971). An attentional aspect similar to that present in the transfer of information from sensory register to short term memory seems to be involved in the transfer of information from short term memory to long term memory. Information is transferred by the mental repetition of information (rehearsal) and by perceiving different aspects, attributes, or conceptual psychological dimensions of the information (Kumar, 1971). The encoding strategies are conscious efforts of the individual involving substitution (a replacement of the incoming information by another symbol), elaboration (the storage of additional information), and scheme formation (the combining of information with past experience).

The long term memory, the most important of the memory systems, is relatively permanent and resistant to forgetting. In comparison to the sensory register and the short term memory, the capacity of long term memory is almost limitless. Everything that is to be retained for more than a few minutes must be placed in long term memory. Here are stored all one's knowledge of the world, language and cultural rules, and strategies for creating meaning out of the world. The problem with long term memory is generally not one of forgetting, but one of retrieving. Recall may be inhibited, assuming the information was truly stored in long term memory, by inadequate search strategies or insufficient information.

The long term memory is relatively resistant to forgetting

Conclusion

The conclusions of Piaget, Guilford, and the cognitive psychologists studying the structure of human memory have many parallel features. They all conceive of thinking as a process in which the information an individual receives from the world is systematically organized. The manner in which the information is catalogued and the strategies comprising the process seem to be dependent upon prior experiences and prior information. Piaget theorizes that the growing child develops an internalized view of the world. This seems to be just another way of suggesting that the child has developed a strategy for encoding information into long term memory. In addition, it seems that the structure of language is

> designed to complement the ability of the human to piece together the meaning of a communication from a few isolated fragments. . . . The redundancy of the language . . . allows us to attend selectively to bits and pieces of a communication, to anticipate what will come next, and to look selectively for the key words and phrases that convey the basic meaning of the message (Lindsay and Norman, 1972).

Memory, like the maturing of a child, appears to develop as a problem solving process in which information is routinely analyzed to determine its consistency with an individual's past experience. The way in which the problem is solved seems to be the result of

Information is routinely analyzed to determine its consistency with past experience

1. The kind and form of information.
2. The manner in which the information is presented.
3. The maturity of the individual.
4. The plans for solving problems devised by the individual.

All of these are acquired as part of the acculturation of the individual and are what we call "learning" and "knowledge."

THE DEVELOPMENT OF LANGUAGE IN CHILDREN

In this section, we will limit our discussion to the development of syntactic structures in the language of children. One reason for this is that the grammatical features of our language provide the framework for conveying meaning; it is through deep structures that one gets to meaning. The discussion of phonological development—that is, the development of the ability to produce the sounds of our language—while interesting, has no direct bearing to the examination of our larger topic, namely, the development of the thinking process in children. Little will be said now about the development of vocabulary because there is much evidence to indicate that vocabulary development reflects the social situations in which the young child grows. Much more will be said about this last point in later chapters dealing with vocabulary development and the instruction of children with special needs.

Language is learned as a process of communication

That language is learned as a process of communication is the most important result of the study of how speech develops in children. Young children seem to possess an innate ability to reduce and restructure adult language in a highly systematic way so as to fit their intellects. As the child matures, there is evidence of a progressive differentiation in word usage and in the use of syntactic structures (Brown and Bellugi, 1966). The child's language is not, however, a miniature copy of adult speech—until the child is almost mature, patterns are used that do not normally appear in adult speech. These patterns are remarkably similar from language to language (Slobin, 1971). Further, it is clear that language cannot develop primarily from the memorization of words and lists of sentences. The known limitations of the memory of children of this age preclude memorization as the mechanism of language acquisition. Also, all speakers of a language are able to produce sentences that they have never heard previously.

Generally, children begin to speak around the age of one and a half years, a period that coincides with the onset of what Piaget calls the "preoperational thought" stage. In fact, language development occurs in most normal children during this period. It should be kept in mind that the preoperational thought stage is characterized by the internalization of the external world and that items and events are classified on attributes that the child can actually perceive.

In the first stage, children imitate adult intonations

The initial phase of speech acquisition begins when the baby creates imitations of adult intonational patterns (Menyuk, 1971). This is then followed by a period in which single words appear. These words, although they have no direct tie to words found in a standard dictionary, are word approximations and carry a symbol to object relationship. At this time children show that they understand words spoken to them. In addition, they use various intonational patterns, and it may be possible to distinguish the consistent use of declarative, emphatic, and question intonations in their utterances.

The next stage of language development occurs when children can combine two words to make a sentence. At first a child constructs a few of these sentences. Then, in a brief period of time, there is an effusion of them. These two word sentences are not random combinations of words, but consist of two classes of words: pivot words, and open class words. The pivot words are high frequency words the child uses. Usually the number in this category is small and stable. They are words such as *on, more, big,* and *allgone.* They are generally representative of a quality or a process of something. The open class consists of a large and growing number of words representative of attempts to name and classify the objects and events encountered by the child. The pivot words may occupy the first or the second position in the sentence, but they are easily recognized by the fact that a large number of open words in the child's vocabulary can be joined with them. Examples of two word sentences with the pivot word at the beginning are:

In the second stage, children combine two words to make a sentence

Allgone milk

See Daddy

Big dog

Two word sentences with the pivot word at the end are:

Baby down

Shoe on

Mommy off

The pivot constructions serve various functions in a child's speech. However, they soon begin to show a subject-predicate construction, modification of quantity and quality, and negation.

Some two word sentences seem to consist of only open class words, but careful examination shows they demonstrate a beginning awareness on the part of the child of the deep structure and surface structure features of language. For example, the utterance, "Mommy bottle," might mean any one of the following:

Mommy has the bottle

Mommy, give me the bottle

Mommy, that is the bottle

One determines the underlying meaning of the statement through the context of the situation. In the example, evidence of a specific interpretation exists, if upon hearing "Yes, I have the bottle," the child walks away, or upon hearing "No, you can't have the bottle," the child cries. Observations of young children indicate that at different times the same statement, "Mommy bottle," will produce different responses by the child's mother and quite different subsequent behaviors by the child. The child, while demonstrating at least some understanding of adult syntactic and semantic structures, may not yet possess the capacity to produce more than two word sentences.

Hierarchial constructions appear in the next stage

After the child has begun to use two word, pivot-open sentences, there begins a stage of hierarchial constructions. The child takes the basic pivot-open sentences and begins to expand them by adding on other syntactic features. The construction, "More cooky," might be expanded to, "Want more cooky," and then to, "Want more cooky now." In each case of expansion, the child is not just stringing words together but is creating a hierarchical pattern that develops according to the grammatical structure of the language.

The child then enters a period of regularization

The child then enters a period of regularization. This period is also marked by deviations from adult speech, and constructions are created that are not usually found in the adult speech the child hears. For example, *came* becomes *comed*, and *feet* becomes *foots*. Most often the high frequency irregular forms are learned correctly first, then they are over-regularized as the child becomes aware of generalizations inherent in the language. The child continuously attempts to create order out of the language that child hears.

In the final stage, transformations are used

The final stage is one of using language transformations. This is a highly complex phase of language acquisition, and investigative study is only starting to reveal how children begin to take basic sentences and create transformations of them. Two early transformations made by young children are questions and negatives. When a child begins to construct questions, the tendency is to invoke the "question marker" rule but not the "subject-verb reversal" rule. For instance, a child who is asked to create a question about what Mommy has in her hand will ask, "What Mommy have in hand?" It seems that children of this stage have a limited performance capacity that blocks the application of both transformations together.

By the time children are four years old, there has been a mastery of basic grammatical structures. During the fifth and sixth years, children begin to control the inconsistencies of language, and by the end of the seventh year—roughly corresponding to the end of first grade—the children have developed a grammar that is almost equivalent to that of adults. What is lacking is the extensive vocabulary and the ability to manipulate the extensive number of grammatical transformations of adult speech.

IMPLICATIONS FOR EDUCATION

A few important implications of the insights gleaned from the research presented in the above sections on the thinking process will be referred to here and others will be cited throughout the remainder of the text.

One important conclusion of Piaget's is that development affects learning. How children learn will change as they mature. Children's thinking is basically different from that of adults. Children's world-views are not "wrong," but they are different.

In addition, some things cannot be taught to children in the usual sense. They must experience objects and activities in order to spontaneously acquire new cognitive structures. Children are constantly learning regardless of their activity, albeit not always what we wish to be learned. School-age children are involved with their world and even apparent daydreaming has some aspects of learning in it.

The results of research based upon Piagetian theory have some relevance for the practices of beginning reading instruction. Children in the later stages of the preoperational period—corresponding to the kindergarten and first grade years—may not have developed "conservation." Such children are characterized by an inability to undo a task they have performed. They cannot deal with a slightly changed situation without thinking it is a new situation. The implication of this is that the use of a code emphasis, rule oriented phonics program in the beginning stages of reading is not consistent with the abilities of "nonconserving" children. In addition, Piaget's work points out the importance of curricula in which activities, including reading, are "carried out in social situations where children are working together, sharing information, and learning to take into account another person's point of view" (Raven and Salzer, 1971).

Children's world views are not wrong; but they are different

Readiness makes way for learning

When something has been learned, whether it is a mathematical concept, a grammatical rule of language, or the names of various objects, that information has been committed to a child's long term memory. The evidence is that what gets transferred into long term memory is under the control of the individual. The control is not actually conscious, rather it is a "predisposition" to gain other information. This control is best conceived as markers that guide the transfer of information from the sensory register through the short term memory into the long term memory.

In the classroom, the predisposition for learning can be facilitated by developing appropriate cognitive readiness. One procedure is to use "advance organizers," which are questions or directions focusing on features of the information that should be retained. This allows the child to attend to the particular information, or to a particular aspect of the information, that is to be learned. Most important, the teacher should help the child to develop general advance organizers so that self-learning strategies can be developed. It is also wise to promote the use of rehearsal or practice. Greater rehearsal is needed for new or different information. Old or additional information being added to an already learned body of information needs much less rehearsal. A final procedure is to guide children in the development of information processing strategies, that is, encoding procedures. Since information is encoded into long term memory in its deep structure form, children need training in processing information according to the nature of the information. Different strategies are needed depending upon

1. The difficulty level of the information.
2. The importance of the information to the individual.
3. The interest of the information to the individual.
4. The amount of information to be acquired.
5. The organization of the material (Kumar, 1971).

The teacher must be committed to understanding the child and the content of instruction. The teacher must develop instructional procedures for bringing the two together productively. Then the desired learning ensues.

THE READING PROCESS

Reading, the process, must be distinguished from reading, the act. Every time we select a book, magazine, or newspaper, we are engaging in an act of reading. We are undertaking the action, the doing, of reading. Our days are filled with many acts of reading, and our purposes for reading may or may not change with each act of reading. But the act of reading is not the process of reading. Reading as a process is a continuing development involving numerous changes. Once the process is started, it continues throughout life and is affected by every act of reading one does.

The process of reading is distinct from the act of reading

Significance of a Psycholinguistic Model of Reading

A reading model is a tool for clarifying behavior. Even though the model should be built on a supportable theoretical base, it still is an artifact, and its usefulness depends upon the clarity with which it categorizes behaviors. A model, useful as it is in decision making, should not be thought absolute. It must be continuously modified, or even discarded as new evidence accumulates. A model of reading should be capable of serving three general purposes:

1. It should explain what the complex phenomenon of reading consists of.
2. It should describe how the phenomenon of reading works.
3. It should provide a basis for predictions about changes that will occur in one aspect of reading when changes are made in other aspects (Geyer, 1972).

FIGURE 3-3: A Flow Chart of Goodman's Model of Reading

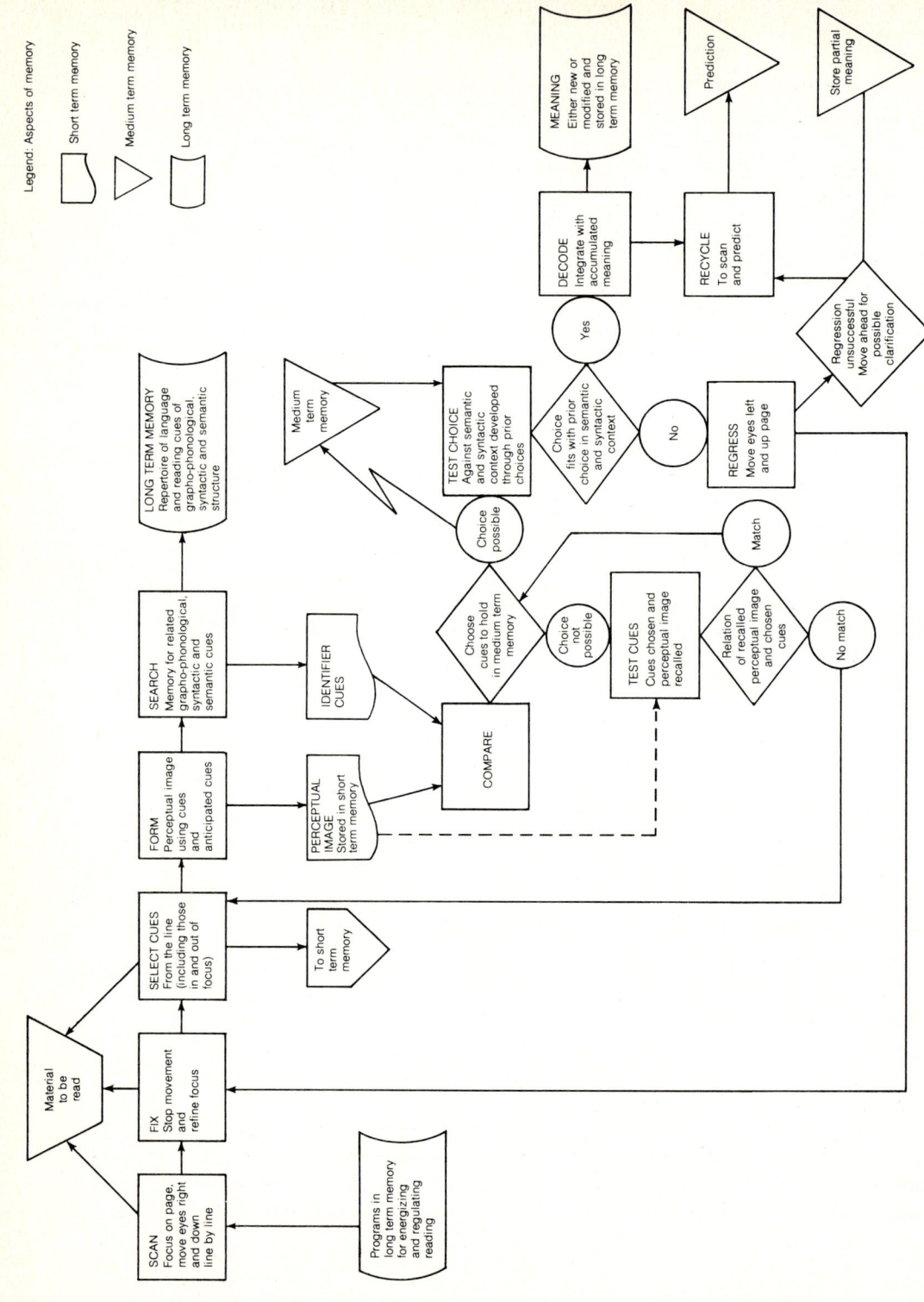

As many as seventy-seven models of reading have been proposed, and about forty eight of them meet the strict definition of a model stated above (Geyer, 1972). Examination of various models—depicting reading from various theoretical positions—will show that a preponderance of them reflects an information processing point of view (Geyer, 1972; Williams, 1973). The present focus of the theoretical models is on the cognitive aspects of the reading process, with a consensus of opinion that reading is a complex of cognitive skills. Reading, it has been concluded, is all of a language process, a psychological process, a psycholinguistic process, and a physiological process combined.

Reading is a linguistic, psychological, psycholinguistic, and physiological process

Ryan and Semmel (1969) examined three aspects of the reading process: (1) the occurrence of graphic-lexical-phonemic correspondences made by a reader, (2) a child's ability to use abstract representations, and (3) the use of language in reading. They concluded that reading is a "constructive, active process in which the reader uses his cognitive and linguistic knowledge to produce a probable utterance from a careful sampling of cues and then matches that prediction for appropriateness" (Ryan and Semmel, 1969). Others, too (Raven and Salzer, 1971; Stauffer, 1971), have shown that the results of Piaget and other cognitive psychologists have important and direct implications for the instruction of reading.

> The search for language structure is an active process of hypothesizing, testing, and confirming or rejecting utilized in real situations and within the constraints of memory and rate under which humans operate. . . . The nature of development is determined by what gets input from the environment and by having the input dealt with intelligently. It is this distinction that is useful in thinking about cognitive development and may result in new and fruitful ways of looking at traditional reading problems (Stauffer, 1971).

A Psycholinguistic Model of the Reading Process

The Goodman Model of Reading (see Figure 3-3) is presented as a representative psycholinguistic model. It does not pretend to describe the reading process totally. At this time, no model of reading does. Yet the Goodman Model does provide usable insights. It has been selected because it has grown from and has been supported by extensive research. The ultimate goal of this research is a completely refined model of the reading process capable of explaining all phenomena occurring during the reading act. Of course, this goal is not achievable; however, the Goodman Model exemplifies the work presently being done by some researchers in the field. The model is put forth as the searching and testing of ideas continue. If contradictory ideas appear, then we should "keep both theories, research both, and search for a general theoretical position which will ultimately reveal one theory as a special case of the other, or which will subsume both theories in a higher consistency" (Weaver, 1969).

It should be kept in mind that the model is an abstraction of what a proficient reader seems to be doing while reading and may not represent the reading process of someone initially learning to read.

Reading is a process of selecting graphic cues that signal meaning

Definition of Reading. Goodman (1968) defines reading as a process of selecting graphic cues that signal meaning, much as listening is a process of selecting auditory cues for meaning. It is supposed that the experienced reader can derive meaning directly from graphic cues without translating them into phonemic cues.

A distinction is made among the aspects of *decoding* (deriving meaning), *recoding* (translating letter patterns into sound), and *encoding* (oral reading). Decoding occurs only when the meaning of the writer is analyzed and understood, in other words, when the reader knows the deep structure of the message as generated by the writer. Encoding can take place only when decoding has preceded it. Recoding is a procedure whereby only the surface structure of the message is perceived and changed into a different form. (In most other sources about the teaching of reading, the term decoding refers to the process of translating the printed symbol into sound, that is, word attack procedures. Goodman prefers to use the term *decoding* in referring to the meaningful unlocking of a message.)

A proficient reader does not use all of the signals built into the writing system just as a proficient listener does not use every facet of the spoken language. The reader anticipates meaning and has it reconfirmed. The less one's thoughts about the message have to undergo change during reading, and the fewer number of cues from the page one needs for arriving at the author's meaning, the more proficient he is as a reader within that reading situation (Goodman 1965a, 1965b, 1967, 1968, 1969a; Ryan and Semmel, 1969).

Research into the Reading Process. Goodman and his associates have been engaged in research in an attempt to classify the responses children make while reading orally. It is from analyses of these responses that he has formulated his theory of the reading process.

One report (Goodman, 1965a) indicates the importance of context in word recognition and the usefulness of regressions—that is, the reader's going back to reread something already read. Other studies (Goodman and Burke, 1968; Y. Goodman et al., 1969) show that incorrect responses are a normal part of the reading process and that concern in diagnosis should be directed toward determining the "quality" of the responses rather than indicating the type or number of these responses. The results of these studies show a proficient reader as one who makes a mistake and is able to recover from it. Further studies (Goodman and Burke, 1969) show that there is a qualitative difference in the incorrect responses of children reading orally. Some mistakes indicate that the reader has no idea of the author's meaning, while others show that the reader has the author's meaning but uses a different word pattern (a transformation) in responding to it. Evidence from miscues that retain basic meaning supports the theory that reading is neither an exact word-by-word nor a letter-matching process.

In a study that examined the reading process of low, average, and high proficiency level pupils in grades two through ten, the analysis indicated that all levels of readers were reading in a manner consistent with the Goodman Model of Reading (Goodman, 1973). Low proficiency readers used the same processes as high proficiency readers, but they used them less well. Low proficiency readers were less efficient in their use of syntactic, graphic, and semantic information. They used more cues than were necessary to decode the message. In addition, they had less productive strategies for using the information on the page and, therefore, lost more of the meaning. No hierarchy of skills was revealed by the analysis, and the single most consistent difference between groups of readers at the different levels of reading proficiency was their ability to understand what they read.

Description of the Reading Process. According to the Goodman Model of Reading, the process of reading by a proficient reader can be compared with information processing. Long term memory holds those learned responses that have become automatic or habitual. Medium memory[1] holds those learnings and responses that are based upon the particular reading act. They are the "guesses" (predictions) and confirmations made during reading. Short term memory holds immediate images and signals needed during reading.

Prior to the onset of an act of reading, the reader has three sets of information stored in long term memory:

1. Procedures for regulating the physical aspects of reading.
2. A language repertoire containing all rules and cues of spoken and written language.
3. Meanings and concepts that have been acquired.

Reading can be compared with information processing

---

1. In the Goodman model *short term* and *medium term* memory refer to the *sensory register* and *short term* memory discussed previously in this chapter.

At the onset of a reading act, the regulating programs get the eyes to move and focus on the material.

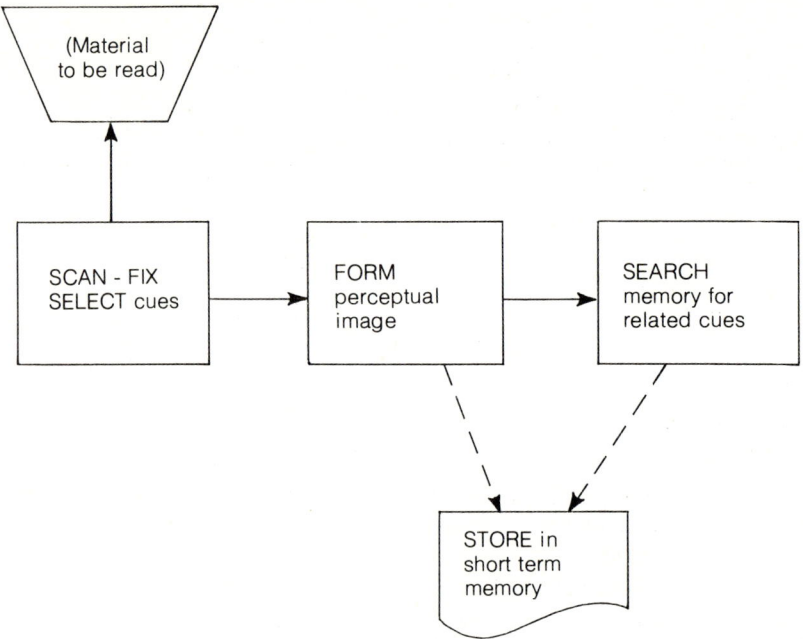

Printed language cues in and around the word are selected for making guesses and then stored in the short term memory. Prior predictions from the medium term memory only aid in the selection of cues after the initial instance of reading.

The selected cues are used to form perceptual images that are also stored in the short term memory. The perceptual cues formed may be anticipatory rather than actual. The proficient reader does not use every cue available or the act of reading would be slow and laborious. Some images formed, therefore, may be anticipations of actual cues that will be substantiated at a later time. There is a search through the language repertoire for known cues (grapheme-phoneme relationships, sentence structures, and meaning structures) that might be related to the present situation. When these cues are identified, they too are stored in the short term memory.

The perceptual images and the identified language cues are then compared. A decision is consequently arrived at to hold these cues in

Understanding the Thinking and Reading Processes 75

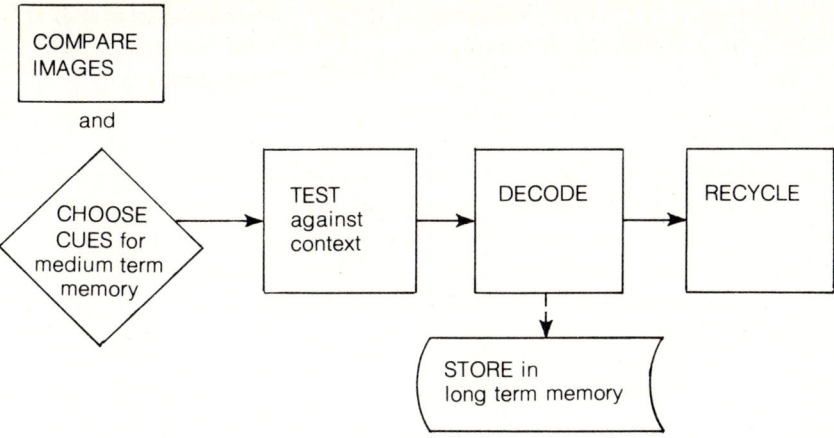

the medium term memory by testing them to see if they fit with prior information (confirmed predictions and stored partial meanings). If they do fit, the message has been decoded. At this point the meaning (deep structure) is integrated with other meanings, predictions are confirmed, and the process is recycled.

There are two places in the process where a decision may be made that the perceived cues do not fit and that the message cannot be decoded. The first occurs after the perceptual image and the identified related language cues are compared.

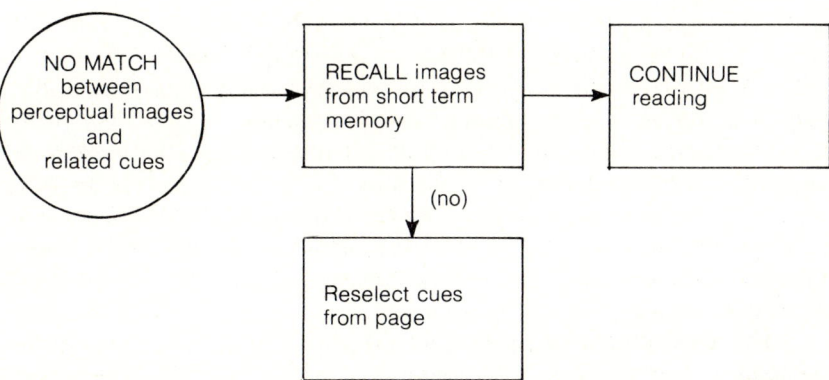

At this point, the perceptual image and the chosen cues are recalled. If there is no match, cues are reselected from the line on the page and the process repeats. If there is a match now, then the cues are held in short term memory and a second test is made.

The second place of decision occurs when the cues are tested against the semantic and syntactic context developed through prior choices. If there still is no fit, the decision is made to regress and to seek the point of inconsistency. If the regression does not produce decoding, the partial meaning, if any, is stored in the medium term memory. The reader moves on with the possibility that additional cues will lead to complete decoding of the message.

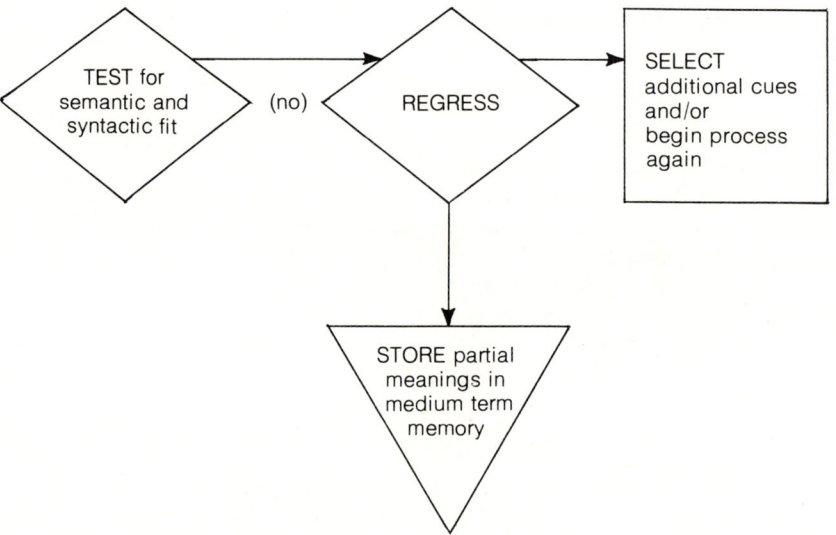

Miscues reveal the use or misuse of language cues

Goodman has analyzed the responses of pupils reading orally and has hypothesized as to the reasons for readers' deviations from the printed text. He does not call these deviations "errors" because the term implies something intrinsically bad or destructive or avoidable. He prefers to call them *miscues* because an analysis of them reveals the use and misuse of available language cues by the reader. In addition, the analysis reveals the process by which the readers utilize the available cues to reconstruct the author's message. Chapter 5 contains a discussion of how an analysis of a reader's miscues can be made and used in formulating an instructional program.

SELECTING APPROPRIATE INSTRUCTIONAL MATERIALS

A surfeit of materials can be found for use in instructional programs. As of this writing, it is in vogue to proclaim that materials are "linguistically" developed. It would be wise to remember, however, that to be "considered linguistically valid, reading materials must be consistent with accurate knowledge of language and how it functions in communication" (K. Goodman et al., 1966).

Reading materials must be consistent with accurate knowledge of language

The following list of critical questions is offered as a guide for use in the selection of materials to teach reading. Linguistics is the study of language, and it is the insights gleaned from this study that have application to the teaching of reading. As teachers, we must judge the accuracy of authors' claims to the relevance and importance of their information.

Choosing Materials to Teach Reading:
   Critical Questions to be Answered (K. Goodman et al., 1966)

   Accuracy of Language Information
      What language information is provided for the teacher?
      Is language information provided for direct instruction to the pupil?
      Are exercises provided which confirm or present language information?
      What is the source of language information?
      Is the language information presented consistent with itself?
      Is the language information presented consistent with scientific knowledge of language?
   Phonemic Considerations
      What provision is made for controlling grapheme-phoneme correspondence?
      Is this provision consistent throughout the materials?
      Is irregularity introduced in a planned and systematic way?
      Are spelling patterns used in building the materials?
      Are spelling patterns used consistently?
      Are phonics (sound-symbol) generalizations taught as such in the materials?
   Morphemic Considerations
      What focus is there in the reading material on words as such?
      Is any assistance offered to the pupil in delineating words and developing a concept of what words are? Are words presented and taught in isolation? If so, how are the problems of intonation and pronunciation handled?
         What attention is given to compound words?
         How are inflectional and derivational suffixes handled?
         Are contractions used in places where adults would normally use them, or are they avoided?

Syntactic Considerations
   Is the language of the material real language similar to the oral language as the learner knows it?
   Do reading materials contain the common language structures of oral language?
   Do these structures occur in the same frequency as in oral language?
   Is any attempt made to proceed from common to uncommon language structures?
   Is any attempt made to proceed from simple to complex fillers of the slots in language structures?
   Is structural and contextual ambiguity avoided?
   How are function words handled in the materials?
   Are there any special efforts in the materials to present syntactic cues in reading?
   Is any special effort made in teacher materials to assist him in helping children to use syntactic cues?

Intonational Considerations
   Do the materials relate punctuation to intonation?
   Are children encouraged to supply the natural intonations in reading?
   Does the material assist the teacher in understanding how intonation functions in communication?
   Does the material assist the teacher in helping children achieve natural intonation?

Dialect Considerations
   Do the materials assume a single "correct" English?
   Do they separate for the teacher and the child learning to read from learning a preferred dialect?
   Are dialect differences recognized? How?
   Is there provision for dialect differences? How?
   Is any attempt made to change oral language: prior to reading instruction; concurrently with reading instruction?
   Is there any attempt to widen the range of oral language comprehension and use?
   What assistance, if any, is given the teacher in understanding dialect problems in reading?

General Language Considerations
   Is the reading material based on child language?
   Does the reading material reflect the view that language learning is developmental?
   Is the teacher provided with help in understanding child language and child language development?
   Does the material draw on the prior language knowledge of the learners?
   Does the material help the teacher draw on the prior language knowledge of the learner?
   What definition of reading is stated or implicit in the reading materials?
   Are early reading materials meaningful?

If so, is the meaning within the range of experience and conceptual development of the learners?

Are pictures used to cue meaning?

Are skills implicitly or explicitly regarded as ends or means in the materials?

Is redundancy considered in constructing the material?

Do the reading materials correspond in redundancy to the oral language of children?

DISCUSSION QUESTIONS AND ACTIVITIES

1. The following statement was made by Andreas Feininger (1966), a well known and highly successful color photographer and author. In what way is his statement substantiated by current research on the thinking process? In what way does his statement help to explain the reading process?

> [The phenomenon of color memory] of the eye-brain combine causes us to *see color as we think it should look*, not as it *actually is*.

2. Observe individual and small groups of children of different ages at play. For example, observe children of ages 2, 5, and 8. Note the language they use when playing alone or with other children. (If possible, tape record about five minutes of their playtime conversations.) How do the children use language in relating to their play objects? How do the children use language in relating to themselves or to the other children?

3. Examine the teachers' manuals to two basal reading series in which it is indicated they were constructed on "linguistic" principles. Use the critical questions on page 77 and determine the validity of the claims.

4. Select two reading passages on different topics that contain information not generally known by a particular group of pupils. Then:

> A. Ask the pupils to read the first passage as they normally would read something. After the reading, test their retention of the main idea and major details of the passage: (a) immediately after the reading, (b) one hour later, and (c) one day later. Determine the type of information that is not retained by the pupils (that is, main ideas or major details).
>
> B. Plan a lesson so that the type of information not retained in the

first reading will be remembered after the reading of the second passage. Again test their retention: (1) immediately after the reading; (2) one hour later; and (3) one day later. Was there greater retention after the second reading?

5. From at least three other texts on reading instruction, obtain definitions of reading. How are they similar to or different from the one presented in this text?

6. The verb *to read* is defined in the dictionary both as a transitive and as an intransitive verb. Explain the confusion that may arise between two speakers who are using different sets of definitions in talking about reading.

FURTHER READINGS

Books written by Piaget himself are sometimes very difficult for the neophyte to read. Two books, which every teacher should read, clearly delineate Piaget's theory and positions on education.
 Furth, Hans G. 1970. *Piaget for Teachers.* Englewood Cliffs, N.J.: Prentice Hall.
 Elkind, David. 1974. *Children and Adolescents: Interpretive Essays on Jean Piaget,* 2nd Ed., New York: Oxford University Press.

The following two books by Smith present a scholarly yet highly readable examination of the psycholinguistic principles underlying the learning of reading. They present in greater depth than presented in this chapter the insights upon which the Goodman Model of Reading was constructed.
 Smith, Frank. 1971. *Understanding Reading.* New York: Holt, Rinehart & Winston.
 Smith, Frank. 1973. *Psycholinguistics and Reading.* New York: Holt, Rinehart & Winston.

Unlike the two books above which do not specifically deal with the methodology of teaching reading, the book by Lefevre explores the contribution that linguistic scholarship has made to teaching the skills of literacy. In it, he proposes a whole sentence method for teaching reading.
 Lefevre, Carl A. 1964. *Linguistics and the Teaching of Reading.* New York: McGraw Hill.

The following contains explanations of a number of different theoretical models of the reading process.

Singer, Harry, and Ruddell, Robert B., eds. 1976. *Theoretical Models and Processes of Reading.* 2nd Edition. Newark, Del.: International Reading Association.

Geyer, John J. 1972. "Comprehensive and Partial Models Related to the Reading Process." *Reading Research Quarterly* 7:541–87.

References

Brown, Roger, and Bellugi, Ursula. 1966. "Three Processes in the Child's Acquisition of Syntax." In Janet A. Emig, James T. Gleming, and Helen M. Popp, eds. *Language and Learning.* New York: Harcourt Brace Jovanovich, pp. 3–23.

Bruner, Jerome S., Goodnow, Jacqueline J., and Austin, George A. 1956. *A Study of Thinking.* New York: John Wiley and Sons.

Carroll, John B. 1964. *Language and Thought.* Englewood Cliffs, N.J.: Prentice Hall.

Carroll, John B. 1966. "Words, Meanings, and Concepts." In Janet A. Emig, James T. Fleming, and Helen M. Popp, eds. *Language and Learning.* New York: Harcourt Brace Jovanovich, pp. 73–101.

Deese, James, 1971. "The Psychology of Learning and the Study of English." In Carol Reed, ed. *The Learning of Language.* New York: Appleton Century Crofts, pp. 157–85.

Elkind, David. 1974. *Children and Adolescents: Interpretive Essays on Jean Piaget,* 2nd Ed. New York: Oxford University Press.

Feininger, Andreas. 1966. *Successful Color Photography.* Englewood Cliffs, N. J.: Prentice-Hall.

Furth, Hans. G. 1969. *Piaget and Knowledge: Theoretical Foundations.* Englewood Cliffs, N.J.: Prentice-Hall.

Furth, Hans G. 1970. *Piaget for Teachers.* Englewood Cliffs, N.J.: Prentice-Hall.

Geyer, John J. 1972. "Comprehensive and Partial Models Related to the Reading Process." *Reading Research Quarterly* 7: 541–87.

Goodman, Kenneth S. 1965a. "A Linguistic Study of Cues and Miscues in Reading." *Elementary English,* 42: 639–43.

Goodman, Kenneth S. 1965b. "Dialect Barriers to Reading Comprehension." *Elementary English* 42: 853–60.

Goodman, Kenneth S. 1967. "Reading: A Psycholinguistic Guessing Game." *Journal of the Reading Specialist* 6:126–35.

Goodman, Kenneth S. 1968. "The Psycholinguistic Nature of the Reading Process," in Kenneth S. Goodman, ed. *The Psycholinguistic Nature of the Reading Process.* Detroit: Wayne State University Press, pp. 15–26.

Goodman, Kenneth S. 1969. "Analysis of Oral Reading Miscues: Applied Psycholinguistics." *Reading Research Quarterly* 5: 9–30.

Goodman, Kenneth S. 1973. *Theoretically Based Studies of Patterns of Miscues in Oral Reading Performance.* Final Report, Project No. 9-0375, Grant No. OEG-0-9-320375-4269. Washington, D.C.: U.S. Office of Education/DHEW.

Goodman, Kenneth S., and Burke, Carolyn L. 1968. *Study of Childrens' Behavior While Reading Orally.* Final Report, Project No. 425, Contract No. OEG-610-136. Washington, D.C.: U.S. Office of Education/DHEW.

Goodman, Kenneth S., and Burke, Carolyn L. 1969. *A Study of Oral Reading Miscues That Result in Grammatical Re-transformations.* Final Report, Project No. 7-E-219, Contract No. OEG-0-8-070219 (010). Washington, D.C.: U.S. Office of Education/DHEW.

Goodman, Kenneth S., Olsen, H., Colvin, Cynthia, and VanderLinde, L. 1966. *Choosing Materials to Teach Reading.* Detroit: Wayne State University Press.

Goodman, Yetta, et al. 1969. "Studies of Reading Miscues." Paper presented at the International Reading Association, Kansas City, Mo.

Guilford, John P. 1967. *The Nature of Human Intelligence.* New York: McGraw Hill.

Guilford, John P., and Hoepfner, Ralph. 1971. *The Analysis of Intelligence.* New York: McGraw Hill.

Kumar, V. D. 1971. "The Structure of Human Memory and Some Educational Implications." *Review of Educational Research* 41: 379–418.

Lindsay, Peter H., and Norman, Donald A. 1972. *Human Information Processing: An Introduction to Psychology.* New York: Academic Press.

Menyuk, Paula. 1971. *The Acquisition and Development of Language.* Englewood Cliffs, N. J.: Prentice-Hall.

Raven, Ronald, and Salzer, Richard. 1971. "Piaget and Reading Instruction." *The Reading Teacher* 24: 630–39.

Ryan, Ellen B., and Semmel, Melvyn L. 1969. "Reading As A Constructive Language Process." *Reading Research Quarterly* 5: 59–83.

Slobin, Dan. 1971. *Psycholinguistics.* Glenview, Ill.: Scott, Foresman.

Stauffer, Russell. 1971. "The Quest for Maturity in Reading." In Carol Braun, ed. *Language, Reading, and the Communication Process.* Newark, Del.: International Reading Association, pp. 9–19.

Weaver, Wendel W. 1969. "The Contribution of Research to Reading Theory." *Journal of Reading Behavior* 1:3–18.

Williams, Joanna P. 1973. "Learning to Read: A Review of Theories and Models." *Reading Research Quarterly* 8: 121–46.

Principles of Analytical Teaching through Standardized Tests

Focus Questions:

1. What is analytical teaching?
2. What are the characteristics of standardized tests?
3. What are the effective uses of standardized tests?
4. What limitations do standardized tests have in analytical teaching?

ANALYTICAL TEACHING

Many teachers view testing and measuring as post-instructional activities. This kind of testing and measuring, however, is only one kind of assessment. Another kind—one that occurs continuously during instruction—is a check to insure that teaching and learning are progressing in the desired direction. Both kinds of assessment are important to the overall instructional program, but the second kind is more important to the classroom teacher. The first type of assessment is *summative assessment.* Examples are the end of course final examinations and comparisons of two or more different types of instructional procedures after they have been in operation for a period of time.

Formative assessment, the other kind, is concerned with evaluating an instructional procedure while it is in progress. It looks at the procedures to determine how many of the instructional goals have been accomplished and how well they have been accomplished according to an established standard. Formative assessment, by providing feedback to the teacher, helps the teacher decide how to proceed.

It is formative assessment that is referred to in this book as *analytical teaching.* The term analytical teaching has been selected over the more common one, diagnostic teaching, because the term "analytical" expresses more of the purposes of what school assessment should be. The term "diagnostic" reflects a medical origin and implies the searching for factors of failure. It implies, when applied to reading instruction, a search mainly for reasons why an individual is not reading well. It seems to exclude assessing a reading performance that is not marked by failure.

Analytical teaching as a rule consists of five steps that the teacher undertakes, not sporadically, but as a continuous classroom activity. All five steps of analytical teaching may be undertaken one or more times a day, or over a period of days.

<small>*Analytical teaching is a continuous classroom activity*</small>

Analytical teaching consists of

Describing: Noting the performance of pupils without using any qualitative or judgmental statements.
Classifying: Placing pupils' reading performances within some schema of the reading process.
Inferring: Judging the quality of a pupil's reading performance by a set of standards. The standards can be applied to individuals or groups and should be consistent with the schema of the reading process.
Predicting: Deciding whether the observed reading performance of the pupil needs to be modified, and planning the teaching and learning that will follow.
Verifying: Deciding whether or not the plan instituted was effective. Verification occurs by describing, classifying, and inferring the reading performance subsequent to the planned instruction and learning.

This chapter is concerned with using standardized tests for teaching analytically. In order to make insightful assessments that can be a basis for an instructional program, one should (1) know something about the principles of testing, (2) know the purposes of school-wide testing programs, and (3) understand the uses and limitations of standardized tests.

OBJECTIVES OF ASSESSMENT

Reading assessment, whether school-wide or within a single classroom, should be guided by certain objectives. Assessment of programs should:

1. Be directed towards formulating methods of instruction.
2. Attempt to place reading performance and reading instruction in relation to the total school or class educational program.
3. Be purposeful in that it has a place in the particular philosophy of education under which the class is conducted.
4. Be efficient to the degree that the greatest amount of pertinent and useful information is collected and analyzed in the least possible amount of time.
5. Be continuous.

An assessment program begins with the selection of a test, or series of tests, that will allow for some useful information to be collected. Yet, tests only describe the performance of an individual or group; they in and of themselves do not give an assessment of someone's performance. For example, if a test shows that a pupil has answered 16 of 25 questions correctly, all one has is a description of that child's performance. On the other hand, what is needed is some measure of the child's reading performance. This is obtained by comparing the difference between the results of two or more tests, or by measuring the results of a single test against some predetermined standard of performance. Still, this record of change or lack of change in reading performance is not yet assessment. Assessment is the application of some criteria for judging, or evaluating, the worth of the performance in a qualitative or quantitative manner. The process of assessing reading performance, then, is the deliberate act of testing, measuring, and evaluating reading performance.

Assessing reading performance means testing, measuring, and evaluating reading performance

Analytical teaching, which is the conscious application of the principles of assessment, is really a matter of degree. The depth and thoroughness of analysis will depend upon the teacher's purpose. A full analysis of different pupils' reading performances one or more times a year may be desired. On the other hand, a briefer, more frequent analysis of different aspects of the reading process may satisfy the teacher's plan. The amount and type of information collected should be usable because it is consistent with one's idea of the reading process and fulfills an instructional purpose.

Information is collected about pupils' reading performance for the purposes of instruction and administration. Information is gathered for instructional purposes when the effectiveness of either the teacher's teaching or the pupils' learning, or a combination of the two, needs to be determined. Administrative decisions are usually out of the realm of the classroom teacher and concern (1) the volatile issue of accountability, (2) school-wide effectiveness in comparison to other schools, and (3) the prediction of long range results of a project or experiment. But as far as a classroom teacher is concerned, the selection and use of tests should help answer instructional questions such as

What has the pupil done in the past?
What can the pupil do right now?
What can be expected of the pupil in the future?

STANDARDIZED TESTS

A standardized test is one that has been experimentally constructed

A standardized test is one that has been experimentally constructed. The test author has followed some commonly accepted procedures and has researched (1) the content of the test, (2) the procedures for administering the test, (3) the system for recording and scoring answers, and (4) the method by which results can be turned into an understandable and usable form. Everything about the test has been standardized so that, if all the directions are correctly followed, the results should be interpreted in the same manner regardless of where in the country the test is given. The results should mean the same thing to different people. A common misconception is that the word *standard* represents a goal to be attained. Standardized means that the methods of administering, recording, scoring, and interpreting have been made uniform.

Characteristics of Standardized Tests

There are two main types of standardized reading tests, norm referenced tests and criterion referenced tests.

Norm referenced tests are used to compare the relative position of individuals in different groups. The test is constructed and then given to a large number of pupils. The "average" score (or median) is found by noting the raw score for which fifty percent of the scores were higher and fifty percent were lower. This score is then designated as the average for the group. As an example, a hypothetical group of fourth grade pupils are given a newly constructed test in the second month of the fourth grade. The middle score of that group would represent a grade equivalent of 4.2. Now, if the test is given to other groups, say of third graders, fifth graders, etc., average scores could be obtained for those grade levels as well. The differences between the average scores for the different grade levels—the

A criterion referenced test can pinpoint pupil strengths and weaknesses

difference between 3.2 and 4.2, and 5.2 and 4.2—would be filled in through a mathematical procedure called extrapolation. It is also possible to obtain "average" scores for different periods of time during the school year. Many standardized test publishers provide different sets of scores or norms for the beginning, middle, and end of each grade level.

A norm referenced test is used to measure the performance of a pupil in relation to the norming, or standardizing, group. If a pupil in fourth grade achieves a grade equivalent of 4.5 during the month of February, it could

A norm referenced test measures a pupil's performance relative to a group

be stated that that pupil has achieved a score equal to the average score in the fourth grade norming group, and the score could be interpreted as meaning that the pupil scored better than fifty percent of the norming population. A score of 5.5 would mean the pupil achieved a score equal to that of the average fifth grader in the norming group. It does not mean that the pupil should be in fifth grade or "is doing" fifth grade work.

The fact that norm referenced tests are useful primarily as indications of how a pupil performs in relation to other children becomes even clearer when two other types of norms, the percentile and the stanine, are considered.

The percentile indicates how a pupil performed relative to all the pupils in the norming group. For example, a pupil with a score at the 60th percentile scored better than sixty percent of the norming group, and forty percent of the norming group scored better than the pupil.

It is possible to create local percentile norms based upon the scores made by the pupils in a particular class, school, or school district. In these cases, a percentile would show a pupil's performance in relation to his immediate peers. It is possible that local norms do not match exactly the national norms provided by the test publisher. A local norm may be higher or lower than the national norm. Take, for example, the following hypothetical percentiles:

	National Norm Percentiles	Local Norm Percentiles
Vocabulary	45	55
Comprehension	45	40

These would be interpreted as meaning that for the vocabulary test, a pupil who scores better than forty-five percent of the national group, in comparison, scores better than fifty-five percent of the other pupils on his grade level in the local school or school district.

The stanine scores are digits which range from one to nine. Like percentiles, their interpretation is based upon a relationship to a particular group. The fifth stanine is considered average and the stanines on either side of the fifth are equally distant from the average. For instance, a pupil who scores in stanine 3 stands the same relative distance from the average as someone who scores in stanine 7. An advantage to the use of stanines over grade equivalents and the percentile ranks is that stanines represent a range of scores rather than one particular score. Three pupils in the second half of the fifth grade with different raw scores could have different grade equivalents and percentile ranks, yet their stanine scores might not differ. If their scores were within the same stanine unit, they could be considered to have performed equally well on the test. The following scores of three pupils on an actual test (Karlsen, Madden, and Gardner, 1966) illustrate this.

Reading Comprehension, Total

	Raw Score	Grade Equivalent	Percentile	Stanine
Martha	38	5.8	40	5
Marc	40	6.0	44	5
Myra	43	6.7	58	5

In many schools, Martha and Myra would not be considered to be performing about equally. The use of the stanine scores, despite the seemingly wide grade equivalent spread, makes it more apparent that all three pupils performed, in comparison to the norming group, in the average range.

Stanines, like percentiles, are relative scores; they indicate performance relative to the group. Myra and Martha performed (from an absolute point of view) differently, but relative to the group of their peers who took the test they performed about the same. (A note of caution: although stanines will classify two different scores as similar, they will also classify two similar scores as different if those scores fall close to one boundary between two stanines.)

Another example of the use of stanines for interpreting scores can be seen in the scores of two fifth grade pupils on another actual test (Kelley et al., 1966). One pupil obtained a raw score of 29 on the paragraph meaning subtest at the beginning (B) of fifth grade. The other achieved the same number of correct answers, but at the end (E) of fifth grade. As can be seen below, they both have identical grade equivalents. However, the scores mean very different things.

	Paragraph Reading			
	Raw Score	Grade Equivalent	Percentile	Stanine
Felice (B)	29	5.3	56	5
Frank (E)	29	5.3	38	4

Felice, who represents a grade score of 5.3 at the beginning of the year, would be considered average in performance in comparison to the norming group. Frank, however, who represents a grade score of 5.3 at the end of the year, would be considered as below average in relation to the norming group.

A criterion referenced test is a set of goals representing tasks pupils are to master

Criterion referenced tests are instruments that determine whether an individual or group has achieved a certain level of mastery. A criterion referenced test is a set of standards, or goals, representing a group of tasks the pupils are supposed to master. Scores on this test, rather than showing placement in relation to a group, show the pupils' placement in relation to a set of goals.

To construct a criterion referenced reading test, the test writer assumes a hierarchy of skills necessary to the reading process. Successful completion of certain tasks are presumed to evidence such skills. If a pupil can perform the task, then that pupil is said to have mastered a particular aspect of reading. For example, an item may ask the pupil to match the letter *b* with the appropriate picture of an object whose name begins with /b/, or the pupil may be asked to read two paragraphs and mark the one that is ordered in a time sequence. For each task there may be one or more items. When the pupil can mark the appropriate answers for a particular task, then mastery of that task is assumed. Like norm referenced tests, criterion referenced tests can be made appropriate for different maturity levels of reading performance.

A standardized test should be valid and reliable

Whether a standardized test is norm referenced or criterion referenced, it should have validity and reliability.

A valid test measures what it says it measures. A reading test should indicate something about reading performance, and the tasks should relate to some aspects of reading. Of course, a test may be valid according to the test writer's definition of reading, but not according to the definition assumed by the test user. Within the definition of reading set forth in this book, a test of reading composed entirely of lists of words would not be considered as valid. Such a test is in no way concerned with testing the child's ability to reconstruct an author's message.

Reliability refers to the consistency with which a test produces its results. Think of an individual who never is able to keep appointments or is constantly disappointing others by failing to follow through with promises. That person lacks reliability. When a reading test cannot be relied upon to give consistent, reliable results, then as far as classroom teachers should be concerned, the test is worthless. The reliability of a test can be determined from statistical information generally provided by the publisher of the test. If a publisher reports a "coefficient of reliability" somewhere between .90 and .99, that test can be accepted as being fairly reliable. A test, however, can have a high degree of reliability, but not have validity: whatever it may test—which may or may not be part of the reading process—it tests it in a consistent manner.

Standardized tests are usually accompanied by a manual of directions that contains a variety of information about the test. This manual should be read very carefully in order to find out (1) the intended purposes of the test, (2) the content of the test, (3) the manner in which the test is organized, (4) the recommended procedures for administering the test, (5) the publisher's estimate of its validity and reliability, (6) the various tables of norms (not included in criterion referenced tests), (7) an explanation of how to interpret the scores, and (8) a discussion of some uses of the test results.

A score is not a judgment

The manuals accompanying norm referenced tests also contain another bit of information which is often overlooked—the standard error of measurement. This number, which is usually but not necessarily expressed in grade level equivalents, is an indication of how much the particular test could be wrong. No test is so precise so as to produce completely accurate estimates of a pupil's actual performance. The standard error of measurement should be used to estimate how much a pupil's score could differ from the one produced on the test. If a pupil scores a grade equivalent of 5.3 on a test with a four month (.4 year) standard error of measurement, it could be assumed about sixty-eight percent of the time that the pupil's real score is between the grade equivalents of 4.9 and 5.7 (obtained by adding and subtracting one standard error of measurement from the pupil's score). It could be assumed about ninety-five percent of the time that the pupil's score is really between the grade equivalents of 4.5 and 6.4 (obtained by adding and subtracting the doubled standard error of measurement).

Standardized Reading Tests

A norm referenced test contains vocabulary and paragraph reading subtests

Norm referenced reading tests usually contain two sections, a vocabulary subtest and a paragraph reading subtest. Separate scores are obtained for each subtest and some tests have a composite score. The vocabulary sections attempt to test a pupil's knowledge of specific words through the matching of the word to its pictorial representation or to an appropriate

---

FIGURE 4-1: Sample Questions from a Norm Referenced Test

To **bake** is to .... ○ eat   ○ cook   ○ cut   ○ stir

A **lamb** is a young .... ○ cow   ○ bear   ○ moose   ○ sheep

To **begin** is to .... ○ race   ○ start   ○ be   ○ come

---

Betty's puppy digs holes in the yard. He barks at people going by. He runs after squirrels and cats. When he gets tired, he lies on the grass and falls asleep.

1. The story tells that Betty's puppy —
   ○ chases other dogs
   ○ barks all the time
   ○ does many things

2. The little dog chases —
   cars   animals   leaves
   ○   ○   ○

3. When does the puppy sleep?
   ○ when he gets tired
   ○ all the time
   ○ while he digs in the yard

Joe and Tom are in the house. They are playing with Tom's trains. They build bridges and hills with the track. Joe likes to watch the engine pull the trains across the bridges.

4. Joe and Tom are playing in the —
   ○ yard   ○ house   ○ car

5. They are playing with —
   ○ trains   ○ toy autos ○ blocks

6. Joe likes to see the engine go —
   ○ over the hills
   ○ through the town
   ○ over the bridges

SOURCE: *Metropolitan Achievement Tests*, Elementary Battery. Copyright 1970 by Harcourt Brace Jovanovitch. Reproduced by permission of the publisher.

synonym. The comprehension of the pupil is tested by means of a series of questions about different paragraphs or short selections. Figure 4-1 contains sample vocabulary and comprehension questions from a representative standardized norm referenced reading test.

The following are representative of some widely used norm referenced reading tests.

> *California Reading Test.* California Test Bureau/McGraw Hill. Intended grades: 1 through 14. Subtests: Vocabulary and comprehension.
> *Gates-MacGinitie Reading Tests.* Teachers College Press, Columbia University. Intended grades: 1 through 9. Subtests: Vocabulary and comprehension (1-9); Speed and accuracy (2-9).
> *Iowa Silent Reading Test.* Harcourt Brace Jovanovich. Intended grades: 4-14. Subtests: Rate, comprehension, directed reading, word meaning, paragraph comprehension, sentence meaning, study skills.
> *Metropolitan Achievement Tests: Reading.* Harcourt Brace Jovanovich. Intended grades: 1-9. Subtests: Word knowledge, word discrimination (2), reading.
> *Sequential Tests of Education Progress (STEP): Reading.* Cooperative Test Division, Educational Testing Service. Intended grades: 4-14. Subtests: Comprehension.
> *Silent Reading Comprehension: Iowa Every-Pupil Test of Basic Skills.* Houghton Mifflin. Intended grades: 3-9. Subtests: Comprehension, vocabulary.
> *S.R.A. Achievement Series: Reading.* Science Research Associates. Intended grades: 1-9. Subtests: Verbal-picture association, language perception, comprehension, and vocabulary.
> *Stanford Achievement Test: Reading Tests.* Harcourt Brace Jovanovich. Intended grades: 1-9. Subtests: Word meaning, paragraph meaning, word study (1-4).

Figure 4-2 contains sample questions from a criterion referenced test.

Although the surface appearance of the criterion referenced test looks similar to that of a norm referenced test, the difference is greater than their layout and format would suggest. The criterion referenced test measures the pupils' mastery of certain specific objectives. Whereas a norm referenced test cannot be used to pinpoint pupil strengths and deficiencies, the criterion referenced tests can do just that without any reference to a norm group.

FIGURE 4-2: Sample Questions from a Criterion Referenced Test

 111   1. In which sentence does <u>play</u> mean <u>to have fun with</u>?
- ○ Do you like to <u>play</u> games?
- ○ Father built me a new <u>play</u> house.
- ○ We are going to give a <u>play</u> in school.

 112   2. In which sentence does <u>fly</u> mean <u>something a bird does</u>?
- ○ There is a <u>fly</u> in the house.
- ○ I wish I could <u>fly</u> over the treetops.
- ○ Bill hit a high <u>fly</u> ball into left field.

 113   3. In which sentence does <u>back</u> mean <u>a part that is not the front</u>?
- ○ We went <u>back</u> to school to get our work.
- ○ We saw the river <u>back</u> up after the flood.
- ○ The <u>back</u> of May's dress has a picture on it.

 114   1. You have to <u>duck</u> to get into the cave.
- ○ a kind of bird
- ○ move your head down
- ○ a place to tie a boat

SOURCE: *Prescriptive Reading Inventory*, Green Book. Copyright 1972 by McGraw-Hill. Reproduced by permission of the publisher.

The following is a representative published criterion referenced test.

Prescriptive Reading Inventory. California Test Bureau/McGraw Hill. Intended grades: 1–6. Subtests: No specific subtest designation; the series of four tests covers the total range of reading behaviors most widely expected of students.

Limitations of Standardized Tests

Both types of standardized test—norm referenced and criterion referenced—have limitations. The tests should be used judiciously with these limitations in mind. Some of the limitations derive from inherent qualities within the tests themselves and some derive from misunderstandings about the capabilities of the tests and what they represent.

Some of the limitations of norm referenced reading tests are:

1. Some tests overestimate an individual's reading performance.
2. The supposedly comparable forms of a test may not in fact be so.
3. The factor of speediness—how much time is allowed for different parts of the test—influences the results.
4. The validity of tests may differ or be lost at different age levels.
5. The scores may be influenced by guessing.
6. The interpretation of scores may be misleading if the norming population differs from the users' pupil population.
7. The revisions made on tests sometimes result in different forms of the test not being comparable.
8. The test results do not always correlate with actual classroom performance.
9. The reading abilities sampled by some of the tests seemed to be limited (Strang, 1968).

Some of the above conclusions warrant further comment. First, in regard to the validity of any particular test, a number of researchers have questioned what it actually is that publishers say a reading achievement test measures. According to one test manual,

> [the paragraph meaning subtest of the test intended for grades five and six is to provide a] functional measure of the pupil's ability to comprehend connected discourse involving levels of comprehension varying from extremely simple recognition to the making of inferences from what is stated in several sentences (Kelley et al., 1966).

The manual goes on to add that exercises were selected "that place a premium on genuine comprehension of the material read." In other words, the test is a measure of whether the pupil can read and understand the material before him. A number of researchers, however, have found some evidence to contradict claims such as the one above.

A set of five different standardized tests were administered and the results were compared to the results of a test consisting of the questions only of these same tests (Tuinman, 1973). If the questions really measured a pupil's ability to read and understand the paragraphs, then the questions should be unanswerable by any pupil who did not read the paragraphs. That is not what was found. On three of the tests, the subjects of the research who did not have the paragraph to read were able to get seventy percent as many answers correct as those subjects who did have the paragraphs to read. From this study it was concluded that the questions on the reading tests were not dependent upon the paragraphs and that pupils can answer correctly a surprisingly large number of questions without ever reading the passages. This seemed to be increasingly true at the higher grade levels.

The results of this study are consistent with other studies. In one study (Pyrczak, 1972), it was found that a substantial number of the subjects knew the point being tested before they even read the paragraph. In another (Weaver and Bickely, 1967), it was found that at least two distinct sources of information existed for completing multiple choice questions (the kind found on most reading achievement tests). The first was concept information brought by the pupil to the testing situation about one or more of the topics on the test samples. The other was a cue within the question itself or a cue in a previous question. In other words, the test itself gave away many of the answers to questions. The conclusion was that some reading comprehension tests are highly dependent upon various reader characteristics and often have little to do with the reading tasks assumed by the tester.

One researcher (MacGinitie, 1973), a test writer himself, indicates that as much difference exists between different edition levels of the same subtest as between differently named tests on the same level. What this means is that a vocabulary test on the primary level may differ from a vocabulary test on the intermediate level as much as it differs from an arithmetic test. It was pointed out how many vocabulary tests on the primary level test pupils' ability to recognize in print a number of well-known words generally found in their auditory vocabularies. On the other hand, the vocabulary test on an intermediate level requires the pupils to deal with less known words and uses minimum contrast clues (distinguishing between two graphically similar words) to measure their knowledge of a variety of words. The titles of the tests remain the same, but the tasks required of the pupils differ radically.

In a comparison of the vocabulary subtests on a reading achievement test and on a test of intelligence (MacGinitie, 1973), there was indication that by the end of third grade the two are indistinguishable. They are the same test—requiring very similar tasks—yet they are interpreted differently by educators.

In a study of nine popular published reading tests intended for group and/or individual administration (Winkley, 1971) it was found that

1. The tests have a wide range of purposes.
2. Most of the tests could not be used to determine a pupil's chief skill deficiency.
3. Most of the subtests of word recognition evaluate spelling ability rather than reading ability.
4. The skills sampled usually require the decoding of single syllable words more frequently than multisyllabic words.
5. Errors existed in many of the tests.

In the matter of validity, then, a reading achievement test may measure something entirely different from reading. It may also test specific aspects of reading that are limited and provide only a partial picture of how a pupil actually does function.

A reading achievement test may measure something entirely different from reading

Another limitation of standardized tests is the manner in which the scores may be interpreted and used for instructional purposes. The following considerations should affect the use of standardized tests in classrooms:

1. *A score is not a judgment.* Judgments must be made by teachers and reflect the value they place upon any score.
2. *A score is not high or low; it is higher or lower than some other score or scores.* This means that any individual score is useless unless it is compared to some other score. Most commonly, the other scores are the national norms. It is inappropriate, then, to compare any scores unless the group from which they were obtained have the same characteristics as the norming group. The manual must be carefully examined to insure that the national norm group contains a sampling of pupils with characteristics similar to those being tested.
3. *Grade equivalent scores from one subtest are not comparable to those from another subtest.* In order to determine whether or not two grade equivalent scores differ, one of two things must be done: (1) check the stanine table to determine if the scores

What is needed is some measure of the child's reading performance

fall within the same stanine. If they do, then no matter how large the difference seems between the two scores, they mean relatively the same thing; (2) add or subtract the standard error of measurement for each subtest to or from the obtained score. If the range of the two sets of scores overlaps, they mean relatively the same thing.
4. *The grade equivalent scores on tests administered at different times of the year represent different performance levels of the pupils.*

If the results from an achievement test are used to compile a pupil's profile—a graphic representation of relative performance on a series of tests—then stanine scores may be the most useful. They are useful because they provide the same kind of information—the pupil's performance on the various tests relative to the performance of a peer group.

Criterion referenced tests, too, have certain limitations. In regard to the validity of the test items, the comments made above hold for criterion referenced tests as well as norm referenced tests. The classroom teacher should be sure that the tasks asked of the pupil represent some aspects of reading. Other limitations of criterion referenced tests are a lack of empirical justification for either the number of items to be used for measuring an ability to perform a task, the percentage of correct items needed for mastery to be demonstrated, or the length of time to be allowed for administration of the test.

When criterion referenced tests are being constructed, the question usually arises as to whether it is necessary to include items which test mastery of every identified skill of reading. Depending on how narrowly the skills are differentiated this might result in an unwieldy test. Researchers are, of course, attempting to determine how many of the individual skills to test and the number of items for each skill to include. Since they are interested in determining pupil flow from performance level to performance level and not in comparing individuals to each other, most criterion referenced test makers are reluctant to engage in the normative procedures used by other test makers. Therefore, when teachers consider the use of criterion referenced tests, the following should be kept in mind: The criterion referenced items should be representative of skills that are essential to learning to read, and the tasks must be evaluated in the context of a normal reading situation (Pikulski, 1974).

The second point is most important. Quite often a pupil is asked to perform a task, say, to match words which contain a similar final consonant' cluster. Yet this task rarely occurs in an actual reading situation. The matching task might be appropriate for a spelling situation, but it has limited utility during an act of reading.

A caution about the "effect of examinations" is offered as a final word about all standardized tests (Bloom, 1969). Pupils, teachers, and administrators are each affected by what each perceives to be the purpose of a test or a testing situation. There may be, then, either positive or negative effects of the entire process of assessment depending upon the attitudes of those involved. If the test is viewed as punitive—as they are in some schools where the results of achievement tests are used for pupil promotion or retention, or for the evaluation of teachers—the entire learning process may be viewed as punitive as well.

Effective Use of Standardized Reading Test Results

Certain information is necessary for a teacher to effectively administer and interpret standardized tests in a classroom. A wise user of tests knows (1) the scope of the school testing program, (2) its relationship to the entire school educational program, and (3) the uses to which test results will be put.

The classroom teacher should know

1. The objectives of the school testing program. What purposes does the administration have for all testing that occurs within the school? How have these objectives been developed, and when was the last time they were reviewed?

2. The content of the tests. What is the relationship between the content of the tests and the objectives of the instructional and testing programs? Who examined the tests to make this decision, and when was the test last reviewed?
3. The pre-testing arrangements. What information about the testing has been provided to the pupils, to the parents, and to the teachers? What attitudes about testing are implicitly and explicitly expressed in this information?
4. The testing schedule. What advance information has been provided to the teachers, pupils, and parents about who will administer the tests, and when and where the testing will occur?
5. The scoring of the tests. How will the tests be marked—by the teacher, by auxiliary staff, by secretaries, by machine? In what kind of scores will the results be expressed—grade equivalents, percentiles, or stanines?
6. The recording of the results. What test data are to be recorded? What forms will be used for recording the results? Which of the derived tests scores will be recorded?
7. The meaning of the scores. What interpretation of the scores will be provided to the teachers, the pupils, and the parents? What is the relation between the test scores obtained and other data available about the pupils?
8. The reporting of scores. How will the test results be reported to the pupils and the parents? When will the reporting take place and in what form?
9. The use of the tests in the school. To what use will the test results be put by the administration, the teachers, the school psychologists, and the guidance counselors? In what way do these uses conform to the objectives of the testing program?

OBTAINING INFORMATION ABOUT ACADEMIC POTENTIAL

The analytic teacher tries to find out if pupils read at the level at which they think

The process of reading is closely related to the entire process of thinking. The analytic teacher attempts to determine whether or not pupils' reading performances are commensurate with their maturity of thinking. To many, this may immediately bring to mind "intelligence"; however, the use of the term intelligence has led to many misconceptions about pupils' performance in school. There are different types of intelligence, and in school there is concern with only one of them. For this reason, the term *academic potential* is used rather than intelligence. Academic potential draws attention to specific abilities that directly influence a pupil's school performance. As it has been stated in the discussion of Guilford's structure-of-intellect model (see pages 56–59), there are different types of intelligence for different types of tasks.

An estimate of a pupil's academic potential may be made from the results of a standardized individual or group test. Individual tests, which should be administered by a psychologist, psychometrician, guidance counselor, or another qualified person, require a great deal of time. Therefore, many schools administer on a regular basis some type of standardized group intelligence, mental maturity, or academic potential test.

The following are representative of some widely used standardized group measures of academic potential.

> California Test of Academic Aptitude. California Test
>   Bureau/McGraw Hill Book Co.
> Lorge-Thorndike Intelligence Tests. Houghton Mifflin.
> Otis-Lennon Mental Ability Test. Harcourt Brace Jovanovich.
> Pintner General Ability Tests. Harcourt Brace Jovanovich.

The academic potential, or mental maturity, tests usually contain a non-verbal, or non-language, subtest and a language, or verbal, subtest. Careful examination of the tests themselves indicates that these terms are not accurate descriptions of the tasks included on the tests. The subsections are tests of non-written language and of written language. In fact, since reading is required on all the language, or verbal, sections of these tests, one can ask whether the test is a measure of academic potential or just another test of reading achievement.

Figure 4–3 contains sample questions from a representative test of academic potential.

Since the results of the verbal forms of group intelligence tests have such a high correlation with performance on reading achievement tests, the differences seem to arise primarily because of the errors of measurement of the two tests. (Strang, 1969). It would seem wise, then, when attempting to gain an estimation of a pupil's potential for doing academic work, to select a test that requires little or no reading, or to use the results from the subtests that require no reading.

Classroom teachers should be alert to any discrepancy between a test

FIGURE 4-3: Sample Questions from a Test of Academic Potential

9. **Injure** means —
    a suffer   **b** bandage   **c** question   **d** hurt   **e** inform

10. The numbers in the box go together in a certain way. Find the number that belongs where you see the question mark (?) in the box.

7	5	3
6	4	?

    f 1   **g** 2   **h** 3   **j** 4   **k** 5

11. ⊗ is to ⊗ as ◨ is to —   **a** ◨   **b** ◧   **c** ◨   **d** ◇   **e** ◇

SOURCE: Otis, Arthur S., and Lennon, Roger T. *Otis-Lennon Mental Ability Test*, Elementary II Level, Form J. Copyright 1967 by Harcourt Brace Jovanovitch. Used with permission.

Teachers should watch for differences between test results and classroom behavior

result and the observed performance of a pupil in actual class settings. When there is a question, the pupil should be referred for further appraisal by the appropriate school personnel.

Some cautionary words about using group tests of academic potential to predict a pupil's reading potential follow.

1. Intelligence tests are not a sure measure of innate ability to learn. They represent "developed ability."
2. Intelligence tests show how an individual is functioning at present, at the time when the test is being taken.
3. Intelligence scores for a pupil fluctuate from test to test.
4. Intelligence tests may have a serious lack of validity.
5. Intelligence tests should be interpreted in light of the pupil's cultural background and home environment.
6. Intelligence test scores should be interpreted with consideration for the pupil's proficiency in language.
7. Intelligence test scores may be raised by practice and coaching (Strang, 1969).

The group tests of academic potential should be used guardedly as part of analytical teaching. If the tests are administered, the results should be used as only one means for comparing a pupil's cognitive maturity to that of other pupils the same age. A pupil who matures at a slower rate or who has not had an equal opportunity to learn cannot be expected to perform in the same manner as the other pupils. The use of group tests of academic potential allows for the identification of those pupils whose performance is markedly different from others, but it will not disclose the cause for the difference. For this, further analysis is necessary.

DISCUSSION QUESTIONS AND ACTIVITIES

1. In order for a test to be valid it must first be reliable. Why isn't the converse of this statement true?

2. Examine a standardized reading test and its accompanying manuals. From your examination of the test items, does the test seem to measure what the author states it is supposed to measure? How many of the questions in the comprehension subsection can be answered from information contained in other questions and answers? Are there features in the layout of the test and its answer sheet that might confuse pupils and cause them to improperly answer the test items?

3. Prepare a statement that could be made to a parents' group. In it, explain in nontechnical language: (1) what the characteristics of a good standardized test are, and (2) some of the advantages to be derived from using standardized reading tests.

4. If there is no single standardized reading test that is best for all pupil populations, all instructional programs, and all school settings, how then should school personnel go about selecting a standardized test that is "best" for their situation?

5. Explain what the following statement means to you: A school instructional program is no better than the means by which it is assessed.

6. The meaning of "grade equivalent" is often misunderstood by many parents and teachers. Explain how confusion may arise between the terms *grade equivalent,* as used on standardized tests, and *grade level,* as used on instructional materials. What procedures might school personnel undertake to clarify the meaning of these terms for both parents and teachers?

FURTHER READINGS

Two short books, addressed to the concerns teachers have about problems of assessment in reading instruction, are:

Blanton, William E., Farr, Roger, and Tuinman, J. Japp, eds. 1974. *Measuring Reading Performance.* Newark, Del.: International Reading Association.

MacGinitie, Walter, ed. 1973. *Assessment Problems in Reading.* Newark, Del.: International Reading Association.

The following is a series of yearbooks which teachers should know about even though the books may not be immediately needed. They contain critical reviews and descriptions of standardized tests in all subject areas. They can be of immense help to teachers wishing to select tests for particular purposes.

Buros, O.K. *The Mental Measurement Yearbooks.* Highland Park, N.J.: Gryphon Press.

For extended discussions of the problems of evaluation of all school programs, not only of reading, the teacher should read the following.

Tyler, Ralph W. 1969. *Educational Evaluation: New Roles, New Means.* Sixty-eighth Year book of the National Society for the Study of Education. Chicago: University of Chicago Press.

References

Bloom, Benjamin S. 1969. "Some Theoretical Issues Relating to Educational Evaluation." In Ralph W. Tyler, ed. *Educational Evaluation: New Roles, New Means.* Chicago: University of Chicago Press, pp. 26–50.

Karlsen, Bjorn, Madden, Richard, and Gardner, Eric F. 1966. *Manual for Administering and Interpreting the Stanford Diagnostic Reading Test, Level II.* N.Y.: Harcourt Brace Jovanovich.

Kelly, Truman L., Madden, Richard, Gardner, Eric F., and Rudman, Herbert. 1966. *Stanford Achievement Test: Reading.* Directions for Administering, Intermediate II Battery. N.Y.: Harcourt Brace Jovanovich.

MacGinitie, Walter H. 1973. "What Are We Testing?" in Walter H. MacGinitie, ed. *Assessment Problems in Reading.* Newark, Del.: International Reading Association, pp. 35–43.

Pikulski, John J. 1974. "Criterion Referenced Measures for Clinical Evaluation." *Reading World* 14: 116–28.

Pyrczak, Fred. 1972. "Objective Evaluation of the Quality of Multiple Choice Test Items Designed to Measure Comprehension of Reading Passages." *Reading Research Quarterly* 8: 62–71.

Strang, Ruth. 1968. *Reading Diagnosis and Remediation.* Newark, Del.: International Reading Association.

Strang, Ruth. 1969. *Diagnostic Teaching of Reading.* 2nd Edition. N.Y.: McGraw Hill.

Tuinman, J. Jaap. 1973. "Determining the Passage Dependency of Comprehension Questions in Five Major Tests," *Reading Research Quarterly* 9: 206–23.

Weaver, Wendell W., and Bickley, A.C. 1967. "Sources of Information for Responses to Reading Test Items." *Proceedings* 75th Annual Convention, American Psychological Association, pp. 293–94.

Winkley, Carol K. 1971. "What Do Diagnostic Tests Really Diagnose?" In Robert Leibert, ed. *Diagnostic Viewpoints in Reading.* Newark, Del.: International Reading Association, pp. 64–80.

5
Strategies for Analytical Teaching through Informal Tests

Focus Questions:

1. What information about a pupil's background and physical condition provides insights for instruction?
2. How may a teacher informally estimate a pupil's potential for doing academic work?
3. What can a teacher do to analyze a pupil's oral and silent reading performances?

Analytical teaching is not prolonged assessment. It is an ongoing activity in which the teacher is constantly on the lookout for the emergence of patterns in the pupils' reading performance. Analytic teaching activities include the selection and recording of information during instances of the pupil's oral and silent reading.

Assessment is only as effective as the individual performing the evaluation. Teachers should be able to devise and administer informal reading instruments and make the necessary instructional judgments that lead to appropriate reading programs for all pupils.

Although useful information about pupils' reading performance may be obtained through group comparisons, the analytical teacher tries to identify individual needs and progress as well. Elementary school pupils might pass through the same developmental stages in their acquisition of reading tasks; however, no two pupils will pass through the stages in exactly the same manner, using the exact same pattern of strategies, or using the same language cues. Analytical teaching attempts to relate the developmental growth characteristics of all children and the individual reading needs of each particular pupil.

An analytic teacher continuously watches for patterns

USEFUL BACKGROUND INFORMATION

An understanding of pupils' backgrounds and prior experiences allows the teacher to keep their classroom performance in perspective. Often, information about the pupils' home situations, prior school and non-school experiences, and attitudes toward reading and other activities gives the teacher insights about pupils' school behavior and, in particular, their reading performance. Although this information in itself may not explain why pupils read the way they do, it may help to explain why they do or do not respond to certain instructional activities and learning situations.

One source of information is the pupils' school records. They often contain notations about previous achievement and home-school interaction, specialized reports or tests on record, and general impressions and evaluations. Where school records are incomplete or unavailable, it might be beneficial to interview the pupils and their parents, being sure to make it quite clear that the information obtained will be used only to help in formulating programs geared to the pupils' needs.

Sometimes pupils will reveal their attitudes toward reading and their preferences in story content during discussions with the teacher or with other pupils. Teachers can be guided by these attitudes and preferences when forming instructional programs with pupils who show reluctance to reading independently or who resist conventional instructional materials.

Classroom teachers should observe pupils' behavior for signs of certain physical conditions that may impede school performance. In general, one should particularly look for general coordination problems, possible visual defects, or possible auditory deficiencies. Pupils who demonstrate speech problems also need special attention. (Speech in this case refers to the physical production of oral communication.) At no time should an attempt be made to correct those deficiencies without proper guidance. It is a fallacy that pupils normally outgrow speech defects, they must in general be corrected by knowledgeable personnel.

Background information may help explain why pupils do not respond to instruction

By noticing deviations from the behavior of the other pupils in the class, teachers can identify those pupils who need further examination by an appropriate specialist. It is good educational policy to bring to the school nurse-teacher, psychologist, speech teacher, guidance counselor, or principal the results of any observations of deviancy. After consulting with the appropriate school personnel, teachers may make a general recommendation to the parents about seeking further professional assistance.

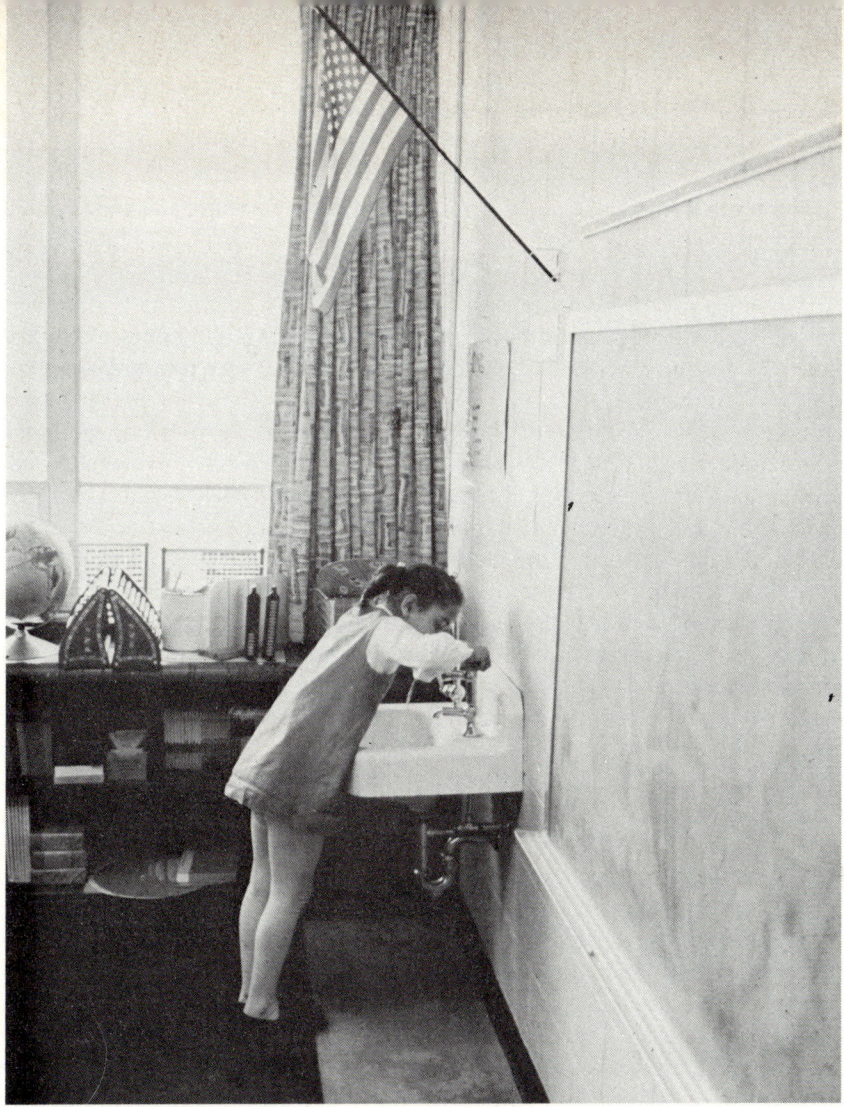

The analytical teacher tries to identify individual needs

Information about Academic Potential

When formal measures of academic potential are not available, a pupil's cognitive maturity and potential for reading can be estimated. Listening comprehension seems to be directly related to reading. Listening comprehension is a reflection, among other things, of a pupil's language development and knowledge of spoken words and sentences (Smith, 1975). Since the cognitive processing of written language seems to be the same as the processing of spoken language, a listening comprehension test can be a good estimate of reading potential.

One means of informally estimating pupils' academic potentials is

A listening comprehension test can be a good estimate of academic potential

through the administration of listening tests. One test series which is available in a standardized form is:

> *Durrell Listen-Read Series,* Harcourt Brace Jovanovich. Intended grades: 1–9. Subtests: listening, vocabulary and paragraph comprehension; silent reading vocabulary and paragraph comprehension.

These tests were designed to measure the difference between pupils' understanding of spoken language and written language. They are included in the section on informal assessment because the reliability of the differences between the listening and reading scores is not sufficiently high for use as anything except an informal procedure.

Other informal tests, however, can be devised that might prove more functional in particular classroom situations. All that is needed is a passage representative of the material with which the pupils are expected to work. After reading the passage aloud to the pupils, they are questioned in order to obtain a measure of how well the material was understood. If the pupils understand the material as it is read to them, then they can be judged to have the "potential" for reading similar material.

In order to devise listening comprehension tests, the procedures discussed in the next section for developing informal tests of reading comprehension may be followed by substituting "listening" for "reading."

Be aware, however, that attempts to measure comprehension may be measuring memory. The pupil who "understands" but does not retain that understanding over a period of time should be identified. This issue is further discussed in a later section. In addition, be sure pupils' reading and listening performances are compared on materials of similar types and difficulties. Reading and listening comprehension often vary from one type of material to another.

OBTAINING INFORMATION ABOUT READING PERFORMANCE

The discussion now focuses on techniques for obtaining and analyzing samples of pupils' oral and silent reading. These assessments are made to determine the strategies the pupils are using while reading. As noted previously, these are analytic assessments that should be made throughout the school year. From these assessments, teachers can determine the specific lessons that need to be developed as part of the instructional program for particular pupils as well as keep track of the progress they are making in using their reading strategies.

Assessing Oral Reading Performance

Research has indicated that proficient readers, as well as less proficient readers, produce miscues (Goodman, 1969). In assessing oral reading performance it is not the number of miscues that is important, but the quality of the miscues. Through an analysis of miscues, it is possible to examine the readers' ability to reconstruct authors' messages.

Miscue analysis reveals the reader's ability to reconstruct authors' messages

A miscue is an actual response in oral reading that does not match the expected response—that is, the reader orally produces a message that is not an exact reproduction of the message on the page. Miscue analyses can be made of pupils' oral reading by asking a series of questions about the miscues. The answers to the questions are then tabulated and summarized and a pattern of the miscues is evaluated (Burke, 1973, 1975; Goodman, 1969).

Obtaining the Miscues. Miscue analyses are done on the oral reading of an unfamiliar story. The story should be moderately challenging, but not one that is so difficult that it will frustrate the pupil. The story should be challenging enough so that the pupil makes at least twenty-five miscues. This can be accomplished by selecting a story from material that is intended for use one year above the grade level at which the pupil is reading.

Miscue analyses are done on the oral reading of an unfamiliar story

By selecting a challenging, but not frustrating, story, the schemes a pupil uses to read are revealed. The miscues produced under frustration usually are not indicative of a pupil's normal approach to reading.

The exact number of miscues per hundred words that indicate "challenging" or "frustrating" cannot be determined through a formula. Only through the process of doing miscue analyses will a sense be developed as to when material may be too easy or too difficult for a pupil. The factors that make a story difficult for one pupil are not the same ones that make another story difficult for a second pupil.

The oral reading of each pupil should be recorded on an audio tape or cassette recorder. This will allow the teacher to replay the pupil's responses at a later time. For the novice in miscue analysis, a recorder is almost a necessity. Quite often, miscues are missed, or need reconfirming. Also, intonational miscues are sometimes difficult to judge without a second or third listening.

Place the recorder in a position that is not distracting to the pupil.

FIGURE 5-1

The Bell of Atri

Atri is the name of a little town in Italy. It is a very old town and is built halfway up the side of a steep hill.

A long time ago, the King of Atri bought a fine large bell and had it hung up in a tower in the marketplace. A long rope that reached almost to the ground was tied to the bell. Even the smallest child could ring the bell by pulling upon this rope.

SOURCE: Fay, Leo, Ross, Ramon Royal, and La Pray, Margaret. *The Young America Basic Reading Program*, Level 10. Produced by Lyons and Carnahan. Copyright 1974 by Rand McNally.

Explain to the pupil why the recording is being made, but do not place excessive stress on this.

Ask the pupil to read the story aloud. Indicate that no assistance will be offered during the reading and that at the end the pupil will be asked to retell the story. Directions can be similar to the following:

Please read this story to me. Read it out loud. While you are reading, I will not help you in any way. If you come to a word you do not know, try to do the best you can. You may skip the word if you cannot figure it out. However, I would like you to try to guess the word. When you are all finished reading, I will ask you to tell me about the story in your own words.

Tabulating the Miscues. All miscues are written on worksheets which are copies of the story being read. The copies should faithfully maintain the line length of the story. On the worksheet each line is numbered for reference. Figure 5-2 shows how a worksheet is prepared for use in a miscue analysis from the original story and how the miscues are recorded on the worksheet.

Miscues are recorded on copies of the story

Each miscue is indicated on the worksheet by means of some commonly accepted markings:

1. *The substitution of a word:* Write the substituted word above the word in the text. Spell nonsense words phonetically. A partial substitution of a word correct to the stopping point and then repeated is not considered as a miscue; however, it is marked on the worksheet.

   look
   He would like to put it
   in the art contest.

   whee —
   I don't want it if it won't whistle.

2. *An insertion of a word:* Indicate the placement of the inserted word by means of a caret.

   fine
   "My prince," said the queen one ˄ day.

3. *An omission of a word:* Circle the omitted word or word part.

   All day (long) the rain fell.   It di(n't) whistle.

4. *A reversal of two or more words:* Draw a *z* shaped figure between the words reversed. If more than two words are involved, extend the horizontal lines to the end of the words.

Once upon a time there ⌐lived⌐a prince.

(Read by the pupil as: Once upon a time a prince lived there.)

5. *A repetition of one or more words* (to correct a miscue, to change a correct response, or to maintain continuity of thought): Underline the repeated word or words. Place a symbol in a circle to show the type of repetition.

A correction:

All day long the prince rode his horse. *house* ⓒ

A repetition of a miscue, but the miscue is not corrected:

He is painting/a picture. *pasting* Ⓗ

A repetition that changes or abandons a correct response:

Jack ran/to Pat's house. *runs* Ⓐⓑ

A repetition to maintain continuity:

And you know/that a prince must marry a princess. Ⓐ

6. *Intonation miscue:* Indicate the pupils' intonation by means of punctuation or by means of arrows.

"Now why don't you get on your horse?

and go looking?"

Tabulating the Retelling. At the completion of the oral reading, the pupil is asked to retell the story. At first, provide the pupil with no assistance. On an outline of the story (see Figure 5–3), record the information the pupil freely recalls. When additional information cannot be provided unaided, guide the pupil through the use of some general questions. The following guidelines should be followed:

After reading the story, the pupil is asked to retell it

1. Questions should not contain any information from the story that the pupil has not already given.
2. Questions should be general. The questions should not be so specific as to lead the pupil to conclusions that would not have been formed from the reading of the story.
3. Questions should retain any mispronunciations made by the pupil (Y. Goodman and Burke, 1972).

Some general questions should be prepared before the pupil retells the story (Y. Goodman and Burke, 1972). These questions should be appropriate to a variety of situations and story plots, yet they can be just the encouragement a pupil needs for retelling the story. The following are sample questions for guiding a pupil's retelling:

Tell me more about . . . (Use information already offered by the pupil.)
Who was in the story? or Who else was in the story?
What did (he, she, they) do?
What kind of person was . . . . ? (Use characters pupil offers.)
What else happened in the story?
Where did the story take place?
When did the story take place?
What was the whole story about? or What kind of problem was the story about?
Why do you think the story was written? or What did the author want you to know when he (she) wrote the story?

FIGURE 5-2: Miscue Worksheet

The Bell of Atri *[©Antarg]* Edward, 3rd grade

101 Atri is the name of a little town in Italy. *[Arter ⓐ]*

102 It is a very old town and is built halfway *[it ... wee ©]*

103 up the side of a steep hill. *[s© ... the]*

104 A long time ago, the King of Atri bought *[artery]*

105 a fine large bell and had it hung up in a *[ⓐ fine large bell]*

106 tower in the marketplace. A long rope that *[© ... ⓐ]*

107 reached almost to the ground, was tied *[v He v]*

108 to the bell. Even the smallest child could *[T ⓒ]*

109 ring the bell by pulling upon this rope. *[ins©]*

201 "It is the bell of justice," said the King. *[ⓐ juist]*

202 When at last everything was ready, the *[re ⓐ]*

203 people of Atri had a great holiday. All the *[artery]*

204 men and women and children came down

205 to the marketplace to look at the bell of *[ⓐ L v It ©I]*

206 justice. It was a very pretty bell and was *[t © ©]*

207 polished until it looked almost as bright

208 and yellow as the sun *[as© A →]*

209 "How we should like to hear it ring!" *[I ... looke© the bell]*

210 they said.

211 Then the King came down the street. *[©]*

Strategies for Analytical Teaching through Informal Tests 119

212 "Perhaps he will ring the bell," said the

213 people. And everybody stood very still

214 and waited to see what he would do.

215 But he did not ring the bell. He did not

216 even take the rope in his hands. When he

217 came to the foot of the tower, he stopped

218 and raised his hand.

219 "My people," he said. "Do you see this

220 beautiful bell? It is your bell. But it must

221 never be rung except in case of need. If

222 any one of you is wronged at any time, he

223 may come and ring the bell. And then the

224 judges shall come together at once and

225 hear his case and give him justice.

301 "Rich and poor, old and young, all alike

302 may come. But no one must touch the rope

303 unless he knows for certain that he

304 has been wronged."

305 Many years passed by after this. Many

306 times did the bell in the marketplace ring

307 but to call the judges together. Many

308 wrongs were righted. Many evil people

```
                    was pun-    Ⓐ
309    were punished ⓑ →

              a,  T              rang
310    At last, the rope was almost worn out.
                  ↑
              louder Ⓞ
311    The lower/part of it was untwisted. Some
                ___
                strings
312    of the strands were broken. It became so

313    short that only a tall man could reach it.

                 w- Ⓐ                           O
314    "This will/never do," said the judges, one
                 ↑
           → w       Ⓒ          1. wrongdid
315    day  "What if a child should be wronged? Ⓝ   2. rung
         ↑                              ___

316    He could not ring the bell to let us know it."
```

FIGURE 5-3: Retelling Outline for "The Bell of Atri"

Characterizations (30 points)

    Identification (1̶5̶) 9   Traits (1̶5̶) 3   *Edward;*
                                                     3rd grade

King of Atri   Hung the bell of justice

Men and women *people* Curious about the bell

Judges   Heard cases of wronged; gave

                       order for new bell rope

Man   Volunteered to fix rope

Knight *minister/master*   Once brave; now a miser

Horse   Mistreated; became lame and sick

Boys   Threw rocks at horse

Theme of story (20 points) 5

Not to be bad.

Justice applies to all creatures: animal and human.

Plot of the story (20 points) 10 *about a King and a horse*

How a faithful horse that is wronged brought retribution
someone was mean to
to his unkind master.

Main events of the story (30 points) 14 *Took place in Italy*

The King of Atri provided the town with a bell that had

a long rope so even a child could ring it.

The King declared it is the bell of justice and proclaimed

that anyone who was wronged should come and ring the bell.

The bell would summon the judges to hear the case of the
king would punish
wronged.

The people of Atri had a holiday when the bell was finished.

Years passed and many cases were heard and settled. Fi-
short
nally the rope became worn and no longer reached the ground.

Only a tall person could reach the bell rope to ring the bell.

Since there was no rope in the town long enough to hang

to the ground, someone climbed up and tied a long grapevine

to the bell, instead. *King said to leave it.*

A knight who was once brave had grown old and became

a miser thinking only of his gold.

All day the miser sat and counted his gold. He neglected *The master was mean to*

his horse who had been his best friend and had carried him

safely through many dangers. The knight could only think of

how much the horse would cost him so he left the horse to

starve. *someone wanted to be minister* / *minister wanted to get the master's gold.*

The horse, grown lame and sick, was chased by the boys

of the town and barked at by the dogs.

One day, the horse wandered into the town when everybody

was indoors. He came upon the grapevine connected to the

bell. The hungry horse began to eat the leaves on the vine.

As the horse ate the leaves, the bell was rung calling

the townpeople and judges.

When they saw the horse, they knew he had been wronged. *at the bell*

They realized that the horse had called for justice against

his master because of the way he had been treated. All the

townspeople explained how they had seen the horse mistreated.

The miser was called for. He was told that he must pay *master*

half of his gold to provide the once faithful horse with

food and shelter.

The miser grieved for his gold, and the townspeople

were happy.

The horse was led to his new shelter and food. *the people put*   *Total = 41*

The following conversation shows how a teacher guided a pupil in the retelling of the story, "The Bell of Atri." From the retelling, the story outline in Figure 5–3 was marked and scored.

Teacher: Can you tell me what you remember about the story?
Child: I don't remember too much.
 T: Well, tell me what you remember.
Ch: A King put up a bell. If someone was being bad they would ring it. And everyone would come and the bell . . . the rope got too short. And then the man, another man got another rope and put a vine on it. And then the King said leave it the way it is. And then the other guy wanted to be the minister. And he got gold and he was mean to his horse. He didn't feed him. The horse ate the leaves off the bell and he rang it and all the judges came. And they brought his master. And then they put him in a stall at the end. And one day there was a . . . the bell string got short and only a tall man could ring it. And then they made a new one. That's all I remember.
 T: Can you tell me more about the horse?
Ch: He was starved. And he had nothing to eat and to drink so they put him in a stable and he began to eat. He had a lot of dinner.
 T: Who put the horse in the stable?
Ch: The people after they found him.
 T: Where did the people find him?
Ch: At the bell.
 T: What was he doing there?
Ch: Eating the vine.
 T: What happened when he ate the vine?
Ch: He rang the bell.
 T: Why did the people think he rang the bell?
Ch: Because someone was being bad.
 T: Who was that?
Ch: The master.
 T: How was the master being bad?
Ch: By not feeding the horse. And not giving him shelter.
 T: Can you tell me more about the judges?
Ch: I don't know. I forgot.
 T: Why did the King put up the bell?
Ch: So if there were any person who was bad, another person would ring the bell and everyone would come.
 T: And then what would happen?
Ch: They would punish him.
 T: Who would they punish?
Ch: The person who did the thing bad.
 T: Who would decide if the person was bad?

Ch: *The King.*
T: *Can you tell me more about the minister and the master?*
Ch: *The minister wanted to get the master's gold but he wouldn't let him. He wanted to keep it himself. That's why he wouldn't feed the horse.*
T: *What happened when the bell string got short?*
Ch: *They fixed it.*
T: *How?*
Ch: *With the pine ivory. No, a grapevine.*
T: *Do you remember where the story took place?*
Ch: *No.*
T: *Can you remember what kind of place it was?*
Ch: *In Italy.*
T: *Can you tell me what the whole story was about?*
Ch: *About a King and a horse someone was mean to.*
T: *What do you call it when people who are bad get punished?*
Ch: *Judges.*
T: *Can you tell me why this story was written? What message did the author want to give you? Can you think of it?*
Ch: *To not be bad.*
T: *Is there anything else you can tell me about the story?*
Ch: *No.*

Analyzing the Miscues. The pupil's miscues are analyzed by asking three groups of questions (Burke, 1975) about each miscue:

> How effective are the pupil's strategies for recognizing words in context?
> How effective are the pupil's strategies for using his knowledge of language?
> How much do the pupil's miscues change the intended meaning of the author?

Word recognition questions are asked only when the pupil substitutes one word for another. Answers to these questions indicate the extent of the pupil's use of grapho-phonological cues and knowledge of grammatical functions.

> Q-1. Does the miscue look like the word in the text?
>   High: There is a high degree of similarity.
>   Some: There is some degree of similarity.
>   None: There is no similarity in any part of the word.

Q-2. Does the miscue sound like the word in the text?
High: There is a high degree of similarity.
Some: There is some degree of similarity.
None: There is no similarity in any part of the word.

(Note: In determining the difference between "high" similarity and "some" similarity, teachers may find the following useful: high similarity exists when two of a word's three parts generally look like the other words; some similarity exists when one of the word's parts is similar to that of the other word.)

Q-3. Does the miscue retain the same grammatical function as the word in the text?
Same: The miscue is the same part of speech.
Questionable: It is difficult to tell whether there is a change in the part of speech.
Different: There is a change in the part of speech.

Knowledge of language questions are asked of every sentence in which a miscue has occurred. Each sentence with one or more miscues—not just substitution miscues, but all types of miscues—is examined. Answers to the following questions give some indication as to whether the pupil is concerned with producing acceptable language during oral reading. The final sentence, with all the pupil's attempts at correction, is evaluated. The criterion for judging acceptability is whether or not the pupil would produce such a sentence in spoken language. (Chapter 12 contains a discussion about judging the acceptability of the spoken language of pupils who speak divergent dialects of American English. The general rule is: If the sentence the pupil reads aloud contains elements of speech and language found in the normal, everyday speech of the pupil, the sentence and its miscues are judged as "acceptable.")

If a miscue extends across a sentence boundary, judge the acceptability of both sentences together in order to maintain the relationship of that miscue to all others in the sentences.

Q-4. Is the sentence as finally produced an acceptable and grammatical sentence?
Yes: The sentence as finally read by the pupil is an acceptable sentence that could stand by itself as grammatically correct.
No: The sentence as finally read by the pupil is not acceptable and could not stand by itself as grammatically correct.

Q-5. Does the sentence as finally produced have an acceptable meaning?
   Yes: The sentence as finally read by the pupil can stand by itself as a meaningful sentence.
   No: The sentence as finally read by the pupil cannot stand by itself as a meaningful sentence.

A comprehension question is asked of every sentence in which a miscue has occurred. The answer to this question indicates the degree the pupil has changed the intended meaning of the author in relation to the rest of the story.

Q-6. Does the sentence as finally produced change the meaning of the story in relation to its plot and theme?
   No: The sentence as finally read by the pupil does not change the intended meaning of the author.
   Minimal: The sentence as finally read by the pupil moderately changes the minor incidents, characters, or sequences in the story.
   Yes: The sentence as finally read by the pupil importantly changes the major incidents, characters, sequence, or theme in the story.

The teacher should be on the lookout for patterns

After the pupil's miscues have been fully transcribed from the recording onto the copy of the story, the first twenty-five substitution miscues are written on the evaluation form. Then the word recognition questions are asked of them. Figure 5-4 contains a sample completed evaluation form. In the first column of the form write the line number on which the miscue occurred. In the second column write the pupil's response. In the third column, write the word as it appears in the text. Then place a check in the appropriate column for answering the word recognition in context questions, Q-1, Q-2, and Q-3.

When the three questions have been answered for the first twenty-five substitution miscues, column totals and percentages are calculated.

The second part of the evaluation form is completed by answering the two knowledge of language questions and the comprehension question for the first twenty-five sentences containing miscues. In the first column of the second part, write the number of the line on which the sentence begins. In the second column indicate the total number of miscues in the sentence. This number represents the sum of all miscues (not just the substitution miscues). In the last columns, complete the appropriate answers to the knowledge of language questions, Q-4 and Q-5, and the comprehension question, Q-6.

When the three questions have been answered for the first twenty-five sentences containing miscues, column totals and percentages are calculated.

The percentages from the two parts of the evaluation form are summarized and compared. The result is a profile of reading strategies indicating both the pupil's strengths and weaknesses. From the individual profiles a composite class profile can be constructed for use in planning instructional procedures and class groupings. Figure 5-5 is an example of a class summary and profile sheet.

Evaluating the Pupil Profiles. The first evaluation made of the pupil's profile is that of the pupil's strategies for word recognition in context. Clues to the strategies the pupil uses are obtained from the answers to questions about the degree the miscue (1) looks like the original word, (2) sounds like the original word, and (3) retains the same part of speech. Answers to these questions do not in and of themselves indicate the pupil's proficiencies as a reader. They only provide some insight into the manner in which the pupil's attempts at reading may affect the interpretation of the story. Miscues that have a low degree of sound or graphic similarity, but which do not change the meaning of the story, are not considered as miscues of prime importance. A miscue that does change the meaning of the story as intended by the author on the other hand is of some concern. Some pupils, in reconstructing an author's message, change the part of speech of some words. Again, if the miscues change the meaning of the story then there is evidence of a deficiency. However, some pupils' miscues result in a change in a part of speech without a major change in the meaning of the story. This is possible because the pupil's miscues result in other miscues, and the sentence is adjusted grammatically. For example, notice how the pupil's miscues in the following sentence resulted in a grammatically and semantically acceptable response.

By the time Niko was part way

home, he had overcome some

of his disappointment.

FIGURE 5-4: Miscue Evaluation, Part I

No.	Reader	Text	Graphic Q-1			Sound Q-2			Grammatical Function Q-3		
			High	Some	None	High	Some	None	Same	Questionable	Different
101	arter	atri		✓			✓		✓		
102	it	is		✓			✓				✓
102	halfwee	halfway	✓			✓				✓	
103	ups	up	✓			✓				✓	
103	the	a			✓			✓	✓		
104	Artery	atri		✓			✓		✓		
109	his	this	✓				✓				✓
201	juist	justice		✓			✓			✓	
205	It	of			✓			✓			✓
208	as	and		✓			✓				✓
209	look	like		✓		✓			✓		
209	the bell	it			✓			✓	✓		
212	Peerhaps	Perhaps	✓			✓			✓		
220	It's	It is	✓			✓			✓		
221	rong	rung	✓			✓			✓		
222	your	you	✓			✓					✓
222	rung	wronged		✓			✓		✓		
301	Richard	Rich and	✓			✓					✓
301	alk	alike		✓			✓			✓	
305	May	Many	✓			✓					✓
306	time	times	✓			✓			✓		
308	rungs	wrongs		✓			✓			✓	
308	right	righted	✓			✓			✓		
309	was	were		✓			✓		✓		
310	rung	worn			✓			✓	✓		
		Column Total	11	10	4	11	10	4	13	5	7
		Question Total	25			25			25		
		Column Percentage	44	40	16	44	40	16	52	20	28

Edward, 3rd grade

FIGURE 5-4: Miscue Evaluation, Part II

Edward, 3rd grade

Sentence or Line Number	Number of Miscues	Syntactic Acceptability Q-4	Semantic Acceptability Q-5	Meaning Change Q-6		
				No	Minimal	Yes
101	1	Yes	Yes	✓		
102	4	No	No	✓		
104	2	Yes	Yes	✓		
106	2	No	No			✓
108	1	Yes	Yes			✓
201	1	Yes	No			✓
202	1	Yes	Yes	✓		
203	3	Yes	Yes		✓	
206	3	Yes	Yes	✓		
209	2	Yes	Yes	✓		
211	1	Yes	Yes	✓		
212	1	Yes	Yes	✓		
216	2	Yes	No	✓		
220	1	Yes	Yes	✓		
220	3	Yes	No		✓	
221	3	No	No			✓
301	4	Yes	Yes	✓		
302	3	No	No			✓
305	1	No	No			✓
305	1	No	No			✓
307	2	Yes	No			✓
308	2	Yes	No	✓		
310	1	Yes	No		✓	
311	1	Yes	No			✓
311	1	Yes	Yes	✓		
Total Miscues 47		Total Y 19	Total Y 12	13	3	9
		%Y 76	%Y 48	52%	12%	36%

On the class summary and profile sheet, enter:

1. The combined percentage of each pupil's *high* and *some* sound similarity totals.
2. The combined percentage of each pupil's *high* and *some* graphic similarity totals.
3. The percentage of miscues that retained the same part of speech.
4. The percentage of the sentences that were grammatically acceptable.
5. The percentage of the sentences that had acceptable meaning.
6. The percentage of sentences that resulted in no change of meaning in the story.
7. The score of the pupil's retelling.
8. The strategies each pupil uses effectively.

The class profile sheet should contain information from each pupil's reading of the same story. If this is not possible, be sure the stories read by the pupils do not differ in style, length, and difficulty of concepts.

The following comparisons should be made for determining the pupils' effective reading strategies. It may be necessary to refer to the evaluation form and the story worksheet for additional information while making these comparisons.

1. Compare the word recognition scores to the knowledge of language scores. Does the pupil primarily use strategies for recognizing individual words to the exclusion of using knowledge of language for deriving meaning from the sentences? Which seems to influence the pupil's use of strategies: the sound relationships in the word? the graphic structures in the word? or the function of the word in the sentence?

2. Compare the grammatical acceptability and meaning acceptability scores. Is the pupil creating sentences that are grammatically correct as sentences, but which do not have any meaning? Is this due to a large number of gross mispronunciations or substitutions that, while maintaining a grammatically correct form, distort the meaning of the author?

3. Compare the grammatical function and grammatical acceptability scores. Is the pupil correcting miscues that change the grammatical function of a word so that the final sentence is grammatically acceptable? Does the pupil make other alterations in the sentence so that a miscue which changes the grammatical function of a word still results in a grammatically acceptable sentence?

4. Compare the meaning acceptability scores and the meaning change scores. Is the pupil producing sentences that are meaningful by themselves but which change the intended meaning of the entire story?

FIGURE 5-5: Miscue Analysis—Class Summary Sheet

3rd grade "The Bell of Atri" Pupil's Name	Q-1 (High + Some %) Graphic Similarity	Q-2 (High + Some %) Sound Similarity	Q-3 (Yes %) Retained Part of Speech	Q-4 (Yes %) Grammatical Acceptability	Q-5 (Yes %) Meaning Acceptability	Q-6 (No %) No Meaning Change	Retelling Score	Effective Strategies
Alfred	90	90	85	65	60	45	40	sound and graphic cues, some language sense
Betsy	60	95	80	80	75	80	75	sound cues, language and meaning sense
Charles	65	50	60	40	35	15	30	some sound and graphic cues
Diane	100	95	95	90	90	85	90	all
Edward	84	84	52	76	48	52	41	*

* What effective strategies does Edward have?

5. Compare the meaning change and effective retelling scores. Does the pupil's retelling reflect the quality of the miscues made on the story? Does the retelling score seem to be affected by memory factors?

6. Compare the miscues per hundred words to the comprehension scores. Are the miscues so spread out over the story that any apparent change in meaning is offset by the sparseness of the miscues? Is the pupil maintaining understanding because the distance between the miscues allows for meaning to be gained from the intervening passages?

A class analysis identifies pupils who need instruction

The final step in miscue analysis is using the results of the profile sheet for formulating classroom instruction. From the class analysis, it is possible to identify some individuals or groups of pupils who need instruction in developing and/or reinforcing strategies.

Pupils who show a need for developing word recognition strategies might benefit from those strategies for using grapho-phonological information discussed in Chapter 9. If their need is in correctly identifying the grammatical functions of words, they might benefit from lessons constructed from the information on sentence reading strategies in Chapter 8 or that on contextual signals to word meanings in Chapter 9. For pupils whose oral reading responses are not syntactically or semantically acceptable, the strategies on sentence reading in Chapter 8 might prove helpful. When pupils create a great deal of meaning change while reading orally, they might receive instruction on the prediction strategies and the paragraph and longer discourse reading strategies discussed in Chapter 8. Pupils who have difficulty in retelling a story after oral reading might benefit from the guided reading and questioning strategies in Chapter 7 and the prediction strategies discussed in Chapter 8.

Assessing Silent Reading Performance

Pupils' silent reading performance can be assessed through (1) the oral retelling of a story read silently, and (2) a cloze procedure silent reading test.

Oral Retelling. An analysis of a pupil's silent reading comprehension is made in a manner similar to that of assessing the oral reading retelling. At the completion of the silent reading, the pupil is asked to retell the story. No help is provided, and the information a pupil recalls is recorded on a story outline. The guidelines and types of questions used to encourage or guide the pupil are similar to those used for the oral reading retelling.

The pupil's performance on the oral reading retelling and the silent reading retelling can be compared to note if there is a pattern of similarity in the types of responses given. The following questions can assist the teacher in determining the degree of difference between recalling stories after oral and silent reading.

> Is there a difference in the recall of the main characters in the stories?
> Is there a difference in the recall of information about the appearance, feelings, actions, and relationships of the main characters?
> Is there a difference in the recall of events in the stories?
> Is there a difference in the recall of the plots of the stories?
> Is there a difference in the recall of the themes of the stories?

The comparison of a pupil's recall from oral and silent reading gives one indication as to whether the estimate of a pupil's reading performance

All readers produce miscues

provided by the miscue analysis can be assumed for silent reading as well. Some of the common patterns emerging from the above comparisons are:

Pattern one: *The silent reading recall score is greater than that of the oral reading recall score.* Possible reasons for this are that the pupil during oral reading is attending primarily to the pronunciation of words. Prior experience may have taught the pupil that correct pronunciation, or at least attempts at such, are the important aspects of reading. Often a pupil is judged in reading ability not by a comprehension check, but by the ability to accurately recode the printed symbol into sound. During silent reading, the pupil can attend to the development of the story without undue concern for the accurate pronunciation of the words printed on the page.

Pattern two: *The silent reading recall score is less than that of the oral reading recall score.* A pupil displaying this pattern may need the conscious effort applied in reading aloud in order to maintain involvement with the story. Such a pupil may only be an active reader when forced to recode the written story into sound. The overt involvement may be keeping the pupil's attention directed at reconstructing the author's message. During silent reading, this pupil may experience difficulty in the selection of cues for reconstructing meaning.

Pattern three: *Both the oral reading and silent reading retelling scores are much below the meaning change score from the miscue analysis.* In this case, the pupil may be processing the story information with meaning at the instant of reading. However, the retention and/or recall of this information may be hindered. A pupil understands a story when miscues do not change the meaning of a story or miscues that do change the meaning are corrected. The problem may lie in the lack of strategies for adequately storing the information. The problem may also lie with a lack of adequate strategies for producing an effective association among the bits of information so that recall is facilitated. As another possibility, a pupil displaying this pattern could have facility in reconstructing surface features; the pupil may not have strategies for reconstructing the author's deep structure meaning.

When the pupil's oral and silent recall scores both fall below the meaning change score of the miscue analysis, one further step may be taken to determine the pupil's ability to understand the material. Keep the story passage open and allow the pupil to refer to it during the retelling. This procedure is not effective with materials in which the entire story plot is carried in pictures. However, most materials above the beginning reading levels have pictures that correspond to the story, but do not reveal the entire plot and theme. If the pupil can produce a greater portion of the story information after referring to the text, then this may be further evidence that the pupil's ability to recall is interfering with the story retelling.

FIGURE 5-6: Sample Cloze Comprehension Test

My uncle is an anthropologist. That (1)_____ he studies all about (2)_____ kinds of people and (3)_____ they act. He travels (4)_____ over the world to (5)_____ people and to learn (6)_____ about them.

My uncle (7)_____ me that one of (8)_____ most important things an (9)_____ does is talk with (10)_____. That isn't as easy as it sounds, since that means he has to know how to speak many different languages.

Answers: 1. means   2. different   3. how   4. all
          5. meet   6. all   7. tells   8. the
          9. anthropologist   10. people

SOURCE: Fay, Leo, Ross, Ramon Royal, and La Pray, Margaret. 1974. *The Young America Basic Reading Program*, Level 10. Produced by Lyons and Carnahan. Chicago: Rand McNally.

Such a pupil, then, may need instruction in developing strategies for retaining and recalling information such as those discussed in Chapters 7 and 8. Recall is a desired trait to develop in pupils, but the ability to recognize information is also a vital comprehension task. A pupil should not be deemed as deficient in comprehension strategies because of a limitation in recall strategies.

Cloze Procedure. A means of measuring pupils' comprehension that has been gaining popularity is the cloze procedure. The cloze procedure is a technique in which words are systematically deleted from a passage and the reader is expected to replace the deleted word while reading. It is a comprehension test that is easy to construct and score; in addition, it can provide teachers with insights into how pupils "think through" material as they read. Figure 5-6 shows an abbreviated sample cloze procedure comprehension test.

> A cloze test reveals how pupils "think through" material as they read

The cloze procedure test is a quick and efficient way for a classroom teacher to estimate the appropriateness of any book for use with particular pupils. It can be used to estimate the appropriate level of a basal reading series into which pupils should be placed. Also, the cloze procedure test can be used to determine whether particular material can be read independently by pupils, whether it can be read only with the teacher's guidance, or whether it will be too frustrating for the pupils.

For example, a teacher could create a series of cloze tests to cover a fairly wide range of texts in a basal series or a content area series. The easiest level test can be administered to the whole class. As pupils' responses indicate that a harder level is inappropriate, they are assigned to a text and the remaining tests are administered to the other pupils. Additional testing might be required for those pupils for whom the first test is too difficult or the last test too easy. Thus, in a few days a teacher can place pupils into texts which are commensurate with their ability to read.

A great deal of research has been done in an attempt to substantiate that the cloze procedure measures an individual's ability to comprehend a written message. First, it seems that the cloze procedure measures the reader's ability to deal with the linguistic structure of the language. Accordingly, it is related to a reader's ability to deal with the relationship between words and ideas (Horton, 1972). Second, since the cloze procedure requires the reader to predict the exact word that was deleted and replace it, the cloze procedure measures an individual's ability to perform comprehension processes. Research based upon psycholinguistic principles has consistently shown that a reader's comprehension is measured by how well the information surrounding the blank is used and how well the information taken from the text is employed to obtain additional information. Also, studies show that a reader's performance on a traditional comprehension test (questions) cannot be distinguished from that person's performance on a cloze comprehension test (Bormuth, 1975). Hence, the cloze procedure measures the mental processes during reading that are commonly called "comprehension."

The procedures for creating cloze tests have become fairly standardized (Bormuth, 1975). For grade three and higher, the procedure is:

1. Select a 250-word passage.
2. Beginning with any one of the first five words of the second sentence of the passage, delete every fifth word until 50 words are deleted. The first and last sentence are always left intact. Punctuation and hyphens are never deleted, and numerals, such as 1975, are deleted as if they are whole words. Apostrophes are deleted along with the words they appear in.
3. Type the passage on a master, double spacing between lines. For each deleted word, type a line fifteen spaces long. The spaces should be uniform in length regardless of the length of the original word.
4. Provide the pupils with instructions and a sample test before giving them the actual cloze tests. The instructions may be similar to the following:

At the bottom of this page is a sample of a new kind of test. Your job will be to guess what word was left out of each space and to write that word in that space.

Remember: Write only one word in each space. Try to fill every blank; don't be afraid to guess.

You may skip hard blanks and come back to them later. Wrong spellings will not count against you (Bormuth, 1975).

This untimed test is scored by counting every response that correctly replaces the exact word deleted from the original passage. Research has shown that when the cloze procedure is used to measure pupils' comprehension, the most efficient means is to use the exact word criteria as the standard for marking (Bormuth, 1975). In Chapter 8 there will be a discussion of the use of the cloze procedure as an instructional procedure. In such circumstances, it will be shown, deviations which still retain the intended meaning of the passage are acceptable. However, in order to maintain some consistency in the interpretation of the cloze procedure as a comprehension test, only exact reconstructions are counted as correct.

After the number of a pupil's correct responses has been determined, convert that number into a percentage. Research has shown that a pupil's ability to obtain a score of approximately 40 percent indicates that the material is appropriate for instructional purposes. When a pupil obtains a score of approximately 60 percent or greater, the material can generally be read independently by the pupil. Scores below 40 percent indicate that the material may be too frustrating for the pupil (Jones and Pikulski, 1974; Bormuth, 1968). Thus, when groups of pupils are tested for placement in any series of texts, the pupils are given higher level materials whenever they score 60 percent or greater. Pupils who score below 40 percent are assigned to the last level at which they scored 40 percent or greater.

Additional insight may be obtained into how the information in a passage is being processed. Simply point to each cloze item and ask the pupil why the word was selected to complete the cloze item. When using this informal procedure, it is unnecessary to have the pupil read the entire passage aloud. In fact, it is preferable not even to ask the pupil to pronounce the answer word. Just request the pupil to explain why the word was selected and note the types of clues the pupil indicates were used to determine the answer.

Although the cloze procedure test seems to be a valid and reliable measure of comprehension, there are certain limitations which should be noted (Pace and Winsch, 1975). Some cloze tests may contain many deletions for which there are no contextual clues. Certain children, particularly those in the primary grades, should not be given cloze tests without some modification. These modifications will be discussed in Chapter 8. Also, major emphasis should not be placed on the written response, but rather on the comprehension of the given passage. In cases in which the pupil is reluctant to write, the teacher may accept an oral response. In such cases, the teacher still can obtain some indication of the pupil's ability to read and understand the passage. Finally, the cloze tests measure global aspects of comprehension and not specific substrategies. Therefore, the test cannot be used for an analysis of specific diagnostic information about a pupil's strategies and skills.

DISCUSSION QUESTIONS AND ACTIVITIES

1. Explain why it may be more practical for a classroom teacher to examine the performance of pupils in classroom situations doing typical classroom work than it may be to examine their performance on standardized tests.

2. Using informal procedures explained in this chapter for assessing oral and silent reading:
    a. compare the oral and silent reading performance of an elementary age pupil;
    b. compare the oral and silent reading performance of two elementary age pupils of the same grade level reading the same story;
    c. compare the oral and silent reading performance of two elementary age pupils of different grade levels while reading the same story;
    d. compare the oral and silent reading performance of an elementary age pupil reading a narrative story and a passage from a content area text.

3. Explain the "significant characteristics" about which Helen M. Robinson (1975) speaks in the following statement; explain how a teacher might identify them.
    > To study the reading process, two essential ingredients must be examined: the reader and the selection read. If the significant characteristics of each could be identified, then the interaction of the reader and the materials could be interpreted.

4. Construct cloze procedure comprehension tests on three different types of reading material for use at the same grade level: a narrative story, a social studies passage, and a science passage. Administer the tests to:
   a. A group of pupils at the same grade level; and/or
   b. Pupils from each of three different grade levels. Identify those pupils for whom the passages: (a) may be used for instructional purposes, and (b) may be read independently.

5. The following statement by John Bormuth (1975) has implications for classroom teachers when they are constructing tests to measure pupil comprehension. Explain how the procedures for guiding retelling after oral and silent reading, discussed in this chapter, may help overcome some of the difficulties about which he is speaking.

> Test writers influence the difficulty of tests: two writers making a test over a single passage could produce tests of quite different difficulty, the one writer's test eliciting mostly low scores, and the other's mostly high scores.

FURTHER READINGS

For those who wish to investigate in greater detail the administration and interpretation of miscues, the following texts will be helpful. The first is the manual for the full miscue inventory. The second contains articles explaining the application of miscue analysis in various educational settings.

    Goodman, Yetta M., and Carolyn L. Burke. 1972. *Reading Miscue Inventory: Manual, Procedures for Diagnosis and Evaluation.* New York: Macmillan.

    Goodman, Kenneth S., ed. 1973. *Miscue Analysis: Applications to Reading Instruction.* Urbana, Ill.: National Council of Teachers of English and ERIC Clearinghouse on Reading and Communication Skills.

The following text contains articles explaining more about miscue analysis and the use of the cloze procedure.

    Page, William D., ed. 1975. *Help for the Reading Teacher: New Directions in Research.* Urbana, Ill.: National Conference on Research in English and ERIC Clearinghouse on Reading and Communication Skills.

The following book has two purposes: to compile informal instruments that can be used for assessing performance in all the language arts, and to compile reviews of these instruments. The tests are listed by area, but there is a cross reference index so that instruments appropriate for a particular age or grade level may be located. It is an excellent source not only of the existing instruments but also of ideas for teachers to use in the construction of their own informal assessment procedures.

> Fagan, William T., Charles R. Cooper, and Julie M. Jensen. 1975. *Measures for Research and Evaluation in the English Language Arts.* Urbana, Ill.: ERIC Clearinghouse on Reading and Communication Skills and National Council of Teachers of English.

The following article is an extensive review of research that has been done on the study of pupils' oral reading errors.

> Weber, Rose-Marie. 1968. "The Study of Oral Reading Errors: A Survey of the Literature." *Reading Research Quarterly* 4: 96–119.

In the following article, the authors explain an interesting variation of the cloze procedure that can be used to identify children with comprehension problems and to monitor pupils' progress in comprehension development.

> Guthrie, John T., Mary Seifert, Nancy A. Burnham, and Ronald I. Caplan. 1974. "The Maze Technique to Assess, Monitor Reading Comprehension." *The Reading Teacher* 28: 161–168.

References

Bormuth, John R. 1968. "The Cloze Readability Procedure." In John R. Bormuth, ed. *Readability in 1968.* Urbana, Ill.: National Conference on Research in English, pp. 40–47.

Bormuth, John R. 1975. "The Cloze Procedure." In William D. Page, ed. *Help for the Reading Teacher: New Directions in Research.* Urbana, Ill.: National Conference on Research in English and ERIC Clearinghouse on Reading and Communication Skills, pp. 60–89.

Burke, Carolyn L. 1973. "Preparing Elementary Teachers to Teach Reading," in Kenneth S. Goodman (Ed.) *Miscue Analysis: Applications to Reading Instruction.* Urbana, Illinois: National Council of Teachers of English and ERIC Clearinghouse on Reading and Communication Skills, pp. 15-29.

Burke, Carolyn L. 1975. "Oral Reading Analysis: A View of the Reading Process." In William D. Page, ed. *Help for the Reading Teacher: New Directions in Research.* Urbana, Ill.: National Conference on Research in English and ERIC Clearinghouse on Reading and Communication Skills, pp. 23-33.

Cazden, Courtney. 1972. *Child Language and Education,* New York: Holt Rinehart and Winston.

Goodman, Kenneth S. 1969. "Analysis of Oral Reading Miscues: Applied Psycholinguistics." *Reading Research Quarterly* 5: 9-30.

Goodman, Yetta M. and Burke, Carolyn L. 1972. *Reading Miscue Inventory: Manual.* New York: Macmillan.

Horton, Raymond Joseph. 1972. "The Construct Validity of Cloze Procedure: An Exploratory Factor Analysis of Cloze, Paragraph Reading, and Structure-of-Intellect Tests." Unpublished Doctoral Dissertation, Hofstra University.

Jones, Margaret B., and Pikulski, Edna C. 1974. "Cloze for the Classroom." *Journal of Reading* 17: 423-38.

Melear, John D. 1974. "An Informal Language Inventory." *Elementary English* 51: 508-11.

Pace, Judy, and Winsch, Jane L. 1975. "The Effectiveness of the Cloze Procedure as an Indicator of Comprehension Ability." Unpublished manuscript, Queens College of the City University of New York.

Robinson, Helen M. 1975. "Children's Behavior While Reading." In William D. Page, ed. *Help for the Reading Teacher: New Directions in Research.* Urbana, Ill.: National Conference on Research in English and ERIC Clearinghouse on Reading and Communication Skills, pp. 9-22.

Smith, Frank. 1975. *Comprehension and Learning.* New York: Holt Rinehart and Winston.

Strang, Ruth. 1969. *Diagnostic Teaching of Reading.* 2nd Edition. New York: McGraw Hill.

Strategies for Developing Readiness for Reading Instruction

Focus Questions:

1. What is "being ready to learn to read"?
2. What factors affect pupils' readiness to read?
3. What strategies must pupils be able to employ in order to be ready to receive formal reading instruction?
4. How can pupils' readiness for reading be assessed?
5. In what ways can pupils be made ready to participate in group activities?

The concept of reading readiness has been the concern of educators for as long as there has been concern about developing reading programs in the elementary schools. Teachers want to know when pupils can begin to receive reading instruction. They often ask, "When are children ready to have a book placed in their hands and to begin reading?" Professional texts and journals contain numerous checklists for identifying those pupils who are ready to read. These checklists are accompanied by suggestions for prescribing programs of "readiness" training for those who are not ready. The general fallacy with using extensive and detailed checklists lies in the conception that readiness is represented by a specific collection of sub-skills that have some demonstrable connection with the act of reading. This thinking also fosters the impression that readiness is a period of time or a specific program that must be completed before reading instruction can begin.

    The aim of this chapter is not to present another checklist nor to list those specific skills that are prerequisites to learning to read. Rather, this chapter will center on what it means to be "ready" to read any type of material at any stage of development. In what follows we will be concerned with identifying the general factors that affect readiness to read, and relating those factors to the initial stage of literacy—commonly called reading readiness. As will be shown in the discussion, although the suggested activities usually occur in school at the kindergarten or first grade levels, readiness activities should precede all learning. Therefore, reading readiness, in the broad sense of the term, is the concern of all elementary school teachers regardless of the grade level they teach.

Readiness activities should precede all learning

READINESS FOR ALL READING

In a Piagetian sense, readiness means possessing those skills and abilities of a preceding stage of development. Or, simply put, "development determines learning" (Elkind, 1974). Every pupil in school, regardless of grade level, is ready to learn something about the reading process. What that something is should be selected and prepared in keeping with the pupil's abilities at the moment. The teacher's responsibility is to identify what the pupil is to learn, and to determine whether the pupil can learn what is expected.

Every pupil is ready to learn something about the reading process

All of a pupil's school experiences affect the manner in which any subsequent school task is undertaken. Although no developmental pattern of school tasks has ever been established, it does seem logical that positive experiences, which have provided a pupil with skill in the various routines of school work, can only aid a pupil in learning. Pupils should have had pre-school exposure to language oriented activities. Those without this exposure will be less likely to undertake the learning of reading with the same facility as those who understand "what school is all about."

Cognitive and linguistic skills, physical-motor abilities, emotional and social development—these constitute what is being called reading readiness. No sequence of skills is presented here because any such sequence would be purely arbitrary. No empirical evidence exists to justify the use of one hierarchy of skills over another. Very little is actually known about what specific skills should be taught. In fact, very little is known about (1) specific student characteristics that are prerequisites to mastery of a given reading task, (2) specific prerequisite characteristics that are amenable to training, and (3) specific alternative training procedures that can be imposed upon children who lack the prerequisites for learning reading tasks (Blanton, 1972a).

The discussion of readiness *is* undertaken here because there is evidence that linguistic preparation for reading can be fostered. However, the evidence only indicates the broad kinds of activities with which children should have experience, and these will be the focus of the following discussion.

Reading readiness seems to be the product of both maturation and environmental factors (Durkin, 1968). Readiness seems to depend upon a combination of children's particular capacities and the kind of learning opportunities made available to them. Most important, readiness does not seem to be one particular combination of abilities or circumstances. When a child is ready to begin reading varies as children vary. The time when readiness to read occurs is a reflection of not only a child's capabilities and interests, but also the degree to which instruction can accommodate both factors. A child is never totally ready or unready to learn to read. "Readiness is not all-or-none; it depends on the method and materials that are used and on the level at which instruction begins" (MacGinitie, 1969). Since reading is a language process, much of what constitutes reading readiness is language related.

Reading readiness is determined by maturity and the environment

DEVELOPMENT OF READING READINESS

The reading readiness program should be one of creative problem solving (Lundsteen, 1974). It should be a program that develops and extends a child's ability to think. In Piagetian terms, the teacher should be causing some sort of cognitive conflict (disequilibrium). The conflict, which should be challenging but not excessive, makes it possible to maintain motivation (McDonell, 1975).

A readiness program extends a child's ability to think

Problem solving depends upon careful and conscious acts by both the teacher and the pupil. Using a variety of school problems that are full of unknowns (Lundsteen, 1974), the teacher can lead pupils to

1. *Clarify the problem.* During the beginning of the problem solving process, pupils are led to recall already known information that is relevant to the problem.
2. *Generate a hypothesis.* Here pupils are guided in generating alternative ways of stating the problem. This stage helps the pupils to further clarify the problem and put it into some form that is answerable.

3. *Plan procedures.* The pupils, with the teacher's guidance, attempt to determine various ways in which the question or hypothesis may be answered. At this time the teacher helps the pupils to determine which of the plans seem more workable and to undertake those first.
4. *Evaluate results.* The pupils are led to examine the various results obtained by working through the procedures used to solve the hypothesis. If the hypothesis cannot be verified at this time, the pupils are guided in how to deal with an unresolved problem. Plans for suspending judgments for future verification or rejection are developed.

Readiness is the ability and desire to take risks (McDonell, 1975). With the teacher's guidance, the pupils discover prediction strategies and develop cognitive skills for selecting, questioning, testing, and generalizing about the information in their world. This, by the way, is how the pupils learned their language in the first place.

In helping to develop pupils' cognitive strategies, the teacher has the task of instructing them about their environment. The pupils' world consists not only of the classroom, but also of home, stores, streets, radio and television programs, and all the people met in these places. To help them to cope with their environment, the teacher can help the pupils focus attention on the immediate problem, realize how information is searched and evaluated, and find alternatives for searching and evaluating the obtained information (Mishler, 1972). Throughout, the importance of language is underscored. Special or important words relating to the pupils' environment are given attention and their roles in helping one think are identified.

The emphasis of a reading readiness program must be on language development

If the process is to be truly a *reading* readiness procedure, then the emphasis of the program has to be on language development. "Because reading is a counterpart of listening in language, children must acquire the ability to respond rapidly to cues they hear in language before they are ready to respond to these cues in graphic form" (Smith, Goodman, and Meridith, 1970). Or, put another way, reading is "parasitic on language" (Kavanagh, 1968). In order to learn to read, one must possess a knowledge of the language.

A program of reading readiness, then, that is concerned with preparing pupils to learn to read effectively and naturally should be concerned with developing *expectancies* in both the oral and written language systems. In one's language system, the expectancies are both verbal and

non-verbal. These expectancies are those referred to in Chapter 3 in the discussion of the representative psycholinguistic model of reading. To review, they consist of

1. Procedures for regulating the physical aspects of reading.
2. A language repertoire containing all rules and cues of spoken and written language.
3. Meanings and concepts that have been acquired.

The development of a readiness to read, therefore, consists of providing a chance for pupils to store in their long term memories the knowledge, rules, and strategies for reconstructing meaning from language. The discussion that follows examines some instructional procedures for readying pupils for reading.

READINESS FOR FORMAL READING INSTRUCTION

Since most "readiness" programs occur in elementary schools within the kindergarten and first grade, the following discussions will seem to be more concerned with pupils of this age range. However, the teacher should be fully cognizant that these procedures are really *readiness for literacy* procedures. Any pupil, regardless of age or grade level, who does not possess the strategies for reading needs readiness developed. It is a simple matter for a teacher to take the procedures and adapt them for older pupils.

The question arises among many teachers as to whether the kindergarten is the time for "formal" reading and readiness activities. The question, in many instances, draws attention to the wrong aspect of the problem of readiness instruction. There is no doubt that a carefully planned, systematic readiness program has more positive and lasting effects on later reading achievement than does an incidental readiness program (Blanton, 1972). This means that the teacher who intentionally fosters readiness activities in an organized manner provides a better foundation for reading than does a teacher who haphazardly or infrequently promotes such activities.

Organized activities are better than haphazard ones

In addition, the question of formal or informal readiness activities many times refers to the use of a particular commercial program for developing reading readiness. The answer to such a question depends not so much on whether the materials are teacher made or commercially produced but on the type of activities and the use made of the materials. There is no inherent wrong in commercial readiness materials as long as they are used wisely by teachers. The activities should indeed foster a readiness to read, and they should be appropriate for the pupils with which they are used. Research indicates that both formal and incidental readiness programs that emphasize language development and experiences appear more successful than those whose use focuses on narrower aspects of reading readiness (Blanton, 1972). In addition, it appears that language development "is neglected when children are placed in a regimented situation whereby all children merely follow directions" (Church, 1974).

One important misconception about readiness, cited previously, is that readiness is a product that must be acquired before reading can begin. This belief is fostered by those who indicate that there is such a thing as reading readiness which exists independently of the methods and materials used and the pace of instruction instituted by the teacher (Mayer, 1975). This is an oversimplification. When pupils are made ready, they are made ready for something. Therefore, what the teacher assumes to be the reading process should determine what it is that constitutes readiness for reading. The reading readiness program cannot be considered apart from the kind of reading instruction that will be available (Durkin, 1968).

One kindergarten teacher has described "reading" in the kindergarten in the following manner:

> "Five year olds" are all ready to learn but differ in their rate of growth, backgrounds of experience, interests, and inborn capacities. Assessing physical, mental, emotional, and social aspects of young children takes a lot of observation and interaction on the part of the teachers. Experiences which build on where the children are and extend their outreach through concrete interaction with materials, people, places, and ideas are the vehicles by which children "arrive." Learning: To "read" facial and body expressions; to see and find meaning in pictures and relate it to past experiences; to "collect" new words (the tools of language and speech development) through trips and interaction with the concrete; to read the labels on food cans in the playstore and the street signs; to recognize letters; to put puzzle fragments together; to coordinate large and small muscles within a given space or task; to represent ideas in paintings and drawings; to see similarities in the way the names of other children begin or end; to listen to poetry and alike sounds; to clap out a rhythm; to hold out one's left foot; to find objects within the classroom that are the same shape; to sew one's name on a beanbag; to classify objects in a lotto game; to guess the outcome of a story or experiment; to make up one's own puppet show to interact with someone else's character; to formulate questions; to express opinions; to make comparisons; to remember sounds and the days of the week; to tie a shoelace; to be read to and beg for the same story again; to read a friend's name on the attendance cards; to learn that H-A-P-P-Y spells *happy* on the birthday cake; to enjoy and utilize one's senses more fully; to extend frustration and accept greater responsibility for one's own behavior; to have concern for the rights of others . . . these are some of the "stuff" of which beginning reading is made.
>
> A climate that encourages growth is established by providing the security of some routines with set limits and some with plenty of room for individual choices and decision making and by designing the classroom so there is interaction among the five year olds with their peers and with "facilitating" adults in an environment consisting of opportunities as well as materials. Five year olds who are already reading extend themselves in an environment where imagination, initiative, and opportunities for verbalization and interaction are in full play. More time for physical and social development will reinforce their skills and self-confidence for a good start in the first grade (Vendig, 1974).

It can be seen in the above statement that the teacher believes a key to readiness is "interaction." Learning to use language can only occur in social situations. Since the purpose of language is to facilitate communica-

The reading readiness program is tied to the reading instruction that follows

tion, there must be ample opportunity for interaction with other children and with adults. The goal of a readiness program is to provide situations that foster cognitive, affective, psychomotor, and linguistic growth. This is accomplished through experiences in which the pupils can act upon the environment and in turn be acted upon by the environment. The linguistic factors are the strand running through all the others and provide for the pupils' internal manipulation of the environment, their organizing of thinking, their development of self-expression, and their interrelating of thoughts and action (Foerster, 1975a).

Strategies for Developing Readiness to Read

Concepts are acquired through experience, verbal explanation, and conceptual explanation

Concepts are acquired in three ways: (1) through direct experience, (2) through direct verbal explanation, and (3) through conceptual explanation (J. Smith, 1972).

When something is learned through direct experience, there may not be a need for explicit verbalization. A pupil can observe the teacher performing some task and then, using the teacher's performance as a model, attempt to perform the same task. Or, the pupil can, through several experiences of the situation, form a concept alone.

Direct verbal explanation may take the form of a definition, as,

This is a hammer,

or it may take the form of an explanation of how or why something functions, as,

The water comes through the pipe at the top and falls into the little buckets. The buckets are now heavy so they move downwards. The falling buckets are attached to the wheel. The wheel turns as each bucket gets full, falls toward the river, empties into the river, and then rises up to be filled again.

In the case of direct explanation, the situation is generally concrete, that is, the situation is within the sight, sound, smell, or touch of the pupil. The success of a verbal explanation depends upon both the speaker and hearer having experiences that match; that is, the speaker and hearer assign the same meanings to the same words because they have had similar direct experiences.

However, in the case of conceptual explanation, verbal message and reality may not be directly connected. Conceptual explanation is abstract; the pupil must have made long term memory storage of other experiences to which the new experience can be related. The success of learning by conceptual explanation requires that the speaker and hearer share a total experience.

In the development of reading readiness with young pupils, the sequence of instruction should move from direct experience to direct verbal explanation to conceptual explanation. If teaching begins at the conceptual explanation level without a base of experience, learning is hindered. When a pupil is able to deal with some experience or concept abstractly, then the pupil is ready to read about that particular topic.

This last point is most important. For every thing about which one can read, there must be a readiness. No singular general skill can account for an individual's ability to read. For example, a reader's strategies that are limited to dealing with the grapho-phonological cues in language cannot be expected to fully reconstruct an author's message. Therefore, initial reading materials should be those which deal with experiences and concepts familiar to the reader. Chapter 7 contains strategies for formally introducing pupils to the reading process through the Language Experience Approach. Here, emphasis is placed on those activities that allow pupils to develop facility with the oral language system so that functioning in the written language system becomes an extension of it. Reading should become as natural and easy as listening.

Initial reading materials should deal with familiar experiences and concepts

The reading readiness program outlined below consists of a variety of activities with differing purposes. Individual activities do not develop single skills, so there will be no attempt to classify them as if they do. The classifications presented, therefore, should not be construed as hierarchical or absolute; rather, they are tentative and heuristic—a means for initiating and stimulating investigation into the nature of reading readiness.

Cognitive Factors. Some teachers refer to these as "comprehension skills." Many of the activities below will seem like "play"; but it should be remembered that play is an integral part of pre-school and kindergarten programs. Play, of course, has an important role in the development of the thinking process (Anastasiow, 1971).

1. *Classifying and patterning.* ☐ Provide pictures or objects of a general category. Once the objects and the categories have been learned, mix up the items of two or three categories and have the pupils sort them. Some classifications that might be used are:

zoo	farm	street
ride on	ride in	jobs
wear	outdoors	indoors
eat	furniture	containers

things used to eat, work, or write with

☐ Provide a series of items. From some additional items, many of which are not related to the items in the series, have the pupil select an item or group of items that will continue the series. *It is important always to ask the pupils why they selected an item. Sometimes they will "see" a pattern not intended by the teacher, but which is logical.* Some series that might be used are:

☐ After pupils understand how to detect series of items, provide them with a matrix. The dimensions of the matrix represent two different series. After pupils have discovered how the matrix works, they should be asked to complete partial matrices. Two sample matrices that can be constructed are shown in Figure 6-1.

FIGURE 6-1

A series of geometric shapes

A pattern of dots

A pattern of sounds

A pattern of colors

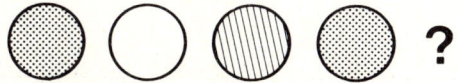

☐ Provide the pupils with objects, or with pictures of objects, placed to show the various relationships that are expressed by the prepositions of our language: *in, on, under, over, behind*, etc. The pupils should be able to complete a statement that indicates the relationship between two or more objects. Or, they should be able to place the objects in a relationship expressed by the teacher. For example, have the pupils identify "The car is next to the tree," or "Put the block under the ruler."

The above activity can be carried out using the adverbial relationship *how*. For example, "The catsup comes slowly out of the bottle."

☐ Provide the pupils with various objects having different characteristics that can be identified by different senses. Have the pupils classify the items according to the sense(s) that provides them with the most information about the item. This activity works well with items that share characteristics. For example, use items that look somewhat alike (sugar–salt), feel somewhat alike (sand–sugar), smell somewhat alike (flower–perfume), etc.

☐ Provide the pupils with samples of various sounds found in their environment. Have them match the sound to the appropriate object by either having the object or a realistic representation of the object at hand. The sounds can be prerecorded so that home and street sounds can be included.

Also, have the pupils compare sounds of objects placed in closed cannisters (for example, plastic film containers). Use objects such as seeds, pebbles, sand, flour, nails, money, or water. Have the pupils classify the sounds by intensity and descriptive qualities—"clinky," "rattlely," "swishy."

The above activities can be extended into other modalities. Have the pupils taste or touch an object and attempt to name the object and/or match the taste or feel to the real object.

☐ Present the pupils with a group of objects that have one or more characteristics in common. Ask them to indicate what the items have in common. The activity can be extended by using items that have one or more characteristics which are different. For very young children, the characteristics must be observable. As the pupils mature, more abstract qualities can be used to group the objects. For example, young children may be asked how objects that are all blue are the same. As the children mature, the objects may be classified by function ("used in cooking"), or higher order quality ("all made of metal"). *It is most important that the* teacher constantly ask the pupils for their reasons in classifying distinguishing features.

☐ Provide the pupils with a sequence of pictures that tell a story. Mix up the pictures and have the pupils rearrange them to tell the story. As pupils gain facility in this task, provide them with a sequence of pictures, but do not show them the completed story beforehand.

☐ Provide the pupils with a problem. Have them generate as many solutions to the problem as possible and then test out each to determine which are the more workable. The alternative solutions do not always have to be workable. Allow the pupils to determine whether a solution is workable or not after it has been tried.

☐ Provide the pupils with various illustrations of completed events and have them indicate what could be possible causes of the activity or incident. The situations can be given to the pupils pictorially or verbally. For example, show the pupils a picture showing the results of a storm, or tell them that a baseball player is being congratulated at home plate. Allow the pupils to generate as many possible causes as they can.

2. *Understanding.* ☐ Let the pupils listen to a story. When the story is completed, ask them what the story was about. Discuss the details or major events of the story, the general plot, and the theme of the story. Pupils who experience difficulty in remembering the events of a story should be allowed to develop strategies for remembering. One such device is to allow the pupils to make simple drawings while listening. Then in the retelling, they may use their simple sketches as "notes."

In order to facilitate remembering, pupils can also develop techniques for ordering the events. As they listen, have them apply sequence cues—first, second, third, etc.—to the events.

☐ Remembering can also be developed through variations of the game of "concentration." This game is played by constructing a deck of playing cards that consists of paired items the same shape, color, use, etc. The deck is dealt out face down in rows. When a pupil turns over two paired cards, they are kept. Unsuccessful matches are turned face down again, and the next pupil takes a turn. Encourage the pupils to develop "tricks" for remembering where the various cards are after they have been returned to the field of play.

☐ To develop an understanding of *plot,* provide the pupils with some sample story outlines. The pupils then try to match the story outline to stories they know or have heard. For example, the pupils should be able to recognize some of the more common fairy tales from outlines such as:

A little girl takes some food to a sick relative.
A girl finds an empty house and tries out the family's food and furniture.
Three young animals try to set up homes but run into trouble from another animal.

☐ To develop an understanding of theme, have the pupils listen to stories, poems, plays, etc., which are all examples of a particular theme. Start with themes within the pupils' experiences and to which they can easily relate. As they hear stories, encourage them to state the theme of the story and classify it with other known stories of the same theme. Some themes around which many stories appropriate for young elementary pupils are written are:

We cannot always do everything we want to do.
Family and close friends can be of great help sometimes.
Some people have different ways of doing things.
We have different feelings when we are personally rejected or accepted.
Things aren't what they always appear to be.

☐ Provide the pupils with opportunities to follow and demonstrate they understand different types of directions. Beginning with simple, one-step directions, have them carry out the instructions. Then move to more complex directions. Allow the pupils to discuss among themselves why certain directions are difficult to follow and others are easy. Let the pupils suggest how directions can be remembered over brief periods of time.

The above activity can be extended to an investigation of the ways people of all ages remember a set of directions. Have the pupils question their parents, relatives, teachers, and other pupils in the school, and any other children or adults they have contact with, about ways they remember directions.

☐ Find examples of directions which are given in pictures or in symbols. Have the pupils translate the directions into verbal directions. (Pictorial directions often accompany toys and games.)

☐ After hearing a story, let the pupils listen to a musical version of the story told without words. For example, read or tell the story of *Peter and the Wolf,* or the *Sorcerer's Apprentice,* then play a record of Prokofiev's *Peter and the Wolf* or Dukas' *The Sorcerer's Apprentice.* After the pupils are familiar with both the story and the musical version, have them narrate the story to the music.

Extend the above activity by having the pupils create their own musical versions of well-known stories. The pupils can orchestrate the story by using rhythm instruments that are either provided by the school or made by the pupils. These activities work best with stories in which the number of characters is not too large and each character is repeated in the story at least two times.

☐ Have the pupils listen to brief vignettes, but do not complete the story. Have the pupils offer possible endings to the stories. This activity can also be done with a long story. At various points in the story, stop reading and ask the pupils to suggest what they think will happen next. (See in Chapter 7 "A Guided Reading-Thinking Lesson." Turn the lesson into a guided *listening*-thinking lesson.)

☐ Read a story about some familiar activity. Include in the story some incorrect information. After the story is completed, have the pupils identify the incorrect information. Be sure to inform the pupils before reading the story what it is that will be expected of them.

Affective Factors. Activities that have as their prime concern the development of attitudes and interests will be considered as fostering readiness in affective factors. Included in this area are activities that lead pupils to make generalizations about themselves as individuals and as members of groups. Language is studied as a key to understanding social relationships (Mishler, 1972).

☐ Provide the pupils with opportunities to differentiate themselves as physical bodies in space. They should develop a sense of their own body as well as a sense of themselves in relation to other individuals and objects.

☐ Play dough or clay can be used to create human and animal shapes. The pupils are encouraged to examine pictures of animals and then to discover what body parts animals and humans have in common. The pupils can discover how the shapes of various body parts differ between humans and animals.

☐ Have the pupils create family portraits either through montages of photgraphs or by drawings. Have the pupils pay attention to the physical characteristics that help to distinguish one individual from another. The pupils should identify how body parts change as people get older.

☐ Play games that require the identification of body parts and their relative positions in space. Use games such as "Simple Simon" and the dance movements that accompany songs such as "Looby Loo" and "Hokey Pokey."

☐ Read stories to the pupils which deal with body parts and individual characteristics (hair, skin, and eye color, shape of face, type of hair, etc.). Let pupils discuss what everyone has in common and how individuals differ.

☐ Play matching games in which the pupils match a piece of clothing to the part of the body for which it is intended.

☐ Use thumb, hand, or foot prints as a basis for creating animal characters or abstract designs. Or, let the pupils lie down on a large piece of paper and have other pupils trace their outline. These figures can then be completed with facial and clothing features.

☐ Provide the pupils with opportunities to express their feelings about themselves in different situations. These activities can be combined with stories about how other children and animals feel in different situations. Lists can be made of various words that relate to the emotions and of words that evoke emotions. In the latter case, connotations of some common words can be explored. For instance, the pupils can discuss what feelings are evoked by words like *bacon, bath, ice cream, vacation, dentist,* etc. (for additional suggestions, see Chapter 9).

☐ Read different types of literature to the pupils (see Chapter 11). Have them discuss the types of stories they prefer. Extend the discussion to include television programs and movies. Let the pupils become conscious of the factors that affect their attitudes, interests, and preferences for such things as choosing a program to watch, selecting a friend, buying dessert in a restaurant, picking clothes to wear.

☐ Give the pupils a number of different roles to act out. At first, the activities may require the pupils just to go through the motions of a house builder, a baker, etc. Then have the pupils act out emotionally charged situations in which they must show fear, happiness, anger, sadness, etc.

A reading readiness program is one of creative problem solving

Extend the role playing to hypothetical situations. Use open ended stories to have the pupils explore answers to questions such as: What could you do? What would you do? What should you do?

☐ Have the pupils survey adults and older children about their attitudes toward reading. Let the class as a whole classify the various feelings expressed about reading and try to hypothesize why people feel differently about it.

☐ Have pupils express their feelings and attitudes through art. Let them examine various pictures or reproductions of artists' work that are grouped according to theme. Have the pupils describe what characteristics of the pictures create different moods. Have the pupils create mood pictures by turning a story or a musical selection into a picture. Encourage the pupils to experiment with realistic and abstract renditions of things, with color, with size, etc., for creating different moods. Let other children try to explain what the pictures mean to them.

Psychomotor Factors. The activities included in this section are aimed at helping pupils to understand that some body movements relate to the culture or group to which one belongs, and some body movements relate to one's own personality (Foerster, 1975b). Cultural body movements are the conventional body movements that can distinguish members of one culture from the members of another culture. Individual body movements distinguish individuals of the same culture and are an expression of personality.

Some body movements are cultural, others are idiosyncratic

☐ Using pantomime, have the pupils communicate some idea to others. Using facial expressions, convey feelings. Using gestures, convey an idea or mood. Make a study of the "body language" people use in different situations. Lead the pupils to notice how most people who grew up in the school area use similar movements with individual variations.

☐ Play games such as "Indian Chief." One pupil leaves the room and someone from the circle of other pupils is chosen to be "chief." The chief initiates different changes of actions or movements that must be followed by the other pupils. The chief must signal changes without any verbal communication. The pupil who was out of the room returns and tries to figure out who the chief is.

☐ Have the pupils engage in activities such as, "Move as if you. . . ." in which the pupils must move their bodies as if they were performing some task or as if they were some other person or animal. Some suggested movements might include being a baby, walking up (down) the stairs, carrying a heavy load, eating something sticky, being bored, finding a dollar. Encourage the other pupils to express verbally the idea or feeling being conveyed by the pupil's movements.

The above activity may be expanded by having the pupils move to different rhythms. Also, the pupils may be asked to do various movements with one or more other pupils. Have the pupils explain how doing something alone differs from doing it with others.

☐ Have pupils lead other pupils who are blindfolded around the room without any verbal communication between them. The pupils may only touch the other pupils' arm with one hand. Have them express how it felt to be totally dependent upon the other pupils.

☐ View a movie or television program without the sound. Have the pupils suggest from the action and body movements of the actors what ideas are being conveyed. Then have them watch a rerun of the same program with the sound turned on. Allow the pupils to discuss how their interpretation coincided with or differed from the intended meaning.

☐ Let the pupils make up dances to musical selections that vary not only in tempo and rhythm, but also in melody, sound, and pitch.

☐ Have the pupils learn and act the movements to songs, such as, "If you're happy and you know it." When the pupils are fully familiar with the song, change *happy* to some other emotion or feeling. Then the pupils must move a body part and make the appropriate facial expression.

☐ Explore with the pupils the various sounds it is possible to make with one's body. For instance, the pupils should be able to make sounds that are represented by the following words: *knock, slap, snap, tap,* "*raspberry,*" as well as various sounds for which there are no words in English.

☐ Have the pupils learn and act various work songs. When the pupils have caught on to the idea of work songs, they may be able to create parodies of them to express their own "work" in school.

☐ Have the pupils learn and play any type of circle game in which the outcome of the game depends upon being able to "read" the body movements of the other pupils. Such games as "Dodgeball," and "Crows and Cranes" are examples.

☐ Have the pupils create artwork out of materials of various textures. Have them create mood stories which can only be "read" by running one's hand over the completed work. Then have other pupils give their interpretation of the various stories.

☐ Have the pupils explain to a fictitious "Martian" how certain physical activities are done. During the explanation, the pupils should not use any physical motions. In fact, this activity can be done by putting the explainer behind a screen. Explain to the Martian what a telephone is, how to tie a shoelace, what a knife, fork, and spoon look like.

☐ Have the pupils repeat various sentences that could be ambiguous except for the intonation and gestures that accompany different meanings. Sentences such as the following can be used:

> That's great.
> I like growing children.
> I ate the whole thing.

☐ Pupils are blindfolded and seated in the middle of the room. Sounds are made from different sides of the room and the pupils have to indicate the direction from which the sound came. The pupils should have ample opportunity to develop eye-hand coordinations and spatial relations. An activity that fosters spatial orientations is block building, especially tall towers!

☐ Pupils should act out stories with puppets. Let the pupils create their own character puppets and perform with them. Puppets can be easily and inexpensively be made from paper bags, fingers, fists, sticks, socks, toilet paper tubes, and old tennis balls.

A variation of puppet plays is "finger plays" in which a story is dramatized with the hands. Unlike using fingers and fists as puppets, in finger plays no additional props or "make-up" is used. In this sense, finger plays almost become a sign language.

Linguistic Factors. Linguistic factors actually permeate all the other factors. However, there are some activities that relate basically to the nature of language itself. To develop linguistic factors is to identify and interpret the

Linguistic development entails identification of language cues

oral and written cues of language themselves. Here the pupil learns how language actually works, what types of activities or situations may or may not promote effective communication, and the appropriateness of different kinds of language in different situations.

Since most material that is read is prose and not conversation, reading readiness instruction should move from conversation to spoken prose before reading instruction is attempted (McDonell, 1975). Part of each day should be devoted to some reading aloud to the pupils. There is support for this suggestion; a body of research shows that a teacher's reading aloud daily is associated with a measurable increase in pupils' language ability (Cullinan, 1974). Stories read aloud to pupils help them to draw inferences at a higher level than when the pupils read the stories to themselves. In addition, a special program in literature using daily oral reading by teachers has been shown to have a significant effect on the pupils' reading ability.

Traditional readiness programs have often assumed that pupils hear words as units of sound within sentences. Also, the traditional programs assume that pupils can recognize and understand the relationship between letters and their sounds or meaning. However, there is evidence that neither assumption is correct. These abilities seem to be a function of experience and maturation (Sawyer, 1975). For children under five, the sentence probably constitutes the basic psychological unit of meaning. For adults the smallest unit of speech processed seems to be the syllable. The ability to analyze speech into units of single words does not begin to appear until after the ages of five or six (Sawyer, 1975; Downing and Oliver, 1973).

☐ The pupils may be introduced to the discussion and investigation of linguistic factors by the question, "How can we communicate with others when they are not near?" This should lead the pupils to recognize how newspapers, magazines, letters and other written material can be effective in preserving ideas for others to deal with at a later time. Also, the pupils should recognize the function of records and films. Have the pupils try to answer the question: When is writing a better way of saving and communicating ideas than record or film?

☐ Discuss the use of picture language and sign language. Have the pupils create their own stories using only picture sequences. Then have them create symbols for many of their activities and their feelings and attitudes. Encourage the pupils to write stories to each other using these symbols. What happens when someone uses a symbol the others do not know? What happens if some of the symbols the pupils devise are similar to others and seem ambiguous?

☐ Let the pupils explore the advantages of the telephone, radio, and television for quickly bringing information to people. Discuss the use of the telephone for reporting a fire or accident. Guide the pupils to an understanding of the techniques for sending and receiving calls on the telephone. (The local business offices of the telephone companies provide many services free to schools, including demonstration telephone kits, films, filmstrips, recordings, and sample telephone information materials.)

☐ Make a collection of words that have multiple meanings. Explore with the pupils how they can tell what meaning a particular word will have.

☐ Read riddles to the pupils and provide them with opportunity to solve them. Let the pupils begin to create their own riddles. For those who do not catch on to the idea, point out how many riddles use words with multiple meanings.

☐ Read or tell the pupils stories in which confusion occurs between two or more individuals because different meanings are applied to words. From these stories, let the pupils explore some of the common idioms of our language. Have the pupils draw pictures of the literal and intended meanings of the idioms to show how confusion may arise when one does not know the use of a particular idiom. For instance, let the pupils illustrate the literal and idiomatic meanings of: They had lunch over my house. We got on the bus.

As an alternative to listening to the teacher, small groups of children or individuals can listen to recordings of the story in the classroom listening center. The recordings can be teacher or commercially produced. This activity works well when copies of the book are available for the pupils to follow along. Be sure the recordings, whatever their source, clearly identify the page being read and allow enough time for the pupils to be able to peruse the illustrations.

☐ Using the basic kernel sentences discussed in Chapter 2, provide the pupils with models of how these sentences may be transformed or expanded. Let the pupils make suggestions for transforming and expanding other sentences. Also, provide sentences which are transformations and expansions of kernel sentences and have the pupils identify the kernel sentences and the embedded sentences. For instance, the activity could start with a sentence like

The player saw the ball.

Have the pupils create a question, a passive, a negative, and a sentence beginning with "there" or "it."
Then a sentence such as

The funny clown rode on the brown horse

could be broken down into the following:

The clown is funny.
The clown rode the horse.
The horse is brown.

(This activity will require a great deal of repetition and a great deal of modeling. The task is not an easy one for young pupils and the teacher should not expect all the pupils to acquire facility in doing the tasks. Many pupils will be able to deal with only a few sentence patterns, and some will be able to deal with a great many. If the teacher constantly asks, "Is there another way to say that?" and "Can we put those two ideas together?" or "Can we take those two ideas and say them separately?" then the pupils will be continuously alerted to the possibilities for dealing with the syntactic patterns of their language. The outcome will be that the pupils develop an appreciation of the English language and greater facility with language in general.)

☐ Read a sentence to the pupils in which a word has been deleted (an oral cloze exercise). Let the pupils generate words that could complete the sentence. Ask them how they selected the word they did. For those pupils who may experience some difficulty at first, provide them with three alternatives—a possible correct response, a word that is the correct part of speech, but semantically incorrect, and a word from another part of speech. Whenever the pupils give the *correct* response, ask them how they came to select that word.

☐ Play word games with the pupils in which their answer is a word that rhymes with the key word. You might employ incomplete rhyming couplets such as

> One fine day
> We went out to _____ .

Or you might use rhyming adjective-noun combinations such as

> fat   cat
> green   bean
> mad   Dad

☐ The pupils can begin to develop a sight vocabulary from various labels and signs that the teacher can place around the classroom. In many instances, teachers use single words to label things on bulletin boards as well as things such as doors, windows, etc. However, it is a more natural lead-in to reading if these labels contain sentences. Instead of controlling the pupils' vocabulary, the teacher could begin to use sentence patterns that are used in many first grade readers (not to be confused with pre-primers, which often use artificial language). For instance, a bulletin board about community helpers could include captions for pictures which read

> This is a fire fighter.
>
> This is a police officer.
>
> This is a postal worker.

Classroom signs that could be put up are

> We go to Art at 9:30 a.m.
>
> Please close the closet door.
>
> The coat hooks are in the back of the room.

☐ Pupils can be introduced to the alphabet through a discussion of how their names are spelled. The pupils can become acquainted with the many alternative forms and shapes in which the letters are drawn by creating montages of words from newspapers, headlines, advertisements, and signs. The pupils can determine how they can distinguish the letters when they have various forms:

cat milk TOOTHPASTE

☐ Let the pupils play games in which they describe a letter to a pupil who cannot see it. In this game use only basic lowercase or uppercase manuscript letters. For example, one pupil might say,

> I see a letter that has one long line going up with a circle on the left side of the line,

and the other pupil should answer, "d."

☐ Have the pupils begin to "read" calendars, maps, globes, thermometers, pictures, simple graphs, etc. On many of these, symbols are used. After the pupils have become familiar with the symbols, have them read the information to other pupils. For instance, using some basic, common symbols used on television weather programs, have pupils create weather maps. Other pupils can then interpret the maps for each other.

☐ Acquaint the pupils with the different parts of a book. As a story is read to them, demonstrate techniques for the careful handling of the book. In addition, identify the cover, title page with author and publisher, main story part, and table of contents.

☐ Sometimes communication between individuals is hindered because the speaker uses many pronouns and other pro-forms. Young children will use pronouns to the extent that the referents of each may become ambiguous. As pupils engage in various oral activities, be alert to their use of ambiguous pronouns. Also, read or tell stories to the pupils in which a great many pronouns have been substituted for the characters' names. Each time a pronoun is said, the pupils must supply the name of the person to whom the pronoun refers.

Another type of substitution is the use of *this* and *does* for entire ideas, as in:

It's raining; because of this, we won't go to the beach.

Sometimes Melissa will not help her mother, and sometimes she does.

As sentences such as those above are read to the pupils, ask them to supply the words for which *this* and *does* are substitutes.

☐ Create a "word of the day" display in which a new word is put up each day. To maintain the pupils' interest, the words may be related to some upcoming school event or public holiday. The display could be changed seasonally—a tree with colors in the fall, a snowman in the winter, children flying kites in the spring. Words may be printed on small signs which fit the decor of the display. A few minutes each day can be spent discussing the word and its meaning or meanings. During the day and succeeding days, the pupils may be encouraged to use the words as many times as they can in "natural" situations. No word is too big to be learned; that is, the length of the word in no way determines its appropriateness for the pupils. However, the teacher should take care to select words which can be conceptualized by the pupils. Words with high imagery work well in this activity.

☐ Provide opportunities for the pupils to become familiar with the melodic qualities of the language. Use echo activities in which the pupils must repeat a sentence exactly as it is said by the teacher or another pupil. This "follow the speaker" activity can be used as a lead-in to choral speaking. Beginning with short poems or rhymes that can be easily memorized by the pupils, interpret each differently by changing the rhythm, intonation, and accent given to the words and sentences. Then let the pupils decide which interpretation they prefer. (In using choral speaking, the teacher should assume an active role as leader. In this activity, the purpose is not to develop individual styles of interpretation, but to develop a sense of a number of individuals working together to produce a group result. After the pupils understand what "leading" and "following" entails in such activities, they may assume the leadership positions.)

DETERMINING PUPIL READINESS TO READ

As stated previously, many teachers would like a nice, neat way to identify those pupils who are "ready" to read. To accommodate individuals with this view, test writers have devised reading readiness tests which are supposed to discriminate between those pupils who are ready to read and those who need additional "readiness activities." However, there is very strong evidence that reading readiness tests cannot clearly distinguish those pupils who are "ready," nor are they so precise that they can specify the areas in which a pupil needs additional instruction (MacGinitie, 1969; Rude, 1973; Pikulski, 1974; Sawyer, 1975; Vogel, 1975).

Reading readiness tests cannot clearly distinguish those pupils who are ready

First, the term readiness means different things to different people. Whatever one's definition of reading, there are some factors that make a pupil ready to read. The question then becomes, What is a definition of readiness that is consistent with what is known about child development in language and thinking? Using a definition of readiness consistent with one's definition of reading, the prerequisites for reading can be determined. In essence, then, any assessment of pupils' readiness to read must take into consideration the methods and materials that will be used to teach reading.

Second, reading readiness tests are predictive, not diagnostic. Since there has been little agreement among authorities as to what constitutes reading readiness skills, the tests were designed to predict which pupils probably would be successful on a reading achievement test after a period of instruction. The discussion in Chapter 4 pointed out how some achievement tests may not be measuring "reading" ability. In the same vein, what the readiness tests may be measuring is general potential for doing academic work.

In assessing readiness to read, then, the wrong questions have been asked (MacGinitie, 1969). Instead of asking "Is the pupil ready to learn to read?" teachers should be asking "*What* and *how* is the pupil ready to learn?"

The predictive value of any task used to estimate the readiness of pupils derives from the resemblance of the task to the process of reading. Since reading is a complex interaction of cognitive, affective, psychomotor, and linguistic factors, "there appears to be no nice, clean way to identify children who are likely to encounter difficulty in reading" (Pikulski, 1974).

Readiness assessments should grow out of classroom activities

Readiness assessments should grow out of the classroom activities. Through the application of analytical teaching procedures (Chapter 3), the teacher can assess the pupils' cognitive and linguistic abilities and how these abilities are used in different situations.

Reading should become as natural as listening

Some formal instruments exist that the teacher can employ for determining those abilities pupils possess and those for which additional learning must take place. One representative standardized instrument, which measures pupils' mastery of concepts considered necessary for achievement in the first years of school, is:

The Boehm Test of Basic Concepts. The Psychological Corporation, 1971 Edition, Forms A and B. Intended level: kindergarten, grades 1 and 2.

Figure 6–2 contains two sample items from the test and the instructions for testing those items. *The Boehm Test of Basic Concepts* may be used to identify pupils with deficiencies in concepts used in common curriculum

FIGURE 6-2: Sample Items from a Test of Basic Concepts

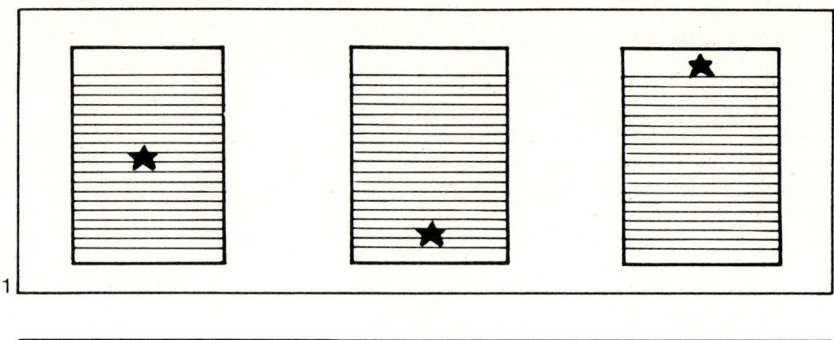

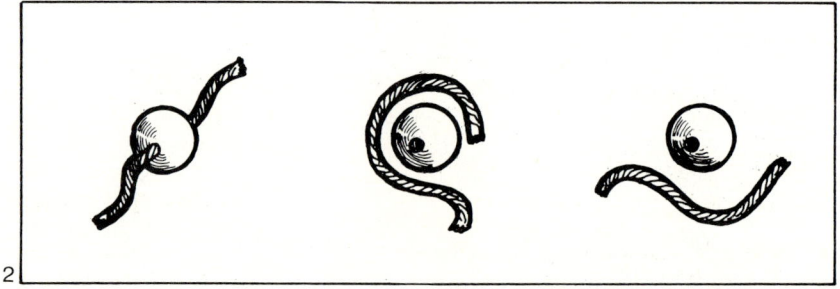

Reproduced by permission. Copyright 1967, 1969 by The Psychological Corporation. All rights reserved.

Directions:

1. Look at the pictures of writing paper with stars. Mark the paper with the star at the *top* . . . . Mark the paper with the star at the *top*.
2. Look at the beads and strings. Mark the bead that has a string *through* it . . . . Mark the bead that has a string *through* it.

Reproduced by permission. Copyright 1967, 1969, 1970, 1971 by The Psychological Corporation. All rights reserved.

materials and to identify individual concepts on which particular pupils could profit from additional instruction. The manual of instructions contains information for the teacher on how to use the test for analytical purposes and includes some suggestions for instructional practices.

Measures for Research and Evaluation in the English Language Arts, by William Fagan and others (cited in Chapter 5, *Further Readings*), can be used or adapted for assessment purposes. The sections on measures for assessing language development and listening should be very helpful. In addition, some of the sources cited in a later section of this chapter, *Resources for the Teacher,* contain suggestions for assessing pupil proficiency in the cognitive, linguistic, psychomotor, and affective areas.

TABLE 6-1. Assessing Individual Language Readiness

Does the pupil:
Respond to his or her name?
Respond to simple questions?
Ask to have questions repeated?
Speak clearly and distinctly enough to be heard?
Repeat spoken words correctly?
Speak spontaneously in sharing time?
Follow simple directions?
Listen attentively?
Listen when other pupils are speaking?
Express himself or herself in telling about things?
Express simple ideas in complete sentences?
Tell a story in sequence?
Ask the meanings of words and signs?
Show interest in reading books?
Recognize rhyming words?
Recognize words that begin with the same sound?
Show an interest in alphabet repeating and reading alphabet letters?
Write his or her name?

NOTE: Adapted from Burns, Paul C., and Broman, Betty L. 1975. *The Language Arts in Childhood Education.* Third Edition. Chicago:. Rand McNally.

Finally, the questions in Table 6-1 can be used for informal assessment purposes.

DEVELOPING READINESS FOR PARTICIPATING IN GROUP ACTIVITIES

Bringing a number of pupils together for a lesson does not mean a "group" has been formed. In the first chapter it was suggested that "flexible" classroom grouping procedures should be used. The intent was to focus on the purposes for forming groups. Teachers should have a variety of reasons for organizing groups, and the requirements for a pupil to join a group or be included in one after it is formed should be flexible.

However, although a number of pupils are brought together for a particular purpose, a group still may not have been formed. Quite often so called "groups" are nothing more than aggregations. A real group has an internal interpersonal structure. When a number of pupils meet with the teacher, and each pupil communicates solely with the teacher, then the

A real group has an internal interpersonal structure

pupils are not functioning as a group. When each of the pupils communicates with the others as well as with the teacher, a true group is functioning.

One common misconception about grouping is that grouping only entails organizing pupils of somewhat equal ability. Usually what is meant is that the pupils are reading "at the same level," or that they need the same skill development. What results is usually an aggregation in which the teacher is presenting a lesson to a number of individuals simultaneously. Although ability may be, at times, a desired criterion for inclusion in a group, it is not the hub about which a group is formed. The primary purpose for organizing any group is to facilitate learning through joint problem solving ventures.

When a true group exists, there are at least three functioning levels:

Groups function at the task level. This usually represents the original purpose for organizing or designing the group. Most groups to which individuals belong have a conscious task need. Quite often, that is the main level at which the members seem to operate.

Groups function at a maintenance level. Groups function with a constantly changing system of relationships among its members. This is the group personality. The members of a real group are aware that they exist as a group, and they are confronted with the need to maintain the interpersonal relationships so that a working system exists.

Groups function at an individual level. Each group consists of individuals who have their own personal needs. The needs can range from the need to share experiences with others to the need for domineering. Too often, because the individual needs of the group members are masked, the functioning of the group breaks down. When members, consciously or unconsciously, place their needs and goals ahead of the main purpose of the group, the cohesiveness of a group lessens.

The group can be efficient only as the members interact and maintain some balance among the three functioning levels. Learning to be a good group member is important. The group process can facilitate a great deal of the learning that occurs in schools. Therefore, teachers should be sure that their pupils are ready to participate as members of real groups.

Group Functions

Although pupils may not overtly identify the three functions of a group, they should have some awareness of a goal and the personal responsibilities for helping the group reach that goal. Below are some of the more common task and maintenance functions that can be carried out by group members (Gorman, 1974). Through guidance and modeling, the

Pupils should share responsibility for helping the group reach some goal

teacher can encourage pupils to assume many of the functions as the group operates.

Task functions. Task functions consist of

Initiating. Group members propose goals, define a group problem, and suggest ways for solving that problem.

Seeking ideas. Group members request information and seek suggestions and ideas.

Giving information. Group members offer information and ideas, and state a belief or opinion.

Clarifying ideas. Group members interpret or reflect on information or ideas already given, give additional information or examples, and suggest alternative solutions.

Summarizing. Group members bring together the ideas of others, and offer a conclusion for the group's acceptance.

Testing. Group members test or check out to see how much agreement exists among the members of a group.

Maintenance functions. Maintenance functions consist of

Encouraging. Group members become responsive to the ideas, suggestions, and opinions of others, accept their contributions, and give them recognition for their contribution.

Expressing feelings. Group members sense the mood and feelings of the group, and express this to the other members.

Reducing tension. Group members get individuals within the group to explore their differences.

Offering compromises. Group members attempt to resolve conflicts through compromise.

Facilitating communication. Group members make suggestions for the sharing and discussing of ideas and reconciling differences.

Setting limits. Group members state standards for evaluating the group's functioning and achievements.

In summary, it is not possible to talk about "grouping" without specifying (1) the purpose of the group, (2) the situation within which it will operate, and (3) the nature of the learning that is expected to result from the group's efforts. For a group to be productive—to achieve its goal—the members of the group must share common concerns and aims, and they should understand how group members constructively work together toward the completion of their goal. With the teacher's guidance and initial leadership, groups can be formed that allow the individual members to function without losing self-respect or experiencing rejection from other group members.

Forming Groups in a Classroom

The nature and size of groups will vary. The duration of a group will depend upon the task and the abilities of the group members. However, before classroom groups can function adequately, the pupils should be familiar with certain routines which prevent chaos.

Some pupils may become effective group workers more quickly than others

Although it may take pupils varying periods of time to learn to become effective group workers—some pupils may learn how in a matter of weeks while others may take years—all should be encouraged to participate in the identification of the task and maintenance level functions. At the kindergarten and first grade level this might be accomplished by organizing, at first, interest groups. For example, some pupils might wish to develop a puppet show from a favorite story, or some pupils might wish to design and build a class store.

Next, pupils must know some of the techniques that will be the basis for their activity. The pupils must know

1. How to handle specific materials such as phonographs, woodworking tools, tape recorders, and filmstrip projectors.
2. How to follow the class routines for using supplies such as paper, crayons, paint, and paste.
3. How to seek help from the teacher and from other class members.
4. How to maintain class decorum so that no one is imposing upon the ability of others to perform whatever activity they wish.
5. What to do whenever an activity is complete or cannot be completed at that time.
6. How to work in special learning centers without adult guidance.

Finally, the pupils must know how to work independently. There will be times when not all the pupils are working at group activities or under the teacher's direct guidance. At these times, the pupils must work on individual projects or assignments. The pupils should understand

1. How to allow others to work without interference.
2. How to stay with a task until it is completed, or at least, to understand how, why, and when a task may be terminated before its completion.

3. How to move from one activity to another without requiring the assistance of others.

That many teachers complain that a class is uncontrollable, or that pupils do not have the maturity to work independently or as effective group members, usually means that the teachers have not effectively established routines for efficient classroom practices. It is widely accepted that children are self-motivating. Without guidance and limitations, they will seek their own ways to relieve boredom and frustration, the prime causes of most uncontrolled classrooms.

RESOURCES FOR THE TEACHER

Any teacher beginning to undertake the development of reading readiness programs is faced with a task of accumulating materials for instruction. When schools have readiness materials from a basal reading program, too often these are only exercises in letter-sound relationships. In such cases, the teacher may wish to supplement the program with activities and materials that will provide a well-rounded program of readiness for reading.

The resources listed below are representative of those that a teacher can use for creating a language centered readiness program. The materials listed here differ from those in the *Further Readings* section. *Resources* contains references to instructional materials, whereas *Readings* contains discussions of a more theoretical nature.

The first materials are manuals from commercial programs. When the entire readiness program is not available for instructional purposes, teachers might find it worthwhile to obtain one or more of the manuals for use as handbooks or guides.

Readiness Experiences, Teacher's Edition. 1973. The Bank Street Readers. New York: Macmillan.

Greater Cleveland Reading Program: Readiness for Reading, Teacher's Guide. 1969. Cleveland: Educational Research Council of America.

Open Court Kindergarten Program: Teacher's Guide. 1970. La Salle, Ill.: Open Court.

Peabody Language Development Kit, Manual for Level #P. 1969. Circle Pines, Minn.: American Guidance Society.

Language Experiences in Early Childhood, Teacher's Resource Book. 1966. Chicago: Encyclopaedia Britannica Press.

Matrix Games Package, Teacher's Guide. 1968. New York: Appleton-Century-Crofts.

The following texts contain suggestions for instructional activities.

Moffett, James. 1973. *A Student-Centered Language Arts Curriculum, Grades K–6: A Handbook for Teachers.* Boston: Houghton-Mifflin Co.

Berger, Allen and Smith, Blanch Hope. 1973. *Language Activities.* Urbana, Ill.: National Council of Teachers of English.

Gerbrandt, Gary I. 1974. *An Idea Book for Acting Out and Writing Out, K–8.* Urbana, Ill.: National Council of Teachers of English.

Forte, Imogene and MacKenzie, Joy. 1969. *Kids' Stuff: Reading and Language Experiences,* Primary Level. Nashville, Tenn.: Incentive Publications.

The following is a source of word and language games for all age levels.

Hurwitz, Abraham B. and Goddard, Arthur. 1969. *Games to Improve Your Child's English.* New York: Simon and Schuster.

There are many books containing suggestions for crafts activities and circle and sports games. The following are only representative of those that exist in this area.

Edgren, Harry D. and Gruber, Joseph J. 1963. *Teacher's Handbook of Indoor and Outdoor Games.* Englewood Cliffs, New Jersey: Prentice-Hall.

Cook, Mayra B., Caldwell, Joseph H., and Christiansen, Linda J., 1967. *The Come-Alive Classroom: Practical Projects for Elementary Teachers.* West Nyack, New York: Parker Publishing Co.

Edkren, Betty Lois and Fishel, Vivian. 1952. *500 Live Ideas for the Grade Teacher.* New York: Harper and Row.

Anthologies can be very useful for teachers seeking stories and poems for listening and acting out activities. Anthologies such as the following provide teachers with a great variety of literature that can be conveniently kept at hand in the classroom.

Arbuthnot, May Hill. 1961. *Time for Fairy Tales.* Glenview, Ill.: Scott Foresman.

Arbuthnot, May Hill. 1967. *Time for Poetry.* Glenview, Ill.: Scott Foresman.

Arbuthnot, May Hill. 1961. *Time for True Tales.* Glenview, Ill.: Scott Foresman.

Hurber, Miriam Blanton. 1965. *Story and Verse for Children.* New York: Macmillan.

Johnson, Edna, Sickels, Evelyn R., and Sayers, Francis Clarke. 1970. *Anthology of Children's Literature,* 4th Edition. Boston: Houghton Mifflin.

The following companies produce recordings and filmstrips for all curriculum areas. Teachers developing readiness programs will find them a good source for recordings of songs, games, and rhythmic activities, and for filmstrips and picture-study-story prints.
Educational Activities, Inc., P. O. Box 392, Freeport, N. Y. 11520.
Singer/Society for Visual Education, Inc., 1345 Diversey Parkway, Chicago, Illinois 60614.

DISCUSSION QUESTIONS AND ACTIVITIES

1. Select a basal reading series and examine the teacher's manual for the readiness materials. In what way do the activities foster the development of a "readiness" to read in light of a psycholinguistic definition of reading? Is the aspect of readiness viewed as a broad, many faceted process or as a limited, one dimensional one?

2. Some of the kindergarten teachers in a school wish to implement a reading readiness program that consists primarily of a workbook purporting "to teach the letters of the alphabet and their sounds." What advice would you offer these teachers to assist them in the selection of a readiness program?

3. A parent of a first grade pupil comes to you and wants to know why the class "plays" so much of each day. The parent is concerned that the pupils in the class are not learning, and will lose out in learning to read, in comparison with the other first grade classes. In actuality, the class consists of a large number of immature pupils. The "games" are activities of the type described in this chapter. What will you answer the parent?

4. Answer Frank B. May's (1967) question:

> But could our biggest mistake be that of focusing classroom learning upon the *acts* of reading, writing, speaking, and listening rather than the *serious problems* of communication which human beings have?

5. Examine several reading readiness tests and their accompanying manuals. In your opinion, what items on each of the tests, although they may

be predictors of possible reading achievement, are not indicative of the strategies used during the reading process?

6. Administer to a pupil in kindergarten or the beginning of first grade a series of informal language and cognitive tasks as discussed in this chapter. Describe the pupil's behavior—apparent cognitive strategies, linguistic proficiency, psycho-motor activity, and emotional reactions—while undertaking the tasks.

FURTHER READINGS

The following short book contains descriptions and critical reviews of many of the common perceptual training and language readiness programs used in kindergarten and first grade.

    Kaufman, Maurice. 1973. *Perceptual and Language Readiness Programs: Critical Reviews.* Newark, Del.: International Reading Association.

The following short monographs originally intended for distribution to parents are available from the International Reading Association, Newark, Delaware. Teachers will find them useful as references when making suggestions to parents.

    Rogers, Norma. *How Can I Help My Child Get Ready To Read?*
    Rogers, Norma. *What Is Reading Readiness?*
    Rogers, Norma. *What Books and Records Should I Get For My PreSchooler?*
    Chan, Julie M. T. *Why Read Aloud to Children?*

The following text is not specifically about reading readiness. However, its aim is to explain human thought and human learning.

    Smith, Frank. 1975. *Comprehension and Learning: A Conceptual Framework for Teachers.* New York: Holt Rinehart and Winston.

The following text is an explanation of how children can have fun and at the same time develop the ability to appreciate, create, and communicate with language.

    May, Frank. 1967. *Teaching Language As Communication to Children.* Columbus, Ohio: Charles E. Merrill Books.

The following two books deal with behavior in the classroom and the relationship of teachers and pupils as encoders and decoders of language.

Clark, Margaret L., Erway, Ella A., and Beltzer, Lee. 1971. *The Learning Encounter: The Classroom As a Communication Workshop.* New York: Random House.

Gorman, Alfred H. 1974. *Teachers and Learners: The Interactive Process of Education,* 2nd. Edition. Boston: Allyn and Bacon.

References

Anastasiow, Nickolas. 1971. *Oral Language: Expression of Thought.* Newark, Del.: International Reading Association.

Blanton, William E. 1972. *Preschool Reading Instruction: A Literature Search, Evaluation and Interpretation.* Final Report. Washington, D.C.: National Center for Educational Communication/DHEW.

Church, Marilyn. 1974. "Does Visual Perception Training Help Beginning Readers?" *The Reading Teacher* 27: 371-4.

Cullinan, Bernice. 1974. "Teaching Literature to Children, 1966-72." In H. Alan Robinson and Alvina Truet Burrows, eds. *Teacher Effectiveness in Elementary Language Arts: A Progress Report.* Urbana, Ill.: National Conference on Research in English/ERIC-CRES.

Downing, John, and Oliver, Peter. 1973. "The Child's Conception of 'A Word'" *Reading Research Quarterly* 9: 568-82.

Durkin, Dolores. 1968. "When Should Children Begin to Read?" In Helen M. Robinson, ed. *Innovation and Change in Reading Instruction.* Chicago: University of Chicago Press, pp. 30-71.

Elkind, David. 1974. *Children and Adolescents: Interpretive Essays on Jean Piaget.* 2nd Edition. New York: Oxford University Press.

Foerster, Leona M. 1975a. "Kindergarten—What Can It Be?" *Elementary English* 52: 81-83.

Foerster, Leona M. 1975b. "Teach Children to Read Body Language." *Elementary English* 52: 440-42.

Gorman, Alfred H. 1974. *Teachers and Learners: The Interactive Process of Education,* 2nd Edition. Boston: Allyn & Bacon.

Kavanagh, James F. 1968. *Communicating By Language: The Reading Process.* Proceedings of the Conference on Communicating By Language: The Reading Process. February 11–13, 1968, New Orleans. Bethesda, Md.: National Institute of Child Health and Human Development/DHEW.

Lundsteen, Sara W. 1974. "Questioning To Develop Creative Problem Solving." *Elementary English* 51: 645–50.

MacGinitie, Walter H. 1969. "Evaluating Readiness for Learning to Read: A Critical Review and Evaluation of Research." *Reading Research Quarterly* 4: 396–410.

May, Frank B. 1967. *Teaching Language as Communication to Children.* Columbus, Ohio: Charles E. Merrill Books.

Mayer, Jeri E. 1975. "Evaluating Reading Readiness: A Reply." *Elementary English* 52: 343–45.

McDonell, Gloria. 1975. "Relating Language to Early Reading Experiences." *The Reading Teacher* 28: 438–44.

Mishler, Elliot G. 1972. "Implications of Teacher Strategies for Language and Cognition: Observations in First Grade Classrooms." In Courtney B. Cazden, Vera P. Johns, and Dell Hymes, eds. *Functions of Language in the Classroom.* New York: Teachers College Press, Columbia University, pp. 267–98.

Pikulski, John J. 1974. "Assessment of the Pre-reading Skills: A Review of Frequently Employed Measures." *Reading World* 13: 171–97.

Rude, Robert T. 1973. "Readiness Tests: Implications for Early Childhood." *The Reading Teacher* 26: 572–80.

Sawyer, Diane J. 1975. "Readiness Factors for Reading: A Different View." *The Reading Teacher* 28: 620–24.

Smith, E. Brooks, Goodman, Kenneth S., and Meredith, Robert. 1970. *Language and Thinking in the Elementary School.* New York: Holt Rinehart and Winston.

Smith, James A. 1972. *Adventures in Communication: Language Arts Methods.* Boston: Allyn and Bacon.

Vendig, Anne. 1974. "'Reading' in the Kindergarten." Unpublished manuscript. Great Neck, N.Y.: Great Neck Public Schools.

Vogel, Susan A., and McGrady, Harold J. 1975. "Recognition of Melody Patterns in Good and Poor Readers." *Elementary English* 52: 414–18.

7
Strategies for Guided Reading Development

Focus Questions:

1. In what ways do instructional objectives aid the teacher in organizing instruction?
2. How can the language experience approach be used as a means of introducing pupils to literacy?
3. How can classroom instruction be organized through the use of thematic units?
4. What are the procedures for developing a guided reading-thinking lesson?
5. What are the different types of questions that can be used to develop and extend pupils' understanding during guided reading?

A distinction has to be made between reading that is guided by the teacher and that in which the pupils independently guide themselves. In guided reading, the teacher assumes the responsibility for directing the pupils in their reconstruction of the author's message. As a safari guide leads the inexperienced hunter to the quarry but leaves the "last shot" for the novice, the teacher structures a lesson so that the pupils arrive at a point where they can capture the author's thoughts. In independent reading, the pupils take full responsibility for initiating and completing a reading act. At such times, they are their own guides.

A reading program that is responsive to the needs of the pupils provides for both types of activities. The teacher guides the reading of the pupils until they possess the maturity for independent reading. Since pupils are always capable of some independent reading, both types of instruction are generally appropriate. This chapter focuses on those strategies a

In guided reading, the teacher directs the pupils in message reconstruction

teacher employs to navigate pupils through a reading selection. The succeeding chapters focus on strategies that permit the pupils to be responsible for finding their own way through a story.

USING INSTRUCTIONAL OBJECTIVES

Much current eductional literature emphasizes the use of instructional objectives. Some confusion arises, however, because a number of authors refer to instructional objectives as "behavioral" objectives, a term that frightens and intimidates some educators and inspires others. In the following discussion, instructional objectives are defined, some of their limitations are enumerated, and some possible procedures for using them effectively are proposed.

Instructional objectives assert what instruction should achieve

Basically, instructional objectives are assertions about what should happen in a particular situation as the result of instruction. Good instructional objectives describe the performance desired, identify the minimum level of acceptability, and may specify the conditions of the performance (Otto et al., 1974).

Objectives indicate what is desired at the end of instruction. They describe the behavior expected after the pupil has mastered a particular task. A distinction is made between the objective and the activities used for instruction. The activities of instruction are the means for arriving at the objective. If the teacher makes the objectives explicit, pupils should know what is expected of them during the instructional period. Further, pupils and teachers may be provided with some standards for evaluating the results of instruction (Vargas, 1972).

Instructional objectives have a potential for analytical teaching. However, in order to understand how they can be used effectively, teachers should be aware of some of the objections raised against them.

One very important objection is that there is an absence of research confirming their effectiveness (Lapp, 1972). To assume, then, that a teaching and evaluation process will be more thorough because instructional objectives are used is to accept a hypothesis supported mainly by conjecture. It must be added, in turn, that there is also little research evidence concerning any negative effects they may possess. A review of empirical studies as to the effect of objectives on learning shows that objectives sometimes help, and they are almost never harmful (Duchastel and Merrill, 1973).

The main philosophical criticism of instructional objectives is that they are "nonhumanistic." One reason for this criticism is that much of their use has been advocated by proponents of behavioral psychology. Critics of behaviorism suggest that what is needed in education are open systems that place a stress on process rather than ends (Combs, 1973). Open systems are accomplished by encouraging human judgment rather than by stifling it. These critics of behavioral objectives would like to see education made accountable from a humanistic perspective through humanistic objectives, that is, those generally concerned with developing affective aspects of learning.

Another objection is that the users of instructional objectives often stress the pedestrian aspects of education. Many educators employ those aspects of instruction that are the easiest to create but may have less importance for instruction. For example, word recognition objectives predominate in some reading programs over those dealing with understanding or attitudes.

Nevertheless, instructional objectives may have a place in the classroom:

1. Instructional objectives are useful as advance organizers. They can provide some direction to the pupils' learning.
2. Instructional objectives organize the instruction. They can give the teacher and pupils structure to their tasks.
3. Instructional objectives can provide for feedback. The teacher expects certain behavior from the pupil and has a means for collecting evidence that the behavior has been attained. The pupil knows what is expected and has an indication as to whether or not the desired end has been achieved (Duchastel and Merrill, 1973).

There is no need for instructional objectives to be pedestrian or to stifle human qualities. The degree of individuality and originality promoted in the classroom through the use of instructional objectives depends upon what behavior the teacher selects, encourages, and requires (Vargas, 1972). Flexibility can be written into many objectives. A worthwhile objective is one that stresses the transfer of learning to new situations. The focus of a well-constructed objective may be on the broad understanding of a concept or on the procedures that are a subclass of that concept.

A worthwhile objective stresses transfer of learning to new situations

For example, instructional objectives can be written for the acquisition of general reading strategies. For the prediction of the meaning of an unknown word within a sentence, the following objectives could be specified:

>Focus on consequences: Given a group of sentences containing an unknown word, the pupil will predict a possible meaning for each word.

>Focus on procedure: Given a group of sentences containing unknown words, the pupil will indicate the contextual signals to meaning in each sentence.

When attention is on library skills, the following may be written:

>Focus on consequences: The pupil will be able to locate a specific book in the library when only the subject of the book is known.

>Focus on procedure: The pupil will be able to explain how to locate a book through a library card catalog when only the subject of the book is known.

Instructional objectives concerned with attitudes may be written as:

>Focus on consequences: During the course of a semester in which discussions about different types of books are held, the pupil will have independently selected and read at least one book in each category.

>Focus on procedure: After a series of class discussions, the pupil will be able to explain why it may be desirable to read different types of books.

A pupil's use of evaluative thinking processes may be fostered by:

>Focus on consequences: Using the class developed criteria, a pupil will judge the accuracy of the information in a particular social studies passage.

>Focus on procedure: The pupil will list criteria for judging the accuracy of the facts presented in a social studies text.

Pupils are led from a concrete experience to the verbalization of that experience

Instructional objectives have a place in teaching and learning plans as long as classroom teachers keep in mind both that reading is not a content subject and that individuals have their own way of organizing and processing information. Objectives are nothing more than a statement of what a teacher might expect of pupils after a period of instruction. With these factors in mind, the classroom teacher should be able to effectively use instructional objectives to show that pupils have acquired meaning from instruction. Created to reflect general instructional goals, they become the basis for continuous assessment of pupils' growth, and they allow the teacher to determine the pupils' future instructional needs.

Instructional objectives become the basis for continuous assessment

THE LANGUAGE EXPERIENCE APPROACH

The language experience approach to reading deliberately attempts to develop reading skills through the natural relationships that exist among all the language processes. The language experience approach is predicated upon the idea that

> reading can be most meaningfully taught when the reading materials accurately reflect the child's own experience as described by his language. The language of instruction then must be that which proceeds from the wealth of linguistic, conceptual, and perceptual experience of the child. A child is more likely to learn to read when the activities associated with the approach have functional relationships with his language, experience, needs and desires (Cramer, 1971).

A common misconception about the language experience approach is that it is an activity normally relegated to the first grade classroom. Nothing could be further from the truth. The language experience approach to reading is a way to foster literacy in any age pupil. Since the difficulty of the material read is controlled by the learner's own language abilities, the material developed by this approach is appropriate for any age pupil.

The language experience approach fosters literacy

It is suggested that

1. Beginning readers are users of language. A teacher should accept the pupils' language as a starting point. (The language of speakers of divergent dialects is taken up in Chapter 12.)

2. Beginning readers should learn to view reading as a communication process.
3. Beginning readers should understand the reading process as the conscious relating of print to oral language.
4. Beginning readers should incorporate the learning of writing with the learning of reading.
5. Beginning readers should learn to read meaningful language units. The minimum meaningful language unit is the sentence.
6. Beginning readers should learn to read with materials written in their own language patterns (Hall 1970; 1972).

Although the language experience approach to reading has been extensively researched, a review of the literature shows findings that reflect a multitude of contrasts (Vilscek, 1968). The conflicting findings seem to be due to differences among the studies in how the researchers (1) selected their subjects, (2) assigned their subjects to experimental or control groups, (3) defined operational guidelines for curriculum practices, (4) treated the study as a novel situation, (5) acquired background information about the subjects, and (6) designed and implemented the research itself.

However, despite the differences among the studies, there seems to be sufficient evidence to favor the language experience approach as an instructional program (Vilscek, 1968); thus, it seems that the language experience approach has some justification as an instructional procedure beyond personal bias.

Another complaint about the language experience approach is that it offers too little structure to the teacher. While it is no panacea and is not necessarily an *easy* program to implement, through the language experience approach the teacher can provide a rich experimental and activity oriented program that uses the child's own language and provides for individualized instruction (Schwartz, 1975). Through its use, a teacher can make learning an active, dynamic process.

The language experience approach informs the teacher as well as the student

As one teacher discovered (Gelb, 1975), the language experience approach can bring revelation to the teacher as well as to the pupil. While working with a ten year old non-reading child on a series of activities related to "colors," the teacher came upon the idea of having the pupil become physically involved in mixing and creating colors. "Finally," the teacher concludes,

> the experience meant something to him. The words were felt because he was living them. That was the key to the whole problem: One must live the words to understand them. I felt I had read this 10 million times, but until this day, they had no meaning because *I had not lived them either.* [Emphasis added.]

Implementing the Language Experience Approach

The language experience approach has as its most important consideration the cultivation of the idea that language communicates meaning. There is no attempt to separate any skill development from the process of thinking. The language experience approach includes planned and continuous activities of the following nature:

The language experience approach includes planned and continuous activities

1. Individual and group pupil dictated stories.
2. Individual pupil word banks of known words.
3. Handwriting exercises.
4. Creative writing situations.
5. Daily oral reading of prose and poetry by the teacher to the pupils.
6. Pupil illustrations of dictated stories.
7. Maintaining of a pupil notebook containing individual and group dictated stories.
8. Opportunities for working at learning stations.
9. Teacher guided reading-thinking lessons.
10. Keeping records of pupil progress (Stauffer and Pikulski, 1974).

Many opportunities are structured into the school day so that:

1. *The teacher works with the whole class.* A teacher might read aloud to them from some book or story related to a class activity, read some children's class discussions, show a movie or filmstrip, introduce a new game, sing or do rhythmic activities, and lead choral reading or speaking.

2. *The teacher works with small groups.* A teacher might do a follow-up to a large group lesson, take dictation, listen to pupils' oral reading, develop a reading skills lesson, lead listening development lessons, and guide the reading of a story.

3. *A teacher works with individuals.* A teacher might engage in many of those same activities carried out with the whole class or small groups.

4. *The teacher works as a resource person.* A teacher might suggest ideas for pupils' creative writing or drawings, guide pupils to fully explore and think out an activity, assist pupils who need help, and be a sounding board for pupils' ideas.

The learning stations within a classroom can consist of library centers, writing resource centers, listening stations, viewing areas, art centers, and

Beginning readers are users of language

game corners. The number and structure of the learning stations will depend upon the facilities of the school as well as the ingenuity of the teacher. For example, a writing center can be established by placing on a table in one part of the room some paper, writing instruments (pens, pencils, brush point pens, crayons, and possibly a typewriter), resources for words such as picture dictionaries, and story motivators such as story beginnings, pictures, and comic strips with the "talk" cut out. A dictating center can be created by placing a tape recorder and some story starters together. At a later time, the teacher and the pupil can listen to the story. The teacher can write it out for the pupil or (in schools where they are available) educational assistants, aides, or volunteer parents can function as transcribers.

Within a language experience approach, the planning and selection of topics and activities should take into account the pupils' experiences with words, their study of the English language, and their experiences with authors' ideas. The activities from each of the three areas of pupil experiences should be simultaneous and continuous throughout the school year. Never should there be a feeling that learning about something is ever finished. The air of things being a little "unfinished" is a great stimulus for independent further learning.

The basic framework of a language experience approach is given in Allen and Allen (1970):

Group One: Extending Experiences with Words
1. *Sharing experiences*—the ability to tell, write, or illustrate something on a purely personal basis.
2. *Discussing experiences*—the ability to interact with what other people say and write.
3. *Listening to stories*—the ability to hear what others have to say through books and to relate ideas to one's own experiences.
4. *Telling stories*—the ability to organize one's thinking so that it can be shared orally or in writing in a clear and interesting manner.
5. *Dictating words, sentences, and stories*—the ability to choose from all that might be said orally the most important part for someone else to write and read.
6. *Writing independently*—the ability to record one's own ideas and present them in a form for others to read.
7. *Authoring individual books*—the ability to organize one's ideas into a sequence, illustrate them, and make them into books.

Group Two: Studying the English Language
1. *Conceptualizing the relationship of speaking, writing, and reading*—the ability to conceptualize, through extensive practice, that reading is the interpretation of speech that has been written and then must be reconstructed, orally or silently.
2. *Expanding vocabulary*—the ability to expand one's listening, speaking, reading, and writing (including spelling) vocabulary.
3. *Reading a variety of symbols*—the ability to read in one's total environment such things as the clock, calendar, dials, thermometer.
4. *Developing awareness of common vocabulary*—the ability to recognize that our language contains many common words and patterns of expression that must be mastered for sight reading and correct spelling when expressing one's ideas in writing.
5. *Improving style and form*—the ability to profit from listening to, reading, and studying the style of well-written material.
6. *Studying words*—the ability to pronounce and understand words and spell them correctly in written activities.

Group Three: Relating Authors' Ideas to Personal Experiences
1. *Reading whole stories and books*—the ability to read books for information, pleasure, and improvement of reading skills on an individual basis.
2. *Using a variety of resources*—the ability to find and use many resources in expanding vocabulary, improving oral and written expression, and sharing ideas.
3. *Comprehending what is read*—the ability, through oral and written activities, to gain skill in following directions, understanding words in the context of sentences and paragraphs, reproducing the thought in a passage, reading for detail, and reading for general significance.
4. *Summarizing*—the ability to get main impressions, outstanding ideas, or some details of what has been read or heard.
5. *Organizing ideas and information*—the ability to use various methods of briefly restating ideas in the order in which they were written or spoken.
6. *Integrating and assimilating ideas*—the ability to use reading and listening for personal interpretation and elaboration of concepts.
7. *Reading critically*—the ability to determine the validity and reliability of statements.

In summary, the language experience approach to reading provides pupils with multi-sensory experiences in observing their world, listening to and reading about what others have observed, experiencing authorship themselves, and understanding the various literary forms.

Pupils are led from experience to verbalization to conceptualization

A specific language experience activity is structured so that the pupils are led from a concrete experience to the verbalization of that experience and then to the conceptualizing of that experience. The sequence of implementing the approach over a few days might be:

Phase I:
1. Provide a concrete experience as an attention getter and as a conversation starter. If possible, the experience should allow the pupils to manipulate objects.
2. Allow the pupils to talk spontaneously about the experience.
3. Through pertinent questions, guide the pupils' attention to relevant features of the experience.
4. Solicit from the pupils some dictation about the experience. In small group settings, allow each pupil to contribute at least one sentence to the narrative account.
5. Read the completed story to the pupils.

6. Have the pupils make a drawing about, or in some other way, illustrate a significant aspect of the experience. On the illustration place a sentence from the dictation that corresponds to the pupil's illustration.

Phase II:
1. Reread the story or narrative to the pupils.
2. Have the pupils, as a group, read the story.
3. Allow individual members of the group to read the story.
4. Have each pupil locate within the story particular sentences, phrases, and words.

Phase III:
1. Reproduce the story for each pupil.
2. Provide the pupils with literature related to their experience. After the material has been read to them, allow them to peruse the material individually.
3. Place into the pupils' word banks all words that they know. Only those words that a pupil can read from the dictated story without teacher assistance are placed in the word bank.
4. Provide the pupils with a skills lesson that develops or extends a pupil's ability to read independently.

The following account by a teacher illustrates how this approach was used successfully with three fourth grade pupils who were experiencing difficulty in acquiring beginning reading strategies (Bercari, 1975). The result was a filmstrip illustrated in Figure 7-1.

> The activity was initiated by reading and carrying out with pupils the instructions for making salt dough which was in a supermarket magazine. My aims in getting the girls to produce the filmstrip were to develop a sense of sequence, exercise their memories, develop written expression of their own experiences, and to give each girl a sense of accomplishment.
>   We developed the strip by: (a) writing individual stories on how we made the salt dough, (b) reading each other's stories and discussing what had been left out of all three, (c) taking the ideas from all three stories and making a master story following the sequence in which the project was carried out, (d) writing sentences on 5 x 7 inch papers for each frame, (e) illustrating those frames in which there was room with ideas that could be drawn, (f) doing a final editing of the story to see what had been left out, and including additional material and frames. When the filmstrip came back from the processing lab, the girls discussed what colors should be added to the filmstrip with permanent marking pens.
>   Finally, the filmstrip was shown to the other pupils. The girls alternated in reading the frames on the filmstrip during the showing.

FIGURE 7-1: An LEA Filmstrip

1. How to Make Salt Dough Art

2. By Crystal Brown Wendy Bailey Paulette Gaskins Miss Bercari

3. We found the recipe in a magazine.

4. This is what we need: 2 cups of flour, ½ cup of salt ¾ Cup of hot water.

5. First we mix the 2 cups of flour and ½ cup of salt in a big bowl.

6. Then we added ¾ cup of hot water. We mixed the hot water with the flour and salt.

7. It made a mushy dough that stuck to your fingers

8. But after we mixed it a lot, the dough started to get thick.

9. When the dough got thick we put coloring in it. Paulette used green and Wendy used blue and Crystal used red.

10. After we mixed the coloring, we rolled the dough out on a cookie sheet covered with aluminum foil.

11. Then we made our shapes.

12.  Crystal made a circle

13.  Paulette made a turtle.

14. Wendy made a fish.

15. After we made our shapes, we brought them home and put them on the radiator.

When the shapes got dry—on the top side, we turned them over.
16

The dough had to dry for about one week.

17

Then we painted our shapes with varnish and had our salt dough art.
18

Be careful not to roll the dough too thin.

19

Do'nt put too much coloring in, and don't let the dough dry out before you finish.
20

If the shape breaks before you get to varnish it, use white glue to put it back together.
21

If the dough is sticky when you roll it out use a little more flour.
22

Now you know how we made salt dough art. Why don't you try it.
23

You can make animals 🐟 or flowers 🌷 or bowls 🥣 or what—
24

ever you want!

25

Good Luck!
26

Individual pupil and small group dictations which are transcribed on class charts can be of four types:

1. Personal language charts, which are the pupil's own dictation in written form.
2. Narrative charts, which are the record of a group's dictation.
3. Work charts, which represent the consensus of a class or small group about how something should be organized or directions for using class resources.
4. Skill charts, which are records of or instructions for carrying out strategies in one of the language areas (Lee and Allen, 1963).

When composing the charts for use in the classroom, teachers should follow certain principles of composition:

1. *Make the charts attractive.* Be sure to letter them neatly and clearly. The final chart should be copied from a draft after the teacher and pupils have made their final editorial changes. Also, allow pupils to decorate the charts with planned illustrations.
2. *Give the charts some measure of literary quality.* Although most of the charts should retain the pupils' own language, the imaginative and resourceful teacher can lead the pupils, through guided questions, to attempt to emulate the literary forms they have become familiar with as a result of daily readings by the teacher.
3. *Give consideration to phrasing.* Especially with younger pupils, the lines should be written to provide the maximum of language redundancy through helpful syntactic and semantic clues.
4. *Compose the charts with consideration for the greatest legibility.* Aside from well-drawn letters, the teacher should give consideration to the spacing of the lines, use of margins, use of typographical clues such as numerals or symbols, use of color, and the use of contrast between the color of the printing and the color of the paper.

Figure 7-2 shows some examples of well-planned and well-executed language experience charts.

Implementing a Thematic Unit

One way to organize the language experience approach to reading is through the use of *thematic units.* The various experiences to which the pupils are exposed are related around a theme, a problem, or an area of interest to the pupils. The contents of various areas are brought together in

FIGURE 7-2: Examples of Language Experience Charts

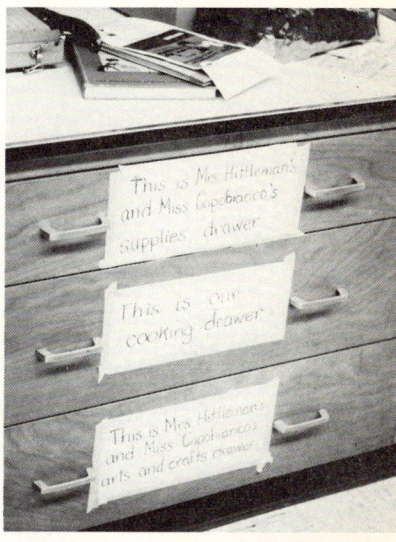
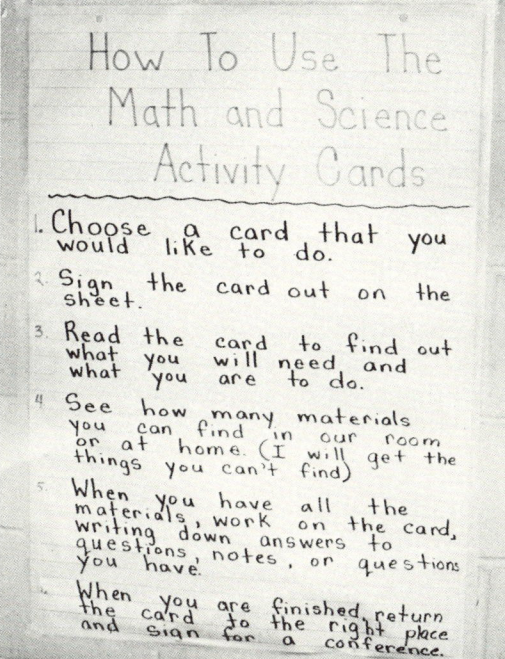

a series of lessons. The basic unit, called a *resource unit,* is developed in advance by the teacher, but flexibility is built in to allow for a great deal of cooperative planning by the teacher and the pupils. Flexibility also allows for changes to be made as conditions within a classroom change.

There is no single pattern for the formal construction and organization of a resource unit. The preparation a teacher does may vary according to the pupils' abilities and needs, the opportunities in the school and community, and the amount of time available for carrying out the unit. In addition, the selection of a theme will depend upon the cognitive and affective needs of the class members, the school and community resources available for developing experiences, and the availability within the school of instructional materials such as textbooks, records, audio-visual aids, maps, reference books, and library facilities. The source of the themes may come from one of the content areas or from the interests of the pupils. The methods of instruction by a teacher should vary depending upon the teaching objectives, the pupil needs, and the materials available. Some of the more common methods used by teachers include whole class and small group discussions, trips, dramatizations, audio-visual materials, and individual and small group research projects.

Resource units contain suggestions for activities

A resource unit is a type of plan which contains suggestions for activities, materials and concepts to be learned. It contains information for both the teacher and for the pupils. The activities, resources, and instructional plans are detailed with specific reference to titles of books, films, and records as well as to the materials that may be needed for carrying through a project. The thematic unit is introduced to the pupils through some stimulating activity that focuses the pupils' attention on the topic. Motivation is usually fairly easy when the teacher capitalizes on the natural curiosity of children.

The two resource units in the Appendix to this chapter (pp. 213–223) were prepared on the general subject of communication. One is prepared for a third grade class, the other for a fifth grade class. The style and content of each differ, yet both have the same general purpose: to help the pupils learn about the process of communication and further develop and extend their own communication skills of speaking, listening, reading, and writing.

RESOURCES FOR THE TEACHER

Some teachers may feel that they lack the background, insights, and resources for implementing thematic units and a language experience approach to reading. This is understandable. However, a teacher who is reticent to use a completely original language-based program can use commercial materials which aim to foster language experiences for reading and writing. The following are selected resources with brief notations about their contents.

> Allen, Roach Van, and Allen, Claryce. 1970. *Language Experiences in Reading.* Teacher's Resource Guides, Levels I, II, III. Chicago: Encyclopaedia Britannica Press.

Each resource book contains five or six thematic units. Although the material is geared toward the primary grades, a creative teacher, using the formats of the units, can adjust the themes for use with older pupils.

> *The Chandler Language-Experience Readers.* 1965. New York: Chandler Publishing Company and Noble and Noble Publishers.

A series of beginning readers that were developed from recordings of the natural language of young children, the books retain the format and style of language experience stories and charts and use photographs of children and events rather than drawings.

> *Peabody Language Development Kits.* Levels I, II, III. 1965, 1966, 1967. Minneapolis: American Guidance Service.

The kits contain detailed lesson plans, picture cards, story posters, recorded stories, puppet and manipulative materials.

> *The Reading Works.* 1975. Plainview, New York: New Dimensions in Education, Inc.

This is a basic reading and language arts program for pupils beyond the initial level of reading instruction. The entire program consists of lesson plans, records, film strips, stories, pictures and pupil worksheets.

Teachers who wish to locate existing publications of thematic units should refer to the following sources:
1. State and city education departments and boards of education.
2. Specialized groups and societies such as natural history and ecology societies, the various associations of manufacturers and industrial groups, and historical and scientific societies.
3. The major encyclopedia publishers who often provide supplementary educational materials.
4. The vertical files in public libraries and in university curriculum centers.

The following publications provide teachers with a source of free materials. The information is listed by subject for easy reference.

> *Educator's Guide to Free Films. Educator's Guide to Free Filmstrips.* Annual. Randolph, Wis.: Educator's Program Service, Inc.

The following text is a guide for providing and coordinating the educational activities that will help young children develop self-confidence, individuality, and creative freedom. The book consists of a series of unit plans organized around major themes appropriate to young children.

Taylor, Barbara J. 1974. *When I Do, I Learn.* Provo, Utah: Brigham Young University Press.

The following series contains activities that encourage pupils to value their own thinking and develop their own resources for thinking. The activities are open-ended and do not imply one right answer.

Myers, R. E., and Torrence, E. Paul. 1966. *The Idea Book Series in Creative Development: Can You Imagine? Invitations to Speaking and Writing Creatively. Invitations to Thinking and Doing.* Waltham, Mass.: Ginn and Co.

STRATEGIES FOR GUIDING PUPILS' READING

The guided reading lesson is built on the premise that reading material communicates directly to the reader. "It is through pupils' actions upon material and their interaction with each other that sound intellectual reading skills and appropriate emotional dispositions are best acquired" (Stauffer, 1975). The guided lesson is a procedure for use with almost any type of reading material.

A guided reading lesson is a guided thinking lesson

Since reading is a thinking activity, the guided reading lesson is in reality a guided thinking lesson. It is adaptable for use as guided-listening lessons as well. Some authorities consider what is here called 'guided reading' as critical reading. All reading, however, is critical thinking.

The three stages of the guided reading-thinking lesson are (1) the act of inquiry, (2) the processing of information, and (3) the validating of answers (Stauffer, 1975). During the lessons, pupils and the teacher both have active roles (Burrows et al., 1972).

> Pupil Actions
>   Predicting (Setting Purposes)
>   Reading (Processing Ideas)
>   Proving (Testing Answers)
> Teacher Actions
>   Activate thought (What do you think?)
>   Agitate thought (Why do you think so?)
>   Require evidence (Prove it!)

FIGURE 7-3

The Lion and the Mouse

One day a big lion was walking in the woods.
He sat down by a tree, and before long he went to sleep.

Just then a little mouse came by.
The little mouse didn't look where he was going.
He walked right up the lion's back.
He walked right into the lion's ear!

SOURCE: Fay, Leo, Ross, Ramon Royal, and La Pray, Margaret. *The Young America Basic Reading Program*, Level 6. Produced by Lyons and Carnahan. Copyright 1974 by Rand McNally.

The strategies pupils learn through use of the guided reading-thinking lesson are those of: (1) examining information, (2) hypothesizing, (3) finding proof, (4) suspending judgment, and (5) making decisions (Stauffer, 1975). These strategies are applied in four steps:

1. Predicting from title and picture clues.
2. Predicting from first page clues.
3. Predicting from one or more subsequent pages.
4. Predicting from the point just prior to the story climax.

The lion could feel the mouse
in his ear.
He got the mouse
and was ready to eat him.

"Oh, don't eat me, great one!"
cried the mouse.
"Let me go! Please, let me go!
You will be very happy if you do.
Someday I will help you."

"You can help me?" the lion said.
"That's very funny.
You are too little to help me.
I'm very big and very strong.
No one has to help me do anything."

"I'm too little for you to eat,"
said the mouse.

The lion laughed.
"You are right about that!" he said.
Then he let the mouse go.

The exact number of lines, paragraphs or pages that a teacher expects the pupils to read will vary in accordance with: (1) the cognitive maturity of the pupils, (2) the amount of data they are capable of processing, (3) the type of information contained in the story, and (4) the nature of the purposes for reading the selection (Burrows et al., 1972).

For example, some teachers may find they have to allow the pupils to read the story one paragraph at a time. In such cases the pupils may have limited experience with making predictions or with processing the information. The concepts contained within the reading material may be so numerous that the pupils experience a tremendous strain on their memory. However, other teachers may find that the nature of the reading material is so familiar that the pupils can process as a unit the information given on two, three, or more pages.

One day when the lion was looking for food, he walked into a trap.

The trap was made of strong rope, and the lion couldn't get out.

The lion jumped this way and that way.

He tried and tried.

All day long, the lion worked to get out of the trap.

But he couldn't get out.

When night came, the lion began to cry.

"Help! Help!" he called.

"Help me get out of this trap."

Many animals heard the lion.

They went to look at him.

But they couldn't help him.

The little animals were scared of him.

And the big animals didn't know how to help him.

"We've never helped a lion before," they said.

"We don't know what to do."

The guided reading-thinking lesson differs from the typical "directed reading lesson" that is advocated by many reading authorities and is popular in the format of the lessons in many basal readers. One major difference is that the responsibility for establishing a purpose for reading the story is shifted from the teacher to the pupils. With the teacher's guidance they identify a purpose or set of purposes for reading the story based upon what they perceive to be the author's purpose for writing the story.

The pupils must establish a purpose for reading the story

Another difference is that so-called "new" words are not presented to the pupils prior to the reading of the story. Only by meeting unfamiliar words in the natural context of a story can the pupils put to use their word recognition strategies. Teachers quite often have a mistaken notion about how pupils should be prepared for reading. The teachers selectively pre-

The lion began to cry again, "Won't someone please help me get out of this trap!"

This time the mouse heard the lion.
The mouse came up to him.

"Don't cry," said the mouse.
"I'll get you out of the trap.
One time you let me go.
I told you that I would help you someday.
Now I can help."

Then the little mouse sat down and chewed one of the big ropes.
Then he chewed another rope.
He chewed and chewed.
Soon he had chewed all the ropes.
The lion was free!

"Thank you, little mouse," he said.
"You are a good friend.
Never again will I say that anyone is too little to help!"

sent the new and unfamiliar words prior to the reading of a story and lead a discussion about their meaning and pronunciation. By doing this, the teacher deprives the pupils of learning through application the purpose of word recognition strategies. Also, what is "new" to one pupil may not be so to another. No basal series author, and few classroom teachers, can accurately predict those words which will be unfamiliar to each pupil. Since the lesson is *guided* by the teacher, whenever a pupil fails to successfully employ word recognition strategies, together the teacher and the pupil can explore why the word was not understood and how it may be processed in the future.

The following two lessons, one constructed on a story from a "first grade" basal reader and one from a "fourth grade" reader, illustrate the

Guided Reading-Thinking Lesson for "The Mouse and the Lion"

Story Theme: No one is too little to help.

Story Plot & Summary: A rather pompous lion catches a mouse. The little creature begs for mercy, appealing to the lion's common sense by pointing out that he, the mouse, would hardly be much of a meal. When the mouse is free, he expresses his gratitude, vowing to help the lion someday. The lion is amused by such a promise and laughs. But it is the mouse who has the last laugh when he rescues the lion from a trap by chewing through the binding ropes (Fay, Ross, and LaPray, 1974).

Guiding Questions:
1. Title and picture, first page of story
   Do you think this is a real story?
   Does the title give you any idea as to what may happen in the story?
   What do you think may happen?
2. First page
   What has happened?
   Do you have any idea from this part of the story as to what may happen next?
   Are there any words you did not know? What did you do when you came to those words?
3. Second and third pages
   Were any of you correct in what you thought?
   If the lion was talking, what kind of voice would he have? What about the mouse?
   What do you now think the rest of the story will be about?
4. Fourth page
   Were any of you right? What do you now think will happen?
   Do you want to change your ideas about what will happen?
5. Fifth, sixth, and seventh pages
   Why did the author write this story? What message did he want to give you?
   Why couldn't any other animal help the lion?
   Were there any words you didn't know and couldn't figure out from the story? What information on the page let you understand the story without knowing what those words were?

---

initial preparation a teacher should undertake for a guided reading-thinking lesson.

During the guided reading-thinking lesson a teacher guides pupils through the reading of a story to help them reconstruct the author's meaning. The guided reading-thinking lesson is a time when the pupils can demonstrate their mastery of various reading strategies. When mastery is not evident, the teacher is prepared to assume the role of guide and assist the pupils in the process of reading and thinking. The teacher is alert for signs that pupils may not be able to apply their reading-thinking strategies in new situations or while reading particular types of material. In the guided reading-thinking lesson the teacher is aware of both the reading tasks the pupils are to perform and the significance that should be attributed to the

The teacher guides the pupils through the story

Guided Reading-Thinking Lesson for "Miss Esta Maude's Secret"

Story Theme: Outward appearances do not necessarily indicate a person's true interests and personality. Even very staid and quiet people may secretly long for excitement in their lives.

Story Plot and Summary: Esta Maude Hay, a school teacher for twenty years, leads what the townspeople think is a pitifully dull and ordered life. Nobody knows that locked in Miss Esta Maude's barn is a powerful red racing car, with which she tinkers every night. On Friday nights, dressed in helmet and goggles, she speeds down the highway and often meets with adventure. She saves a stray flock of lambs, brings a sleepwalking boy home, and successfully races the stork to the hospital.

Central to the story is the contrast between Miss Esta Maude's outwardly quiet life and her secret love of speed. However, the car is not her only source of happiness. Miss Esta Maude enjoys teaching and likes to help people: the car merely adds a note of excitement and adventure to her life (Fay and Anderson, 1974).

Guiding Questions:
1. Title and pictures on first and second pages
   What do you think this story is about?
   What kinds of feelings do the pictures give you?
2. First and second pages
   What do you think now?
   What have you learned about Esta Maude?
   Are there any clues as to what her secret might be?
   Are there any words you could not figure out from the story? Was the word important to understanding the story?
3. Third and fourth pages
   Were you right about her secret?
   What have you learned about Esta Maude?
   Which description shows the "real" Miss Maude?
   What type of adventures might she have?
   Why wouldn't people know who she is while riding in the sports car?
4. Fifth, sixth, and seventh pages
   Do you think people will ever find out about Esta Maude's secret?
   What might happen if many people started talking about a "stranger in a sports car"?
   What message did the author want to get across to the reader of this story?

---

pupils' behavior in the performance of these tasks. The analytic teacher observes the pupils' application of various reading strategies during silent and oral readings. Based upon these observations, follow-up lessons on specific strategies for making the pupils independent readers can be planned and implemented.

Analytic teaching is a process whereby the teacher continually adjusts the teaching, learning pace, and methods to meet the needs of the pupils. The guided reading-thinking lesson provides an opportunity for pupils to be observed and assessed in actual reading situations.

STRATEGIES FOR QUESTIONING

The thought provoking questions of the guided reading-thinking lesson are only one kind of question teachers should use to generate the pupils' thinking strategies. In addition, the teachers should tap different thought processes through the use of questions that require different cognitive operations. (Some may find it useful to review the Guilford structure-of-intellect model as it is described in Chapter 3.)

Teachers should ask questions that require different cognitive operations

The following types of questions are suggested (Torrence and Myers, 1972):

1. Recognition Questions—
   a. Multiple choice:
      In the story, Chun Toy was allowed to
      build the boat
      paint the boat
      row the boat
   b. Matching:
      Match the character in the story with a word that describes the person

      Li Lun   ashamed
      Teng Lun   wise
      Sun Ling   afraid

2. Analysis Questions—
   a. Interpretive:
      What did Sun Ling mean when he said: "There are other things than fishing?"
   b. Comparison:
      In what ways was the kitten like the tiger?
   c. Analysis of series or process:
      How do the animals and insects in the story get ready for winter?
3. Synthesis or Hypothesis Formation Questions—
   Based upon how Josie felt about her brother, what might you expect her to do?
4. Convergent Thinking or Redefinition Questions—
   Which of the solutions offered by Pierre would be acceptable here in our school?
5. Open-ended or Divergent Thinking Questions—
   What are some other ways Chun Toy could have helped his brothers as they worked on the boat?

6. Evaluation Questions—
   a. Judgmental:
      In this story, do you think the grasshoppers are thieves?
   b. True-false:
      Is the following statement true or false? "Megan's actions in the story were more because of fear than of love."
   c. Provocative or extension of thinking:
      If an earthquake were to hit this school five minutes from now, what things would we do?

Teachers should be aware of some of the positive and negative features of the above question patterns:

1. Questions that focus on remembering may be of limited value in that (a) no further learning is compelled, (b) answering them may be interpreted by the pupil as either a punishment or a reward, and (c) the information received by the pupil is only as accurate or complete as that provided by the teacher.

2. Recognition questions are popular and can be used to identify incorrect thinking. However, they may foster unstructured guessing.

3. Analysis questions may have limited use if the pupils do not have enough background information to make interpretations or comparisons. Also, too many of this type may become tedious for pupils.

4. Synthesis questions are good in that they can lead pupils to discover generalizations. But, they are limited in that the responsibility lies with the pupils to select the significant details. Therefore, pupils may never arrive at a generalization.

5. Convergent thinking questions require that pupils already know what would be "best" or "acceptable" in a given situation.

6. Open-ended, or divergent thinking, questions provide pupils with the opportunity to give a number of responses. They may be of limited value for immature pupils who may be unable to generate alternatives. Also, some pupils become upset or frustrated by questions that do not have a "right" answer.

7. Evaluation questions are good in that they stimulate rational thinking. They are limited to the degree that (a) pupils have been provided with appropriate criteria for forming judgments, (b) pupils have had experience in decision making, and (c) pupils have the ability to do extended thinking activities (Torrence and Myers, 1972).

Many of these limitations can be overcome. Over a period of time, a variety of questions can be developed which foster different thinking operations. Not all stories lend themselves to all types of questions, yet a good teacher directs pupils through a variety of questions about a variety of reading materials where possible.

Beginning readers should learn to view reading as a communication process

Good instructional questions can be constructed by using the following guidelines. (The answer, of course, to each of the guideline questions should be yes.)

Do the questions tap more than a limited number of thought processes?
Do the questions focus on information that is significant to the general plot and theme of the story?
Do the questions imply that there is no "right" answer all the time, and do they allow for possible alternative responses?
Do the questions require pupils to undertake a type of thinking for which they are cognitively ready?
Do the questions challenge but not frustrate the pupils so

information is obtained as to how they perform in problem solving situations?

DISCUSSION QUESTIONS AND ACTIVITIES

1. Examine a set of instructional objectives that accompany a basal reading series. Do any of the criticisms of instructional objectives presented in this chapter apply to those you are examining?

2. Create a set of instructional objectives that focus on consequences to show what you as a teacher would expect of pupils during a guided reading-thinking lesson.

3. Prepare a teacher's resource unit on a particular theme. Be sure the unit contains the age or grade level for which it is intended; the major skills that will be developed, stated in terms of instructional objectives; the period of time the unit will cover; the particular experiences and activities in which the pupils will be engaged, the school and community resources that are available; and, examples of the books, records, and films that will be available for the teacher's and pupils' use.

4. Present an argument that either supports or refutes the following statement by Idella Lohmann (1968): "The teacher who is unfamiliar with the relationships in language, unfamiliar with concept development, and unfamiliar with ways to assess growth in language might find [the language experience] approach, in total, beyond her [or his] capacity to use."

For students who are currently teaching:

5. Select a story and prepare a guided reading-thinking lesson for a group of pupils. Use the lesson. In what ways did you have to modify your original plans because of the responses given by the pupils?

6. Create a language experience lesson and use it with two groups of pupils of different age and grade levels. In what way did you have to modify the lesson to meet the cognitive, affective, and instructional needs of each group? In what way did the language performance of the groups differ?

FURTHER READINGS

The following book might be considered one of the most concise statements on the use and construction of instructional objectives.

    Mager, Robert F. 1962. *Preparing Instructional Objectives.* Palo Alto, Calif.: Fearon Publishers.

The following three books provide detailed instructions about implementing a language-experience approach to reading.

    Dunne, Hope W. 1972. *The Art of Teaching Reading: A Language and Self-Concept Approach.* Columbus, Ohio: Charles E. Merrill.

    Hall, Mary Anne. 1970. *Teaching Reading as a Language Experience.* Columbus, Ohio: Charles E. Merrill.

    Veatch, Jeanette, et al. 1973. *Key Words to Reading: The Language Experience Approach Begins.* Columbus, Ohio: Charles E. Merrill.

For the teacher who desires guidance in developing activities and techniques for constructing with the pupils instructional materials as part of thematic units, the following book is recommended.

    Calder, Clarence R., Jr., and Antan, Eleanor M. 1970. *Techniques and Activities to Stimulate Verbal Learning.* New York: Macmillan.

The following text provides teachers with a discussion of the rationale for using thematic units as well as explicit instructions for creating series of learning experiences.

    Hanna, Lavone A., Potter, Gladys L., and Reynolds, Robert W. 1973. *Dynamic Elementary Social Studies: Unit Teaching,* Third Edition. New York: Holt Rinehart and Winston.

References

Allen, Roach Van, and Allen, Claryce. 1970. *Language Experiences in Reading.* Chicago: Encyclopaedia Britannica Press.

Bercari, Joan. 1975. Personal correspondence.

Burrows, Alvina T., Monson, Dianne L., and Stauffer, Russell G. 1972. *New Horizons in the Language Arts.* New York: Harper and Row.

Cramer, Ronald L. 1971. "Dialectology—A Case for Language Experience." *The Reading Teacher* 25: 33–39.

Combs, Arthur. 1973. "Educational Accountability From a Humanistic Perspective." *Educational Researcher* 2: 19–21.

Duchastel, Philippe C., and Merrill, Paul F. 1973. "The Effects of Behavioral Objectives on Learning: A Review of Empirical Studies." *Review of Educational Research* 43: 53–69.

Fay, Leo, and Anderson, Paul S. 1974. *The Young America Basic Reading Program, Level 11 Teacher's Edition.* Produced by Lyons and Carnahan. Chicago: Rand McNally.

Fay, Leo, Ross, Ramon Royal, and LaPray, Margaret. 1974. *The Young America Basic Reading Program, Level 6 Teacher's Edition.* Produced by Lyons and Carnahan. Chicago: Rand McNally.

Gelb, Larry. 1975. "Developing an Experiential Reading Program." Unpublished manuscript, Queens College of the City University of New York.

Hall, Mary Anne. 1970. *Teaching Reading as a Language Experience.* Columbus, Ohio: Charles E. Merrill Publishing.

Hall, Mary Anne. 1972. "Linguistically Speaking, Why Language Experience?" *The Reading Teacher* 25: 328–31.

Lapp, Diane. 1972. *The Use of Behavioral Objectives in Education.* Newark, Del.: International Reading Association.

Lee, Doris, and Allen, Roach Van. 1963. *Learning to Read Through Experience.* Second Edition. New York: Appleton Century Crofts.

Lohmann, Idella. 1968. "Reactions to Using Language Experience in Beginning Reading." In Elaine C. Vilscek, ed. *A Decade of Innovations: Approaches to Beginning Reading.* Newark, Del.: International Reading Association.

Otto, Wayne; Chester, Robert; McNeil, John; and Myers, Shirley. 1974. *Focused Reading Instruction.* Reading, Mass.: Addison-Wesley.

Schwartz, Judy I. 1975. "A Language Experience Approach to Beginning Reading." *Elementary English* 52: 320–24.

Stauffer, Russell G. 1975. *Directing the Reading Thinking Process.* New York: Harper and Row.

Stauffer, Russell G., and Pikulski, John J. 1974. "A Comparison and Measure of Oral Language Growth." *Elementary English* 51: 1151–55.

Torrence, E. Paul, and Myers, R. E. 1972. *Creative Learning and Teaching.* New York: Dodd, Mead and Co.

Vargas, Julie S. 1972. *Writing Worthwhile Behavioral Objectives.* New York: Harper and Row.

Vilscek, Elaine C. 1968. "What Research Has Shown About the Language Experience Program." In Elaine C. Vilscek, ed. *A Decade of Innovative Approaches to Beginning Reading.* Newark, Del.: International Reading Association.

APPENDIX

COMMUNICATION UNIT—THIRD GRADE. The purpose of the unit is to help children gain an appreciation of people's ability to communicate.[1] The activities and objectives are by no means conclusive. They should stimulate continued interest and study in this area.

Of the activities suggested, the children will begin by drawing upon personal experience to show what they know about the subject. They will be led into gathering information from a variety of sources, summarizing, interpreting, reasoning, problem solving, and critical thinking. Skills will be broadened and understanding developed through the use of conversations, questions, discussions, dramatic plays, creative writing, and readings.

The unit attempts to provide activities for the total class, small groups, and individuals so that the children can develop skills in working cooperatively and in individual study.

1. How people communicate to make thoughts and needs known.
   A. Talk about the methods of communication that the children are aware of: expressions, gestures, signs, signals, speech, writing, numerals.
   B. (1) Dramatize the ways feelings and ideas can be communicated without words: nodding of the head, waving a hand, dancing.
   (2) Use magazines, books, and newspapers to collect pictures that show communication through expression or gesture. Write captions or quotations that might express the tone of the picture.
   C. Look at, collect, and draw pictures of signs and signals that are quick and easy methods of sending messages: traffic signs, American Indian sign language, deaf sign language.
   D. Sounds have meaning: bells, sirens, whistles, music.
   (1) Listen to and keep a record of sounds heard during the day in school and at home.
   (2) Find out what causes sounds and how to make different sounds.
   (3) See a filmstrip about sound.
   (4) Read poetry that communicates its message through alliteration.
2. Communication requires a sender and a receiver.
   A. Begin a list of communication words. Learn their meanings and usage.
   B. Learn about the responsibility of the sender and receiver.

---

1. This section was prepared by Marilyn Okrent.

Dramatize the conveying of messages accurately and inaccurately. Use gestures, expressions, and words to convey messages. Dramatize how a receiver can be certain he understands a message. (Skits are possible here involving role playing by children as people who speak different languages.)

C. Each of our senses is a communications receiver.
   (1) Small groups can list the things our ears, eyes, noses, mouths, and skin tell us.
   (2) Individual or group projects (including research) can be started on some aspect of the senses. (Reports, models, skits, posters.)
D. How does the ear work?
   (1) Discuss the difference between hearing and listening.
   (2) There are various situations we need to learn to listen in: pleasure, safety, information.
   (3) Listen to a story read aloud. Listen to a poem. Draw what you hear. Discuss the sounds we need to hear in order to avoid danger.
   (4) Try to imagine what the world would be like without sound.
   (5) Experiment with part of the school day: try to get messages communicated without sound.
   (6) Individual or group projects can be started on sounds important to animals and humans.
E. How does the eye work?
   (1) We receive information through pictures, reading, signs which are useful for play, safety, work.
   (2) Discuss what it would be like if we could not see.
   (3) View a film about the eye.
   (4) Read and learn about eye care.
   (5) Perceptual activities: use rolled up paper to test for eye dominance. Discuss binocular vision. Let children explore optical illusions.
   (6) Individual or small group projects about the blind and their care, communication through braille.
   (7) Visit a Lighthouse center or have a representative speak to the class.
F. How do we smell, taste, and feel? Discuss how these senses help us communicate. Collect items to smell, taste, and feel. Use them in games. Use words to describe what is being identified.
G. Read or write poetry or stories about how we communicate through our senses.

3. We communicate with people in many ways.
   A. Find out some of the means of communication that are used at home.
   B. Bring in samples of interesting letters, postcards, telegrams. Discuss the value of the various types of written communication forms. Imagine what it was like for families before we had these means of communication.
   C. Explore the classroom to find items that communicate: clock, bell, chalkboard, maps.
   D. Think of the ways communication is used in school.
   E. Visit the secretaries to find the ways communication is used by them: stenography, duplicating machines, telephone, mail.
   F. Write thank you notes to the secretaries.
   G. Communication enables us to give information and express thoughts, needs, and feelings. Create posters about how "danger" can be communicated. Discuss how misunderstandings can arise and how they can be resolved.
4. The newspaper keeps us informed about people, places, and things.
   A. After children browse through copies of newspapers, have them select their favorite part and explain why.
   B. Discuss what is found in newspapers. Make a list of the major sections.
   C. Create booklets containing a sample of each of the major newspaper sections.
   D. Discuss the importance of headlines and how they aid in communication.
   E. Experiment with various types of type and printing.
   F. Begin a class newspaper. Children can determine the content of the paper. Assign jobs to different children.
5. Communication is our means of sharing information, thoughts, and feelings. Communication lets us learn about past, present, and future events.

   This section is devoted to individual or committee projects. Written research reports and physical representations such as dioramas would be acceptable. Some topics are:

   mail service   cameras—still or movie
   telephone   signs and signals
   telegraph   labels, trademarks, advertising
   photographs   radar
   radio   communication satellites
   television

Resources for the Teacher—Books:

Batchelor, Julie F. 1953. *Communication: From Cave Writing to Television.* New York: Harcourt Brace Jovanovich.

Epstein, Sam, and Epstein, Beryl. 1974. *The First Book of Printing.* New York: Franklin Watts.

Miner, Irene. 1960. *The True Book of Communication.* New York: Childrens Press.

Radlauer, Ruth. 1969. *Good Times with Words.* Melmont Publishers.

Schneider, Herman, and Schneider, Nina. 1965. *Your Telephone and How It Works.* 3rd. Edition. New York: McGraw Hill.

Sootin, Laura. 1956. *Let's Go To A Newspaper.* New York: G. P. Putnam's Sons.

Resources—Films, Filmstrips, and Records:

FILMSTRIPS
Telezonia—A Series. American Telephone and Telegraph.
Communication—A Series. Encyclopaedia Britannica Educational Corp.
FILMS
Communication. Encyclopaedia Britannica Educational Corp.
Communication: A First Film. BFA Educational Media.
RECORDS
The Ways We Talk—A Series of Records. South Holland, Ill.: H. Wilson Corp.

References

How People Meet Their Needs for Communication: A Social Studies Unit for the Third Grade. Chula Vista, California: Chula Vista City School District.

COMMUNICATION MODULE—FIFTH GRADE.

I. Introduction: What is communication?	2 weeks
II. Nonverbal communication: gestures, body movements	1 week
III. Speech and listening	1 week
IV. Writing and reading	2 weeks

Introduction to Class. We will be working on a unit about communication.[2] To communicate means to give information to another person or thing. The person who gives the information out is the sender or transmitter. Right now I am the transmitter. The person who gets the information is the receiver; you are the receiver. The sender and receiver are involved when any communication takes place; otherwise, the communication is not complete.

Let's look at some different ways to communicate. Suppose you are across the street and I want you to come to me. How many ways can I send this message to you?

Let's experiment and see whether some means of communication are more effective or easier than others. Everyone think of some pose you can make to get an idea across to the receiver (e.g., boxer's pose, salute).

1. Get pupils to pose. Does everyone understand the meaning?
2. Communicate another idea to a receiver by adding something to your pose. Can we still understand the message? Was it easier or harder?
3. Now communicate an idea through movement and voice. Do we understand the message? Is it easier or harder to understand now? Why?
4. Everyone write a paragraph about any subject. Read it to a small group of your classmates.
    a. Communicate the idea of the paragraph in one sentence.
    b. In one word.
    c. With one letter.
    d. Discuss which is easier to understand and why.

---

2. This section was prepared by Patricia Batine.

Teacher Activities for Module
Ideas for Pantomime
1. Playing with a Yo-yo.
2. Using a pencil sharpener.
3. Playing with a mechanical toy.
4. Being a sky diver.
5. Being a skier going off a jump.
6. Working a toaster.
7. Using a can opener.
8. Breaking open an egg.
9. Using a tube of toothpaste.
10. Filling a ball with air.

Ideas for Listening
1. Pouring water.
2. Bouncing ball.
3. Turning eggbeater.
4. Rubbing sandpaper.
5. Crinkling cellophane.
6. Hitting rhythm sticks.
7. Hitting a triangle.
8. Snapping an elastic.
9. Letting air out of a balloon.
10. Playing a music box.

Commands
1. Stand close to a building, face the building, stretch to look at someone in a very high place.
2. Try to push a wall over without striking the wall.
3. Play with a bug in your hand.
4. Hang a picture on a wall.
5. Eat a peanut butter sandwich.
6. Slice a piece of cake.
7. Polish your shoes.
8. Have an itchy foot and you can't take off your shoe.
9. Get gum off your shoe.
10. Step on a thumbtack.

Communication Module

Objectives
1. You will be able to define *transmitter* and *receiver*.
2. You will be able to define *communication*.
3. You will be able to tell why people commmunicate.
4. You will be able to list at least five ways people can communicate.
5. You will be able to discuss ways that communication can take place without talking.

6. You will be able to tell the part that facial expressions play in communication.
7. You will understand the function of body movements or gestures used to communicate.
8. You will know what *language* is.
9. You will be able to tell what part listening plays in communication.
10. You will be able to explain the importance of intonation in oral language.
11. You will learn the different types of writing and some reasons for writing.
12. You should be able to explain:
    a. What *propaganda* is.
    b. Why propaganda is used.
13. You will learn some codes.
14. You will be able to tell how art can be used to communicate.
15. You will be able to tell how music can be used to communicate.
16. You will learn about different signals of meaning used only in writing.
17. You will be able to tell how "reading" is communicating.

Suggested Books:

Bueher, Walter. 1957. *Sending the Word: The Story of Communications.* New York: Putnam Sons.

Bathelor, Julia. 1953. *Communication: From Cave Writing to Television.* New York: Harcourt Brace Jovanovich.

McGough, Elizabeth. 1974. *Your Silent Language.* New York: William Morrow. Ill. by Tom Huffman.

Lubell, Winifred and Cecil. 1972. *Pictures, Signs and Symbols.* New York: Parents' Magazine Press.

Wise, William. 1970. *From Scrolls to Satellites: The Story of Communication.* New York: Parents' Magazine Press. Pictures by Hans Zander.

Suggested Audio-visual Materials:

FILMSTRIPS
Newspapers in the Classroom—A Series. Copley Productions.
Story of Communication Series. Eye Gate House.

FILMS

Communication—Let It Begin Now. Mountain States Telephone and Telegraph.

Signals for Survival. New York: McGraw-Hill Textfilm.

Requirements

1. You must do a minimum of five activities:
   a. One must be chosen from activities 1–4.
   b. One must be chosen from activities 5–8.
   c. One must be chosen from activities 9–11.
   d. Two must be chosen from activities 12–18.
2. You must listen to the presentation of five other pupils' activities.
   a. Submit a list of six things you learned from the presentations.

ACTIVITY ALTERNATIVES	REPORTING/SHARING ALTERNATIVES
1. Show what the jobs of the receiver and sender are.	Make a chart and set up a color code.
2. Locate as many different definitions of *communication* as possible.	Create a transparency overlay. Compare the different definitions.
3. Research and discover five different reasons for communication.	Make a picture chart showing this information. Make an outline showing this information.
4. Show five ways that people communicate.	Prepare a picture chart.
5. Imagine that you were unable to talk for 24 hours.	Prepare a list of all the ways you could communicate with others.
6. Show the importance of facial expressions to speech.	Make a list of the different emotions. What words describe the facial expressions of these feelings? Find pictures of facial expressions showing different feelings. Make a chart.

7. You are a pantomime actor or actress.

Pick an idea or role to act out. This may be done with another pupil.

8. Investigate the sign language of the deaf.

Make a presentation showing and explaining how these people communicate.

8a. Investigate the sign language of a referee or umpire for some sport.

Give a demonstration of the signs and explain what they mean.

9. You are to become a sound detective.

Listen to the "Sound Tape" and list the sounds you hear.
Tell a story to a group using only sounds to show the action and the characters.

10. Investigate how gestures help a spoken message.

Select a poem or story and read it orally to a group:
   First, without gestures.
   Then, with gestures.
Get the group's reaction to the two readings.

10a. Observe the different gestures used by people you meet for one day.

Make a list of all the gestures you saw people use. Explain how some of the same gestures were used differently.

11. You are a politician and want to know the importance of *intonation* in speech.

Find out what *intonation* is and what part it plays in communication.
Read a speech (yours or someone else's):
   First, without intonation.
   Second, with intonation.
   Third, with a different one.

12. Compare how the same thing is written about in at least two different books or magazines.

Find a paragraph in either your science or social studies book. Look up the same topic in an encyclopedia. List how the styles of writing differ.

13. You are a government agent and your job is to research propaganda techniques.

Prepare a composition or a short talk telling what it is, and why it can be used to change people's thinking. Make a scrapbook with examples of the different types of propaganda.

14. You are a code expert.

Find out what you are called.
Using *Codes to Captains*
(1) Decode the Indian message on page 24, or the cowboy code.
(2) Send messages using these codes.
(3) Make up a code of your own using the rules on page 31.

15. Tell a story through art.

Using "circle symbol" characters, create two stories:
One, familiar to the others.
Two, not familiar to the others.

15a. You are an Indian cave artist.

On brown paper, draw a story of a tribal event.

16. Communicate through music.

Select music without words that gives you different ideas or feelings. See if these same ideas and feelings are communicated to others.

17. Investigate all the communication signals in writing other than letters and words.

Prepare a poster showing the different writing signals and explain what each communicates.

18. Investigate how there can be a breakdown in communication.

Read one of the following stories and discuss why there is a breakdown in communication.
    "Henny Penny"
    "40 Thieves"
    "Emperor's New Clothes"
    "Tale of Peter Rabbit"
    "Amelia Bedelia"

KEEP A RECORD OF YOUR WORK HERE:

1. I have performed the following activities:
   a.
   b.
   c.
   d.
   e.
2. I have listened to the following OTHER activities:
   a.
   b.
   c.
   d.
   e.
3. I have learned:
   a.
   b.
   c.
   d.
   e.
   f.

Strategies for Reconstructing Meaning

Focus Questions:

1. What is the function of prediction strategies in understanding an author's message?
2. What typical sentence constructions do authors use?
3. How can knowledge of the structures and functions of paragraphs increase one's understanding of an author's message?
4. What are the steps in developing a reading strategy lesson?

When an author constructs a message, a communication with a reader or group of readers is initiated. The author usually has some intended audience in mind; though, of course, there can never be total assurance that the message will reach the intended audience. The author, then, builds a message using knowledge of

1. The subject area and topic to be discussed.
2. How much the intended audience knows about the subject area and the topic.
3. The style of language in which the message is to be written, and the manner in which the ideas are to be organized.
4. The language maturity of the intended audience.

Once the message is formed, the author's meaning lies in strings of words. Whether the message is meaningful to the reader depends upon factors residing within the reader. A message is potentially meaningful when the reader's knowledge of the subject area and topic, the reader's

Copyright © 1975 by United Feature Syndicate, Inc.

language maturity, and the reader's familiarity with language styles are at least equal to that used by the author.

Traditionally, the process of dealing with an author's message has been called *comprehension,* which is conceived to be a set of skills the reader must possess in order to understand the author. It is traditionally assumed that the set of comprehension skills can be separately defined, sequentially developed, and are generally applicable in any and all reading situations (Harker, 1973a).

These skills are usually identified as the abilities to get the main idea, understand stated and implied details, follow a sequence of events, make inferences, and understand vocabulary in context. Through the application of these so-called skills, the reader is supposed to be able to know what the author is talking about.

However, research dealing with the development of models of comprehension seems to indicate that the traditional view of comprehension is in error (Harker, 1973a). The research suggests that comprehension is a multidimensional process involving the cognitive processing of language. The traditional comprehension skills do not refer directly to language. Rather, they are concerned with the way people classify information (Bormuth, 1969b); the skills themselves are just a manifestation of the inner cognitive processing of language (Harker, 1973a). From a psycholinguistic viewpoint, on the other hand, *the features of language provide the information upon which the comprehension processes operate* (Bormuth, 1969b).

The comprehension processes are mental operations that occur while an individual is reading. The so-called traditional comprehension skills (getting the main idea, sequence, details, etc.) are really products of the comprehension process. They represent what is produced after comprehension has taken place (Simons, 1971). The traditional skills explanation of comprehension seems to be deficient on two counts:

> Comprehension is a multidimensional process involving the cognitive processing of language

1. Confusion exists over what cognitive activities can be characterized as comprehension. The traditional skills approach fails to specify those skills unique to reading and those found in general mental processes.
2. There is a failure to distinguish between the *how* and the *what* of something that is comprehended.

Instructional programs, then, are inadequate when reading comprehension skills are viewed as if they are reading specific, and do not treat the ends of comprehension differently from the processes of comprehension.

The strategies for reconstructing an author's meaning that are presented in this chapter are based upon the following premises:

1. Information is more easily gained when it is learned as a process rather than as a collection of facts.
2. Comprehending involves the cognitive processing of language and language cues.
3. Understanding oral language and oral language cues is preparatory to understanding written language and written language cues.

THE READER RECONSTRUCTS THE AUTHOR'S MESSAGE

The strategies suggested in this chapter are those that a teacher helps develop in pupils so they may function as independent readers. The following discussions deal with (1) techniques for fostering pupils' prediction strategies, (2) pupils' strategies for reading and understanding sentences, paragraphs, and longer pieces, and (3) pupils' strategies for reading and answering questions that appear in instructional materials.

Prediction Strategies

Often teachers' attempts at encouraging the development of prediction strategies are dismissed as the encouraging of "guessing." The negative connotation of the term "guessing" is unfortunate here. To some, the term implies a random, unstructured, wild attempt to hit upon the correct answer. Yet, guessing is in fact an important strategy that people use constantly throughout their lives. When looked upon as a proper activity, it is usually referred to as *hypothesizing,* or *predicting.* Individuals who spend a great deal of their lifetime in trying to guess the outcome of sporting events rarely refer to their endeavors as "guessing"; rather, they state that they are making predictions based upon the best, currently available information.

Pupils should be encouraged to predict

In school, pupils should be encouraged not to guess, but to engage in hypothesis testing, or predicting. Activities should direct the pupils' attention to the information that language provides so that they can accurately make predictions about the meaning of a particular word in a context or the overall meaning of a story as the author intended it.

An important aspect of prediction strategies is the setting of purposes. As stated previously, authors have very definite purposes when they write something. On the other hand, many readers undertake reading acts without a purpose of their own. Or, if they do have one, it often is not consistent with the purpose set by the author. "When students are encouraged, indeed required, to set logical purposes for reading non-fiction and to make predictions when they are reading fiction, they soon discover that the ideas and sense of form of the author are frequently different from their own" (Cramer, 1970). Thus, it is important for students to make predictions about and set purposes for any reading they undertake.

Predicting requires the use of prior knowledge relevant to the material being read (Smith, 1975). Individual words have a great many possible meanings out of context so a reader must have had some experience with the topic and its related vocabulary in order to come up with a meaning consistent with that of the author's. And often the spelling of a word does not give any clues to the manner in which it should be pronounced, so the reader must already know what the word should be. (More on this subject will be found in Chapter 9.) Since there is a limit to how much visual information the brain can process during reading, the reader must have some prior knowledge so that the author's ideas can be associated with already known information and more readily stored in memory.

Simply, the act of making predictions is the act of eliminating any unlikely alternatives (Smith, 1975). When considered as such, predicting is not wild guessing; it is systematically evaluating alternatives and selecting those that seem to match the reader's expectations of the author's meaning. It should be evident, then, that predictions are most difficult, and most likely to be incorrect, when the reader has had limited experience with the topic and is unfamiliar with or cognitively not ready to process the language and stylistic features used by the author.

How well pupils are able to predict depends on the pattern of questions the teacher has asked in prior lessons

There are advantages to having the reader regularly make decisions to accept, modify, or reject assumptions about the author's meaning. The reader will be working at a level of meaning. The reader does not have to worry about loading short term memory with a great deal of visual and auditory information. It is when teachers stress the "accurate" processing of every visual clue provided by the author that many readers deal with only the surface features of a passage instead of being concerned with the message at its meaning level.

Pupils can develop prediction strategies just by being encouraged to predict. Some pupils have an intuitive sense of prediction. Others have learned not to predict. Their instruction has instilled in them a sense that

FIGURE 8-1

SOURCE: Fay, Leo, Ross, Ramon Royal, and La Pray, Margaret. *The Young America Basic Reading Program*, Level 9. Produced by Lyons and Carnahan. Copyright 1974 by Rand McNally.

To predict, pupils must know what information is pertinent

only accuracy should be valued; they withhold any attempt at prediction making for fear of being considered "wrong."

In order to make predictions, pupils must know what information to select and how to confirm their predictions. In this entire chapter we will discuss some of the types of information pupils should use in making their predictions. Here, in this section, we will be concerned with a general prediction strategy, that is, one that is used for getting the overall message of the author.

The type of information used for prediction making will differ among pupils. We know that children at different stages of development differ in how they think and use language. For example, in one research study, third grade pupils showed a different cognitive style when they selected a more concrete "best" answer in comparison to sixth graders who selected a more abstract choice (Lundsteen, 1974). Therefore, teachers must be aware of the level of thinking that each pupil is capable of doing.

One method for fostering prediction strategies for the general meaning of a story is to use a technique similar to the one described in Chapter 7 for a guided reading-thinking lesson. The involvement level of the teacher makes the difference between a guided lesson and one in which the pupil develops a sense of creating predictions. When the teachers' actions totally structure the pupils' actions, the lesson is a guided one. When the teacher places the greater responsibility for selecting information and creating purposeful questions upon the pupils, they are then moving toward their own independence as readers. For example, the introductory sequence of questions for a guided lesson of "The Eagle and the Boy" might be:

> Title and picture, first page of story—
> What do you think the story is about?
> Where do you think the story took place?
> Have you ever read any other story that dealt with a human and an animal?
> Based upon the title, what do you think the story will be about?

After pupils have been guided through a number of stories in which the teacher has employed the principles of a guided reading-thinking lesson, they are ready to begin making their own predictions about a story. The repetitive use of the guiding questions by the teacher should have established a pattern for the pupils to follow. The introductory sequence of questions for a lesson that fosters the pupil's independent prediction strategies might be:

> Title and picture, first page of story—
> Looking only at the picture and title of the story, what questions can you ask about it?
> After reading the first page of the story, what questions can you now ask about the story?
> Do you want to change any of the questions you asked before you read the page?

The above sequence of questions illustrates how the responsibility for setting purposes for reading the story is shifted to the pupils. The following responses show how the pupils with different levels of thinking and language maturity react:

"I bet this story is just like the one I saw on television where the boy helps the eagle and then later when the boy's in trouble, the eagle helps him."

"We could probably ask, 'What's going to happen between the Indian boy and the eagle?' Usually when a story has two people in the title, the story is about what happens to them. What's going to happen to the Eagle? The eagle probably won't die because they wouldn't have put him in the title if he did. The story's probably about how the Indian and the eagle become friends and help each other."

For anyone who knows the story, the above predictions, although produced by pupils of different maturity levels, are quite accurate. Now both pupils have definite, self-created purposes for reading the story. How well the pupils are able to predict depends upon the pattern of questions the teacher has asked in prior lessons.

Predictions need to be confirmed

Unless confirmation is expected, asking pupils to make predictions is not effective for developing an understanding of the relationship between reading and thinking. The pupils should be asked whether their predictions were accurate and their responses can be justified. In this way, reading does not become the mundane activity of reading and answering "ten questions." It becomes an active, purposeful endeavor. The students are made conscious of reading as an attempt to match the purpose of the reader to that of the author so the latter's message can be understood.

A second procedure for developing a sense of prediction is the cloze procedure. In Chapter 5, the use of the cloze procedure as a silent reading test was discussed. Here, we will talk about its use as a means for developing pupils' prediction strategies.

A cloze passage constructed for teaching differs in two ways from one constructed for testing. First, the systematic deletion is not limited to every fifth word. The cloze procedure can be used to teach first and second grade pupils with as few deletions as every tenth word. In the other grades, passages with deletions of every seventh word can be used. The second difference is that synonyms are accepted since the purpose is to foster a sense of anticipating what the author intended.

When introducing the procedure, use short passages with a total of about five deleted words. As pupils gain in their ability to predict, longer passages with an increased number of deletions are used. After the pupils independently complete as many items as they can, let them discuss the reasons for their choices. This activity is most effective when pupils question each other and must substantiate their own selections.

No emphasis should be put on attaining the "correct" answer. Teachers should guide the pupils with questions like: Does the word keep the meaning that the author wanted?

A third procedure for developing pupils' sense of predicting is somewhat similar to that used in the cloze procedure (Pehrsson, 1975). Unlike the cloze procedure, in which only single words are systematically deleted, this procedure involves the deletion of more than one word at a time. Instructional material is prepared by deleting in every other sentence the main verb phrase and all the information following that verb.

For example, a prepared passage might look like this:

Faster and faster raced the little bark canoe. The black rocks (1) _____

_____

The roar of the terrible waters became like thunder in the boy's ears. But still Waukewa (2) _____

_____

He would face his death as a brave Indian should (Fay et al., 1974).

The materials should be selected from any reading matter appropriate for any independent or instructional level. The passage may be read orally or silently, and the pupil may be asked to write all responses or tell them to the teacher. The pupil's responses are then used as the basis for discussions about the use of semantic clues found in the story.

The instruction associated with this procedure of developing anticipatory thinking involves an examination of three types of information: (1) grammatical acceptability, (2) semantic acceptability, and (3) contextual acceptability.

In response to the passage above about Waukewa, the Indian boy, a pupil offered the following:

(1) "The black rocks bumped the boat."
(2) "But still Waukewa was not afraid."

The two responses are grammatically acceptable as independent sentences. The first response, while it may not be quite semantically acceptable (the boat would bump the rocks), does maintain contextual appropriateness. The second response is appropriate both semantically and contextually.

However, the following responses by another pupil are not contextually appropriate although they may be grammatically and semantically acceptable:

(1) "The black rocks were shining in the sun."
(2) "But still Waukewa kept paddling his canoe faster and faster."

In these responses, the pupil does not relate appropriately to the information in the surrounding sentences. The first answer does not indicate that the rocks were seen as a source of danger as suggested by the phrase "terrible waters" in the succeeding sentence. The second answer seems to indicate that the pupil responded to the "faster and faster" of the first sentence as a clue that Waukewa wanted his canoe to go faster.

Practice and instruction in anticipatory thinking should help to focus the pupils' attention on acceptable sentence patterns and appropriate meanings.

Another activity that shifts the responsibility for asking questions to the pupils and away from the teacher is the use of "inquiry lessons" (Olmo, 1975). This activity aims at increasing pupil involvement in a lesson, thereby decreasing the amount of teacher talk, and increasing the level of the pupils' thinking from fact stating to problem solving.

An inquiry lesson is devised as follows:

1. The pupils, who have been randomly divided into four to six groups, are provided with packets containing different material about the same general theme. The material can be in a variety of forms: textual material (books, magazine articles, etc.), pictures, recordings, and graphics.
2. As a group, the pupils examine, read, and analyze the material in the packet and begin to prepare answers to questions the other pupils will ask of them.
3. In turn, based upon the type of information in their folder, the pupils should begin to develop questions they will ask the other pupils. (It should be pointed out that the type of information in each folder is the same, only the particulars differ.)
4. As a group, the pupils attempt to find a solution to the common problem that "ties" together the information in all the packets.

In a third or fourth grade classroom, the teacher might confront the pupils with the following question: What problems do people who live in desert areas have? Four packets might then be prepared, each of which illustrates the life and problems of people in four desert regions—the Sahara, the Gobi, the Australian desert, and the American Southwest. The resources in the folders might contain information about the problems desert dwellers have in getting water, food, shelter, and clothing. For sources the pupils can use library books, articles from newspapers, magazines and children's school newspapers, filmstrips, records, maps, articles from an encyclopedia, and large pictures or study prints.

As the above lesson unfolds, the pupils are given an opportunity to simultaneously gather information for questions that might be asked of them and to create questions to ask of other pupils.

Throughout this activity, which might last from one to five days, the teacher acts as a resource, providing additional information or suggesting where the pupils might find it on their own, and as an interpreter, clarifying anything that is not fully understood by the pupils.

Strategies for Understanding Textual Material

As the pupils are developing a sense of predicting and confirming, they should work on strategies to reconstruct the author's meaning. These strategies fall into three catagories: (1) sentence reading strategies, (2) paragraph reading strategies, and (3) longer selection reading strategies. A study of language cues will reveal how authors have built their messages. By recognizing and responding to these signals, pupils can develop independence as readers.

A study of language cues will reveal how authors build messages

To reiterate a point made previously, these strategies do not go by the traditional names usually associated with "comprehension skills." These strategies should, however, increase the pupils' understanding (as revealed through the pupils' "getting the main idea," "following directions," etc.).

The idea of having pupils take cues from language structure is not a new one. What is new in the present approach is that the structures are not treated in isolation. They are dealt with in a manner that allows the pupils to realize that comprehension is a set of processes operating on specific features of language (Bormuth, 1969a). These specific features are visual presentations of language signals the pupils generally respond to in oral language. They can learn to respond to the language signals correctly without having conscious knowledge of formal grammar and rhetoric (Bormuth, 1969a). Therefore, the study of the language signals can lead pupils to be able to answer the following questions (Christapherson, 1974) without their knowing the correct grammatical terminology:

Who or *what* caused an event?
Who or *what* was directly affected by the event?
What was used to perform the event?

Where did the event take place?
Who or *what* benefited or suffered from the event?
What was the outcome of the event?
What descriptions and identifications were given about the event?

According to Bormuth (1969a), some of the general signaling systems of which elementary pupils can develop an awareness are:

The meaning of words.
The ways word affixes affect meaning and syntactic function.
The ways deep structures are assigned to sentences.
The ways surface and deep structure of sentences govern word and phrase meanings.
The ways structures are assigned to paragraphs and larger units of discourse; and, how those structures are used to modify sentences, paragraphs, and section meanings.
The identification of antecedents of pronouns and other referring words.

Identifying what certain words refer to often poses problems for pupils. Take, for example, the following forms:

Pronouns

Some spiders are hairy all over. *They* are called wolf spiders.

Deleted nouns

Then the cloth is put into different liquids. *One* cleans the cloth. *Another* makes the cloth stronger.

Proverbials

He was not very smart, but he knew he could not stop. If he were to *do so,* the tiger would eat him up. So he continued.

Synonymous terms

The horse arrived at the barn door just before feeding time. *The building,* however, was locked up.

The pin was set with precious jewels. Each *gem* glistened in the sunlight.

Arithmetic pronouns

As the group approached, Bill could recognize the *three* who had visited him last night—Mr. Watkins, Mr. Stevens, and Mr. Olivera. The latter seemed to be the leader of the group.

Prosentences

When you talk or sing or shout, the air passing between your vocal cords makes them vibrate. *This* **is what makes the sound of your voice.**

The strategies that follow are not hierarchical. Although it may be logical to begin with sentence reading strategies before dealing with paragraph reading strategies, there is no need to limit pupils' instruction only to sentence reading until all these strategies are mastered. The result would be unnatural. It is rare to find sentences isolated from paragraphs, and paragraphs isolated from longer discourse. Thus, the specific strategies in which pupils receive instruction will depend upon their capabilities in processing units of language. The strategies are to be learned cyclically rather than hierarchically. The pupils are alternately exposed to sentence and paragraph reading strategies as they are able to deal with more mature discourse.

Students are alternately exposed to sentence and paragraph reading strategies

Sentence Reading Strategies. The specific strategies pupils need to understand sentences are:

1. Recognizing "who" or "what" the sentence is about.

   Felice got into the blue truck.

   The animals in the zoo stared back at the children.

2. Recognizing "what is being done" by the "who" or "what" of the sentence.

   Raymond *hugged his aunt and uncle.*

   More and more people *are interested in how to protect wild birds and animals.*

3. Recognizing and using the signals for information that indicates "where" something is or is done. The signals for "where"-information are *under, over, in, on, at, to, between, among, behind, in front of, through.*

   The class had its morning recess *in the school gym.*

   Jocie took careful aim and shot the ball *right through the hoop.*

4. Recognizing and using the signals for information that indicates "when" something is done or happens. The signals for "when"-information are *before, after, later, while, as, now, then.*

Frank was able to get inside his house *before the thunder and lightning started.*

After breakfast, **we all started to clean up the yard.**

5. Recognizing and using the signals for information that indicates "how" something is done. The signals for "how"-information are the adverbial endings *-ly, like, as.*

They walked *quietly* **up the steps.**

Like safari hunters, **the children crept through the weeds stalking their older brothers.**

6. Recognizing and using the signals for information that indicates "how long" or "how much" something is. The signals for "how long"- and "how much"- information are *for, about, almost, as long (much) as, until* (and information dealing with any sort of measurement).

The cat sat *for hours* **waiting for the canary to leave its cage.**

The teacher gave Alice *until Monday* **to finish her project.**

7. Recognizing and using the signals for information that indicates a "condition" exists. The signals for "condition"-information are *is, seems, appears.*

Harry *is* **the name of my pet cat.**

Nobody *seems* **happy with my answer!**

8. Recognizing and using information that indicates "what kind of" thing something is. The clues for "what kind of"-information are the possible transforms of the "condition" sentences.

The *tired* **quarterback looked at the clock and wished the game was over. (The quarterback is tired.)**

High in the tree sat a *reddish* bird I had not seen before. (The bird is reddish. The bird appears red.)

9. Understanding how some information in a sentence can be moved without changing the meaning of the sentence.

The architect skillfully drew the lines of the house.

Skillfully, the architect drew the lines of the house.

Once in a while we like to bring pizza home for supper.

We like to bring pizza home for supper once in a while.

10. Understanding that different sentences can have practically the same meaning.

Sandra painted the furniture to match the drapes her mother made.

The furniture was painted by Sandra to match the drapes made by her mother.

11. Recognizing and using the signals for information that indicates certain information about someone or something has been placed within the sentence. The clues to this extra, descriptive information are *who, which,* and *that.*

Guessing is an important strategy that people use throughout their lives

Once there was a little grey mouse *who* lived with his mother.

Since everyone *who* wanted to help had arrived, it was now time to think of some way to get the skunk out.

All of a sudden, Jean remembered the cows *that* were waiting to be milked.

The test questions, *which* seemed unanswerable by all the students, covered everything *that* they had learned about the geography of Asia.

12. Recognizing and using the signals for information that indicates certain information has been replaced. The clues to the replaced information are *I, you, he, she, it, they, we, us, them, their, his, her, your, our, him, this, these.*

As the young mouse grew, *he* became more curious about the world.

Aunt Harriet landed the plane on *her* ranch.

Fran liked to tease *her* cat, but Sally thought it was a silly thing to do.

"Wait until you see *this*," shouted Randy, running to the other kids with *his* stamp collection.

The teacher should note that *it* and *this* and *these* many times do not replace just one word. Often these pronouns replace groups of words or entire ideas.

13. Understanding that words are often left out of a sentence and that the reader has to mentally replace the omitted information. The clue that information has been omitted is that questions beginning with *what* or *did what* can be asked at the point the information was omitted.

While everybody was eating the hot pancakes, Leslie made some more. (More *what?*)

When the coach shouted, "Run!" all the players began. (Began doing *what?*)

14. Understanding how different sentences can be connected together, and conversely, how sentences can be separated into other sentences. The signals to understanding the connecting of sentences are a variety of conjunctions that seem to signal four types of relationships:

a. Joining. The relationship is one of bringing together ideas that are similar. The common signals to joined information are: *and, moreover, furthermore, in addition, too, also.*
b. Excluding. The relationship is one of discriminating, negating, or rejecting ideas. The common signals are: *not, this . . . not this,* and *neither . . . nor, but, except.*
c. Selecting. The relationship is one of taking from a larger category a subset of items. The common signals to selected information are: *one, the other, both, some, part, a few, either . . . or,* and the quantitative pronouns.
d. Implying. The relationship is one of effect/cause, result, necessity, proof, or condition. The common signals are:

if . . . then, if not this . . . then that, although, though, because, since, so, in order, as, unless, before, where, when, how, why, however, therefore, nevertheless, hence (Henry, 1974).

In addition to the instruction the pupils receive about the various sentence reading strategies, they should receive instruction in recognizing, using, and understanding these strategies as they apply to groups of two or more sentences. Quite often, authors place additional information (of say, the *when* or *where* type) in a subsequent sentence. Pupils must be directed to note the signals that indicate the additional information and to understand the relationships between the sentences. In the examples below, additional information, or the referent of replaced information, is in a previous sentence. The signals are in italics.

They all tried to lift the first bar. *But* only Stan Mojeski, Pete Pussick, and a stranger from Johnstown could lift *it*.

Then Pete and Stan and the stranger moved on to the next bar. Pete and Stan each got *her* off the ground, but the stranger from Johnstown had to give up.

So Esther filled the big jug again and hurried home. *Her* mother was awake when *she* got there.

That's what people all over the world do. *They* wear what the people around them wear.

Another young woman from a different tribe in South Africa wears a blanket of wool. *She* folds *it* into a cape around her shoulders.[1]

Paragraph Reading Strategies. Paragraph reading is more than just reading individual sentences that have been grouped together. A paragraph is a set of relationships among the sentences it contains. The teaching of paragraph reading strategies focuses on the manner in which paragraphs are structured as well as the function they perform in longer discourse. The discussion here will deal first with following the flow of an author's ideas through a paragraph and the various structures authors use in constructing paragraphs.

To understand paragraphs, pupils need to recognize "who" or "what" a paragraph is about. The normal signals for determining "who"

Teachers should focus on the structure and function of paragraphs

---

1. These examples and those following in this chapter—except where otherwise noted—are from Fay et al. (1974).

or "what" a paragraph may be about are repeated and replaced words.

Repeated words are content words found in practically all of the sentences of the paragraph. By noting these words, a reader is able to follow the flow of ideas and determine the agent of the paragraph. It is not too often that paragraphs with the same word or words repeated throughout are found in literature. The following paragraph has been constructed for illustration and would be used only to introduce pupils to the concept of a paragraph "agent."

> **There are many kinds of storms. Some of the most common storms are rain storms, ice storms, blizzards, and snow storms. Hurricanes are another kind of storm that are known for their strong winds. Another type of wind storm is called a typhoon. Storms of different kinds occur all over the world.**

More often, authors use various words to substitute for words that would be repeated throughout a paragraph. The most common category of substitute words is pronouns: *he, she, him, her, his, hers, it, its, their, them, they.* By mentally replacing the substitute word with its referent, pupils can follow the author's flow of ideas as above.

> **A dolphin cannot live out of the water. Its whole life is in the ocean. It is born in the ocean. The dolphin's mother teaches it how to stay alive in the ocean. It eats nothing but fish from the ocean.**

It is commonly held that all paragraphs have a "main idea." This does not seem, in fact, to be the case (Robinson, 1975). All paragraphs have a topic, but not all paragraphs have a single "main" point. Some paragraphs do. For example, the following paragraph has a main point, or generalization, that is stated in its first sentence.

> **A dolphin is among the fastest swimmers in the ocean. It can swim faster than the fastest person, and faster than many fish. Often it follows ships. It can keep right up with a ship, swimming and jumping and playing.**

However, the following paragraph, while it has a topic, cannot be considered to have a specific "main idea." Rather, it is part of a larger main idea and only serves to add more information in a descriptive form.

Now the monkey knew the name of the older sister too. He waited until they had left the tree, and then he climbed down and went home.

The topic has to do with some action of the monkey, which is part of the larger idea of the monkey employing various schemes to obtain information and pass it on to another animal.

Readers have to realize that authors organize ideas about a topic in various ways. The notion of "main idea" is only one of the major organizational writing patterns an author may use (Robinson, 1975). Readers need to learn the various patterns and the signals that help them to recognize these patterns. The various writing patterns are not unique to one particular level of reading material. They are found at all levels and in all subject areas. The differences that will be found between the same pattern at different levels are in the concepts, sentence patterns, and vocabulary that an author uses. There are six main paragraph patterns (Robinson, 1975).

1. *Enumeration.* The enumeration pattern is one of the easiest to recognize. It usually consists of a statement and then a number of other subordinate statements that list subtopics of the major topic. The common signals of the enumeration pattern are:

> one, two, three, etc.
> another, more, also
> one kind, another kind, etc.

The following paragraphs illustrate an enumeration pattern.

> Musical instruments are often played together in an orchestra. There are four main kinds of instruments used: strings, woodwinds, brass, and percussion.

> There are many different sounds. There is the sound of the wind rushing through the trees. There is the sound of raindrops hitting against your window. There is the sound of a train whistle, of a door closing, of footsteps, of a cat's meow. There are the sounds of birds singing, of a baseball when it is hit by a bat, of your mother calling you home from playing, of chalk on a chalkboard.

Sometimes the enumeration pattern spans a number of paragraphs. Signals within the title, topic heading, or one of the paragraphs indicate the use of this pattern. In the example below, the story title along with the signals in the first two sentences indicate that the enumeration pattern will be used in succeeding paragraphs.

All Kinds of Spiders, All Kinds of Places

There are many different kinds of spiders. Spiders live in almost every part of the world. They live in dry places. They live in the far north and in the highest places in the world.

Sometimes the enumeration pattern is introduced within a longer selection. The following paragraph introduces the enumeration pattern and subsequent paragraphs would complete the pattern by listing other kinds of horses.

To us, probably the most familiar work animal is the horse. There are many different kinds of horses. One kind is the *draft horse*. It was bred in England and France hundreds of years ago.

2. *Generalization.* The generalization pattern is the one that comes closest to what traditionally is referred to as the "main idea." In the generalization pattern, authors usually make some broad statement and then provide supporting evidence of this statement. The supporting evidence may take the form of examples, explanations, or reasons. The generalization pattern can be distinguished from the enumeration pattern in that the generalization is some statement containing an idea or belief. The enumeration pattern just indicates that there are various types or kinds of a particular thing. The generalization can usually stand alone without the supporting ideas, whereas the enumeration statement is incomplete without any additional information.

In the following paragraph, the generalization is found in the first sentence. Notice how the words "for example" can be included after the first sentence to introduce the other sentences.

With his hands the conductor tells the players just what kind of sound he wants. He may want the violins to be the loudest and the timpani to be very soft. Or maybe he wants the trombones to be the loudest with no violins playing at all. Maybe he wants everyone to play softly, or slowly, or as fast as possible.

In the following paragraph, the generalization is found by combining the information found in the first two sentences. The other sentences just provide information illustrating the generalization.

> Some very small spiders live on flowers and leaves. They change color to look just like the flowers they are sitting on. On red flowers, the spiders are red. On sunflowers, they are yellow. On leaves, they are green.

3. *Comparison/contrast.* In this pattern, two ideas that are related are compared and/or contrasted. Sometimes the two contrasting ideas are signaled by *but, however, although, yet,* and *even though,* as in the following paragraphs.

> Even though burros look sad and sleepy, they are very intelligent animals. People are always surprised at the clever tricks burros think up to get out of working.

> Ned thought that his father looked both funny and sad as a clown. The white and red and black paints made his father look funny. So did the bits of red hair stuck on all over his head. But the black rings around his eyes and the big white mouth he painted made the face seem sad.

4. *Sequence.* The sequence pattern may seem similar to the enumeration pattern at first glance. However, in the sequence pattern the order in which the ideas are presented is important. In the enumeration pattern, the order of the ideas can be changed without substantially altering the author's intended meaning. There is no way to reorder a sequence pattern without changing the author's meaning. The common signals of a sequence pattern are: *first, second, third, last; before, after, while; then, later.*

The following sequence of paragraphs illustrates the sequence pattern:

> After the cotton is dried and cleaned at the gin, men put the cotton onto trucks, and the trucks take it to cotton mills.
> At the cotton mills, the cotton goes through many machines. Some machines clean the cotton. Other machines make it into thread. Other machines make the thread into cloth.

(Notice how the enumeration pattern is also a part of the paragraph development of the second paragraph above. These paragraphs were taken from a selection in which the main pattern is sequencing. However, one step in the sequence is further explained by the enumeration of examples.)

5. *Effect/cause.* The effect/cause pattern is really one of implication. One idea is subordinated to another in a relationship to show that it is dependent upon that idea. Commonly the effect/cause relationship is signaled by the word pair *if . . . then.* Other signals also show this pattern: *because, so, in order that, unless, as a result of, since, so that, where, when.*

The following paragraph illustrates an effect/cause pattern. Notice the absence of signal words which forces the reader to supply the relational signals.

> **Frogs and toads go deep under the water and into the mud. The mud keeps them warm, and they can sleep all winter.**

In the following paragraphs, the effects and causes are in separate paragraphs.

> **Trash and garbage caused other problems. Garbage dumps made fine homes for rats, flies, and other pests. These pests were often the cause of sickness.**
>
> **So garbage men tried digging deep pits in the ground for the trash and garbage. But trash and garbage sometimes made drinking water bad.**
>
> **Drinking water comes from the ground. When underground water ran through the trash and garbage pits, the water became bad.**

Also notice how the first paragraph above contains an effect/cause relationship that is signaled by *cause.*

6. *Question/answer.* In the question/answer pattern, both parts are needed to complete the idea of the author. Too often, either the question alone or the answer alone is thought to be the "main idea" of the paragraph.

In the following paragraph, the kind of information that is needed to answer the question is signaled by the word *why.* The information should be a "reason." In other paragraphs, the type of information required to complete the pattern may be signaled by words such as *how, when, where, what.*

> **But why doesn't the spider stick to its own web? For one thing, the spider knows which threads are sticky and which threads are not sticky.**

And the spider has a special oil on its feet. If the spider has to walk on a sticky thread, the oil keeps it from getting caught.

(Notice how the signals "for one thing," and "and" signal that two answers will be enumerated for the question.)

Reading Longer Discourse. Rarely does a reader meet individual paragraphs that stand alone. The paragraphs are generally part of a longer discourse. Within these longer selections, the paragraphs serve some function. Each paragraph is not autonomous; rather, each serves to expand, clarify, or change in some way the main concept the author wishes to convey to the reader.

According to Robinson (1975), the reader can follow the flow of an author's ideas in longer discourse when the reader can recognize the following paragraph functions: (1) introductory, (2) explanatory, (3) narrative, (4) descriptive, (5) definitional, (6) transitional, and (7) concluding.

1. *Introductory paragraphs* can begin a whole selection or they can begin a new idea within a selection. The following paragraphs contain common signals that inform the reader that a story is beginning. Some of the signals are figures of speech. Pupils acquire the ability to recognize these signals through being made aware of them and experiencing them as often as possible.

In longer discourse, paragraphs are functional

> A long time ago, at the edge of a dark and gloomy forest, there lived an old man and his wife. They were very poor, and their only pleasure lay in eight beautiful children. Even though they loved all eight of their children dearly, their favorite was the youngest, Erendel.
>
> Maybe I should tell you a little bit about Caeser before I begin my story. Caesar was a big, dapple-gray horse. He and I used to work for the fire department. You see, a long time ago the fire wagons were pulled by very big, fast horses.
>
> I had heard a lot about a young dolphin that spent a summer with the people of Opononi. I thought it would make a good story for my newspaper. So I went to Opononi to talk with the people there.

When a paragraph introduces a new idea within a longer selection, it often follows a transitional paragraph. Therefore, the recognition of introductory paragraphs within longer selections is dependent to some degree upon the reader recognizing that the author has changed the flow of his ideas and has introduced another idea or set of ideas.

2. *Explanatory paragraphs* explain, inform, tell about, or provide some factual support to an author's idea. The internal organization of the paragraph may take the form of one of the paragraph patterns discussed previously. This category encompasses the vast majority of paragraphs within a long selection. Quite often, the paragraph has a signal that relates it to the ideas in a previous paragraph.

In the following paragraph, the first sentence ties the paragraph to a preceding paragraph and continues an explanation of an idea.

> Not too many years ago, it was simple. Garbage men took trash and garbage far outside of town to dump it. The garbage dumps and trash heaps were ugly and smelly. But they were far from town so people did not see them or smell them.

The following paragraph is signaled to be an explanatory one through the use of the expression "the oxen" rather than just "oxen."

> In America, the oxen helped settle the western part of the country. They pulled settlers' large, heavy wagons thousands of miles across the country. In India they pull big, clumsy carts filled with grain. In Portugal they plow the muddy fields in the spring, and they pull carts loaded with wine barrels and other goods.

The word "too" in the first sentence of the next paragraph signals that the paragraph continues to explain an idea introduced elsewhere.

> Some kinds of butterflies fly south, too. One kind is a big orange and black butterfly. Every year, on the same day, these butterflies begin their trip. It takes them a long time to get where they are going.

3. *Narrative paragraphs* are usually found in story type selections and are used to advance the story line or explain the actions of a character. The following paragraphs are examples of paragraphs that continue the narration of a story.

> Lee ran back through the MAIL ROOM door. She saw another door marked OUT. She pushed the OUT door, but on the other side was a door marked IN. People came and went through both doors.

Mr. Pepperkorn whistled the song all the way to the hospital. He wanted to whistle it there, too. But there were signs everywhere that said QUIET PLEASE. So Mr. Pepperkorn walked quietly up the steps and into Ruthie's room. Then he hugged Ruthie and she hugged him right back. Ruthie loved her grandfather very much. She thought she had the nicest grandfather in the world.

He went on for miles and miles. Sand was getting in his shoes. The hat made his head hot. The trunk was beginning to hurt his back. Even the boxes he had carried for his master had never hurt his back. And he still didn't know what was over yonder. It seemed as far away as ever.

4. *Descriptive paragraphs* serve the function of providing a description for the reader of an event, a person, or a thing. These paragraphs do not usually advance the story line. They usually provide descriptive information in the explanation of an author's story.

One music box had a golden bird. The bird sat on top of a tree. On another box girls and boys danced up and down. On another, Goldilocks ran around the three bears.

Draft horses have large bones and heavy, strong muscles, especially in the chest and legs. They are usually over five feet tall at the shoulder. They are gentle and patient, and they can work long, hard hours without getting tired.

5. *Definitional paragraphs* provide the meaning of some term used by the author. In narratives, these paragraphs usually do not advance a story line or add further information about the author's main concept. They often can be omitted from the selection without breaking up the flow of the author's ideas.

The smallest particle of mercuric oxide that you can see is still much larger than the smallest particle of a compound, called a molecule. A molecule is the smallest particle into which a compound can be divided and still have the properties of the compound (Brewer et al., 1972).

6. *Transitional paragraphs* have the function of indicating that the author is changing the flow of his ideas. Some transitional paragraphs, in addition to signaling a change of ideas, introduce a new idea. The follow-

ing paragraph makes a transition to a story that has its own introductory paragraph.

> **Can you guess what happens to a landfill? Here is a story about what one town did with a landfill.**

The following paragraph makes a transition and introduces a new idea of the author.

> **But there are some parts of the world where a horse cannot go. A horse cannot live where the weather is very cold, and cannot run through deep snow. So people in very cold countries have found other animals to work for them.**

7. *Concluding paragraphs* draw a close to a story or to an author's ideas. Readers can learn to recognize various signals authors use to indicate the conclusion of their selection. The following paragraph has the traditional signals ending a fairy tale.

> **The enchantment was broken. Erendel and the Prince returned to their palace, where they lived happily ever after. And Erendel was always very kind to bears.**

The following paragraphs contain signals that the author is concluding a discussion or explanation. One common signal authors use is to relate to some idea introduced at the beginning of the selection or to provide some sort of brief summary or restatement of the important ideas presented in the selection.

> **And now we begin our long swim up to the top of the ocean. Back we climb toward the sun and sky and trees and people and animals that we know. But we shall never forget, you and I, the wonderful watery world that lies deep within the Atlantic Ocean. And we shall never forget our sea monster, the octopus.**

> **All over the world animals are moving loads for people. In some places machines are doing the jobs animals used to do. But there are some places in the world where machines cannot go.**
> **And some people may never want to use a machine instead of an**

animal. After all, you can't pet an airplane or milk a tractor or whisper into a truck's ear.

Although the seven paragraph functions enumerated above have been illustrated with isolated paragraphs, the teaching and learning of the paragraph functions should not occur in isolation. Pupils should be given the opportunity to examine and make generalizations about the various paragraph functions only during the reading of longer selections.

Pupils should examine paragraph functions only in longer discourse

DEVELOPING STRATEGY LEARNING LESSONS

In order for the pupils to make good predictions about an author's message, they must possess information. One kind of information (that discussed in this chapter) is contained in the various signals to meaning we have in our language. When pupils can recognize and use these signals, then it is more likely that they can reconstruct an author's message. The language signals in sentences and paragraphs can be learned intuitively by the pupils. However, a much more expedient procedure is for the teacher to teach them.

When the teacher has determined that a pupil, or group of pupils, can not consciously use the language signals to reconstruct an author's message, lessons should be developed to have the pupils learn strategies for recognizing and using those signals. The lesson below uses five steps to develop a reading strategy: (1) the identification of a situation, (2) an example of the situation, (3) the strategy for recognizing the situation, (4) guided application of the strategy, and (5) independent practice in the use of the strategy.

The first four steps in the strategy learning lesson are under the direct supervision of the teacher. The final step allows the pupil to work out some problems independently and to gain facility in the use of the strategy.

The identification step establishes the point of the lesson. During this step, the teacher provides the pupils with information about what signals, patterns, or organization an author uses. The pupils are not asked to identify the signal or pattern. (If they could identify it, there would be no point in having them complete the lesson.) Usually, the identification step ends with a paraphrase of the "strategy" that will be stated in step three.

The example step is, again, a teacher directed step in which another instance of the situation is provided for the pupils. In the lesson below, the example step provides an opportunity to demonstrate a second and third signal. The teacher should decide how many examples will be provided during this step.

The third step, the strategy, is where the pupils are given the statement of the strategy and all of the signals that are to be learned with the strategy. The signals for the strategy should be placed on poster paper and hung in the room for the pupils' reference during the guided application and practice portions of the lesson. The poster can remain hanging until the pupils are completely familiar with the signals and no longer need to refer to it.

In the guided application step, the teacher provides extensive guidance during the first example. Less guidance is provided for the second example, and practically no direct guidance is provided for the last. This procedure—almost a weaning from teacher direction—lets the teacher observe the pupils in situations of increasing independence. The last part of this step should be identical to the practice step. Therefore, if the pupils are observed to experience difficulty, the teacher can repeat the first four steps using other sentences. Some pupils may need more than one "step through" before they are ready to do independent practice.

The sample lesson deals with the strategy for recognizing and using signals for a *cause* and a *result*. The material was prepared for use with pupils in the fourth grade. The pupils are provided with a worksheet containing all of the example sentences. Although this exercise could be done by writing the examples on a chalkboard, teachers' experiences have shown certain drawbacks to this practice. First, if the related activities are done on the chalkboard, not all of the pupils receive a chance to perform all of the tasks. Second, if the pupils are required to copy the example sentences onto paper at their desks, the task could be tedious for many pupils and could direct their attention away from the main purpose of the lesson. Therefore, two worksheets are recommended: one containing the examples of steps one to four, and one containing the practice sentences of step five.

(Note: Prior instruction was undertaken to ensure that the pupils understood the concepts *cause* and *result*.)

I. Identification of Situation

Teacher: *In the first sentence, the writer has given two ideas. One is a cause, and one is a result. The sentence has a signal to help you see which idea is the cause and which idea is the result. The signal word, "so," is* circled. "So" tells you that the cause comes first. Going out in the rain without an umbrella caused Sara to get wet. The result is Sara got wet.

cause
Sara went out into the rain without an umbrella

result
(so) Sara got wet.

The signal word, "so," tells you that the cause comes first in the sentence. The result comes after the word, "so."
Writers sometimes use other words to signal a cause and a result.

II. Example

Teacher: For example, in the next sentence,

result
Mrs. Polanksy's class could not go on their

cause
picnic (because) the bus broke down.

the word "because" is circled. It is a signal that the result comes first in the sentence and that the cause comes second. The bus breaking down was the cause of the class not going on its picnic. The idea after the word "because" is the cause.
Another signal writers use is "as a result of." In the next sentence,

result
The little rabbit was safe in its nest (as a

cause
result of) fooling the hound dogs chasing it.

the cause of the rabbit being safe was fooling the dogs. The words "as a result of" signal that the idea following them are the cause.

III. Guided Application

Teacher: Look at the next sentence. This sentence has a cause and result signal in it.

The dog hid under the bed because it was afraid of the lightning.

Find the cause and result signal and draw a circle around it. (Pause) What word did you circle?
Pupils: "Because."
Teacher: *What does the word "because" signal, a cause or a result?*
Pupils: *A cause.*
Teacher: *Draw a line under the words that show the cause. Write the word "cause" above the part of the sentence with the cause in it. (Pause) What words did you underline?*
Pupils: *"It was afraid of the lightning."*
Teacher: *What is in the other part of the sentence?*
Pupils: *The result.*
Teacher: *Draw two lines under that part and write the word "result" over it. (Check pupils' work.)*

Look at the next sentence. It also has a cause and a result. Find the signal word and circle it. Then draw a line under the cause and two lines under the result. Write "cause" and "result" above the correct parts of the sentence. (Pause) Look at the answer. (Write the correct answer on a chalkboard or poster.) Does your answer look like this?

cause   result
<u>I was hungry</u> (so) <u><u>I bought two pretzels.</u></u>

If pupils have incorrect answers, discuss their answers to discover why they may have answered as they did. Some pupils may need continued guidance such as was given on the first sentence. Such pupils may need more than three applications to be able to undertake the task independently. Other pupils may not understand the concept and may need a repeat of the Identification and Example steps with additional sentences. Since the final sentence in the Guided Application is a test to see whether or not the pupils can do the task independently, do not move on until you are sure the pupils understand the concept and the task.)

Teacher: *Do the next sentence the same way. (Pause) Does your sentence look like this?*

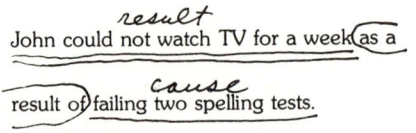

(Discuss any different answers with the pupils. At this time, a decision is made as to which pupils are ready for the Practice and which pupils may need additional guided instruction.)

IV. Practice Sheet

Teacher: *Each sentence below has a cause and result. Each sentence also has a signal word that can help you find the cause and the result.*

Draw a circle around each signal word. Then draw one line under the cause and two lines under the result. Write "cause" and "result" above the correct part of each sentence.

The coyote was eating the farmer's chickens so the farmer shot it.

My tooth ached because I ate two pieces of candy.

He put water on the flower seeds so they would grow.

Saul had two broken legs as a result of his skiing accident.

Everyone on the street stopped to look because the girl in the window was waving.

Teacher: *When you are finished, take the answer sheet and mark your work. After you have marked your work, take your paper to the teacher.*

The five step lesson can be followed for the teaching of any of the sentence and paragraph reading strategies. Once there is assurance that the pupils understand the concept and that they can recognize and use the signals, lessons can be developed that focus on the authors' ideas. For example, the following exercise can be used after the pupils are able to recognize and use the signals for *cause* and *result:*

Teacher: *Read the sentence and answer the question after it.*

The pitcher's wild throw went over the second baseman's glove into center field so Carlos was able to run to third base.

Which of these statements is true?

1. Carlos went to third base because of the pitcher's wild throw.
2. Carlos' run to third base was the cause of the pitcher's wild throw.
3. The pitcher's wild throw was the result of Carlos' run to third base.

Exercises such as the above one do not teach the pupils about reconstructing the author's ideas. They do, however, place the pupil in situations in which the strategy must be used and in which the pupil's ability to use the strategy is tested.

ACTIVITIES TO DEVELOP USE OF READING STRATEGIES

An author's plan may be illuminated with an idea map

A technique for making pupils aware that authors use plans for organizing their ideas is to provide the pupils with a "map" of the flow of ideas of the author. This map can be duplicated so that it fits alongside the pages of the selection being read. On the map, the various paragraph functions found within the selection are identified. In addition, various paragraph structures may be identified. In this manner, the pupils gain insight as to how an author constructed a particular piece of reading matter. Most importantly, the pupils may come to see that authors have definite plans for organizing their ideas when they write and that ideas are not just haphazardly or randomly placed on the paper.

The development of the author-idea map can begin as soon as pupils are reading selections of any length. The maps can be made to fit a typical story type selection or they can be constructed to follow the ideas in informational, nonfiction type selections. To illustrate that this technique can be used with young readers, the following example was taken from material originally prepared for use at the first grade level. Too often, comprehension development is left until after the pupils have learned "basic word recognition" strategies. It should be obvious after reading this far in the text that understanding must precede the recognition of individual words. That is why the chapter on vocabulary and word recognition strategies follows rather than precedes the chapter on comprehension.

No pupil is too young to begin understanding the strategies authors use for writing selections. What has to be varied with pupils differing in cognitive and linguistic maturity is the language the teacher will use for explaining the ideas to the pupils.

The author-idea maps are constructed by dividing a duplicating master into columns to correspond to the pages of the selection. The idea map is aligned with the page and each column is identified by its corresponding page in the selection. Some selections, such as the one in the example, may need more than one duplicating master. The less mature the reader, the more there is a need to write out complete sentences on the idea map.

As the reader gains maturity, sentence fragments, phrases, and single words can be used to identify the author's organization and development of ideas.

The idea map in Figure 8-2 identifies the patterns used by the author. The map does not explain the author's ideas; it merely points out how the author put the ideas together. Whether the pupils understand the author's ideas can be determined through the guided thinking strategies and the questioning techniques discussed in the previous chapter. Remember, however, that the prime purpose of the strategies discussed in the present chapter is to develop in the pupils a sense of independence. Therefore, this portion of the reading instruction should emphasize techniques the reader can use to recognize the organizational and writing patterns of the author as a means of locating what it is the author is saying.

The map shows how the author put the ideas together

Although the story, "The Terrible Lizzards," does not contain paragraphing in the usual sense, typographical features are used to differentiate between ideas. Notice the use of double spacing between certain groups of sentences. Examination of the entire piece reveals that these spacings correspond to paragraphing. All the sentences between such double spacing are intended, it appears, to be read as a unit.

The use of the author-idea map, then, allows teacher and pupil to identify the various writing patterns used by authors. By recognizing these patterns, pupils can more easily locate what it is authors wish to communicate about a topic. However, the mere location of an author's ideas does not mean that there will be understanding. Whether pupils understand these ideas depends upon their knowledge of the concepts presented and their understanding of the relationships established between these ideas.

Pupils' proficiency in reading longer selections can also be aided by developing a sense of story organization. Narrative stories are generally constructed with five main elements:

1. *Characterization.* Every story has a cast of characters. Some are important to the main story line while others play incidental or minor parts. In addition, each character can be identified by some distinguishable, identifying trait.
2. *Plot.* Every story is constructed around some general outline or problem. The plot is the basic framework within which the story unfolds and the characters operate. Quite often the plot takes the form of a problem that provides the impetus for the characters to act. Many stories can be recognized as having similar plot structures; they differ, however, in the characters and specific events.
3. *Events.* The events of the story are the specific, sequential

FIGURE 8-2: A Sample Idea Map

SOURCE: Fay, Leo, Ross, Ramon Royal, and La Pray, Margaret. *The Young America Basic Reading Progcam*, Level 6. Produced by Lyons and Carnahan. Copyright 1974 by Rand McNally.

1. This tells <u>when</u>.

2. This gives a meaning.

3. This tells what they were like.

4. This tells what will come next.

5. This describes, or tells about, one kind of dinosaur.

❻ It was hard to be a giant.
　A thunder lizard was so big that it could not run.
　It was so big that it had a hard time walking.

　The brontosaurus was so big that it had to eat a lot.
　It ate plants.
❼ In the water, there were many plants.
　So the thunder lizard lived in the water.
　The brontosaurus needed the water for other things, too.
　The water helped hold the big lizard up.

　The water helped keep enemies away.
　Some of these enemies were meat-eating dinosaurs.
　The meat-eating dinosaurs wouldn't go into the water.

❽ But the thunder lizard had other enemies.
　Time was one of them.
　Time changed everything.
　Time changed the land.
　The land changed from hot to cold.
　The land wasn't wet anymore.

6. This tells more about it.

7. There is a cause and result here.

8. This gives a list. What is it a list of?

Strategies for Reconstructing Meaning   **261**

❾ When the land changed, the plants changed.
  But the brontosaurus did not change.

❿ The brontosaurus couldn't eat the new plants.
  It couldn't find food.
  And where there was no food, the brontosaurus couldn't live.
  After a long, long time, all the thunder lizards were gone.

⓫ Today we find these things that the brontosaurus and other dinosaurs left.

⓬ Lizards are still around today. Dinosaurs are the great-great-great-granddaddies of these lizards.

  But the great-great-great-granddaddies, the terrible lizards, are gone.

9. There are two different ideas here.

10. This information is given in an order.

11. The last sentence tells about the picture.

12. There are two different ideas here.

happenings that provide the flow of the story. The events can be recognized as those things the characters do, or as those things that happen to the characters.
4. *Other information.* Stories often contain information that cannot be considered as "an event." This information may take the form of explanations about what or why something is happening or happened. It might also take the form of description. Although this other information may be important to the overall understanding of the story, it does not convey the story action.
5. *Theme.* Most stories have a theme or message. The message relates to one of the moral issues humans face during a lifetime. In the case of expository or informative writing the "message" is the main thesis of the author. The theme in narratives should not be confused with the statement of the plot. A statement such as, "A young girl seeks the help of her brother in finding out what a 'shadow' is only to find out what a 'silhouette' is," states the plot of a story. This story outline could be developed to exemplify various themes, one of which is, "Sometimes it's hard to get answers to your questions."

Pupils can be introduced to these five elements of a story as soon as they are confronted with their first story, either oral or written. Once pupils understand these five aspects of stories, they can begin to identify them in the stories they read or hear. Also, they can begin to use the story elements as a basis for reconstructing an author's idea and as a scheme for recalling the story. During lessons, an author-idea map can be used to identify the different aspects of the story.

The following activities are briefly stated in order to illustrate the many types of activities that can be used to foster proficiency in the use of the strategies for reconstructing an author's meaning.

☐ Provide the pupils with pictures and sentences. The pupils must read the sentences and match them correctly to the appropriate picture. This task can be made more difficult by using pictures that have similar scenes or activities. Only by using the information in the sentences can the pupils distinguish among the pictures. The length and complexity of the identifying sentences can be adjusted to meet the reading and language maturity of the pupils.

This activity can be used with paragraphs. Instead of limiting the paragraphs to descriptions of the pictures, paragraphs can be written, or selected from other sources, that relate to, but do not fully describe, the information in the picture. For example, a series of pictures may be used that shows a scientist in a laboratory, someone preparing a meal, and a mechanic working on a car. The paragraphs could be a recipe, steps in an experiment, and directions for repairing a flat. Or, using the generalization paragraph organization: a reason for safety in the laboratory, the need for cleanliness in the kitchen, and an appeal for wearing safety clothes while using tools.

☐ Provide the pupils with opportunities to read the directions of real situations. Many pupils do not have the opportunity to play certain games at home. They can learn to play these games by reading the directions. Other sources for learning to read and follow directions are in the constructing of model planes or cars, and the learning of card games. Many books exist which explain card games of varying complexities for various ages. The reading of directions such as these should not be considered as a frivolous activity. Board games and card games provide many of us with enjoyable, challenging recreational activities. Model building is not an activity engaged in by the young alone. Many adults have as their hobby the building of model railroad cars and the constructing of model ships. Since the formats of the directions are generally the same within each of the three categories mentioned, pupils can begin to learn about them and acquire the necessary vocabulary as part of their school learning.

☐ Provide pupils with sentences that contain the same words but different punctuation. The pupils read the sentences orally using the correct intonation to convey the intended meaning. For example, one group of sentences might be:

"Frank," said Marty, "Let Jimmy do it!"

Frank said, "Marty, let Jimmy do it?"

Or, let the pupils read sentences such as the following to show, through different intonations, what may be the meaning of the sentence.

I like boxing bears.

He can't imagine flying fish.

☐ Provide the pupils with an opportunity to expand basic sentence patterns through the addition of different information. For example, information such as *where, when, how,* and *why* can be added to:

The puppy cried.

The teacher gave everyone a book.

An alternate activity is to give the pupils sentences with one type of information omitted. The pupils have to complete the sentence with the appropriate type of information.

The cat sat _____ watching the birds at the bird feeder.
(where)

_____ gave me a new pen for my birthday.
(who)

This activity can be extended to paragraphs. A paragraph is constructed in which different types of information are omitted. The teacher, or another pupil, asks for the information. The pupil supplies answers without knowing the story. After the pupils' answers have been added to the paragraph, the paragraph is read in its entirety.

☐ Provide pupils with sentences in which some information has been moved to other parts of the sentence. The pupils are to determine whether the meaning has been changed by the shift of information. *Ask the pupils to justify their decisions.* For example,

The cow ate the apples behind the barn.
The cow behind the barn ate the apples.
Behind the barn, the cow ate the apples.

Slowly, Jaye opened her eyes and got out of bed.
Jaye slowly opened her eyes and got out of bed.
Jaye opened her eyes slowly and got out of bed.
Jaye opened her eyes and slowly got out of bed.
Jaye opened her eyes and got out of bed slowly.

☐ Provide the pupils with a sentence. Have them select from a group of other sentences which of the sentences indicate accurate information about the sentence. For example,

It is important for students to have a purpose for any reading they undertake

Atri is a very old town and is built halfway up the side of a steep hill.
1. Atri is a very old town.
2. Atri is the side of a steep hill.
3. The hill is built on the old town.
4. Atri is built half way up the side of a steep hill.

One hot afternoon when no one was upon the street the old horse chanced to wander into the marketplace. He saw the grapevine rope that hung from the bell of justice.
1. He saw the bell of justice.
2. He hung the rope on the bell of justice.
3. The grapevine rope hung from the bell of justice.
4. He hung the bell of justice.
5. He saw the rope hanging from the bell.

The complexity of the sentences—that is, the number and types of transformations which the sentences have undergone—should fit the language and reading maturity of the pupils. *Always discuss with the pupils why they selected the answers they did.*

☐ Provide the pupils with a basic sentence and other information that should be added to the first one (Peltz, 1975). Have the pupils place the information in different places and then discuss with them any changes in meaning imposed upon the original sentence. For example,

Mother planted five new rosebushes in the garden.

Add: only.

Some possible constructions:

**Only Mother planted five new rosebushes in the garden.
Mother only planted five new rosebushes in the garden.
Mother planted only five new rosebushes in the garden.
Mother planted five new rosebushes only in the garden.
Mother planted five new rosebushes in the garden only.**

Or again,

My brother plays with the toy duck.

Add: in the bathtub.

Some possible constructions:

**In the bathtub, my brother plays with the toy duck.
My brother in the bathtub plays with the toy duck.**

My brother plays in the bathtub with the toy duck.
My brother plays with the toy duck in the bathtub.

☐ Provide the pupils with cut up sentences. First, type the sentence on construction paper or oaktag. Then cut up the sentences into word groups or into individual words. Have the pupils arrange the parts of the sentence to make a logical statement. For example, the sentence parts could be:

the	we	check	landlord
rent	the	for	the gave

in the race	this Saturday
will be running	Harold

This activity can be extended by typing out the sentences of a paragraph. Clues can be provided to the pupils as to what type of paragraph organization they should construct from the sentences.

☐ Provide the pupils with a variety of puns, jokes, and riddles. Examine cartoons and comic strips to identify how meanings are conveyed through dialectal writing and typographical features. Have the pupils explain what in the joke or cartoon creates the humorous situation. What creates the humor in the following?

Why is the letter *f* like Paris?
(Because it is the *capital* of *France*.)

Discuss what a reader must know before a joke, pun or riddle is humorous.

☐ Provide the pupils with domino type cards. On the cards write the words *who, what, when, where, how* or words that provide similar information. Sample "dominoes" are:

where	where		where	who		Harry	in the car

at home	how		ran	Sally		how	slowly

The game is played following typical domino rules. For example, a domino with "where" and "where" can be matched at either end to a domino with "where" or one with "at home." A domino with "Harry" and "in the car" can be matched at one end to a domino with "Sally" or "who" and at the other end to a domino with "where" or "at home."

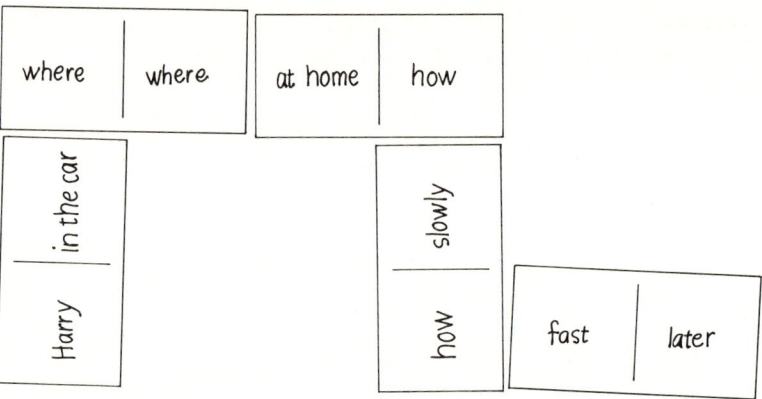

☐ Provide the pupils with a story in which there is a great deal of simultaneous or overlapping action. Have the pupils identify the signals for this action: as soon as, meanwhile, at the same time, while, etc. On a time line, have the pupils map out the time relationship among the various events.

☐ Provide the pupils with sentences or short paragraphs that describe a situation. The pupils must act out the situation as it appears on the paper and other pupils must determine what is being enacted.

☐ Provide the pupils with a story that has accompanying illustrations. Have the pupils determine which sentences in the story relate specifically to the pictures. Have them determine whether the pictures provide information needed for understanding the story that is not provided in any of the sentences or paragraphs.

RESOURCES FOR THE TEACHER

The following resources were selected because they contain exercises that relate specifically to the strategies discussed in this chapter. Many basal reading series contain lessons and exercises that correspond to the reading strategies for reconstructing meaning previously discussed. However, the following were selected because they have easily identifiable components relating to one or more strategies. Often exercises are provided in these components at varying levels of difficulty or maturity.

Teachers should not expect these materials to teach. They rarely teach. They are excellent sources of examples for use in a teacher's lesson. As with all instructional materials, teachers should examine them beforehand, and only select those that are appropriate for the age, language development and reading maturity of the pupils.

CROFT Skillpacks: Reading Comprehension. 1974. Old
    Greenwich, Conn.: Croft.

Two separate skillpacks, primary and intermediate, provide classroom practice in the objectives of: selecting details, translating details, identifying signal words, selecting the main idea, determining implied details, identifying organizational patterns, and inferring the main idea.

Specific Skill Series. 1970. Baldwin, N.Y.: Barnell Loft.
Supportive Reading Skills. 1975. Baldwin, N.Y.: Dexter and
    Westbrook Ltd.

Two series consisting of multi-leveled sets of booklets providing exercises in a number of specific areas. Titles in the *Specific Skill Series* that complement the strategies in this chapter are: Detecting the Sequence, Using the Context, Drawing Conclusions, Getting the Main Idea, and Following Directions. Appropriate titles in the *Supportive Reading Skills* series are "Understanding Word Groups" and "Understanding Questions."

New Practice Readers. 1962. New York: Webster
    Division/McGraw-Hill Book Co., 1962.
Reading for Concepts. 1970. New York: Webster
    Division/McGraw-Hill Book Co.

These multi-leveled series contain stories on a large variety of topics. Each story is followed by a series of questions that require a different type of thinking strategy.

SRA Schoolhouse: Comprehension Patterns. 1975. Chicago:
    Science Research Associates.

A kit containing multi-leveled exercises in determining the meaning of words, sentences, and paragraphs. The exercises, on individual activity cards arranged in units, provide practice with a variety of sentence and paragraph patterns.

The Thinking Skills Development Program. 1973. Westchester, Ill.: Benefic Press.

Consists of a kit of activity cards, filmstrips, and cassettes. The activities are structured around various thinking operations and draw their content from a variety of subject areas. The maturity of the language makes this program appropriate for upper elementary grades only.

Interaction: A Student Centered Language Arts and Reading Program, K – 12. 1975. Boston: Houghton Mifflin.

An integrated language arts program that treats language as a process through which individuals communicate. Learning to read is totally integrated with learning to speak, listen, write, and act out.

Reading Thinking Skills: Elizabethtown, Penn.: Continental Press.

Multi-leveled sets of spirit duplicating masters that contain exercises under the headings of: inference, organization, relationship, imagery, and vocabulary.

Reading Comprehension Series. Englewood Cliffs, N.J.: Scholastic Book Services.

A series of four books intended for use in grades 3 to 6, each of which contains short stories with follow-up exercises in finding the main idea, important details, sequence, and understanding word meanings.

Spectrum of Skills: Reading Comprehension Booklets. 1973. New York: Macmillan Publishing Co.

A set of multi-leveled booklets intended for use at the intermediate and upper elementary grades. Unlike the other resources listed, these booklets do provide some direct instruction to the pupils.

Re-Com: The Reading Comprehension Game. 1975. Plainview, N.Y.: New Dimensions in Education, Inc.

A board game in which the progress of the game is determined by the pupils' ability to perform activities under headings such as: sequence, inference, and cause and effect. The game requires the pupils to make decisions while manipulating play money, buying and selling properties, avoiding penalties, and pursuing bonuses. The game is intended for use by children 8 years and older.

Schaffer, Frank. 1974. *Task Cards and Wise Owl Task Cards.* Palos Verde Peninsula, Cal.: Frank Schaffer Publications.

Sets of index-size activity cards which require the pupils to read, solve problems and riddles, create things, work out relationships, and use their imagination and creativity. The activities are appropriate for use with pupils in the middle elementary grades.

DISCUSSION QUESTIONS AND ACTIVITIES

1. Rewrite the following statement by Ronald E. Johnson (1975) so that it would be understandable to a group of teachers who do not have an understanding of psycholinguistic principles.

> Whether a concept is meaningful thus depends upon the associational background of the learner and also the semantic structure of the concept within the linguistic community.

2. The following statement by Frank Smith (1971) has implications for teachers whenever they make reading assignments for pupils. Does Smith mean that pupils should never be asked questions?

> The more a reader expects to be asked questions on what he reads the more he will rely on visual information, and the more difficult will reading become.

3. Construct a series of lessons to demonstrate to a group of pupils the following principle as stated by John W. Miller (1974):

> Certain words place restrictions on the meaningful occurrence of other words within a sentence.

4. Select a story appropriate for use with a group of primary grade pupils. Construct an author-idea map that:
    a. Identifies the main characters of the story.
    b. Shows the flow of the main events of the story.
    c. Identifies information important to the story but which does not carry the main action.
    d. Points out where the theme or moral of the story is stated (or implied).

Use the "map" as the basis for a lesson in which the pupils are to recall the major information of the story.

5. Select two stories—one appropriate for use with primary grade pupils and one appropriate for use with upper grade pupils—and analyze the sentence and paragraph patterns used in each story. How do they differ in

construction? Use the patterns that occur most frequently as the basis for an informal test to determine whether the pupils can recognize and understand those structures.

6. Review current reading instructional materials to determine whether their authors would agree with the following statement by W. John Harker (1973b):

> Comprehension results from a dynamic cognitive process and not from the rigid application of a set of predetermined skills.

7. Select some current and popular reading instruction materials. From the materials select sentences that show description, attitude, or mood. Devise a lesson using those sentences to develop the concept that sentences do not necessarily show action.

8. Create different cloze procedure exercises from the same passage for the following purposes:
   a. To develop a "sense" of predicting and confirming.
   b. To develop an understanding of a particular syntactic structure of English.

FURTHER READINGS

For individuals who feel the need to obtain additional information about the construction of English sentences, the following two small books present this idea clearly and concisely.

Waddell, Marie L., Esch, Robert M., and Walker, Roberta R. 1972. *The Art of Styling Sentences: 20 Patterns to Success.* Woodbury, N.Y.: Barron's Educational Series.

Elgin, Suzette Haden. 1975. *A Primer of Transformational Grammar for Rank Beginners.* Urbana, Ill.: National Council of Teachers of English.

The following monograph contains an explanation of the general nature of syntactic complexity and some questions about the nature of the readability of materials.

Dawkins, John. 1975. *Syntax and Readability.* Newark, Del.: International Reading Association.

In order to better understand the structure and function of paragraphs, teachers might find it helpful to consult references on rhetoric and style.

Teachers often feel the need to improve their own reading procedures. One popular book that does not follow the traditional "how-to-do-it" format is the following. From a reading of it, teachers should also get greater insight into the teaching of the reading of longer discourse.

Adler, Morimer J. and Van Doren, Charles. 1972. *How to Read a Book: The Classic Guide to Intelligent Reading.* New York: Simon and Schuster.

Many of the ideas about the teaching of paragraph structures dealt with in this chapter were drawn from the following text. Although it is written primarily with examples from high school materials, elementary teachers will gain great understanding about how authors construct textual materials at all levels from reading the book in its entirety. It is one of the few books that provide specific techniques for strategy lessons on the structures of English.

Robinson, H. Alan. 1975. *Teaching Reading and Study Strategies: The Content Areas.* Boston: Allyn & Bacon.

References

Bormuth, John R. 1969a. "An Operational Definition of Comprehension Instruction." In Kenneth S. Goodman and John T. Fleming, eds. *Psycholinguistics and the Teaching of Reading.* Newark, Del.: International Reading Association.

Bormuth, John R. 1969b. "Research on Literal Comprehension." Paper read at the Symposium on Application of Psycholinguistics to Key Problems in Reading. International Reading Assoc., Kansas City.

Brewer, A.C., Garland, Nell, and Notkin, Jerome J. 1972. *Elementary Science: Learning by Investigating.* Chicago: Rand McNally.

Christapherson, Steven L. 1974. "The Effect of Knowledge of Discourse Structures on Reading Recall," Paper read at the Annual Meeting of the American Educational Research Association, Chicago. ERIC No. ED 090 531.

Cramer, Ronald L. 1970. "Setting Purposes and Making Predictions: Essential to Critical Reading." *Journal of Reading* 13: 259-62, 300.

Eisenhardt, Catheryn T. "The Structure of Meaning." Paper read at the Annual Meeting of the International Reading Association, New Orleans. ERIC No. ED 095 484.

Fay, Leo, Ross, Ramon Royal, and LaPray, Margaret. 1974. *Young America Basic Reading Program.* Chicago: Rand McNally.

Harker, W. John. 1973a. "Classroom Implications from Models of Comprehension." Paper read at the Annual Meeting of the International Reading Association, Denver. ERIC No. ED 089 226.

Harker, W. John. 1973b. "Teaching Comprehension: A Task Analysis Approach." *Journal of Reading* 16:379-82.

Henry, George H. 1974. *Teaching Reading as Concept Development: Emphasis on Affective Thinking.* Newark, Del.: International Reading Association.

Johnson, Ronald E. 1975. "Meaning in Complex Learning." *Review of Educational Research* 45:425-59.

Lundsteen, Sara W. 1974. "Levels of Meaning in Reading." *The Reading Teacher* 28: 268-72.

Menzel, Peter. 1970. "On the Linguistic Bases of the Theory of Writing Items." Appendix to John R. Bormuth, *On the Theory of Achievement Test Items.* Chicago: The University of Chicago Press.

Miller, John W. 1974. "Linguistics and Comprehension." *Elementary English* 51:853-54, 857.

Olmo, Barbara G. 1975. "Teaching Students to Ask Questions." *Language Arts* 52: 116-19.

Pavlak, Stephen A. 1974. "Significant Research on Comprehension (1948-72)." Paper read at the Annual Meeting of the International Reading Association, New Orleans. ERIC No. ED 095 506.

Pehrsson, Robert. 1975. "The OP-IN Procedure." Paper read at the Preconvention Institute, "Psycholinguistics and Reading Instruction," New York State Reading Association Annual Conference, Kiamisha Lake, N.Y.

Peltz, Fillmore K. 1975. "Handling Questions About Reading Materials." Paper read at the Preconvention Institute, "Psycholinguistics and Reading Instruction," New York State Reading Association Annual Conference, Kiamisha Lake, N.Y.

Robinson, H. Alan. 1975. *Teaching Reading and Study Strategies: The Content Areas.* Boston: Allyn and Bacon.

Simons, Herbert D. 1971. "Reading Comprehension: The Need for a New Perspective." *Reading Research Quarterly* 6: 338-63.

Smith, Frank. 1975. "The Role of Prediction in Reading." *Elementary English* 52: 305-11.

Smith, Frank. 1971. "Overloading the Competent Reader." Paper read at the National Council of Teachers of English Annual Conference, Las Vegas. ERIC No. 085674.

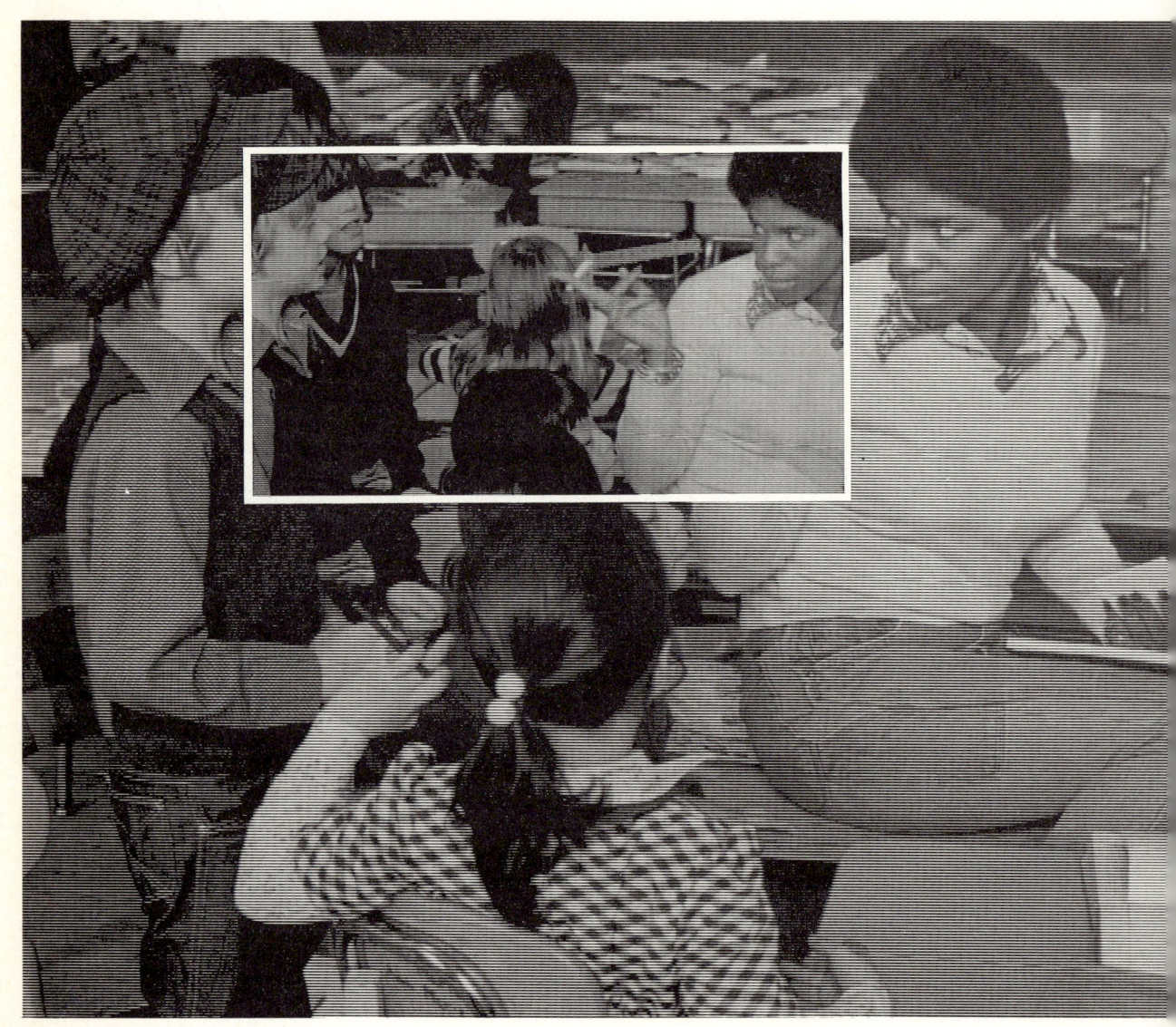

9

Strategies for Vocabulary Development and Word Recognition

Focus Questions:

1. How can pupils' knowledge of concepts and words be developed and extended?
2. How can pupils use context as an aid to word recognition?
3. What strategies should pupils have for recognizing an unfamiliar word in print?
4. How should pupils use dictionaries?

The discussion of vocabulary development and word recognition is purposely placed after the discussion on recovering an author's meaning. Psycholinguistic investigations suggest that individual word recognition occurs after the reader understands the author's message. Meaning is not derived from the synthesis of identified and understood words. Rather, psycholinguists have discovered that the opposite seems to be true—the reader recognizes the constituent words of a sentence after assigning meaning to the sentence.

The discussion in this chapter is based upon the assumption that pupils come to school with a basic speaking and listening vocabulary. In previous chapters it has been demonstrated how a pupil's vocabulary, no matter how limited, can form the basis for literacy through a language experience approach. Strategies for understanding can then be developed for all levels of language maturity.

The purpose of the present chapter is to present ideas for (1) extending pupils' word knowledge, (2) developing pupils' strategies for determining the meanings of unknown words in context, (3) teaching pupils to use grapho-phonological information together with sentence and other mean-

Individual words are recognized only after the reader understands the message

ing signals for recognizing words, and (4) developing pupils' strategies for using the dictionary.

One clarification should be made first. The term *word recognition* is used vaguely in the professional literature. In fact, it is used interchangeably with at least five other terms: decoding, word perception, word identification, word analysis, and word attack. In the present text, *word recognition* indicates the processes by which a reader realizes what word an author has used and the meaning intended for it. A word is recognized in various ways: the reader already knows the word, the reader surmises what word is intended because the general meaning of the passage is understood, the reader translates an unknown graphic form into a recognizable oral form, or the reader relies on some other source—for example, a dictionary.

A word is recognized when the reader realizes what the author meant it to mean

STRATEGIES FOR DEVELOPING AND EXTENDING WORD KNOWLEDGE

Every individual comes to school with a listening vocabulary and a speaking vocabulary. As the individual becomes educated two other vocabularies are acquired—a reading vocabulary and a writing vocabulary. For most people, the listening vocabulary is usually the largest because it has been developing the longest. The size of one's listening and speaking vocabularies at the time of entering school is in a large part determined by the individual's prior language environment. The more restricted one's language background is, the less extensive one's vocabulary and language patterns will be. All pupils, however, are capable of increasing their vocabularies by acquiring new concepts and their labels, or by acquiring additional labels for already known concepts.

All pupils can increase their vocabularies by acquiring new labels

A significant factor for developing and extending pupils' vocabularies seems to be the excitement about words that a teacher can generate. An extensive review of research concerned with the teaching of vocabulary (Manzo and Sherk, 1971) revealed that many different activities can successfully lead to increased vocabularies; yet, unless the teachers demonstrated enthusiasm for words and were able to transfer this excitement to the pulils, no instructional activity was any better than any other. Assuming the teacher possesses this positive attitude, the following are features of a successful vocabulary development program:

1. The teacher's attitude toward vocabulary development is contagious and is rapidly acquired by the pupils.

2. The program provides continued and systematic attention to words and word acquisition.
3. Almost any technique that draws attention to word parts and/or word meanings can positively influence word acquisition.
4. A game-like atmosphere, which fosters incidental learning, can often provide a major source of vocabulary stimulation.
5. Guidance is given in the development of contextual awareness, dictionary strategies, word derivations, and structural elements.
6. Words are encountered in many different contexts.
7. The study of a few words in depth results in their greater usage than does exposure to a large number of words.
8. Although it may be possible, it is not practical to teach words which are not part of the pupil's verbal community.

Increasing General Vocabularies

Too often vocabulary development procedures encourage pupils to memorize just lists of words. Individual words are of no help to pupils unless the concept for the word is also learned. Vocabulary development, then, should be concerned with the teaching and learning of a variety of conceptual relationships (Williamson, 1974). The pupil must be able to recognize (1) members of the concept, (2) what is not a member of the concept, (3) unique characteristics that place members within a concept, (4) the range of sizes of members within a concept, (5) an act or activity peculiar to members of the concept, (6) the effect one concept has upon another, (7) the cause and effect relationship between two or more concepts, and (8) what members of a concept depend upon for continued existence. For example, developing the concept mammal through an exploration of these relationships will result in greater understanding by the pupils than if they are just required to learn the label and memorize a definition. Some concepts, of course, such as "possessing aspects of a color" (bluish, greenish) do not require exploration in all of the above relationships.

Vocabularies can be developed and extended through the systematic study of semantics (Burns and Broman, 1975). Throughout a school year, effort can be made to identify and use meanings as follows:

1. *Understanding symbols:* Symbols may be nonlinguistic: expressive gestures, traffic lights, road signs, flags, emblems. Language itself is a symbol, along with its derivatives: shorthand, Morse and other codes, Braille alphabets, the symbols of mathematics, and so on.

2. *Understanding referents:* A *referent* is something that refers or is referred to. For communication to occur, there must be an agreed-upon

meaning for the referent—an accepted meaning for the sender and receiver. It is at this point that much of the confusion of communication can be traced, particularly of multi-referent words. For example, what different meanings might *run* have for a baseball player, a stocking salesman, a playwright? Understanding a referent often involves gleaning meaning from the context—verbal, social, emotional, or historical.

In addition to the problems cited in the preceding paragraph, there are terms without tangible means of referential support: *generosity, patriotism, truth, happiness, goodness, democracy, justice, cooperation.* What such a term means will depend upon who uses the word, what this person values, his purpose for using the word, and his definition of the word. When a writer or speaker uses such terms, it is necessary to pause and think: "Here is a word worth examining. What does this person mean? Is it used to stir emotion or express opinion? Does the word mean to him what it seems to mean to me? Do I really understand what he is saying?"

3. *Understanding the denotative meaning of a word:* This appears to be a fairly straightforward concept, but dictionaries are not published frequently enough to keep up with all the new words (or new meanings of words)—particularly technical words—nor do they generally contain slang expressions.

4. *Understanding the connotative meaning of a word: Connotation* refers to suggested or implied meaning associated with a word apart from the thing it explicitly names. This is one of the more difficult aspects of understanding words, for there are so many words that have multiple and/or changing connotations. For example, a generation or so ago the word *square* carried the connotation of true, honest, and forthright when used in describing a person; today, the same word is used to describe a person who is socially inept and out of touch.

5. *Understanding euphemisms: Euphemism* is the substitution of an agreeable expression for one that may offend or be unpleasant: e.g., *mortician* for *undertaker.* The word *plump* is less offensive than *fat,* and *slender* is more pleasing than *skinny.* Euphemisms require constant updating, as they occur in usage long before they appear in dictionaries.

6. *Understanding functional shift: Functional shift* requires an understanding not only of connotative shifts, but also shifts in parts of speech, as a change from a verb to a noun; for example: *They* walk *to the bus stand each day,* or *Joe went for a* walk.

7. *Understanding the purposes of slang and various groups who use slang:* An activity could be the compiling of slang words and expressions used by class members and defining the slang words in standard language. Discussion could include who uses these expressions, when they are ap-

propriate, and special slang used by different groups—ethnic, geographical, age, occupational.

8. *Understanding technical language:* Technical terms are important, for people are increasingly exposed to technical fields such as space, medicine, and ecology.

9. *Understanding all forms of affective language:* Social adjustment and consumer wisdom are absolutely vital to everyone, as they affect every aspect of life. It is important to realize that every form of communication contains a bias because the sender is expressing the concept from one subjective viewpoint and the receiver is accepting it from another subjective viewpoint. When the two viewpoints are not clearly understood, confusion and/or propagandizing results. Children should know that catchwords and slogans, such as *brotherhood of man,* and *good citizen,* can produce stock reactions.[1]

Activities for Developing General Vocabularies

For pupils to acquire new words—new concepts and labels and new labels for already known concepts—they must be actively involved intellectually, emotionally, and physically (Donlan, 1975). This means that hearing a word or being given a word and its meaning or finding the meaning of a word in a dictionary may not result in actual vocabulary growth. Pupils should be totally involved so that the new words and concepts are assimilated. Once so learned, these words will remain part of the pupil throughout life.

In general, the factors that seem to affect the acquisition of new vocabulary items are utility, application, and memory load (Bruland, 1974). Without some purpose for using new words, pupils will discard them in a shorter time than it took to learn them. Pupils should be able to use new vocabulary within their daily lives—both in school and out of school. Without some opportunity to put the words to use, the pupils will forget them. Once words are learned, there should be planned times for the pupils to practice the words as part of their daily assignments. If too many words are attempted at any one time, however, only a few of them will be acquired.

Without some purpose for using new words, pupils will discard them

In order to develop and extend pupils' vocabularies, teachers should

☐ Develop action packed vocabularies (Toothaker, 1974). Over an

---

1. From Burns, Paul C. and Broman, Betty L., 1975. *The Language Arts in Childhood Education,* 3rd Edition. © 1975 by Rand McNally College Publishing Company, Chicago, pp. 313-15.

extended period of time, words that suggest actions, conduct, motions, responses, or behavior can be introduced to the pupils. The advantage of this approach is that it promotes physical experiences. Two categories of words can be developed:

1. *Muscular action words* are included in classifications such as traveling, driving, reactions, motion with object in front (behind), contracting, facial, eating, rubbing, upward (downward), leaping, to and fro, circular, irregular, fast (slow), exertion;
2. *Mental action words* are included in classifications such as memorization, language response, dramatic, musical, artistic, social, creative, mathematical, scientific and analytical, discriminatory.

The difference between the two classifications is that the first deals with those actions that are more automatic or habitual than the second.

☐ Provide ample opportunities for new and interesting experiences. Field trips, movies, classroom demonstrations, classroom visitors, and seasons and holidays provide the situations in which new concepts and words can be introduce.

☐ Provide opportunities for different social experiences. Identify situations in which the pupils have limited experiences, such as using the telephone to seek information or order something, seeking advice or help from an adult of little acquaintance, reporting emergencies to the police or fire departments, or visiting the home of a new friend who belongs to a different ethnic or cultural group.
The activity can be extended to cover other topics such as developing a sense of social responsibility. Role playing provides controlled opportunities for pupils to practice various roles: givers of orders or information, receivers of orders or information, questioners, mediators. In each situation there is the need for a careful examination of words that increase rather than hinder communication.

☐ Develop an interest in the natural environment. There is an almost universal concern with conserving resources and lessening pollution. The outdoors allows many opportunities for physical as well as emotional involvement as pupils learn to appreciate the beauty of nature. When it is not feasible to explore natural environments, articles or specimens can be brought into the classroom and set up in "hands-on" exhibits.

☐ Encourage the study of a hobby. Displays of the work of pupils or teachers who already have hobbies can provide many pupils with the stimulation to undertake one of their own. Even though some pupils may never develop hobbies of their own, they can develop an appreciation of others' hobbies. These activities provide many opportunities for vocabulary development through labeling, organizing, and classifying.

☐ Develop words around a theme. School events, special studies, literary units, and holidays provide pupils with opportunities to acquire words and concepts related to the theme. Sometimes the theme can be of a more general nature such as friendship, humor, or moods.

☐ Develop an understanding of the figurative and idiomatic expressions in our language (Foerster, 1974). Idioms—expressions that convey meanings other than the literal one—necessitate a degree of language

I think that English is sickly.
Words change their meanings so quickly.
"Time goes *fast*," simply means that time's fleeting.
When you *fast*, it just means you're not eating.
And "stuck *fast*" means you're glued to the spot.
So if you go *fast*, you will never be *last*,
If you *fast*, you may *last*, or may not.

SOURCE: From *Would You Put Your Money in a Sand Bank?* by Harold Longman, illustrated by Abner Graboff. Copyright 1968 by Harold S. Longman. Used by permission of Rand McNally.

sophistication in order to be fully understood and appreciated. Idioms can be analyzed by illustrating both their literal and figurative meanings and pantomiming their meaning. Idioms can also be categorized according to their main source of metaphor: color, parts of the body, animals, food, clothing, solar system, plants, and marine life.

☐ Provide opportunities to explore the meanings of familiar words in new contexts (Deighton, 1959). In addition to the figures of speech mentioned above, pupils should be allowed to develop an extended understanding of: (1) words frequently used figuratively such as ear, eye, face, foot, head, river, mountain, road: (2) relationship words with close meanings such as over/above, across/over, near/by/at/in, along/with/among/together, lower/under, still/yet; (3) judgment words that can be used in a variety of situations, but which may change in meaning due to their usage, such as cold, bad, beautiful, better, best, big, dark, deep, far, fast, fine, good, great, hard, heavy, high, hot, long, new, old, poor, rich, short, strong, sweet; (4) synonyms such as stay/remain, sure/certain, small/little, glad/happy, build/make; (5) indefinite words that change in meaning depending upon the situation in which they are used, such as all, always, certain, every, sure, never, right, true, whole; and (6) idioms constructed from words such as hold, bring, buy, clear, come, cut, put, make, get, go, in, down, up, around.

☐ Develop a sense that the vocabulary of our language is constantly undergoing change. The pupils should be aware of words that are in current usage but which were not so a few years ago. The fields of science and technology provide numerous examples of newly created words. Pupils with more mature language skills may also be able to undertake a study of words that are no longer in current usage.

The change in our vocabulary can also be noted in the changing meanings of known words. As words are used more and more frequently, new meanings become attached to them. Although many professional writers contend that words are being used "incorrectly," the final judge as to the acceptability or correctness of a word in any given context is whether or not it is so used by a significant portion of the population.

☐ Provide the pupils with a vocabulary "capsule" (Crist, 1975). The capsule is comprised of a list of words related to a specific topic that has been identified through a survey of the pupils' interests. The new words are introduced by the teacher in a talk to the pupils. The pupils then talk among themselves using the words. The pupils become the judge as to whether the others are using the words in the same manner as the teacher. At another time, the pupils can be involved in writing activities using the new vocabulary.

To recapitulate, the pupils' general vocabularies—spoken, listening, writing, and reading—can be developed through planned activities that involve direct teaching as well as incidental learnings. The enthusiasm of the teacher appears to be a key ingredient to a successful vocabulary development program. The pupils are sure to respond to the learning of new words that are useful to their everyday lives and schoolwork in situations that make vocabulary acquisition a pleasant and pleasurable experience.

USING CONTEXT TO DETERMINE UNKNOWN WORDS

To use context clues, pupils need to know language patterns

As pupils acquire new vocabulary and extend their understanding of already familiar words, they should be developing strategies for determining the possible meaning of an unfamiliar word met in context. In order to use context clues effectively, the pupils should be aware of the various language patterns and signals from which information concerning the author's intended meaning of the word can be obtained. In context, a number of textual constraint variables are in operation. These variables point out segments of the printed language which the reader is likely to use in determining word meanings at the sentence level (Aulls, 1970). These variables seem to be: (1) the position of the word in the sentence, (2) the grammatical class of the word, and (3) the types of grammatical structures in which the word is found.

The use of context for determining word recognition has some limitations. The results of a study of words and their use in contexts (Deighton, 1959) show

1. Context *reveals* meaning far less frequently than is normally supposed. Although it is true that context "determines" meaning, it does not always *reveal* it.
2. Context reveals only one of a word's meanings. Since no word has a fixed unalterable meaning, no one context will suffice for all uses of that word.
3. Context seldom clarifies the whole meaning of a word. At best, context only provides clues from which the reader may infer the meaning of the unfamiliar word.
4. Vocabulary growth and expansion through context revelation is slow and gradual.

Therefore, as strategies for using context clues are developed, teachers should realize that

> What a context reveals as to the meaning of an unfamiliar or unknown word depends upon the reader's past experiences and knowledge.
> The portion of the context revealing, or providing clues to, the meaning of the unfamiliar word must be in relatively close proximity to the word.
> There must be a clear-cut connection between the unfamiliar word and the context which clarifies the meaning of that word.

Contextual Signals to Word Meanings

Contextual signals are aids to determining the possible meaning of an unfamiliar word. Contextual signals work partly because of: (1) the reader's reasoning ability, (2) the reader's store of possible word meanings, and (3) the extent of the reader's knowledge about the topic (Burns and Schell, 1975). If the reader has the basic prerequisites for determining the possible meaning of a particular unfamiliar word, the application of strategies for using context consists of hypothesis generating and confirming.

Contextual signals help determine the meaning of an unfamiliar word

According to Deighton (1959), context may reveal the possible meaning of words through

1. *Definition.* Sentences containing forms of the verb *to be,* alone or in a verb phrase with the word *called,* often give the reader an explicit definition of an unfamiliar word.

    A sculptor is a person who models, carves, or casts a work of art in solid material.

    A person who believes in and campaigns for the careful use and protection of natural resources is called a conservationist.

2. *Example.* Sentences provide clues to possible meaning when they contain expressions such as: *for example, such, such as, like, especially, other, this,* and *these.* If the reader has a knowledge of the item used as an example, it may be possible for a meaning of the unfamiliar word to be inferred.

Many new sporting arenas such as Cobo Hall in Detroit and Madison Square Garden in New York are being built in the form of an amphitheater.

3. *Modifiers.* Sentences often contain unfamiliar words that can be understood because of a modifier used with that word. Modifiers can be single words, phrases, or entire clauses. Two very important modifiers are relative clauses and predicate adjectives.

My grandfather's chronometer, which had a bright face, glistening black hands, and a loud tic, always brought excitement to all of us when he removed it from his vest pocket.

Delphinium are beautiful perennials that bed nicely with white lilies.

4. *Restatement.* Sentences containing appositives, the punctuation marks of parenthesis and dashes, and the words *in other words, that is,* and *or* provide numerous signals to unfamiliar words.

The parcels were all sent down a chute—a kind of slide—into the storeroom below.

The photograph was finished in sepia, or dark brown tones.

5. *Inference through established connectives.* Sentences may reveal the possible meaning of an unfamiliar word through various grammatical patterns:
   a. Parallel sentence structure. The use of a series—either within the same sentence or in succeeding sentences—often allows the reader to determine the meaning of unfamiliar words.

Each child brought a favorite musical instrument: Fred, his drums, Mary, her tambourine, and Warren, his horn.

   b. Repetition of key words. Often a writer will repeat the unfamiliar word throughout a paragraph. Each time the word is used, more information is provided about its possible meaning. Or, the writer may restate an idea, thereby providing the reader with additional clues to the meaning of an unfamiliar word.

c. Familiar connectives. Sentences containing coordinating and subordinating connectives provide the reader with various clues to the possible meaning of an unfamiliar word.

Although Frances kept her room immaculate, her twin sister's was untidy and always messy.

Other ways readers can unlock the possible meaning of an unfamiliar word are through the use of the sentence and paragraph reading strategies found in Chapter 8. Readers can begin to perceive the meaning intended by an author as they begin to question how the word is used:

Does it seem to be the "who" or "what" of a sentence?
Does it seem to indicate "what is being done"?
Does it seem to mean "what kind of thing something is"?
Does it seem to mean "how," "how much," or "how long" something is happening?
Does it seem to mean something about "where" or "when" or "why" something is happening?
Can the meaning be derived from other "examples" or "reasons" in the paragraph?

As pupils gain experience in utilizing the sentence and paragraph reading strategies, they are also gaining strategies for determining the possible meaning of an unfamiliar word.

Contextual aids can also be found in the illustrations, charts, tables, and maps that often accompany textual material. For example, the meaning of "pedipalps" in figure 9-1 may not be fully grasped by pupils until they refer to the drawing in the text. However, teachers should not assume that the presence of an illustration assures that pupils can and will use them. Relating visual information to its printed counterpart is a necessary strategy and skill that should be developed in all readers. (See Chapter 10 for further discussion of this.)

Activities for Using Context Signals

Pupils should be taught not only the various signals, but also the manner in which these signals may be used for determining an author's intended meaning. The most practical beginning place for obtaining teaching and practice material is the instructional materials for the pupils. The specific contextual strategies and the precise order in which they are pre-

Pupils should be taught the signals and their uses

FIGURE 9-1

> Let's look at the spider's head. Most spiders have a very strange-looking head.
>
>
>
> This is because many spiders have four or six or eight eyes. Even so, a spider cannot see very much. A spider can tell only if it is light or dark or if something is moving.
>
> Most of the other parts of a spider's head help it to catch food. The spider has two small leg-like things, called *pedipalps*. It has one pedipalp on each side of its head. The pedipalps help the spider to hold an insect.
>
> The spider has two jaws just in front of its mouth. These jaws have fangs at the end. When the spider catches something, it bites the insect with these fangs. Poison in the fangs puts the insect to sleep until the spider is ready to eat it.
>
> 65

SOURCE: Fay, Leo, Ross, Ramon Royal, and La Pray, Margaret. *The Young America Basic Reading Program*, Level 7. Produced by Lyons and Carnahan. Copyright 1974 by Rand McNally.

sented to the pupils can be determined after an examination of the school texts. When a basal series is in use, it is best to follow the sequence of that series. Some basal series, however, do not provide continuous instruction in the use of contextual signals. When they do provide exercises, quite often they merely ask the pupils to "use the context" without specific instruction as to what they are to use and how they are to use it.

The format of the strategy lesson explained in Chapter 8, pages 251 to 256, should be used for teaching the contextual signals and the strategies for using them. After the pupils have learned various signals, they should be provided with opportunities for applying their knowledge and gaining proficiency in using the contextual aids. The activities that are suggested below can be used, with slight modification, for practicing most of the contextual signal strategies.

☐ Provide a modified cloze passage. Instead of deleting every "*nth*" word, selectively delete one or two words from the paragraph. For each deletion give the pupils three or four possible choices that are grammatically correct. By examining the contextual signals, the pupils should be able to select a response that is meaningful. Afterwards, allow the pupils to discuss the reasons for their choices. For example,

> **A cotton gin cleans the seeds from the cotton lint. Lint is the part of the cotton that is made into thread, then woven into cloth. Cleaning the cotton with a gin is called _____ .**
>
> linting   ginning   clothing

☐ Provide an opportunity for the pupils to construct their own sentences or paragraphs that reveal the meaning of an unknown word. Each pupil is given a card on which is written an unfamiliar word. The pupils are to use a particular contextual signal in writing their sentence or paragraph. Afterwards, the pupils' sentences and paragraphs are distributed among the other pupils, who must indicate the meaning of the unfamiliar word. For example, the pupils would be given cards similar to those below.

escapade:	a reckless or daring adventure
signal:	restatement using <u>or</u>

character:	someone in a story or play
signal:	example

☐ Play a variation of the game "Twenty Questions." Select a word which is unfamiliar to the pupils. They may ask a total of twenty questions about the word: the first ten dealing with how the word can be used in a sentence, the other ten dealing with the meaning of the word. For example, the pupils can establish the function of the word through such questions as: Can it do something? Does it describe or tell what kind of thing something is? Can it be moved around in a sentence without changing the meaning of the sentence? Then, the pupils can focus on the meaning of the word once its function is known. The aim, unlike the original game, is not necessarily to guess the stimulus word. The purpose of the game is to arrive at the function of the word and a possible meaning of that word.

STRATEGIES FOR USING GRAPHO-PHONOLOGICAL INFORMATION

One aspect of reading instruction which is often misconceived is that set of word recognition strategies dealing with grapho-phonological signals. In most traditional approaches to word recognition three categories of subskills are identified: phonics, structural analysis, and sight vocabulary. Under phonics are the sound/letter relationships and the various rules for translating the printed symbol into a speech symbol. Under structural analysis are the various rules for syllabication and the use of "root" words and affixes. Under sight vocabulary comes any word that cannot be translated through the use of phonic or structural analysis rules or information. A "basic" sight vocabulary usually refers to the function words of our language which do not have a direct referent, such as *of, from, there*.

The traditional interpretation of reading assumes that reading progresses from a "decoding" of the word to the recognition of that word to the creation of sentences through the reading of all the words together. As stated previously, the psycholinguistic interpretation of the reading process has suggested how sentences, instead of being the sum of the words they contain, are rather a major determiner of the words within their boundaries. A reader, therefore, can only "recognize" the constituent words when the meaning of an entire statement is known.

This is not to say, however, that grapho-phonological information is

not useful. It is, providing one has a clear understanding of its importance. The main purpose for learning about grapho-phonological information is that it is a help in turning ideas that are unrecognized in graphic form into sound in order to determine if the ideas are recognized aurally (Durkin, 1974). It is quite possible that certain words are familiar when they are heard—that is, they may be only within a person's listening vocabulary. By translating the visual form into a sound form, the pupils might recognize the word. If the word is not within a reader's speaking or listening vocabularies, no amount of "decoding" is going to be of benefit to the reader. In order to reconstruct the author's intended message, the reader, then, must rely upon the contextual reading strategies discussed previously.

A word spoken may be recognized while the same word written may not

Clarification of Misunderstandings about Grapho-phonological Information

Of the three traditional word recognition categories, two, phonics and structural analysis, are of questionable value as they are usually taught. Any examination of instructional materials will reveal that more pages are devoted to phonics than to understanding. This seems a strange phenomenon since often the meaning of a sentence determines its sound representation!

Phonics instruction developed as an attempt to use the characteristics of our alphabetic writing system. Alphabetic writing developed not for the convenience of the reader but for that of the writer (Smith, 1972). Normal reading does not involve decoding: we do not understand words on the basis of their sounds. Rather, we attend to the meaning of the spelling patterns of the words. If we did respond to the "sounds" of the words

Alphabetic writing aids the writer

rather than to their spellings, the following sentence (from Smith, 1972) would not provide the reader with a modicum of confusion:

> The none tolled hymn she had scene a pare of bear feat inn hour rheum.

In addition, the alphabetic system is only partially phonetic. We have within our written language two sets of relationships: (1) words that are related should look alike—*medicine, medication,* and (2) words that are not related should look different—*fare, fair.* Obviously, these deviations from the original purpose of alphabetic writing (that is, the opportunity to maintain a simple letter to sound relationship) have been to aid the reader. The complex sound-spelling system is the basis for an idealized phonics instruction program. There is little relation in much of this phonic instruction to the realities of how beginning readers recognize words. Many of the practice exercises found in reading materials require the pupil to identify phonic principles in already visually recognizable words. An example of this point is found in exercises that ask the pupil to mark the so-called long and short vowel sounds in words given on a list. Experienced teachers will verify that pupils experience most difficulty in correctly labeling the vowels in those words with which they are unfamiliar.

In a study that looked at the way in which young children develop the logic of orthography, it was found that beginning spellers go through certain patterns in the acquisition of English orthography (Henderson, 1974). In fact, it appears that the trial and error pattern of the subjects is similar to the trial and error pattern made by beginning speakers. The researcher suggested that instead of forcing pupils to acquire the grapho-phonological relationships in a set manner, teachers should allow them the opportunities to try and test what will work best for them. In fact, this point has been reiterated often throughout this book: Learning to read and write should be as easy for pupils to learn as it was for them to learn to listen and speak.

In many current reading instruction texts, much space is devoted to the teaching of the rules of syllabication. This instruction is based upon the misconception that language in any significant sense is written (Zuck, 1974). A careful examination of many of the rules of syllabication will reveal that they can only be applied after the pronunciation of the word is known. The reason for that is simple: syllabication was devised for the convenience of the typist and typesetter (Waugh and Howell, 1975). The syllable divisions found in most dictionaries indicate the standard units of

Syllabication was devised for the convenience of the typist and typesetter

word divisions. They are not, however, intended as guides to pronunciation. For many English words, the pronunciation division differs from that of the written division. For example, the words *double, strengthen, pleasing,* and *molding* are just a few of those for which dictionaries show a different syllable division for writing and for pronunciation. Dictionaries do divide words within the pronunciation guides only as a visual aid in sounding out the word—these divisions have nothing to do with the various rules found as supposed aids to decoding. Teachers, then, should understand the rationale for various dictionary subdivisions and use them for their intended purposes (Waugh and Howell, 1975).

In summary, the syllable division of the written word often differs from the syllable division of the spoken word. Because of erroneous instruction, and because syllable boundaries differ in speech and writing, pupils may: (1) apply syllable rules strictly and mispronounce many words, (2) pronounce words with additional syllables, (3) stress each syllable equally, thereby distorting the word, and (4) introduce additional sounds into the word (Zuck, 1974).

Effective Instruction in Grapho-phonological Information

In order to intelligently instruct pupils in the use of graphophonological information, teachers should clearly understand (1) the sound structure of English, (2) the relationship between the sound structure and the written form of English, and (3) the spelling structures of written English.

The teacher is referred to Chapter 2 of this text for a review of the sound structure of English. Teachers can assume that pupils of all ages are "familiar" with the sound structure when they come to school. (For a discussion of pupils who speak a divergent dialect, see Chapter 12.) What the pupils must become familiar with is the written representation of the sounds they know. Word recognition instruction should be directed toward teaching the written representation of the language and its relationship to the spoken language, and, more importantly, its relationship to the meaning of the message. The focus of word recognition instruction, then, is on the spelling structures of written English.

Pupils must become familiar with the written representation of the sounds they know

A pupil's ability to recognize "words" as such is a learned ability. One study (Mickish, 1974) showed that even after a full year of instruction many pupils were not able to indicate word boundaries in a written sentence. It also seems that this learning may develop in stages depending upon the pupils' cognitive development. One study (Cohen and Schwartz, 1974) revealed that word recognition stages may be identified through an analysis of a pupil's oral reading responses. It seems that pupils learn to recognize words in developing stages: global, analytic, and synthetic. The teaching of word recognition strategies, therefore, should consider the pupils' cognitive level of functioning.

The learning of these strategies should occur with the understanding that the purpose of the written code is to communicate the feeling and ideas of a writer (Downing, 1975). The pupil's first and subsequent experiences with the written language should stress its communicative function. The teaching and learning of the letter-to-sound relationships should always be within the genuine context of encoding or decoding the thoughts and feeling of the author.

There are two kinds of word recognition: immediate and mediated (Smith, 1972). Immediately recognized words are those the reader can translate automatically into both sound and meaning with no conscious attention to their graphic features. This is what has traditionally been considered as "sight vocabulary." Mediated word recognition occurs when the reader cannot immediately recognize a word. For mediated word recognition, the reader uses knowledge of syntactic relationships, meaningful word structures, and sound/spelling associations.

Immediate Word Recognition

Word recognition begins with a repertoire of immediately recognized words

Word recognition begins with acquisition of a large repertoire of immediately recognized words. These may seem like the traditional "sight vocabulary"; however, instead of learning to recognize large numbers of words in isolation, the pupils learn to recognize the printed form of objects and behaviors with which they are familiar. The relationship words (structure or function words) should be learned as part of sentences or phrases that clearly indicate the meaning they represent. For example, the classroom can be filled with labels containing whole sentences rather than just single words. Also, complete sentences containing function words can be used with pictures that clearly illustrate their meaning. These activities, while common in primary classrooms, do not need to be considered immature for the upper elementary grades. Teachers of grades five and six might find labeled illustrations helpful in clarifying the meanings of *before* as the pupils expand their understanding of its usage—*before* as an adverb, as a preposition, and as a conjunction. Other opportunities for developing immediate word recognition are classroom displays, bulletin boards, and readings containing many repetitions of the words. The pupils' immediate word recognition repertoire should be constantly expanding throughout their school years.

Mediated Word Recognition

Most of the exercises found in instructional materials deal with information and techniques for mediated word recognition. Much of this instruction (or practice, as is more often the case) attempts to develop in the pupils an ability to "decode," or translate into sound, any unrecognized word. The teacher should not overlook the fact that mediated word recognition strategies allow the pupils to recognize words that are within their oral vocabularies but not within their visual vocabularies. If the word is not within the pupils' oral vocabularies, the pupils must use the contextual strategies discussed previously. No amount of "sounding out" will aid the pupils in recognizing a word they do not already know by sound. Their only alternative is to attempt to approximate the word's meaning by using the surrounding context.

Mediated word recognition strategies help pupils recognize words in their oral vocabularies

In order for mediated word recognition strategies to be meaningful to the pupils, they should understand how the conventional spelling of words corresponds to meaning rather than some surface feature—that is, rather than to the word's pronunciation (Chomsky, 1973). Spellings are related to an underlying abstract level of meaning. The mature reader does not need first to pronounce a written word to recognize what it means. Rather, the reader seeks and recognizes the correspondence of the written symbol to some abstract lexical spelling of words. Lexical items are the meaning bearing items of language. Therefore, instruction in mediated word recognition strategies should direct the pupils' attention to features of the written word that, when combined with contextual signals, will allow them to identify the unfamiliar written word.

The acquisition of mediated word recognition strategies depends upon the understanding of two sets of information: (1) common letter clusters, and (2) morphological units.

Letter Clusters. The results of investigations into how pupils actually translate printed symbols into sound representations indicate that readers seem to use a "structures approach" (Glass and Burton, 1973). Pupils who were successful readers, when asked to read aloud, were not seen to use either rules of syllabication or rules of vowel control when they came upon an unfamiliar word. Rather, they seem to group sounds according to various letter clusters appearing in the word. Examination of the materials commonly used in the elementary grades revealed that 119 common letter

TABLE 9-1. Common Letter Clusters Embedded in Whole Words.

sat	bed	fall	fowl	her
sing	big	saw	bus	ha*ir*
set	lip	tel(l)	fil(l)	pal
sit	mud	de*ck*	bite	t*ied*
hot	lid	nice	mes(s)	few
him	den	tick	Tom	fire
top	hug	clif(f)	poke	hear
ran	hut	sink	tore	real
say	far	cob	t*ow*	tea
sad	hem	sod	cast	bee
jam	cup	fog	cane	care
sun	mate	tub	meat	dea*f*
tin	tent	cuf(f)	glas(s)	bo*at*
rap	test	rush	Bev	cue
s*and*	rake	table	kind	too
t*ack*	hide	sight	toss	o*ut*
sum	lock	mis(s)	team	p*ound*
tab	made	Ron	most	cure
bag	came	for	rol(l)	nat*ure*
told	cape	ful(l)	bone	fur
rash	face	fact	pale	fir
fish	sang	taf(f)y	save	ra*id*
	sank	cook	rove	*auto*
	song	nation	folly	bo*il*
			sage	

SOURCE: Glass, Gerald. 1973. *Teaching Decoding as Separate from Reading.* Garden City, N.Y.: Adelphi University Press.

clusters appeared in the materials (see Table 9-1) It is possible and natural for three- and four-letter clusters to be learned as easily as single-letter phonic units. These letter clusters should be learned through an examination of words within the pupils' listening vocabularies that are not immediately recognized. This system helps to alleviate the problem of teaching vowel sounds. A vowel has a "sound" as part of a cluster and not because of some rule (Glass, 1965).

The clusters are presented to the pupils as part of whole words. Through direct teaching, the pupils learn to recognize the cluster and associate it with a common phonological unit. For example, the letter cluster found in *mate* can be presented to pupils once they have within their speaking and listening vocabularies such words as *crate, date, fate, gate, plate, rate, state, skate,* and *slate.* As pupils learn other common clusters, they will be able to recognize such words as *inflate, debate, re-*

bate. This approach can easily be combined with a program in which the pupils learn to employ mediated writing strategies.

Morphological Units. A practical approach to word recognition uses word parts that have invariant meanings and which, when combined with the reader's topical experience and knowledge of contextual signals, produce enough meaning so that the reader can continue reading (Deighton, 1959). The difference between the learning of letter clusters and the learning of morphological units lies in the amount of information about the meaning of the word contained within the graphic unit. For example, the letter cluster contained in the word *fish,* while it may provide clues to the phonological representation of that word, does not reveal any indication as to what the word may mean. On the other hand, the morphological unit *equi-* found in the word *equinox* gives the reader some idea of "equal." Table 9-2 contains some of the morphological units that have invariant meanings. Pupils in grades four, five, and six should receive specific instruction in recognizing and understanding these units. Pupils in the primary grades may receive instruction in many of them as the need arises.

TABLE 9-2: Morphological Units with Invariant Meanings.

Units found at the beginning of words

anthro- (man)	hydro- (water)	phil(o)- (love of)
auto- (self)	iso- (equal)	phono- (sound)
biblio- (book)	lith- (stone)	photo- (light)
bio- (life)	micro- (small)	pneumo- (breath)
centro- (middle)	mono- (one)	poly- (many)
cosmo- (universe)	neuro- (nerve)	proto- (first)
heter(o)- (different)	omni- (everywhere)	pseudo- (false)
homo- (same)	pan- (all)	tele- (far)
	penta- (five)	uni- (one)

Self-explaining compounds (beginning and ends of words)

out	under	self	wise
over	up	way	

(Each of these has two clear meanings except *self,* which has only one.)

Common prefixes with invariant meanings

apo- (different from)	extra- (additional)	mal- (bad)
syn- (same)	circum- (around)	intra- (within)
mis- (not)	com- (with)	equi- (equal)
intro- (within)	non- (not)	
in- (in)	in- (not)	un- (not)

Noun suffixes meaning *agent* or *one who*

-eer	-ess	-grapher	-ier
-ster	-ist	-stress	-trix

Common noun suffixes with invariant meanings

-ana (collection)	-fer (bearing)	-meter (mount)
-archy (rule)	-fication (process of making)	-metry (measuring)
-ard (one who)	-gram (written)	-phobia (fear)
-aster (mimic)	-graph (written)	
-bility (able)	-ics (facts)	-scope (something for viewing)
-chrome (color)	-itis (illness)	
-cide (kill)	-latry (worship)	-ee (one who receives)

Common adjective suffixes with invariant meanings

-est (superlative)	-wards (direction)	-most (superlative)
-ferous (bearing)	-wise (way)	-like (like)
-fic (process)	-less (without)	-ous (full of)
-fold (times)	-able (can)	-ose (sugar)
-form (shape of)		-ful (full of)

In devising teaching lessons, teachers may find it necessary to identify the letter cluster or the morphological unit in words out of the context of a sentence. This may be done during the "identification" and "example" stage of the teaching lesson. The teacher, however, should be sure to develop within the "guided application" portion of the lesson an understanding of how the grapho-phonological information is combined with contextual information in recognizing unfamiliar words.

DICTIONARY USAGE STRATEGIES

Dictionaries are books that tell what words often mean; they are not books that tell what words ought to mean (Downing and Sceats, 1974). An individual turns to the dictionary because a word is encountered (1) whose meaning is not revealed through the context, (2) that is not within the reader's oral vocabulary, (3) whose precise meaning needs verification, or (4) whose pronunciation cannot be determined through mediated word recognition strategies. In such cases the reader finds a need to use a dictionary.

A dictionary helps clarify meaning

Dictionaries often may not be of any help to a pupil because

1. The demands for skill in using it are too great. Some dictionaries are complicated in their format and presentation of information. Pupils are required to possess skills for selecting information, but they may not know what to select.
2. The information may be presented in a manner that is inappropriate for the cognitive level of the pupils. More recent dictionaries are overcoming this failing through the use of more concrete examples and the elimination of definitions more complicated than the entry word (Downing and Sceats, 1974).

In order to use a dictionary successfully, a pupil needs to know certain things. The fundamental skills for using a dictionary include the following:

1. Locating a word. In order to locate an entry word pupils should understand how to use
   a. Alphabetical order,
   b. Guide words,
   c. An inflected or derived form of a word.
2. Deriving the pronunciation of a word. In order to pronounce an entry word, pupils should understand and be able to use
   a. The pronunciation key to identify consonant and vowel sounds and associate them with the dictionary symbols,
   b. The pronunciation guide for blending the consonants and vowels into spoken syllables,

c. Primary and secondary accent marks of the visual syllabic divisions.
3. Deriving the appropriate meaning of a word. In order to determine the meaning of an unfamiliar word in relation to the context in which it is encountered, pupils should understand and be able to use
   a. The basic dictionary definitions,
   b. Illustrations, diagrams, and example sentences or phrases,
   c. The appropriate meaning when an entry word has multiple entries or multiple meanings,
   d. Strategies for adapting the appropriate definition to the context of the word.

Some dictionaries currently being prepared for the elementary levels are being constructed to overcome the limitations stated previously. One way this is being done is by providing separate dictionaries of differing formats for different maturity levels. The illustrations on page 304 show two levels of dictionary entries as published by one company. In addition, supplementary pupil-guides or exercise booklets to dictionary use and practice can be obtained that provide instruction in the fundamental skills of dictionary usage. Figure 9-2 shows one such practice lesson.

An important adjunct to the dictionary is a thesaurus. A thesaurus is a book of synonyms, antonyms, and related words. Pupils can begin to use a thesaurus almost as soon as they learn to use a dictionary. What it helps to do is develop a sense of words. It can also help pupils realize that synonyms do not always mean the same things and that different synonyms may be more appropriate in one situation than in another. Just as dictionaries should be written for the cognitive and linguistic maturity of the pupils, so should thesauri. The illustration on page 305 is from a beginning thesaurus.

In order to use a thesaurus successfully, a pupil needs to understand certain things. Some of the fundamental skills (in addition to the basic dictionary skills) for using a thesaurus are:

1. Locating a word in the index. Since a thesaurus is used for finding related words, the pupils should first understand the principle of locating the word for which a synonym is desired and identifying the page on which that word and its synonyms are located.
2. Understanding the entries. In order to be able to select an appropriate synonym or antonym for a word, the pupils should understand the form of a thesaurus entry.

Many different activities can successfully lead to increased vocabularies

FIGURE 9-2: A Sample Dictionary Use Exercise

Guide words

Look at that page.

It is the same as page 183 of **My Second Picture Dictionary**.

All the entry words on page 183 come between **oh** and **onion**.
They are the guide words.

Look again at that page.

Is the entry word **once** there?
If it is, draw a circle around it.

Below are some more entry words.

Look for each one on that page.

If you find it there, draw a circle around it.

What if you don't find it there!
It is on another page, between two other guide words.

---

oil	**Oklahoma**	**one**
olive	**orange**	**old**

SOURCE: From *My Second Picture Dictionary Exercise Book* by William A. Jenkins and Andrew Schiller. Copyright 1975 by Scott, Foresman. Used by permission.

3. Understanding cross references. In order to successfully locate a desired word, the pupils should understand the various means of cross referencing to other related terms.

The above skills seem to form the basic requisites for effective dictionary and thesaurus use. Pupils of all ages and grade levels may acquire them, or be deficient in them. Once the teacher has determined the performance level of the pupils, instruction can be instituted to extend the pupils' abilities.

---

oh a word used to express surprise, joy, pain, and other feelings: *Oh, dear me! Oh! Joy!* **ohs.**

Ohio one of the fifty states of the United States. See page 362.

oil 1. a thick liquid from animal fat or vegetable fat or a liquid taken from the earth. 2. put oil on or in: *Did you oil the lawn mower?* **oils; oiled, oil ing.**

oh or **Oh** (ō), **1** word used before a person's name in beginning to speak: *Oh, Mary, look!* **2** word used to express surprise, joy, pain, and other feelings: *Oh, dear me! interjection.* Also spelled O.
O hi o (ō hī′ō), one of the north central states of the United States. *noun.* [*Ohio* got its name from the Ohio River. It may have come from an Iroquois Indian word meaning "fine" or "beautiful."]
oil (oil), **1** any of several kinds of thick, fatty or greasy liquids that are lighter than water, burn easily, and will not mix or dissolve in water but will dissolve in alcohol. Mineral oils, such as kerosene, are used for fuel; animal and vegetable oils, such as olive oil, are used in cooking and medicine. **2** petroleum. **3** put oil on or in: *oil the squeaky hinges of a door.* **4** paint made by grinding coloring matter in oil. 1,2,4 *noun,* 3 *verb.*

SOURCE: From *My Second Picture Dictionary* by William A. Jenkins and Andrew Schiller. Copyright 1975 by Scott, Foresman. Reprinted by permission.
From *Scott, Foresman Beginning Dictionary* by E.L. Thorndike and Clarence L. Barnhart. Copyright 1976 by Scott, Foresman. Reprinted by permission.

CARRY

bring
take
transport
fetch
tote
deliver

CARRY means hold something while you move. *The cat **carried** her kitten across the street. Then she dropped it in the grass. The movers **have carried** all the furniture outside. Will they leave it there?*

You **bring** a package if you carry it from some other place to where you are now.

You **take** a package if you carry it from where you are now to some other place. ***Bring** your camping equipment to my house tonight, and I'll **take** it to school for you tomorrow.*

Transport means move or carry something or someone from one place to another—a bus **transports** passengers; a truck **transports** objects. *Before railroads were built across the country, pioneers **transported** their furniture to the West by wagon trains.*

Fetch means go and get. A dog **fetches** a stick when you throw it. *Jack and Jill were supposed to **fetch** water from the well.*

Tote is used by people in some parts of the country to mean carry in your arms or on your shoulders or on your back. Students **tote** their books to school. *Sailors **tote** their clothes in duffel bags. They carry the bags on their shoulders.*

Deliver means bring or send to a person or place. *When can you **deliver** the groceries we ordered this morning? He had to get up early in the morning to **deliver** his papers.*

Look up SEND. You may find more good words for what you want to say.

ANTONYMS: leave, drop, let go

transport

CARVE   Look up CUT.

SOURCE: From *In Other Words*, II, by W. Greet, W. Jenkins and A. Schiller. Copyright 1969 by Scott, Foresman. Reprinted by permission.

Activities for Developing Dictionary Strategies

Once the pupils know the names and sequence of the twenty-six letters of the alphabet, activities such as the following can be implemented.

☐ Provide the pupils with four to six noncontiguous letters. Ask the pupils to arrange them in alphabetical order. For example, the pupils would be required to arrange these letters in order: *y, b, m, d, l, v.*

☐ Provide an interrupted sequence which the pupils are to complete. The sequence ran be of contiguous letters: a _____ c, d, _____ , f, or the sequence can contain noncontiguous letters with the pupils given items from which to select the correct response: d, _____ , g, l, _____ , o, (z, a, f, h, n).

☐ Provide a list of words that begin with the same letter. The pupils must then alphabetize by the second or third letters of the words.

☐ Provide sample guide words and a list of words all beginning with the same letter. The pupils should select those words from the list that could be found on the page represented by the guide words. For example, the words *bear* and *began* are indicated as guide words. Which of these words would be on that page in a dictionary: beat, beach, beg, below, bid, beaver, beef?

☐ Provide a list containing words with inflected or derived forms. The pupils are to indicate what the original form of the word is.
The first stage of this activity could have the pupils match the derived form to the original. As pupils become familiar with various spelling patterns and changes occurring with the addition of inflected endings, they should provide the original word without other assistance.

☐ Provide a list of words spelled phonetically according to a dictionary pronunciation key. Have the pupils match the phonetic spellings to the original spellings. As pupils gain proficiency in this task, provide only the phonetic spellings and have them pronounce the word.

☐ Provide dictionary definitions. Pupils are expected to read the definition silently, then explain to another pupil what the entry word means.

☐ Provide separate dictionary definitions and illustrations. The pupils are to read the definitions and locate the illustration that seems to match the definition.

☐ Provide the pupils with dictionary definitions and example sentences or phrases that help explain the word. The pupils are to create their own example phrases and sentences in explaining the word to another pupil.

☐ Provide the pupils with a sentence that contains a word with multiple meanings. The pupils are to refer to a dictionary and indicate the number of the definition that fits the meaning of the word as used in the stimulus sentence.

☐ Provide two sets of sentences, each containing the same multiple meaning word. If the word has three meanings, each set would contain three sentences. The pupils are to match the sentences from each set that reveals the same meaning for the word.

☐ Provide sentences in which the definition of the word does not "fit" without some adaption. The pupils are to rephrase the sentence so the definition fits. For example,

>**Michael grimaced with pain when the doctor gave him the injection.**
>
>**grimace: twisting of the face; ugly or funny smile.**

☐ Provide the pupils with a set of riddles. Each riddle is followed by a question containing two dictionary references. The pupils must solve the riddle after referring to each of the references. For example, provide the pupils with riddles and questions such as:

>**I am a long-armed ape that lives in the trees of Asia. Am I a chimpanzee or a gibbon?**
>
>**I am sitting on a large porch alongside my house. Am I sitting on a piazza or a plaza?**

RESOURCES FOR THE TEACHER

Many modern elementary school dictionaries are written for different cognitive and linguistic maturity levels. The following publisher provides dictionaries and thesauri for all elementary grades through the sixth. Each book begins with a series of lessons directed to the pupil for developing the fundamental skills for using the particular dictionary or thesaurus. Each book also has an accompanying pupil exercise book.
Scott Foresman and Company. Glenview, Illinois.
    My Pictionary (1975)—for kindergartners and beginning first grades
    My First Picture Dictionary (1975)—for first graders
    My Second Picture Dictionary (1975)—for second graders
    The Thorndike-Barnhart Beginning Dictionary (1974)
    The Thorndike-Barnhart Intermediate Dictionary (1974)

In Other Words: A Beginning Thesaurus (1968)
In Other Words: A Junior Thesaurus (1969)

The following is a set of multi-leveled booklets intended for use at the intermediate and upper elementary grades. Pupils are asked to answer questions, complete statements, supply details, and form generalizations.

Spectrum of Skills: Vocabulary Development. 1973. New York: Macmillan Publishing Co.

The following series consist of multi-leveled sets of booklets providing exercises in a number of specific areas. Titles in each series that complement the strategies in this chapter are listed. These materials do not provide direct instruction, but they are useful as sources of materials for teaching and practice lessons.

Specific Skill Series. 1970. Baldwin, N.Y.: Barnell Loft, Ltd.
Supportive Reading Skills. 1975. Baldwin, N.Y.: Dexter & Westbrook, Ltd. Especially *Rhyme Time, Reading Homonyms, Learning to Alphabetize, Using Guide Words, Reading Homographs, Reading Heteronyms, Mastering Multiple Meanings, Recognizing Word Relationships, Word-O-Rama.*
Picto-cabulary Series. Baldwin, N.Y.: Barnell Loft, Ltd. (Booklets of various titles that present vocabulary within a particular theme.)

The following publishers provide various booklets and duplicating masters of word puzzles and games. Teachers should review the materials to determine their appropriateness for a particular pupil population.

The Continental Press, Inc. Elizabethtown, Pennsylvania, 17022.
Milliken Publishing Co., c/o AV Sales & Service, 166 Western Avenue, Albany, N.Y. 12203.
Scholastic Book Service, 904 Sylvan Avenue, Englewood Cliffs, N.J. 07632.

The following reference is an excellent source of word games for extending pupils' vocabulary and understanding of word usage. Activities are graded by difficulty.

Hurwitz, Abraham B., and Goddard, Arthur. 1969. *Games to Improve Your Child's English.* New York: Simon and Schuster.

There are a great many trade books that can be used to advantage for stimulating pupils' interest in words. The following is only a partial list of the many interesting and colorful books available.

Longman, Harold. 1968. *Would You Put Your Money in a Sand Bank?* (Fun with Words). Illustrated by Abner Graboff. Chicago: Rand McNally.

Rothman, Joel. 1974. *The Antcyclopedia.* Illustrated by Shelley Freshman. New York: Phinmarc Books Inc.

Hanson, Joan. 1973. *Antonyms: Hot and Cold and Other Words That are Different as Night and Day.* Minneapolis, Minn.: Lerner Publications Co. (This book is part of a series of books dealing with homonyms, homographs, synonyms, and antonyms.)

Davidson, Jessica. 1972. *Is That Mother in the Bottle: Where Language Came From and Where It Is Going.* New York: Franklin Watts.

Applegate, Maurece. 1962. *First Book of Language and How to Use it.* New York: Franklin Watts.

Kraske, Robert. 1975. *Story of the Dictionary.* New York: Harcourt Brace Jovanovich.

Without some opportunity to put the words to use, pupils will forget them

Kohn, Bernice. 1974. *What a Funny Thing to Say!* New York: Dial Press.

Adelson, Leone. 1972. *Dandolions Don't Bite: The Story of Words.* New York: Pantheon Books.

Paulson, Russell Soveig. 1959. *A is For Apply and Why: The Story of Our Alphabet.* New York: Abingdon Press.

White, Mary Sue. 1961. *Word Twins.* New York: Abingdon Press.

Teachers may want to refer to the following articles, which are the source of the idea for the development of an "action packed" vocabulary discussed in this chapter.

Toothaker, Roy. 1974. "Developing an Action-Packed Vocabulary." *Elementary English* 51: 861–97.

Fraizer, Alexander. 1970. "Developing a Vocabulary of the Senses." *Elementary English* 47: 176–84.

DISCUSSION QUESTIONS AND ACTIVITIES

1. To what kinds of word recognition instruction is Kenneth Goodman (1972) referring when he says:

> Schools may be teaching kids not to comprehend. They may be teaching them to match oral language with written language, which is very different from comprehending.

Examine some commercial reading instructional materials and determine to what extent Goodman's statement applies to each.

2. Observe a group of primary grade pupils engaged in an activity. Through either note taking or recording, obtain samples of the variety of words the pupils use. From the sample, select those that have multiple meanings. At another time, question the pupils to determine whether they understand all the meanings the words may have.

    Repeat the above activity using the pupils' instructional materials as the source of the words.

3. Examine the various reading materials with which the pupils in a particular grade will have contact for the authors' use of contextual signals to

unfamiliar vocabulary and concepts. How often are difficult or abstract concepts introduced without contextual aids to their meaning? Collect samples of good use of context in revealing the meaning of a word that might be unfamiliar to the pupils in that grade.

4. Examine various dictionaries for use at the elementary grades, paying close attention to the vocabulary used to explain the entry words. How many of the explanations seem confusing because they use abstract language? How many of the explanations require the pupils to refer to other possible unfamiliar words in order to understand the meaning of the entry word?

5. Prepare a short talk that might be given at a parent association meeting about the parents' role in developing a child's vocabulary. What suggestions would you make, assuming that the audience contains parents of varying degrees of educational background?

6. Plan a bulletin board display for motivating pupils at a particular grade level to an interest in the etymology of words.

7. Develop a series of informal tests to determine pupils' performance in the following areas:

   a. The understanding and use of contextual signals to meaning.
   b. The use of grapho-phonological information to pronounce unfamiliar written words.
   c. Locating a word in the dictionary.

FURTHER READINGS

The following articles will provide the teacher with additional information about the structure and function of written English.

Hodges, Richard E. 1972. "Theoretical Frameworks of English Orthography." *Elementary English* 49: 1069–1105.

Groff, Patrick. 1973. "Fifteen Flaws of Phonics." *Elementary English* 50: 35–40.

Goodman, Kenneth S. 1972. "Orthography in a Theory of Reading Instruction." *Elementary English* 49: 1254–61.

The following texts, which have been cited in previous "Further Readings" sections, contain chapters dealing with the lack of effectiveness of traditional phonics instruction.

 Smith, Frank, 1973. *Psycholinguistics and Reading.* New York: Holt Rinehart and Winston.

 Smith, Frank. 1971. *Understanding Reading.* New York: Holt Rinehart and Winston.

The following is a useful reference for additional techniques for developing and extending pupils' vocabulary.

 Dale, Edgar, and O'Rourke, Joseph. 1971. *Techniques of Teaching Vocabulary.* Chicago: Field Educational Publications, Inc.

References

Aulls, Mark W. 1970. "Context in Reading: How It May Be Depicted." *Journal of Reading Behavior* 3: 61–73.

Brewer, A. C., Garland, Nell, and Notkin, Jerome J. 1972. *Elementary Science, Learning by Investigating.* Chicago: Rand McNally.

Bruland, Richard A. 1974. "Learnin' Words: Evaluating Vocabulary Development Efforts." *Journal of Reading* 18: 212–14.

Burns, Paul C. and Broman, Betty L. 1975. *The Language Arts in Childhood Education,* 3rd Edition. Chicago: Rand McNally.

Burns, Paul C. and Schell, Leo M. 1975. "Instructional Strategies for Teaching Usage of Context Clues." *Reading World* 15: 89–96.

Chomsky Carol. 1973. "Reading, Writing, and Phonology." In Frank Smith, *Psycholinguistics and Reading.* New York: Holt Rinehart and Winston.

Cohen, Alice Sheff and Schwartz, Elaine. 1975. "Interpreting Errors in Word Recognition." *The Reading Teacher* 28: 534–37.

Crist, Barbara I. 1975. "One Capsule a Week—A Painless Remedy for Vocabulary Ills." *Journal of Reading* 19: 147–49.

Deighton, Lee C. 1959. *Vocabulary Development in the Classroom.* New York: Bureau of Publications, Teachers College, Columbia University.

Donlan, Dan. 1975. "Teaching Words Through Sense Impression." *Language Arts* 52: 1090–93.

Downing, John. 1975. "What Is Decoding?" *The Reading Teacher* 29: 142–44.

Downing, John and Sceats, John. 1974. "Should School Dictionaries Be Banned?" *Elementary English* 51: 601–3.

Durkin, Dolores. 1974. "Phonics: Instruction That Needs to be Improved." *The Reading Teacher* 28: 152-56.

Fay, Leo, Ross, Roman Royal, and LaPray, Margaret. 1974. *Young America Basic Reading Program.* Produced by Lyons & Carnahan. Chicago: Rand McNally.

Foerster, Leona. 1974. "Idiomagic!" *Elementary English* 51: 125-27.

Glass, Gerald. 1965. "The Teaching of Word Analysis Through Perceptual Conditioning." In John Figurel, ed. *Reading and Inquiry.* Newark, Del.: International Reading Association.

Glass, Gerald G. and Burton, Elizabeth H. 1973. "How Do They Decode? Verbalizations and Observed Behaviors of Successful Decoders." *Education* 94: 58-64.

Goodman, Kenneth S. 1972. "Orthography in a Theory of Reading Instruction." *Elementary English* 49: 1254-61.

Henderson, Edmund H. 1974. "Correct Spelling—An Inquiry." *The Reading Teacher* 28: 176-79.

Manzo, Anthony V. and Sherk, J. K. 1971. "Some Generalizations and Strategies for Guiding Vocabulary Learning." *Journal of Reading Behavior* 4: 78-89.

Mickish, Virginia. 1974. "Children's Perceptions of Written Word Boundaries." *Journal of Reading Behavior* 6: 19-21.

Smith, Frank. 1972. "Phonology and Orthography: Reading and Writing." *Elementary English* 49: 1075-88.

Toothaker, Roy. 1974. "Developing an Action-Packed Vocabulary." *Elementary English* 51: 861-97.

Waugh, R. P. and Howell, K. W. 1975. "Teaching Modern Syllabication." *The Reading Teacher* 29: 20-25.

Williamson, Leon E. 1974. "Teach Concepts, Not Words." Paper read at the Annual Meeting of the Western College Reading Association, Oakland, California. ERIC No. ED 092 925.

Zuck, L. V. 1974. "Some Questions About the Teaching of Syllabication Rules." *The Reading Teacher* 27: 583-88.

10
Developing Strategies for Content Area Reading

Focus Questions:

1. What are the reading demands of content area textbooks?
2. What writing patterns, vocabulary, and graphic displays are commonly found in content area texts?
3. How can reading be guided in the content areas?
4. What strategies are needed for locating and using information in reference materials?
5. What strategies are needed for reading newspapers?
6. What strategies are needed for organizing information?

To some degree, a controversy exists among content area specialists in regard to the place of textbooks in content area instruction and learning. The intent here is not to become involved in the controversy. Since, however, there are a great number of content area textbooks currently in use in the elementary schools, teachers should have an understanding of how they may be used effectively. If school personnel choose to use a social studies, science, or mathematics textbook, or series of texts, then the teacher should understand the typical reading demands imposed by those textbooks.

Textbooks can be an important part of classroom instruction. Too often, textbooks are blamed for inadequacies that in reality result from their misuse by some teachers. In classroom instruction, textbooks can be used effectively to provide

1. An introduction or overview to a topic.
2. New terms or concepts.
3. Descriptions of events or processes.

Teachers should understand the reading demands of textbooks

4. Initial background or common experiences.
5. Specific facts.
6. The substantiation of an idea or opinion.
7. A source for instruction in the study skills and in the reading of graphic materials.
8. The summary of a topic (Michaelis, 1972).

Many authorities in the areas of social studies, science, and mathematics instruction now emphasize a "process" approach to the teaching and learning of concepts, facts, and generalizations. What they call the "process" approach has been termed in this book the problem solving approach. The goal of both is to involve the pupils in experiences that promote the development of language abilities so pupils can communicate their ideas. The "process" in content area instruction differs little from the creative problem solving activities suggested in Chapter 6 (pages 150–167).

In order to help pupils to read content area texts, teachers should know the specialized patterns used in writing and organizing such material (Smith, 1964a). The following discussion synthesizes the findings of investigators who have analyzed the questions, directions, explanations, and the various types of exercises used in content area texts. It is through the structures and patterns of those components that the content area specialist indicates how the pupils are expected to think and work in the particular field (Smith, 1964a).

THE STRUCTURE OF CONTENT AREA MATERIALS

Each content area has its vocabulary and paragraph patterns

Content area materials contain many of the same sentence and paragraph patterns discussed in Chapter 8. What makes content area reading different from direct narrative is that certain patterns show up more often in content area texts. Also, the vocabulary load of content area materials is generally greater than that found in narration. The vocabulary load of content area texts may produce reading difficulties because of the large number of unfamiliar technical terms, the unusual meanings given to some "familiar" terms, and the large number of different concepts found within the same paragraph. Each content area, however, has its particular recurring patterns of vocabulary and paragraphs, and each pattern can be found in combination with other patterns.

The patterns to be described are most prevalent in texts that are intended for use at grades three to six. Usually, texts written for use at the primary grade levels have a style quite similar to that found in the basal reading instructional materials for that level. Teachers should be aware, however, that specialized information in a narrative style can also present problems for readers. Teachers should examine the texts they use so they may determine which patterns appear and may cause reading difficulties for their pupils.

WRITING PATTERNS IN CONTENT AREA TEXTS

The writing found in content area textbooks is examined in three ways: (1) vocabulary, (2) paragraph structures, and (3) graphics. Vocabulary includes the use of technical or specialized terms and the concepts they represent, as well as the use of familiar terms and concepts. The paragraph structures basically are those discussed in Chapter 8 with particular attention to how patterns are used in content areas. Each content area has illustrative materials necessitating certain reading strategies.

Vocabulary

Each content area has a highly specialized or technical vocabulary. For example, the following chart has representative vocabulary from three content areas. The terms and the concepts they represent are generally unique to each individual area.

Each content area has a specialized vocabulary

Specialized Vocabulary

Social Studies	Science	Mathematics
coastal	cochlea	parallelogram
mountain	bacteria	numerator
cases	spore	numeral
government	glucose	improper fraction
Tropic of Cancer	cytoplasm	congruent figures
adobe	molecules	divisor
latitude	particle	perpendicular

During instruction, concepts and their labels are to be acquired by the pupils. In mathematics and science the specialized terms often are composed of morphological units that can facilitate the learning of related terms. For example, psychrometer, thermometer, barometer, and chronometer can all be learned as instruments of measurement. However, scientific and mathematical writing can be difficult to read because of the large number of special symbols and abbreviations that are used.

Common Mathematical and Scientific Symbols and Abbreviations

− (minus)	9° (degrees)	kph (kilometers per hour)
+ (plus)	< (less than)	C (Celsius scale)
= (equals)	> (more than)	∡ (angle)
× (times)	÷ (divided by)	+ (positive charge)
cm (centimeter)	l (liter)	− (negative charge)
g (gram)	mm (millimeter)	→ (direction of a force)

Mathematics reading may be difficult because much of the writing contains a mixture of words, numerals, letters, symbols, and geometric shapes. The reader is required to constantly shift from one "vocabulary" to another. In the two mathematics passages in Figure 10-1, typical of those pupils meet in texts, what demands are placed upon the reader by the combined use of standard vocabulary and mathematics vocabulary?

FIGURE 10-1: Typical Passages from a Mathematics Text
___

Whole numbers are either even or odd.

A whole number times 2 is an even number.
An even number plus 1 is an odd number.

$$\text{whole number} \xrightarrow{\times 2} \text{even number} \xrightarrow{+1} \text{odd number}$$

A *polygon* is made of line segments. It has sides and angles. A polygon is a simple closed curve.

Polygon $ABCDE$ has five sides: $\overrightarrow{AB}$, $\overrightarrow{BC}$, $\overrightarrow{CD}$, $\overrightarrow{DE}$, and $\overrightarrow{EA}$.

Polygon $ABCDE$ has five angles: $\angle ABC$, $\angle BCD$, $\angle CDE$, $\angle DEA$, and $\angle EAB$.

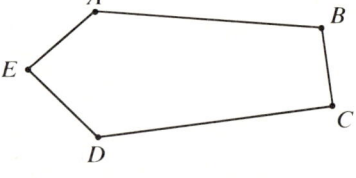

SOURCE: *SchoolMath/4* by Klaas Kramer et al. Produced by Lyons and Carnahan. Copyright 1974 by Rand McNally.

Whenever pupils encounter unfamiliar terms and concepts, they (and their teachers) become aware of the problem almost immediately. But the technical and scientific vocabulary presents only one type of problem. Familiar terms may be used that have specialized meanings. Notice how the sentences below contain a generally familiar term that is used in a special manner.

> Look at the vertical section of finely ground material in the *fault* between the layers of rock.

> What *forces* made the boat move?

In addition, authors may use terms that have different meanings in the various content areas. The sentences below illustrate this point.

> During the long months in prison, Austin's ideas began to *change.*

> If I give the salesperson $10, how much *change* would I get back?

> The force caused a *change* of state.

Other words that may mean different things in the various content areas are *operation, difference, division, property, product, revolution, planes,* and *positive.* Whenever such words are encountered, teachers should take care to insure that the pupils understand the meaning of the word within the context of the particular content area being read.

Another problem pupils may encounter in reading content materials is the use of figurative language. Social studies materials, for instance, contain many concepts stated figuratively. Some of these may be important to the topic, some may not. In the example below, from a text intended for use at the fifth grade level, figurative language is used freely. What kinds of problems may some pupils experience in reading this paragraph?

> Eager to get rid of Louisiana, Napoleon offered it at a low price which Jefferson delightedly accepted. In a single stroke, the United States expanded from the Mississippi to the Rocky Mountains. Though, at the time, many complained that most of the land seemed worthless and too dry to farm, later it would become the breadbasket of the nation. In making the Louisiana Purchase, Jefferson stretched the constitutional powers of the Presidency to the breaking point. The man who feared a strong central government helped to set a pattern for a long series of strong Presidents (Davis et al., 1971a).

Paragraph Structures

The writing patterns used in the content areas make certain common demands upon the reader (Smith, 1964a). Generally, the reader is required to: (1) select and evaluate information, (2) organize the information, (3) recall the information at the end of different time periods, (4) locate information, and (5) follow directions. Although these abilities are common to all reading, the reader's success can only be assessed after the act of reading. For example, if pupils do not know what information to select nor how to use the techniques and patterns of organizing the information, they are judged as ineffective readers. By teaching pupils to recognize and use the structures and patterns in content materials, teachers will be preparing pupils to meet the demands imposed by textbook reading.

Pupils need to recognize patterns in order to read textbooks

In Chapter 8, six paragraph patterns were discussed: enumeration, generalization, comparison/contrast, sequence, cause/result, and question/answer. These patterns not only appear in general narrative and informational writing, they also appear extensively in textbooks. For a review of the discussion of these patterns, refer to Chapter 8, pages 243 to 247. Additional information about the above patterns that is relevant to the structure of content area texts is presented here.

When used in social studies materials, the sequence pattern may be used to present events in a chronological order. The reader is required to understand the particulars of large periods in a specific order. Or, the reader has to fix an important date within a large unit. In addition to the time word signals, the reader needs to recognize the sequence of dates. In science writing, the sequence pattern may provide an explanation of a technical process, or provide detailed instructions for a demonstration (commonly called "experiments" in many texts). Intermixed with the sequence may be questions requiring pupil answers based upon an observation of the demonstration. While in the course of reading a sequence pattern in science, pupils may be expected to follow explicit directions, make an observation of events, provide some explanation of the results, and draw some conclusions.

In the comparison and contrast pattern, an idea, event, person, or process is compared to and/or contrasted with another. In some comparisons one whole idea is presented through an explanation of a closely related, more familiar idea. Or, the comparison is made by detailing the specifics of the idea and comparing them one by one. In another type of comparison, two ideas are given, but the comparison is implied. The reader is left with the task of matching the similar and dissimilar aspects of the two ideas.

In social studies writing, the cause/result pattern may consist of a chain of causes and results, especially when the discussion concerns large periods of history.

In addition to these, content area writing may contain other patterns (Smith, 1964a and 1964b; Robinson, 1975).

What we shall call *topic development* is not a simple paragraph pattern. A particular idea (topic) is developed over a number of paragraphs. This pattern can be recognized by a title or heading followed by an introductory sentence stating the topic. The complete development of the idea may extend over two or more paragraphs. The paragraphs within the topic development may contain a variety of other patterns. The passage below, from a text intended for use at the third grade, shows how the development of the topic extends over a number of paragraphs. As is the case with many topic developments, the section contains a heading and a general statement about the topic that serves to introduce it.

Use of Microscopes

The microscope is an important tool. Scientists have discovered many things that they could not have learned without it.

Louis Pasteur was the first scientist to use a microscope to learn about bacteria. He found that bacteria cause milk to sour and food to spoil. They make some materials decay.

Bacteria may also cause plant and animal diseases. Since Pasteur's time, other scientists have used microscopes to find ways to fight diseases.

The microscope has helped us learn about our bodies. We have learned what blood is made of and what it needs to be healthy. We know how muscles and bones work, and why we can see, smell, and hear. When we are sick, the doctor can use a microscope to find out what is wrong.

Microscopes help police. Sometimes the police find bits of hair and skin where there has been a crime. The bits are studied with a microscope. Then the police can tell if they match the hair or skin of someone suspected of a crime.

When hit-and-run accidents happen, bits of paint or glass may be left. These bits can be matched to the car that they came from.

Microscopes can be used to tell how strong a piece of metal is. They will show any tiny cracks. This is important in making airplanes. The metal must be so strong that it will not break when the airplanes are moving very fast.

Having a microscope of your own can be very interesting. But you can be disappointed by some that are sold as toys. Most advertisements tell about high-magnifying power. How well you can see is more important than high power.

If you want to buy a microscope, have the clerk show you how to use it. Look at salt or sugar. You have already seen these things and know how they should look. Then you can tell whether the microscope is a good one for you (Brewer et al., 1972).

A pattern that at first appearance may seem to be an enumeration pattern is *classification*. It is commonly found in science textbooks. Although the classification pattern may list various subclassifications, the emphasis is on the conceptual subdivisions of information rather than on itemization of information. Like other patterns, the classification pattern may span a number of paragraphs.

There are many objects around the robin. Some of these are clouds, rocks, and plants. There may be other objects you cannot see.

> Many events may be happening around the robin. The sun may be shining, the wind may be blowing, or it may be raining.
> Different places may have different conditions. Heat, dryness, sunlight, and sandy soil are conditions.
> All of the things around the robin are called its environment. The objects, the events, and the conditons are all part of the environment (Brewer et al., 1972).

Another pattern found in elementary content area texts is *problem/solution*. In order to understand the entire idea of the author, the reader must understand both the problem and its solution.

> Although there are many goods and services to choose from today, some families do not have enough money to buy some of the things they would like to have. Many families want color television sets, but it takes a long time for some people to save enough money to buy one. If they do not want to wait for the set until they save enough money, there is a way they can get it with only a small down payment. It is called installment buying, and it is a form of credit. The family can buy the set with a down payment if they promise to pay a certain amount each month. The set will cost more if it is bought this way, for the store will charge a fee for credit. But the family could be using the set while it is being paid for (Davis et al., 1971b).

Lastly, a pattern that is not considered a paragraph pattern but does represent a style of writing found in social studies and its related materials is that of *propaganda*. At all levels of school, pupils should become familiar with the general techniques of propaganda and develop an ability to realize an author's intent. The techniques of propaganda include glad words or glittering generalities, unpleasant words, testimonials, plain folks implications, and stacking the cards. While it is rare to find textbook authors using these techniques, at times authors will allow their beliefs or feelings about a topic to sway their presentation. For example, in the discussion of desert tribes, the expression "have never even learned to store water" seems to have a connotation that the people of the tribe are incapable of learning. Also, the use of exclamation marks to indicate surprise or emphasis, or plain folks implications and glittering generalities, may have connotations of sarcasm or condescension. Finally, some ideas may be presented broadly and loosely, resulting in inaccurate statements. To offset its use, pupils at all levels should be made aware of both overt and covert propaganda in textbooks and related content area materials.

FIGURE 10-2: Typical Textbook Graphic Displays

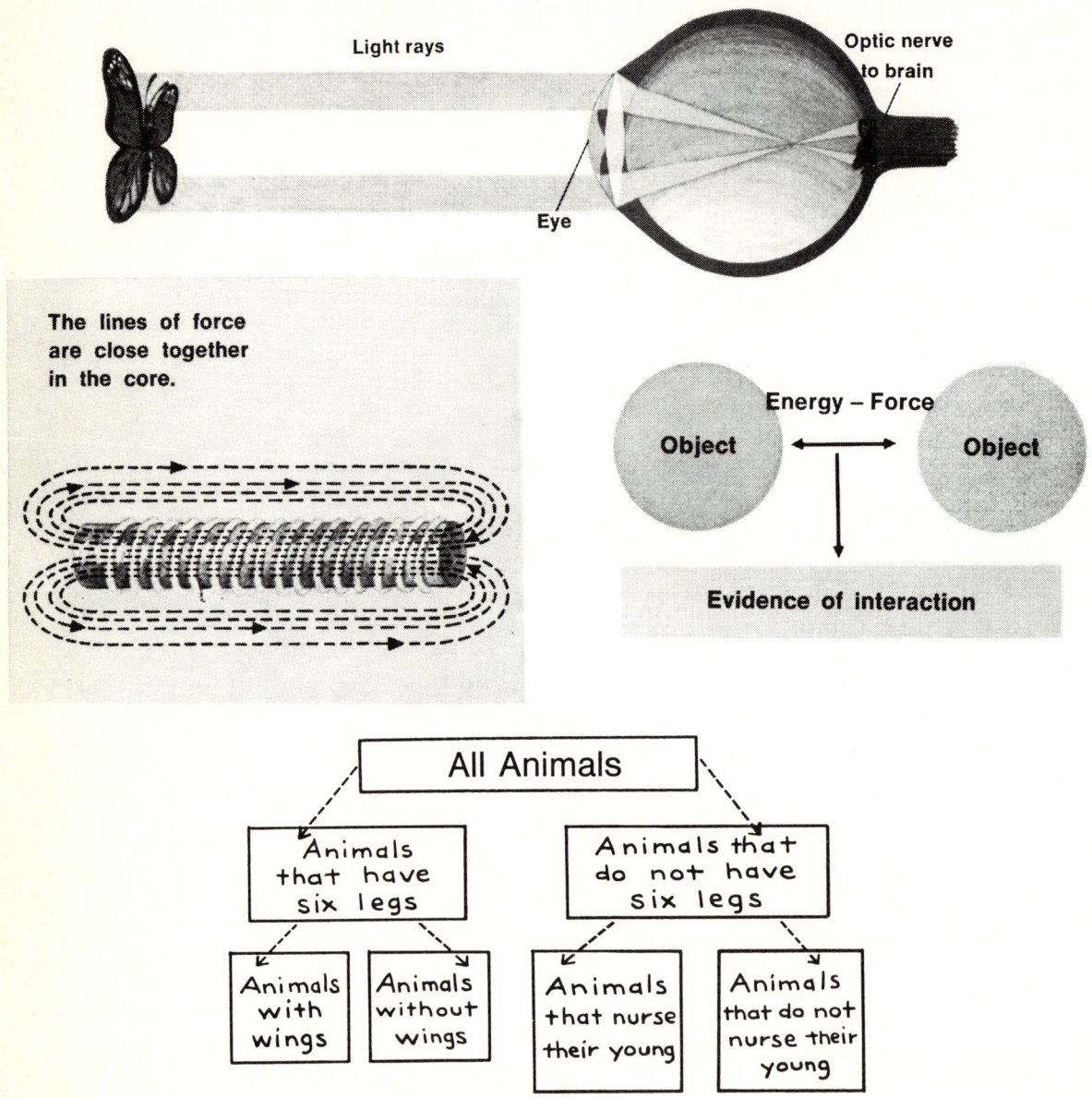

SOURCE: *Elementary Science: Learning By Investigating*, Book 4, by A.C. Brewer, Neil Garland, and Jerome J. Notkin. Copyright 1972 by Rand McNally.

Graphics

Whenever graphic material appears in content area textbooks, teachers should not assume that pupils fully understand the related concept or process just because it is accompanied by an illustration. Care should be taken to insure that pupils are able to interpret a particular graphic display and alternately read verbal and graphic information.

Pupils should be able to interpret graphic displays

In content area textbooks, various kinds of graphic displays are used. Depending upon the nature of the concept and the item to be illustrated, the following types of graphic displays may be found in textbooks. (See Figure 10-2.)

1. *Photographs.* Science, social studies, and mathematic texts use photographs to support and help explain the textual material. The photographs may be in black-and-white or in color.
2. *Realistic illustrations.* Almost all texts make extensive use of drawings. These are realistic representations, in either black-and-white or color, of various objects. Some of the drawings may be used to directly support the textual materials. In such cases, the drawings may or may not have various parts of the drawings labeled. In addition, many content area texts contain illustrations that serve only as decoration. In these cases, the illustration may indirectly support the text by showing a related object or event.
3. *Representational illustrations.* At times, texts may contain drawings in which real objects are recognizable; however, the drawing may be stylized in order to highlight various components of the object. Color is sometimes used to differentiate the components.
4. *Diagrammatic illustrations.* When an object or process is shown symbolically, various geometric shapes may be used to represent real objects or events. While diagrams are used in order to illustrate a process or a relationship, they may not show the entire structure of an object or its complete function. In such cases, the diagram forces the viewer's attention to a particular aspect of the process or relationship.
5. *Charts, graphs, and figures.* Some information is represented in a symbolic form that allows the reader to compare or contrast quantities. In such cases, graphs or figures allow the viewer to realize degrees or amounts of difference or similarity without having to process a great deal of numerical information.

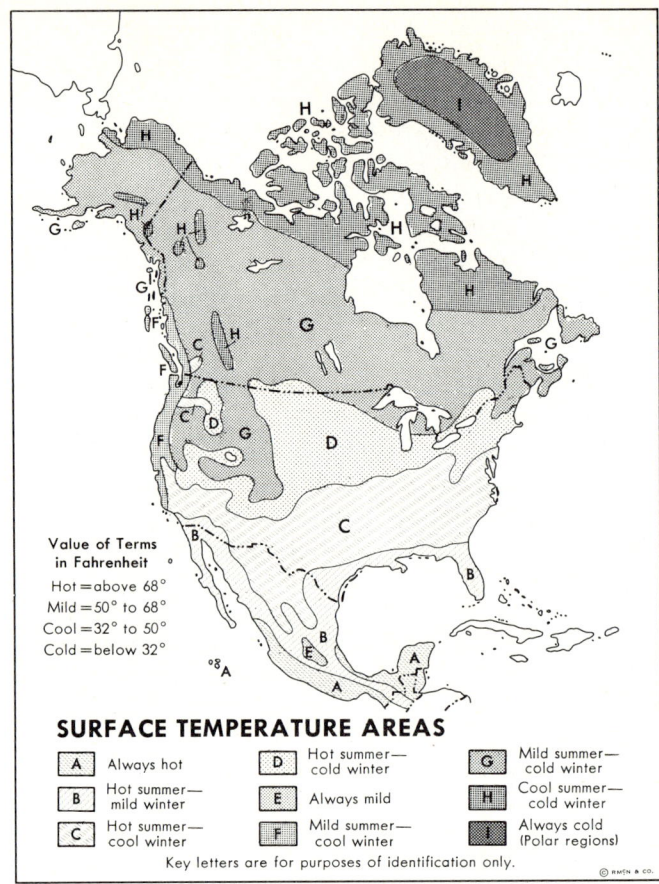

6. *Maps.* Maps are representations of geographical areas. In order to understand maps, the relationship between the physical world and the symbolic representation has to be realized. Maps may be: (a) political—showing governmental boundaries of nations, states, cities or towns, (b) physical—showing land forms and altitudes, (c) specialized—showing such information as weather patterns, population dispersion, industrial development or natural resources, or (d) a combination of any or all of the three.

The use of graphics in content area textbooks, however, does not always facilitate learning. When readers cannot cope with, or do not possess adequate strategies for, the demands of switching from reading verbal material to reading visuals, then they are unable to process the author's message. Some authors have referred to the reading of visuals within textual material as interrupted reading. However, since the visuals are often an integral part of the message, the constant shifting back and forth might be better described as *staccato* reading (Albert, 1971).

Pupils must be able to switch from verbal material to graphics

In order to help pupils learn to read graphic displays effectively, teachers should be aware of some confusion that can be caused by visuals.

Photographs and illustrations. The reading of pictures requires pupils to relate the information to what they already know. When the illustrations contain a great many details, the viewer must have a scheme for processing the information or else some irrelevant details might become distracting. Pictures are not real objects, only abstractions, so the viewer must realize that they show only a fraction of reality. Further, pictures cannot show something in its totality; pictures depict parts. Drawings and diagrams may oversimplify a continuous process by representing it in stages, thus leaving the viewer with a feeling that the process is not continuous. Nor is it uncommon for an illustration to depict the exception and not the rule.

Estimating size. Photographs, maps, diagrams, and illustrations may not always reveal the scale of objects. Also, the scale from illustration to illustration within the same text may not be consistent. Small objects may be shown in enlargements while large objects may be scaled down in order to be represented on the page of a book. Close-ups may reveal details that are not always vital to the understanding or recognition of an object. Finally, the perspective of objects may be distorted by the manner in which they are shown.

Color. Color can serve two purposes: functional or decorative. When color is functional, it distinguishes the various components of an object. When it is purely decorative, it may give the viewer a false impression of the object. In addition, some colors may get in the way of the message of the illustrator. Also, decorative color may direct the viewer to focus on unimportant details.

Movement. All illustrations are static. On the other hand, they are often used to represent movement. Lines and arrows may be used to indicate enlargement, energy release, simultaneous action, movement, and reactions. Since these indicators do not exist in the natural world, the viewer must superimpose them on reality whenever there is to be a transfer of information from the graphic display (Albert, 1971).

GUIDING READING IN THE CONTENT AREAS

The same distinctions made in Chapter 7 between guided reading and independent reading in narrative applies to the reading of content area materials. For the less proficient readers, the teacher should structure the reading activity so that they may more easily determine the meanings intended by the author.

To reiterate, the guided reading-thinking lessons consist of five strategies:

1. Examining information in order to determine what is or is not already known.
2. Hypothesizing about probable meanings based upon the information examined.
3. Finding proof of one's hypotheses by a reading of the text and an analysis of the accompanying graphs or illustrations.
4. Suspending judgment whenever information is not available for confirming or rejecting one's hypotheses.
5. Making decisions whenever the information is available to confirm or reject a hypothesis, or deciding to seek additional information elsewhere.

Teachers guide reading by asking questions that require predictions to be made

The teacher guides the reading by asking questions that require predictions to be made. For example, using the information contained in a selection entitled "New Forms of Transportation and Communication" (King et al., 1974), the teacher would ask for predictions about specific segments of the passage. The number of paragraphs that the pupils read is determined by the amount of information they are capable of processing. Since content area materials are often more demanding, pupils should not be expected to process the same number of sentences or paragraphs as they might be capable of with narrative material.

The following lesson illustrates how a guided reading-thinking lesson might be structured for the reading of a social studies text intended for use at the fifth grade.

Guided Reading-Thinking Lesson for "New Forms of Transportation and Communication" (King et al., 1974)

Concepts: 1. City growth calls for new forms of transportation.

2. Efficient transportation routes must be provided among cities as well as among cities and their suburbs.
3. As a country grows there is a need for improved communications systems.

Purpose: To provide the pupils with new terms and concepts and specific facts about the growth of transportation and communications systems in our country.

Guiding Questions:
1. Subtitle page and pictures, first subsection, "Links among cities." What ways do you know of for getting from one city to another? Why would we need more than one way to get things and people from one city to another?
2. Second subsection, "Links among suburbs and central cities." What questions did the author want you to answer while reading? Did you have an answer for them? What did you do when you couldn't answer the author's questions?
Were there any words you could not figure out from the passage? Was the word important to understanding the author's ideas? What did you do when you couldn't figure out a word? In what way might the transportation needs between a city and its suburbs be the same or different from transportation between cities?
3. Third subsection, "Linking the parts of cities." (Repeat questions about the author's use of questions and unfamiliar vocabulary.) In what ways might the transportation needs within a city be the same or different from the transportation needs between cities and suburbs?
4. Fourth subsection, "A network of communications." Why do we need more than one way to get information to other people? What would make us choose one means of communication over another for sending information?

The guided reading-thinking lesson is an opportunity to direct the pupils' efforts in applying their reading and thinking strategies. All through the lesson, teachers should be conscious of pupils' efforts to apply their sentence reading, paragraph reading, and word recognition strategies in reconstructing the author's ideas. The aim of a guided content reading-thinking lesson is the acquisition of information—that is, the concepts and facts related to the topic—so efforts should always be directed toward that end. The guided reading-thinking lesson is used whenever the pupils can-

The aim of a guided content reading-thinking lesson is the acquisition of information

not gain that information independently. As pupils gain greater proficiency in applying reading strategies, teachers can use the lesson for directing attention to the application of those strategies.

For example, embedded within the text of the sample lesson above are questions or directions for pupils to provide some information on their own. In the case of this lesson the questions require the pupils to already know something about the topic. Such questions as: "Why do you suppose that airports are usually built far out from the center of cities?" and "Why do you suppose subway trains are preferred to elevated trains?" may interrupt the reading and cause the direct flow of the author's main points to be lost. During the course of the lesson teachers should guide pupils around the questions that may interrupt their train of thought. After the entire lesson has been read, you should return to those questions for further discussion. It is quite possible that some pupils cannot create answers to them. In such instances you should determine whether or not the answering of these questions should be delayed until additional information has been acquired by the pupils.

Also, the teacher's guidance may be needed to clarify the referential expressions in this passage, which is quite typical of elementary school social studies textbooks. Depending upon the pupils' understanding of referential constructions, teachers should guide them in identifying the referents in statements such as:

"The picture on this page shows how this is done."

"What do you think this advantage is?"

"Name at least one disadvantage."

"They are called cable cars."

"The railroads call this piggyback service."

STRATEGIES FOR INDEPENDENT READING IN THE CONTENT AREAS

SQ3R is a system for independent reading in the content areas

Pupils need a system for independently reading textbooks in the content areas. One system that is popular is known by the acronym SQ3R (Sargent et al., 1970). The SQ3R process consists of five stages: survey, question, read, recite, and review. The technique may be beneficial for pupils in that

1. The pupils are led to an independent approach to reading and using textual materials in the content areas.
2. The pupils develop procedures for adapting their reading strategies to the reading of an expository style of writing.
3. The pupils develop strategies for integrating the reading of textual and graphic information.
4. The pupils extend their understanding of creative problem solving to the acquisition of the specific knowledge and generalizations in the content areas.

The SQ3R technique should be taught to all pupils. The format of the strategy teaching lesson in Chapter 8 can be modified for presenting the steps to the pupils. The technique can be introduced to pupils at any grade level. Although the procedures may be modified to meet the individual proficiencies of each pupil, the SQ3R plan, once learned, can serve pupils throughout their school years. It provides them with a format into which they can fit their ever-increasing reading strategies and skills.

The steps of the SQ3R plan are:

1. *Survey.* The purpose of the survey stage is to determine what kinds of knowledge or information the author expects the reader to understand. It is a "taking stock" of what one already knows about the topic as well as determining what one does not know. Through a survey of the reading material, one becomes aware of the reading demands that will be imposed by the material and what possible difficulties may be encountered in reading the materials.

Specifically, the survey stage consists of examining the heading and subheadings, looking for terms that are written in boldface or italics, examining the graphic displays for the kinds of information they portray, and looking for any signals to the organization of the textual material.

During the survey stage, the reader is to establish an idea about the topic and to determine the reading demands that may have to be met.

When pupils encounter unfamiliar terms, they and their teachers become aware of the problem almost immediately

2. *Question.* The purpose of the question stage is to set tentative hypotheses about the author's ideas. These hypotheses or predictions become the purposes for which the pupils will read the text. During the questioning stage, pupils should ask themselves what they already know about the topic and what is it the author wishes them to know after they have read it.

Specifically, the question stage consists of establishing questions that may be answered from reading the passage. One source is the list of questions posed by the author at the beginning or end of each subsection. Another source is the collection of subheadings of each section. For example, the subheadings of the passage "New Forms of Transportation and Communication" are:

New Forms of Transportation and Communication
    Links among cities.
    Links among suburbs and central cities.
    Linking the parts of cities.
    A network of communications.

From a survey, it could be determined that the new forms of transportation have been developed to provide connections between cities as well as between cities and their suburbs and within cities themselves. To form specific purposes for reading, pupils might pose questions such as:

What are the new forms of transportation?
What are the new forms of communication?
What are the ways cities are linked together?
What are the ways cities and suburbs are linked?
What are the ways the parts of the cities are linked?
What is a network of communication?

In addition, it could be predicted that the passage will contain information to answer questions such as:

Why are new forms of transportation and communication necessary?
When were the new forms of transportation and communication developed?
Are all cities connected in the same ways?

    The question and survey stages may be combined so that information from the photographs (a highway, a railroad loading, a subway train, and a television studio) is used to alter the questions or suggest different ones.
    Since textbooks usually contain the same format and structure throughout, the SQ3R procedure is facilitated through continued use of the same texts. Pupils should easily acquire the strategy of forming predictions about a selection since they will be able to anticipate the location of those "cues" to the author's message.
    3. *Read.* The purpose of the read stage is to locate the information suggested by the questions posed during the previous two stages. Specifically, pupils should know that they are reading during this stage for two general purposes: (1) to find the answers to the questions they created, and (2) to locate other important information that they did not predict

through specific questions. This latter aspect of the reading is important since their questions might not have covered all the author's main points. They now should distinguish between information contained within the passage that they predicted would be there and that which they did not predict.

Some authors use aspects of the survey and question stages in structuring their textual materials. The passage below provides the pupils with a preset question to focus their attention on some important ideas. However, it should be noticed that the last two paragraphs provide information that does not directly relate to the purpose setting question. Only through reading as creative problem solving will the pupils realize this.

> **How are forests of the Rockies important?**
> Many of the lower peaks and slopes of the Rockies are covered with trees. Ponderosa, pine, spruce, fir, larch, and cedar all grow well in the mountains.
> Wood from these trees is used for fuel and lumber. Wood is also used to make such products as paper, chemicals, and plastics.
> In addition to these uses of the trees themselves, the forests help to keep the soil of the slopes from eroding. Tree roots prevent wind and rain from moving the soil away. Leaves, twigs, and trees falling to the ground decay and help to make the soil rich.
> Much of the forest land in the Rockies is owned by our government. The government hires many men called foresters to see that the forests are used wisely. The foresters also help to prevent forest damage due to tree diseases and forest fires.
> Notice the small trees near the bottom of the picture. Government foresters gave a company permission to cut large trees that had been growing in this part of the forest. What do you think the foresters did after the trees were cut? Why was this a good idea? (King et al., 1974).

4. *Recite.* The purpose of the recite stage is to answer the questions posed during the survey and question stages. The recitation is actually the immediate recall of information from the portion of the passage just read. Some pupils will be able to read only one subsection at a time. Others may be able to read the entire section. In either case, the pupils receive immediate feedback about the success of their reading strategies. It is during the recite stage that decisions are made about what information the author intended to be remembered and what information was provided as supporting ideas or just for additional, "human interest" effect.

Specifically, the recite stage consists of taking each question and forming an answer to it. The answers may be given in an oral or a written form depending upon the purpose for the lesson. After all the questions for a section or subsection have been answered, the pupils should then identify other information given in the passage. If the information is deemed important to the topic, then a question should be formed for which this additional information is an answer. A discussion should ensue as to why, if the information seems to be important to the author's main idea, its occurrence was not predicted. The answer may be that some clue was missed or, possibly, no clue was provided.

It is during the recite stage that pupils demonstrate their ability to reconstruct the intended message of the author through a self-guided reading-thinking activity.

5. *Review.* The purpose of the review stage is to answer at a later time the questions formed during the survey and question stages. Since a purpose for studying a content area is to develop a store of information and concepts, remembering is a desirable characteristic of proficient students. However, understanding an author's message should not be considered synonymous with remembering; one's understanding of a topic does not insure recall of its ideas (Pauk, 1973). Therefore, some additional steps should be taken by pupils to insure the retention of learned information. The previous stage, recite, was concerned with the immediate remembering of information. The review stage is concerned with the long term retention of information. The most efficient time to institute this stage is within twenty-four hours of completing the recite stage, and then periodically thereafter.

Specifically, the review stage consists of taking each question created during the survey and question stages, together with those added during the recite stage, and attempting to answer them. At first, no referral is made to the text or to the answers generated during previous stages. Then the new answers are checked against previous answers or the text. This provides immediate feedback to the pupils about the amount of information that is remembered. Pupils realize for themselves what information may need additional effort to be retained. Or, they, together with their teachers, may wish to decide whether the information that was forgotten (and there is strong evidence that forgetting is a natural occurrence) is important and should be relearned.

If relearning is needed, there is some evidence that a mere rereading of the text will not result in remembering (Pauk, 1973). What may occur during rereading is the "seeing" of already known information—that is, the eye and mind see learned information and not any unlearned information. What is needed after a first reading may be a different approach to the same information.

The content area text should not be used as the singular source of learning. There are limitations to the effectiveness of texts as informational resources. The technique suggested here, the SQ3R procedure, may assist pupils in becoming proficient independent readers. Yet, because of factors that exist within the pupils, the reading materials, or the situations in which the reading acts are undertaken, the technique may not be successful at any particular time. Other learning and teaching procedures should then be sought.

ACTIVITIES FOR DEVELOPING CONTENT AREA READING STRATEGIES

The activities discussed in Chapter 7 for developing questioning strategies, in Chapter 8 for developing the use of sentence and paragraph reading strategies, and in Chapter 9 for developing general vocabularies, contextual signals, and dictionary usage should all be continued and extended for use in content area reading. Pupils should be given extensive opportunities to use their strategies independently in both narrative and expository reading materials. In addition to those activities, the teacher can employ any of the following.

Pupils should be given opportunity to use strategies independently

☐ Extend the use of the SQ3R procedure to the reading of word problems in mathematics (Maffei, 1973). The new procedure becomes an SQ4R procedure:

1. Survey. Skim the word problem and locate any unknown words. List them.
2. Question. Write a direct question of the problem.
3. Read. Read the problem and list all word facts in a logical order.
4. Reflect. Translate all the word facts into number facts.
5. Rewrite and solve. Write the word problem as a mathematics problem and solve.
6. Review. Reread the word problem, putting the answer into the correct statement.

☐ Provide an opportunity for the translation of diagrammatic information into standard English sentences. In the beginning phase of this activity, the pupils are to match a sentence to the appropriate diagram. As they become more proficient at interpreting visual displays, they should be asked to create their own sentences. For example, provide the pupils with an illustration and three sentences from which they are to select the one that matches the drawing according to the ideas being studied.

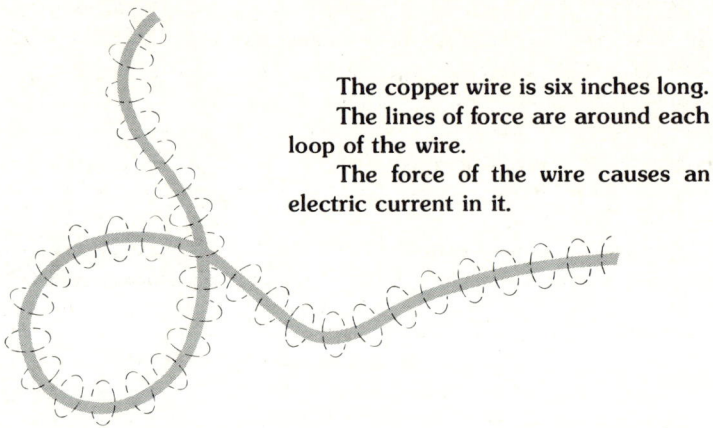

The copper wire is six inches long.
The lines of force are around each loop of the wire.
The force of the wire causes an electric current in it.

This activity can be extended for use with maps or incidental or decorative illustrations. Have the pupils select information from the passage that comes closest to explaining the illustration. Or, have pupils write a paragraph or explain to another pupil about the information given in the map or illustration.

☐ Provide opportunities for the information learned in the content areas to be used in other situations. Have the pupils create stories, plays, poems, radio broadcasts, or murals in which the information has to be used. The source of the information may be from any of the content areas. For example, after studying erosion in science, let the pupils act out situations in which they assume the roles of town engineers planning the construction of a new road in the hilly section of town. Or, after studying the customs and cultures of the inhabitants of South American countries, let them assume the role of a travel agent preparing a tour group for a visit.

☐ Provide an opportunity to relate the lives of interesting or important individuals to the study of a topic. Have the pupils read and discuss the biographies of individuals who either contributed to the topic or were greatly influenced by it. For example, during the study of plants, the lives of

Heinz, B. T. Washington, Burbank and others can be studied and their contributions explored.

☐ Provide an opportunity to explore the everyday application of content area concepts. For example, during a science unit on machines, pupils should have access to repair manuals and "how-to-fix-it" books. Or, during social studies units, to travel books.

☐ Provide "simulation strategies" that approximate what a reader does when reading independently (Herber and Nelson, 1975). This procedure provides direct instruction in reading with good understanding. It begins with the teacher reading a passage and asking questions about the author's major ideas. Then, the answers to the questions are used as a guide in making up a set of exercises:

1. The first set provides the pupils with a number of statements to which they are to react and the pages and paragraphs where information to support or refute those statements can be found. The pupils are to indicate whether they agree or disagree with the exercise statements.
2. The next provides the pupils with a set of statements similar to the preceding, but the teacher does not tell them where additional information may be found.
3. The third provides questions to be answered along with the location of pertinent information.
4. In this set of exercises questions are provided without any reference to pages or paragraphs.
5. When pupils are able to do the preceding exercise, they are given an assignment to read, and they are required to create their own questions and answers.
6. Finally, when pupils are proficient in reading the content area text at their level, they should be able to read a passage and come up with their own statements of concepts and ideas.

☐ Use children's literature as an aid in content area instruction. Trade books can be effectively used to make complex ideas clear, to illustrate many of the practical ideas of the content areas, to further encourage and stimulate expression in speaking and writing, and to foster the growth of vocabulary. There are many informational books dealing with the physical world, people and places, history, and mathematics that can be easily used to extend pupils' knowledge and understanding. Also, after acquiring the background through class exercises, the pupils will have the necessary prerequisites for undertaking the reading of many more books independently.

☐ Provide exercises that lead to the understanding of the relationship between standard English sentences and mathematical sentences. The findings of research on reading in mathematics underscores the importance of a particular language factor. That factor seems to be one of verbal reading ability (Aiken, 1972). The exercises should promote the understanding of the mathematical sentence as an English sentence through examples of mathematical structures that parallel English structures (Lacey and Weil, 1975). The first step is to establish that the mathematical sentence is read from left to right. Then basic symbol and word associations should be established:

"and"	is synonymous with "plus"
"is"	is synonymous with "equals"
$=$	is the equivalent of "is"; also, $=$ is the same as: "these are the same number of things"
$+$	means "and, increased by, plus"
$-$	means "minus, subtract, decreased by, diminished by"
$\neq$	means "is not equal to"
$>$	means "is greater than"
$<$	means "is less than"
$\times$	means "times, product, multiplied by"
$\div$	means "quotient, divided by, ratio"

Using these symbol and word associations, the following activities can be developed:

$$\text{seven and four is eleven}$$
$$7 \ + \ 4 \ = \ 11$$

(1) Read the English sentence and write as a mathematics sentence.
(2) Reverse (1)
(3) Establish that an addition mathematics sentence may be represented by many English sentences.

Seven added to four equals eleven.

Adding seven and four is eleven.

Follow this with sentences about subtraction, multiplication, and division. Compound sentences can be written after some other symbols are learned:

- $\vee$ means the conjunction "and"
- $\wedge$ means the disjunction "or"
- $\geq$ means "is greater than or equal to"
- $\leq$ means "is less than or equal to"
- $\not< $ means "is not less than"
- $\not> $ means "is not greater than"

Sample sentences that may be developed are:

Six plus ten is less than twenty, $\qquad$ $6 + 10 < 20$
and $\qquad\qquad\qquad\qquad\qquad\qquad\qquad\quad$ $\vee$
twelve plus ten is greater than four. $\qquad$ $12 + 10 > 4$

Nine minus one is not equal to two, $\qquad$ $9 - 1 \neq 2$
or $\qquad\qquad\qquad\qquad\qquad\qquad\qquad\qquad$ $\wedge$
nine plus two is greater than ten. $\qquad\;\;$ $9 + 2 > 10$

STRATEGIES FOR LOCATING INFORMATION AND USING REFERENCE MATERIALS

Fully independent readers are able to use almost any type of reading material for obtaining information. The strategies discussed in this section are those needed in order to: (1) locate information in books, (2) locate information in libraries, (3) locate information in encyclopedias, and (4) locate information on maps, globes, and atlases. In some of the literature about reading in the content areas, these strategies are referred to as "study skills." In other places they are labeled "functional reading skills." It does not matter what specific name they are given; they are prerequisites for independent, lifelong self-instruction.

Independent readers can get information from any type of reading material

The strategies that follow are discussed without reference to a specific grade level. What is here listed represents the totality of the locational and reference strategies that should be acquired by the end of elementary school. Instruction should be provided after determining the reading demands placed upon the pupils by the instructional materials in use and the abilities of the pupils to meet those demands.

Locating Information in Books

Pupils should learn the purpose of the various parts of a book

Beginning with their first contact with books, pupils should learn the purpose of the various parts of a book as well as procedures for using those parts to locate information. Specifically, pupils should develop the ability to use

1. The title page to obtain information about the author, illustrator, and publisher of the book.
2. The table of contents to locate topics and general areas of information.
3. The index to locate specific facts or details.
4. The introduction, preface, and foreword to find out both the author's purpose for writing the text and the basic framework of the book.
5. The copyright page to obtain information for estimating the relevance and/or recency of the information in the book.
6. The glossary for the definitions of words as they are used by the author.
7. The bibliography to locate other sources of information on the topic or to check the author's source of information.
8. The appendix to obtain supplementary information about the topic.

In addition, authors use other signaling devices to identify important information. Such signaling devices are italicized words or boldface type, colored type, brackets, underlining, and colored or shaded boxes around sentences or whole paragraphs. A careful analysis of various book formats should reveal other techniques that authors and publishers employ to help readers identify and locate information.

Locating Information in Libraries

Once one knows how to use a library, that knowledge should be useful for a lifetime

Libraries are organized so that information can be conveniently found. Once one knows how to use a library, that knowledge should be useful for a lifetime. Some people erroneously think that the purpose of a library is to store information. Museums are the storehouses of information; libraries are the circulators of information.

In order to effectively locate and use the information in a library, the reader needs strategies for using

1. *The card catalog.* The card catalog contains a listing of all the books in the library. From the catalog it is possible to locate a book if one

TABLE 10-1: Two Popular Library Classification Schemes

The Dewey Classification

000	General Works	500	Pure Science
100	Philosophy	600	Technology
200	Religion	700	The Arts
300	Social Sciences	800	Literature
400	Language	900	History

The Library of Congress Classification

A	General Works—Polygraphy	M	Music
B	Philosophy—Religion	N	Fine Arts
C	History–Auxiliary Sciences	P	Language and Literature
D	History and Topography (except America)	Q	Science
		R	Medicine
E-F	America	S	Agriculture—Plant and Animal Industry
G	Geography—Anthropology		
H	Social Sciences	T	Technology
J	Political Science	U	Military Science
K	Law	V	Naval Science
L	Education	Z	Bibliography and Library Science

knows the author of the book, the title of the book, or the subject area of the book. Some libraries use separate file drawers for each of the three references; however, most school libraries intermix the three types of cards. The strategies needed for using the card catalog are:

Identifying the author's name,
Identifying the book's title,
Identifying the subject heading,
Understanding the library classification code.

2. *The library arrangement.* Most school libraries use the Dewey classification scheme to order and arrange their books. This is only one of a number of ways in which libraries can identify the location of a book. Table 10-1 shows the two most popular classification schemes—the Dewey and the Library of Congress.

Most school and public libraries, however, do not catalog popular fiction or biographies by means of the Dewey system. General fiction is arranged according to the first letter of the author's last name, and biographies are arranged according to the first initial of the subject of the biography, preceded by the letter "B".

3. *Special collections.* Libraries have material in the form of pamphlets and pictures that are arranged alphabetically according to topic in vertical files. In addition, libraries may have record and filmstrip collections and magazines. Older pupils may find it convenient to learn to use the *Reader's Guide to Periodical Literature* in order to locate information in the magazine collection.

Strategies for Using the Encyclopedia

The encyclopedia is an excellent source of information

The encyclopedia can be an excellent source of information about a wide range of topics. It is sometimes thought that the encyclopedia is an irrefutable source. A commonly heard statement is, "It must be right . . . I read it in the encyclopedia" (Wehmeyer, 1975). An encyclopedia, while it may look more authoritative than other written works, can, of course, be in error. The "facts" about the same event may be recorded differently in different encyclopedias (Wehmeyer, 1975). Pupils, therefore, should be encouraged to note and investigate contradictions whenever encountered, and they should not accept information as fact just because it is in the encyclopedia.

Before using an encyclopedia, pupils need to understand (1) the type of information contained in them, (2) the purposes for which the information has been collected, and (3) the relative value of the information contained in them.

In order to effectively locate and use the information in an encyclopedia, the reader needs strategies for using

1. The encyclopedia index.
2. The information on the spine of each volume.
3. The guide words.
4. The cross references.
5. The boldface type and parentheses used in the main entries.
6. The bibliographies at the end of articles.

While encyclopedias are often scholarly attempts at presenting information concisely, they do have limitations:

1. The size and scope of encyclopedias do not allow them to be current on all topics. This is especially true in the fields of natural and political science, where essential data may change within the course of a few weeks' time.

2. Some encyclopedias are cognitively and linguistically too demanding for children in the lower grades.

These limitations are being overcome by some encyclopedia publishers. Specialized, limited scope encyclopedias, for example, are available that deal with science. Also, many publishers are producing limited scope encyclopedia series written especially for young children. These child oriented encyclopedias are written in a style and format approximating that found in many elementary content area textbooks.

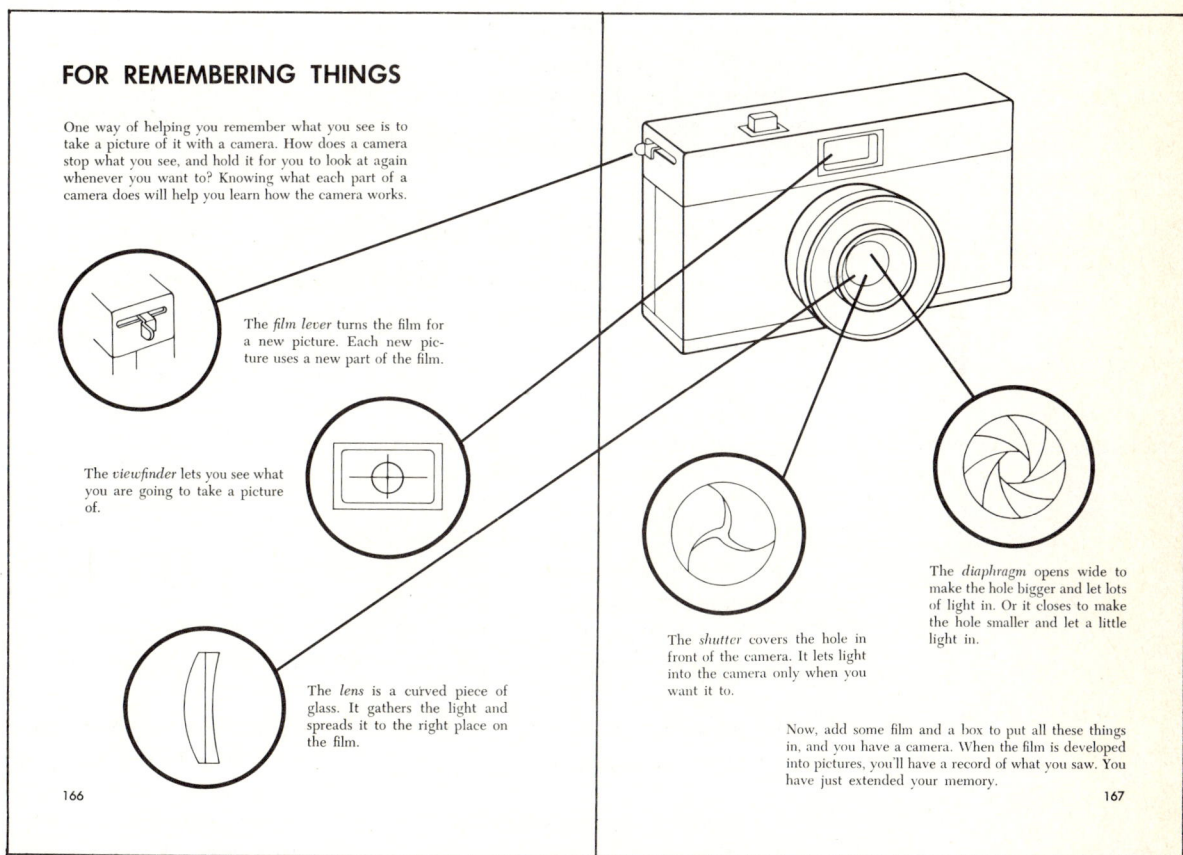

SOURCE: From Vol. 6, *Childcraft—The How and Why Library*. Copyright 1976 by Field Enterprises Educational Corporation.

Teachers should guide pupils around questions that may interrupt their train of thought

Strategies for Locating Information on Maps

Maps are only representations of physical features on the earth. The type of representation that most closely approximates the earth is the globe. However, it may not be practical to use globes for all the different kinds of information maps can provide. Therefore, a basic prerequisite for using maps is the understanding of the element of distortion that occurs when maps are drawn. The distortion affects the size and location of many features of the surface of the earth. The greatest amount of distortion occurs on world maps, the least on maps of extremely small areas of the earth.

Distortion occurs when maps are drawn

In order to effectively locate and use the information found on maps and globes, the reader needs strategies for using

1. Different map projections. The two most common map projections used in elementary content area texts and school atlases are the mercator projection and the polar projection. In order to develop true perspective of the relative size, shape, and placement of geographical positions, the amount and type of distortion created by each projection should be understood.
2. Different types of maps. The purpose of physical or relief maps, political maps, and certain special maps needs to be understood as well as the features that make each kind of map different.

3. Map symbols. Map makers generally use standard symbols for indicating geographic locations: lakes, cities, rivers, highways, political boundaries, and direction.
4. Map colorations. Understanding the relationship between map color and actual land color is essential to effective map use. While some colors on physical maps seem to relate to actual land formations—blue for water, green and brown for landforms—the use of color on political and special purpose maps usually has no relationship to the concept they represent.
5. Scales of distance. Not only are maps not representative of the actual distances found on earth, the scale of distance and size from one map to another may differ.
6. Map legends. Most maps provide a concise reference for interpreting map symbols, color, and scale in the legend.

STRATEGIES FOR READING THE NEWSPAPER

The newspaper generally fits in with any school's content area programs. It is a current, constant source of information about events that is relatively inexpensive and easily available. In addition, it can accommodate a wide variation in reading abilities—something in almost every newspaper can be read by pupils in elementary school.

Newspapers can accommodate various reading abilities

Any newspaper can be used for instruction, but it is probably best to use one that is familiar to the pupils and that will be read by them independently. Once the basic strategies for reading newspapers have been acquired, two or more newspapers can be compared in regard to the same information.

The strategies needed for locating and using the information in newspapers concern, broadly,

1. The content of a newspaper. Every newspaper contains a variety of information. Generally, this information consists of:

   a. News stories. News stories may be factual, interpretive, or speculative.
   b. Human interest stories.
   c. Opinion articles. Opinion articles may be either editorials or essays signed by columnists.
   d. Sports stories.
   e. Business and finance articles.

f. Entertainment articles, news, reviews, time tables.
g. Comics and puzzles.
h. Weather reports and forecasts.
i. Advertisements.
j. Obituaries.

2. The organization of the contents. Each newspaper organizes its contents in a particular manner that remains fairly constant over a period of time. Familiarity with the organization of a newspaper facilitates the locating of information on a particular topic.

3. The organization of news and feature articles. News stories are written so that the most current news is at the beginning of the article. The introductory paragraph usually contains answers to the five "W's": who, what, when, where, why. As one reads further into an article, information that appeared in earlier stories may be found. Feature stories and opinion articles are generally written in a more narrative style.

The newspaper is a source of information that can be used in developing skills and strategies in all of the content areas. Daily, words that are related to social studies and science topics can be located in the newspaper. What is most important, these words are available to the pupils in a context that often discloses their meanings. Photographs, maps, charts and diagrams are used extensively and can be used to supplement the graphic displays used in the content area textbooks. Human interest stories, reviews, opinion articles, and political cartoons can be used to show how the "facts" found in textbooks and encyclopedias can be used by different people to influence others in their thinking. Finally, advertisements, radio, television, and movie schedules, the business pages, and the sports sections can provide vivid examples of the utility of arithmetical skills in the pupils' daily lives.

Activities for Developing Newspaper Reading Strategies

The following strategies for effective newspaper reading can be employed in specific units at different grade levels. If funds are available, it is worthwhile to provide each pupil with a copy of a newspaper. (This is not unreasonable since every pupil can receive a newspaper for an entire month for the cost of a typical "workbook.")

☐ Develop a sense of the content of a newspaper. Have the pupils work in small teams to make a list of all the different types of information that are in a newspaper. This activity can be modified to meet the reading abilities of a wide range of pupils. Younger pupils can name the different types of information and the teacher can record them on the chalkboard or a permanent chart. Older pupils can make their own lists.

☐ Develop a sense of current events. Each day have the pupils locate news articles of local, national, and international concern. This activity can be related to the study of maps by pinpointing on the class map the locale of each story.

☐ Develop a sense of the organization of a news story. Have the pupils use their knowledge of sentence information to figure out that news writers often employ the same signals to the location of that information as do other authors.

☐ Develop a sense of headline writing. Use the headlines of a variety of stories and have the pupils locate the information in the story that was used as the basis for the headline. Extend this activity to develop a sense of the use of figurative language, puns, and connotations in headline writing. Have the pupils write their own headlines for stories, or rewrite the headlines of stories in the newspaper.

☐ Develop a sense of purposeful letter writing. Have the pupils select something from the newspaper—a job advertisement, an editorial, a mail order ad—and then write a letter in response to that item. Where it is appropriate, have the pupils mail their letters.

☐ Develop a sense of the newspaper as a continuous resource and reference. Provide the pupils with a topic study sheet. The topic should be one that is current and that will be reported on almost daily for an extended period. Such topics could deal with politics, social issues, or a sports series. The format and content of the study sheet should guide the pupils' thinking towards drawing some conclusions about the topic. The guide in Figure 10-3 can be used as a model that may be modified to meet the abilities of the pupils.

☐ Develop an understanding of the use of propaganda techniques. Starting with the advertisements and then moving to articles of stories and events with which they are familiar, the pupils can begin to analyze how propaganda techniques are employed. They can try to determine through

FIGURE 10-3: A Topic Study Sheet for Use with the Newspaper

Topic: SOCIAL ISSUES   21

COMIC STRIP: ROLE ANALYSIS
Select 4 or 5 comic strips from your local paper. Analyze them according to the criteria below for at least a 4-week period. Write a report which summarizes your findings, indicating what the comic strips are saying about the "American way" of life.

Occupations
1. What occupations do the male characters have?
2. What occupations do the female characters have?
3. Keep a list of the main characters for whom **no** occupation is mentioned.
4. If children or teenagers discuss future occupations, which jobs are boys interested in? girls?

Environment
1. What is the location of the action of each comic strip? (home, office, parks, city streets, etc.)
2. In which of the above settings do women most often appear? In which settings do men most often appear?
3. In "home" or "family" settings, what activities are men engaged in? women?

Dialogue
1. What topics are discussed in each comic strip (politics, education, the home and the family, etc.?)
2. What can you tell about the attitudes of the characters towards each other from the dialogue?
3. Who discusses what? (that is, can you make any generalizations about topics that women discuss? that men discuss? teenagers?)

Copyright © 1974 by The Associated Press

SOURCE: *The Associated Press Newspaper Reading Skills Development Program*, Project File. Copyright 1974 by AP Newsfeatures.

a comparison with the advertised product (whenever possible), or through a comparison of a number of articles written about the same event or topic, whether propaganda techniques were employed and the extent to which they might influence an individual's thinking.

☐ Develop an interest in the biographies of interesting or important people. Through the reading of newspaper obituaries, pupils can appreciate the contributions of various people to the topics they are studying in the content areas.

STRATEGIES FOR ORGANIZING INFORMATION

Once pupils have located information, it may become necessary to put that information in a form that can be easily retained for a variety of purposes. When pupils are working on projects, or the writing of reports, some form of note or outline form may be necessary. The strategies for organizing information should be developed as the pupils acquire an understanding about different writing patterns. However, unless they realize a definite purpose for organizing information, the activities may become meaningless tasks.

Pupils should develop strategies for organizing information

The most common form of organizing information is the outline. In elementary school instruction, the outline may take a variety of forms. At times, a simple list is all that may be required. At other times a more detailed outline with multiple levels will be appropriate. Whatever form is used, the pupils should realize the relationship between it and the writing patterns from which the information is obtained.

In many instructional materials, outlining is used exclusively with paragraphs written in the generalization pattern discussed in Chapter 8. However, other patterns can, and should, be used to illustrate the uses of outlining. These patterns include topic development, comparison/contrast, enumeration, and classification.

The outline is not the sole manner in which information can be organized. Depending upon the purposes for organizing the information, the uses to which the information will be put, and the amounts of information to be recorded, other usable forms of organizing information are charts, graphs, time lines, and diagrams.

For example, if the learner's attention is on the general categories of behavior one can observe in zoo animals, then the outline form may be appropriate.

> Some behaviors you may observe in zoo animals are:
> the way they move
> the sounds they make
> the food they eat
> the ways they protect themselves
> when they rest and when they move about

If, on the other hand, attention will be given to the differences or similarities among the behaviors of the various animals, then a chart form may be more appropriate for recording and organizing the information.

Animal	Where it makes its home	What it eats	How it moves	How it protects itself	Other behaviors
Walking stick	twig	insects	crawls jumps	looks like a twig	eats every insect in sight

Strategies for Using Outlines

The concept of outlining can be introduced through the simple listing of materials needed to test the properties of various minerals. For example, the simple outline could be:

> **Materials needed to test minerals**
> set of minerals
> hand lens
> scissors
> piece of glass
> penny
> piece of granite
> magnet
> steel file
> piece of tile

More complex outlines can result from using the paragraph patterns to identify the important ideas of the author. For example, in the paragraphs below, a contrast is made. A useful outline would emphasize that contrast.

Who Was Right?

Ptolemy watched the moon change its shape and sometimes disappear as it moved east to west. He believed that the moon reflected light from the sun.

Ptolemy thought the moon, like the sun, was on a glass ball inside the large sphere surrounding the earth. He believed the moon was between the sun and earth. Ptolemy discovered as you did that the moon is not in the same place at the same time every day. He explained this by saying that the moon moves more slowly around the earth than the sun does.

Copernicus thought that all the spheres except the moon's turned around the sun. He believed the moon's sphere turned around the earth.

Copernicus believed that all the objects in the sky seemed to move because the earth is moving. He believed that the earth turned on its axis toward the east and the moon moved around it more slowly in the same direction. This would make the moon seem to move more slowly than the sun and be farther east each day (Brewer et al., 1972).

Explaining Why the Moon Moves

Ptolemy believed
1. the moon and sun are on glass balls around the Earth.
2. the moon is between the Earth and the Sun.
3. the moon moves more slowly than the Sun.

Copernicus believed
1. The Earth moves around the Sun.
2. the moon moves around the Earth.
3. the Earth turns on its own axis towards the East.
4. The moon moves around the Earth slower than the Earth turns on its axis.

Only after the pupils have an understanding of the relationship between the major concepts and the supporting concepts should the formal structure of an outline be introduced. Then, the most common outline form is:

    Title

I. Major concepts

    A. Supporting concepts
    B.

II.

    A.
    B.

Activities for Developing Outlining Strategies

Outlining should be introduced in stages

The concept of outlining should be introduced in stages. The first stage is concerned with developing a sense of the relationship between the main concept(s) and the supporting concepts. The second stage extends this but requires the pupils to locate the appropriate supporting concepts. In the third stage, the pupils are given the outline form and must locate both the major concept and the supporting concepts.

Stage one. Provide the pupils with a paragraph and a list of the major and supporting concepts. After reading the paragraph and identifying the paragraph pattern, the pupils complete the skeleton outline.

> All kinds of energy can be classified as either potential energy or kinetic energy. A moving object has energy because it can cause a force to act. The energy that an object has because it is moving is called kinetic energy. A *moving* object has kinetic energy.
> An object can also have energy because of its position—even if it is not moving. A pendulum held at the top of its swing will move if released. And if it moves, it has energy. This energy of position is called stored energy, or potential energy (Brewer et al., 1972).

I. _____

    A. _____

    B. _____

Potential energy is stored energy
The two kinds of energy
Kinetic energy is in moving objects

Stage two. Provide the pupils with a paragraph and a partially completed outline. After reading the paragraph and identifying its pattern, the pupils complete the outline.

> Nomads depend on their animals for almost everything they need. How does this remind you of the Plains Indians and the buffalo? The animals give good milk, from which tasty cheese can then be made. The desert people shear the hair of their goats and camels. Then they weave clothes or blankets or tents. The nomads sleep on rugs made of sheep wool. When a group of nomads is ready to move, they pack up all their belongings and load them on their camels. Do you think nomads have a lot of things to pack? Could your family pack all their belongings and load them on an animal? Why or why not? (Davis et al., 1971b)

    I. Nomads depend upon their animals for their needs

        A. _____
        B. _____
        C. _____

Stage three. Provide the pupils with a paragraph and a skeleton outline of the major and supporting concepts. After reading the paragraph and identifying its pattern, the pupils complete the outline.

> All cells in any animal must have food and oxygen. The cells also give off waste materials, which must be carried away. These materials are carried to and from the cells by a system of circulation. In higher animals, such as fish, chickens, and man, the circulatory system is made up of a heart, blood, and blood vessels. The heart is a pump that keeps the blood moving through the blood vessels (Brewer et al., 1972).

    I. _____
        A. _____
        B. _____

The strategies for organizing information should be allowed to develop over an extended period of time. Pupils should be encouraged to experiment with different forms of organizing information. Through such opportunities, they will begin to understand, as they develop organizational strategies, what patterns are better suited for use with particular kinds of information. The logic of organizing information can only result from emulating models and attempting—sometimes unsuccessfully—to put information in some sort of rational form.

RESOURCES FOR THE TEACHER

Many instructional materials provide exercises in more than one content area. The resources that follow, therefore, are grouped according to format rather than by specific area. Teachers should find that whenever a resource is more extensive in one area than the others, it still provides a great many ideas for developing one's own exercises.

Units. In order to develop content area reading as a language experience, teachers may find it helpful to have a series of prepared thematic units from which they can develop classroom lessons and activities. One source of such units is the curriculum bulletin prepared and distributed by city and state Boards of Education and Departments of Education. Instructional units for newspaper reading in the content areas may be obtained from the educational services departments of many local newspapers.

The resource that follows is an example of such work, which includes statements of instructional objectives, lists of skills, numerous language experiences and activities, and multimedia materials.

> Board of Education, City of Chicago. 1972. *Curriculum Guide for Social Studies, Grades 1-6.* Chicago: Chicago Public Schools.

The following is a series of units for instruction in the social studies area.

> Michaelis, John O., ed. 1966. *Teaching Units in the Social Sciences.* Chicago: Rand McNally.

The following resource emphasizes a discovery approach. Each kit contains a pupil booklet, a wall chart, a filmstrip, a record, and a toy.

> *Who Am I?* Discovery Workshop, 100 Garfield Avenue, New London, Conn. 06320.

The following resource is a program for developing library skills from the simplest understanding to note-taking for research. It contains ninety-six objectives that cover the entire range of elementary school knowledge about the library.

> Margrabe, Mary. 1973. *The "Now" Library Media Center: A Stations Approach with Teaching Kit.* Washington, D.C.: Acropolis Books, Ltd.

Kits. The first resource is a series of kits that cover three important aspects of content area reading. Within each kit, specific instruction and practice materials are provided.

    Robinson, H. Alan and others. 1968. *Study Skills Library.* Revised Edition. Grades 3–9. Science, Social Studies, Reference. New York: EDL/McGraw Hill.

The next two resources provide instruction and practice in the strategies of organizing information.

    Research Lab. Grades 4–8. Chicago: Science Research Associates.
    Organizing and Reporting Skills Kit. Grades 4–6. Chicago: Science Research Associates.

The following resource provides instruction in the reading of graphic displays.

    Map and Globe Skills, Kit. Grades 4–8. Chicago: Science Research Associates.
    Graph and Picture Study Skills Kit. Grades 4–6. Chicago: Science Research Associates.

The next resource contains specific instruction in the reading and use of the newspaper. The kit is to be used in conjunction with the pupils' own newspaper.

    Newslab. 1972. Chicago: Science Research Associates. Kit I: Grades 4–8. Kit II: Grades 5–9.

Workbooks. The workbooks of many basal reading series contain numerous activities for reading in the content areas. The following are workbooks prepared specifically for content area reading strategies.

    Smith, Nila Banton. *Be a Better Reader: Foundations A, B, C.* Englewood Cliffs, N.J.: Prentice-Hall.
    Barnes, Donald L. and Burgdorf, Arline B. *Study Skills for Information Retrieval.* Boston: Allyn & Bacon.
    Thorn, Elizabeth et al. 1974. *Beginning Stories to Study* and *Stories to Study.* IA, IB, IIA, IIB. (Primary grades). New York: William H. Sadlier, Inc.
    Herber, Harold. 1973. *Go: Reading in the Content Areas.* Grades 4–8. New York: Scholastic Book Services.
    Perkins, Terry William. *Understanding the News:* In Newspapers, Magazines . . . on Radio, TV. *Gathering the News:* For Newspapers, Magazines, Radio, TV. New York: Scholastic Book Services.

In addition, the following company publishes a variety of materials about reading maps and other graphics.

    Weekly Reader, Educational Center, 1250 Fairwood Avenue, Columbus, Ohio 43206.

Books. One reading series that has been devoted exclusively to applying reading skills in content area materials is the following. It contains, at each grade level, a general reading skills unit, and units on reading social studies, mathematics, science, and literature.

    Subject Matter Reading Pattern. New York: Harper & Row, Inc.

The booklets that follow are titles in the International Reading Association's Reading Aids series.

    Earle, Richard A. 1976. *Teaching Reading and Mathematics.* Newark, Del.: International Reading Association.

    Cheyney, Arnold G. 1971. *Teaching Reading Skills Through the Newspaper.* Neward, Del.: International Reading Association.

    Thelen, Judith. 1976. *Improving Reading in Science.* Newark, Del.: International Reading Association.

DISCUSSION QUESTIONS AND ACTIVITIES

1. Explain what the following statement by Ned D. Marksheffel (1969) means to you in regard to reading in the content areas:

> Because reading has no subject matter of its own, whatever the reader reads is reading.

2. Explain what you think David L. Shepherd (1969) means by the statement:

> The scientific method is as applicable to student development in the skill of reading science material as in learning scientific understandings.

3. Obtain oral reading protocols of one upper elementary grade student while reading a passage from a basal reader and a passage from a content area text. Score the miscue analyses of each and compare the results. Does the pupil's pattern of miscues differ on the two passages? If so, to what do you attribute the difference?

4. Select a passage from a content area textbook for use with middle grade elementary pupils. Construct an author-idea map that:
   a. Identifies the major concept of the passage.
   b. Shows the location of the important generalizations.
   c. Indicates the location of the important information supporting the major concept and/or the generalizations.

5. Examine one chapter on the same topic in three different texts intended for use at the same grade level. Compare and/or contrast:
   a. The organization and format of the chapter.
   b. The use of graphic displays and their relationship to the text.
   c. The style of language and vocabulary diversity.
   d. The amount of information within subheadings that does not relate directly to the subheadings.

   Overall, rate the three texts for their effectiveness in communicating with elementary level pupils.

6. The following statement by Robert Karlin (1975) represents a commonly held view of primary grade reading. How would someone who holds a psycholinguistic perspective of the reading process answer this statement?

   > Most of the reading children do in the primary grades is for the purpose of learning how to read, and the use of narrative materials is entirely appropriate. The emphasis of the reading program is on learning and practicing reading skills, not on the ideas the materials contain.

FURTHER READINGS

Those engaged in teaching the reading of content areas in the elementary school should have a background in and understanding of the concepts and generalizations in each area. The following texts provide teachers with such information. The first is especially useful since it contains a series of "discovery lesson plans" that provide the basis for language experience units on a variety of topics at all grade levels. Within each lesson, the thinking processes for each lesson and the thinking processes for each activity and question are identified.

Carin, Arthur A., and Sund, Robert B. 1970. *Teaching Science Through Discovery,* 2nd Edition. Columbus, Ohio: Merrill.

Copeland, Richard W. 1972. *Mathematics and the Elementary Teacher,* 2nd Edition. Philadelphia: W. B. Sanders Co.

Welton, David A., and Mallan, John T. 1976. *Children and Their World: Teaching Elementary Social Studies.* Chicago: Rand McNally.

The following texts were written primarily for use with secondary school students. However, many of the ideas discussed can be adapted for use with elementary school pupils.

Herber, Harold L. 1960. *Teaching Reading in Content Areas.* Englewood Cliffs, N.J.: Prentice-Hall.

Laffey, James, ed. 1972. *Reading in the Content Areas.* Newark, Del.: International Reading Association.

Thomas, Ellen Lamar, and Robinson, H. Alan. 1972. *Improving Reading in Every Class: A Sourcebook for Teachers.* Boston: Allyn & Bacon.

References

Aiken, Lewis R., Jr. 1972. "Language Factors in Learning Mathematics." *Review of Educational Research* 42: 359-85.

Albert, Burton, Jr. 1971. "Purple Marbles and Little Red Hula Hoops." *The Reading Teacher* 24: 647-51.

Brewer, A. C. et al. 1972. *Elementary Science: Learning by Investigating.* Chicago: Rand McNally.

Davis, O. L. et al. 1971a. *Exploring the Social Sciences: Asking About the U.S.A. and Its Neighbors.* New York: American Book Co.

Davis, O. L. et al. 1971b. *Exploring the Social Sciences: Investigating Communities and Cultures.* New York: American Book Co.

Herber, Harold L., and Nelson, Joan B. 1975. "Questioning Is Not the Answer." *Journal of Reading* 18: 512-17.

Karlin, Robert. 1975. *Teaching Elementary Reading: Principles and Strategies.* Second Edition. New York: Harcourt Brace Jovanovich.

King, Frederick et al. 1971. *The Social Studies and Our Country: Concepts in Social Science.* River Forest, Ill.: Laidlaw Brothers.

King, Frederick et al. 1974. *The Social Studies and Our Country: Regions and Social Needs.* River Forest, Ill.: Laidlaw Brothers.

Lacey, Patricia A., and Weil, Philip E. 1975. "Number—Reading—Language." *Language Arts* 52: 776-82.

Maffei, Anthony C. 1973. "Reading Analysis in Mathematics." *Journal of Reading* 16: 546–49.

Marksheffel, Ned D. 1969. "Reading in the Content Areas: A Framework for Improvement." In H. Alan Robinson and Ellen Lamar Thomas. *Fusing Reading Skills and Content.* Newark, Del.: International Reading Association.

Michaelis, John O. 1972. *Social Studies for Children in a Democracy: Recent Trends and Developments.* 5th Edition. Englewood Cliffs, N.J.: Prentice Hall.

Pauk, Walter. 1973. "Two Essential Study Skills for the Community College Student." *Reading World* 12: 239–45.

Robinson, H. Alan. 1975. *Teaching Reading Study Skills: The Content Areas.* Boston: Allyn & Bacon.

Sargent, Eileen E., Huus, Helen, and Andresen, Oliver. 1970. *How To Read a Book.* Newark, Del.: International Reading Association.

Shepherd, David L. 1969. "Reading and Science: Problems Peculiar to the Area." In H. Alan Robinson and Ellen Lamar Thomas. *Fusing Reading Skills and Content.* Newark, Del.: International Reading Association.

Smith, Nila Banton. 1964a. "Patterns of Writing in Different Subject Areas: Part I." *Journal of Reading* 8: 31–37.

Smith, Nila Banton. 1964b. "Patterns of Writing in Different Subject Areas: Part II." *Journal of Reading* 8: 97–102.

Wehmeyer, Lillian M. 1975. "It Must Be Right . . . I Read It In The Encyclopedia!" *Language Arts* 52: 841–42.

11

Developing Strategies for Literature Reading

Focus Questions:

1. What is the purpose of a literature program in the elementary school?
2. What are the different types of literature available for pupils to read?
3. How can literature of exceptional quality be identified?
4. How can the pupils and literature be brought together?
5. What means are available to assist teachers in selecting literature for the pupils?

A most important objective of a literature reading program in the elementary school is the creation of an environment so filled with books that pupils develop the desire to spend part of their lifetime in the act of reading. The reading of literature (as part of a total reading program) should lead pupils:

Pupils should want to spend part of their life reading books

1. To enjoy books and stories of all sorts.
2. To be acquainted with the literary heritage of their society.
3. To understand what constitutes "literature."
4. To apply knowledge gained from literature to their lives.
5. To evaluate and appreciate literature, and develop a personal taste from among the wide varieties and forms of literature (Huus, 1975).

What actually constitutes "literature" is difficult to state. To one, it is classical or contemporary writing of such quality that children can understand what is read or heard (Huus, 1975). To another, it calls for power in the use of words, actions that lead to a well-knit plot, a strong theme that presents a basic truth, and realistic characters. It is seen as writing that reveals an author's knowledge of literary form and from which some wisdom may be apprehended (Painter, 1975). To still another, literature "portrays life and mind in language" and has three qualities: substance, sincerity, and memorable language (Lundsteen, 1976).

Precisely what constitutes "literature" probably could not be defined to the satisfaction of all. Yet similarities can be seen in the three definitions. It is probably best to consider literature not as something good or bad, but as a continuum on which all the writings of all authors reside. At one end can be found the writings that are almost universally accepted as representative of what is meant by "literature." The aim of this chapter is to consider the elements that have been agreed upon by many as representing literary quality. The more a piece of writing contains these elements, the more it can be considered literature.

Literature is neither good nor bad

READING IN A PLURALISTIC SOCIETY

The United States has long been considered a melting pot in which various cultures meld. There is in American society, however, a growing appreciation of the pluralistic nature of the culture. The literature program in elementary schools should aim at studying and developing a respect for the contribution all cultural groups make through their literature. The teaching of literature should seek to broaden and deepen the experiences of pupils. When a reading program omits the exploration of literature that reflects the varying segments of society, the pupils are deprived of a complete and fully rounded education (Reed, 1976).

Through literature, pupils develop respect for other cultures

The reading of literature that treats society as pluralistic is not incongruent with the general purpose of any literature program. A literature program is one of the important ways in which pupils can learn to relive the experiences of others and broaden and deepen their own personal experiences (Smith, 1960). The study of literature that reflects the diverse cultural groups in American society can lead to an open-minded generation of pupils who accept the uniqueness and necessity of other life-styles (Jenkins, 1973). It is through reading the literature of other cultural groups that an understanding of the many similarities between those groups and one's own is developed (Reed, 1976).

For pupils who themselves come from minority groups, the study of multi-ethnic literature is important to developing a healthy self concept, which depends on a knowledge of and sense of pride in one's family and cultural background, and understanding that one's own group is not the "center of the universe."

CURRENT TRENDS IN CHILDREN'S LITERATURE

The content of the literature used should reflect the realities that the pupils face in their everyday lives. This is not to aver that the pupils should be nourished solely on a diet of "realistic" literature. Rather, it is an acknowledgement of various trends that are occurring in the book industry. For quite a long time it was felt that children's literature should avoid presenting life as many children actually knew it. However, it now seems that children may be "forsaking innocence in their reading habits to peruse stark realities" (Merla, 1972). What is being seen in current children's literature are numerous themes that previously were found only in adult literature (Merla, 1972; Sims, 1976): alienation, unwed motherhood, suicide, mental retardation, senility, poverty, racial themes, the plight of the American Indian, war, adolescent sex, homosexuality, divorce, drugs and alcohol abuse. Adults are not necessarily idealized models in the literature, being portrayed as sometimes weak and incompetent individuals. Many of the books no longer have the traditional happy ending and no longer leave the reader with the feeling that the problems of life are always answerable.

Although many of these themes are found primarily in literature intended for young adolescents, some seem to be moving down to books for children in the lower grades (Sims, 1976). Younger siblings are being influenced by what older youths in the house are reading, and children seek books with the realistic themes that are almost daily fare on television. Children of elementary grades are facing these "stark realities" in their sources of recreation as well as in their personal lives.

However, there are dangers in saying that because the authors of children's literature are presenting contemporary realism that the children always want or should be exposed to these situations in their reading matter. When adults select children's books that have relevance to the pupils' lives, they are assuming that their (i.e., the adult's) view of "relevant" is shared by the children. When adults state, as do, for example, Arth and Whittemore (1973), that it is the responsibility of the school to prepare children for the realities of life, they are assuming that only realistic, "close to home" fiction is what prepares children for coping with their world. In reality, it may be the unfamiliar, not the familiar, that intrigues children. Fantasy in reasonable amounts may be essential to the full realization of a child's intellectual potential (Elkind, 1972). It is while children engage in fantasy that they learn to distinguish between what is appearance and what is fact. Realistic fiction may be a mirror, but fantasy can be a window for escape (Sims, 1976).

STRATEGIES FOR DEVELOPING A LITERATURE PROGRAM

Children may not learn from literature without guidance

The teaching of literature does not seem to be widely accepted as a critical part of the school reading program. A review of research dealing with the teaching of literature reveals that literature is most often used as a supplement to other subject areas or as material for the teaching of reading skills (Cullinan, 1974). Children will not develop a sense of literature as enjoyment or as a means of understanding the world without specific guidance. Pupils, therefore, need a planned, balanced program of literature instruction that provides for

1. The free choice of reading materials. Free choice is the opportunity to select, read, and even stop reading, something selected without any intervention from an adult.
2. The daily reading aloud of a story or poem by the teacher. The teacher conveys to pupils a feeling that something is "good," not by extolling its merits, but by the enthusiasm and feeling put into the reading of it. The selection can be one that will bring delight to the children because of the sheer magic of the author's words, or it may be one that leaves the pupils with a newer understanding of some aspect of life.
3. The guidance to find a desired book. Teachers should help pupils find books. Through a teacher's or librarian's recommendation, pupils should be made aware of various books on any given topic, or in relation to topics being studied in the content areas.
4. The focus on a common element in the literature through topical units. The units can focus on a specific topic or subject area, on a type or form of writing, or on a style of writing.
5. The creative sharing of the books. Children can generate interest in the books they are reading, or become interested in

the books others have read, as they share their ideas through discussions, reports, artwork, or dramatic presentations (Huus, 1975).

Within the planned literature program, provision should be made for developing in the pupils

1. Strategies for distinguishing between real and make-believe.
2. Strategies for recognizing the author's craft.
3. Strategies for recognizing the mood, feeling or tone of a story or poem.
4. Strategies for recognizing and interpreting figurative language.
5. Strategies for recognizing the major forms of fiction.
6. Strategies for extending one's personal reading interests.

While attempting to develop a planned literature program, teachers may face certain problems or difficulties (Huus, 1975). The lack of materials or the structure of the school-wide program may not always permit pupils to have a "free" choice of reading matter. Solving the problem of limited materials may be easier than dealing with a situation in which pupils are restricted by a policy of required reading. While reading aloud, teachers should be careful not to inject their personalities into the story. Too often the focus of the daily reading may be on the performance and not on the literature. The guidance a pupil receives from teachers and librarians depends upon their experience and expertise. The development of topical units may be limited by the availability of material on that topic and by the availability of material appropriate and appealing to the intended pupils. Finally, the sharing of books all too often replaces the literature itself. Although reports, art projects, and dramatizations may be desirable, within the structure of the planned literature program they should not take precedence over the literature itself.

Recognizing the Categories of Literature

The literature that pupils encounter in a balanced literature program should be drawn from both the classic literature and the "new" literature. Classic literature is comprised of those stories, poems, and plays that provide some continuity with the literary heritage of society. These consist of folk and fairy tales, the myths and legends of other countries, and the stories and books that have endured as children's works for long periods of

Readings should be drawn from classic and new literature

time. The newer literature consists of the modern fanciful stories and poems and the "realistic" works discussed previously. These, unlike the classics which tie the reader to a cultural heritage, more closely mirror the immediate world of the child.

Children's literature can be studied in various ways. One way in which the study of "literature" can be structured is through literary forms, structural elements of style, and use.

Recognizing Literary Forms

The major forms of writing in children's literature may be placed into quite arbitrary categories, and many books could be placed in more than one. However, the following categories are useful in a guided literature program.

Fiction. The forms of fiction include those that can be considered to be

1. Realistic. Within this classification are books and stories set in historical and contemporary periods. Many of these are the everyday adventure stories to which so many children are attracted. Also included are fictionalized biographies that portray real persons in realistically set, fictionalized conversations and thoughts.

2. Fantasy. Within this classification are both the modern and the traditional stories of magic and romance. The traditional fairy tales, myths, legends, and folktales, have withstood the test of time in their appeal to children. Modern fantasy, the stories of science fiction and American folklore, retain the ancient quality of magic as found in the traditional fairy tales (Higgins, 1970). (Some authorities classify animal stories as a separate category of literature and this is discussed below.)

3. Pop literature. This category contains forms of literature that many would not consider "literature"—comics, jokes, chants in children's games, graffitti, posters. However, there are many forms of pop literature and much of it meets the criteria for "literature."

4. Picture books. These are the books intended primarily to be read to young children. Their stories, although told in words, are carried through the sequence of illustrations. Once the story has been heard, the children can often view the pictures and retell the story.

5. Animal stories. Animal stories seem to remain popular with children and adults. There are three types of animal stories: those in which the animals are talking beasts; those in which the animals act as animals, but talk; and those in which the animals are objectively reported. The purpose of each is different. When the animals are talking beasts they really are

humans in disguise set to tell a story portraying human foibles. Stories in which animals talk but are still animals are stories of fancy. When animals do not talk or act like humans, the author is not free to interpret the animals' emotions, attitudes, or intentions. The animals, central to the plot, remain always animals and readers are free to create their own interpretations of the animals' behavior (Lundsteen, 1976).

Nonfiction. Classified as nonfiction are works that present information on topics in a literary style: biographies, personal narratives, technical or scientific explanations, essays, and books about other people, places and cultures.

Poetry. Poetry seems to be something that is given little attention in class, is seldom read to children, and is infrequently encouraged as a writing form (Terry, 1972). One reason may be that teachers themselves are unfamiliar or uncomfortable with poetry.

A poem depends upon a formal structure and a carefully chosen sequence of words. The sturucture and sequence of those words can take a variety of forms; some of the ones popular with elementary pupils are:

1. *Haiku.* Haiku, a form of poetry composed in Japan, consists of a seventeen syllable statement about nature in which the topic is usually not named. The form is arranged so the first line has five syllables, the second line has seven syllables, and the third line has five syllables.

>   **Rustling green branches,**
>   **Sweet music of singing birds**
>   **Outside my window (Fay and Anderson, 1974).**

2. *Cinquain.* Cinquain, a short poetic form of five lines, deals with a topic by:

   a. Stating in the first line a single thing—a noun
   b. Giving two words in the second line that tell what the thing might do—verbs
   c. Describing the thing in the third line—adjectives
   d. Stating in the fourth line a phrase that describes the thing
   e. Repeating the word in the first line.

>   **Snow**
>   **Floats, dances**
>   **Cold white sparkling**
>   **Sitting on my lashes**
>   **Snow (Fay and Anderson, 1974).**

Copyright © 1975 United Feature Syndicate, Inc.

3. *Limericks.* Limericks are a nonsense form of rhyme that have five lines: lines one and two rhyme, three and four rhyme, and the last, rhyming with the first two, usually provides some humorous statement.

> There was an old man with a beard,
> Who said, "It is just as I feared!—
>   Two owls and a hen,
>   Four larks and a wren,
> Have all built their nests in my beard" (Lear, 1966).

4. *Narrative.* The narrative poem, usually telling a long tale, may use a variety of forms and patterns.

5. *Free verse.* Free verse does not follow any rhyme patterns. The poetry of free verse is obtained from the sound, rhythm, and cadence of the words and phrases.

6. *Quatrains.* Quatrains are poems in four line units in which the second and fourth lines rhyme. Poems can consist of a number of quatrains.

7. *Couplets.* Couplets are two line rhyming units. Many poems consist of a number of couplets, sometimes of alternating rhythms, cadences, and rhymes.

Plays. One form of literature that pupils seem to enjoy is plays. It is a form, like poetry, that is intended to be spoken and heard. Yet, when plays are read, they are literature.

The reading of plays can lead pupils to appreciate the amount of information that the reader has to supply in order to fully re-create the "message" intended by the author. Although there are various hints—stage directions and scene settings—the reader is the one who must provide much of the running commentary and interpretation that is usually provided in prose. Therefore, the study of plays for elementary pupils should be the study of the relationship between a playwright's scripts and the narrative of a prose writer. This experience can provide the readiness pupils need to fully appreciate and understand the dramas they will encounter in secondary school.

Recognizing Elements of Style

The study of *how* literature is constructed leads pupils to the full appreciation of the author's craft. Enjoyment is often derived from watching an artisan when one understands the intricacies of the craft and the criteria for judging the artistic quality of the product. A book is more than just a "story" when one follows an author in the development of a complex thought or the timbre of a phrase.

Characterization. In the development of believable characterizations, authors contend with three elements: credibility, portrayal, and uniqueness (Cullinan, 1971).

Characters are credible when they can be believed within the framework of the particular story. They need to exist as integral parts of the author's story and to make the action move in believable ways. Credibility ceases when a character performs some action or makes some statement that defies what the reader has been led to accept as the character's pattern.

Characters are portrayed in varying ways depending upon the author's intent. Some characters may be fully described; the reader is left with little to construct in order to "know" the characters. Others may be vaguely delineated because they are not central to the plot of the story or because the author wishes the character to be indistinct. In order to fully appreciate an author's character portrayals, pupils should be familiar with various personality types in humans.

Each character in a story should have some unique qualities that set that individual apart from all the others, yet each should have some qualities that are universal and common to all humans.

Plot Development. In simplest terms, a plot is the basic story outline; the plot development is how the story unfolds. If the author does not provide for a purposeful sequence of events and a logical conclusion, readers are apt to dismiss the story as unbelievable. In most narration the order of the plot follows the sequence of introduction, development of a "problem," solution of the problem, conclusion.

Four basic plots have been identified in children's literature: romance, tragedy, irony-satire, and comedy (Sloan, 1975). Romance is basically literature in which wishes are fulfilled. The central character, or hero, is involved in a dangerous or marvelous journey, a struggle or ordeal, and a return. Tragedy is the exploration of the limitation in the central character's ability to have or make wishes come true. Central to tragedy is the death or catastrophic fall of the hero. Irony and satire express the contrast that exists between ideals and reality—irony illustrating the limitations of humans, satire attempting the change of humans through ridicule. Comedy presents a positive view of the human experience, a picture of hope and renewal.

Figurative Language. The craft of an author is most often appreciated through the language used. The author's choice of words determines how the reader constructs the images of the story characters and settings. An author might use language that is straightforward in its reporting:

> As Jock nudged the cow into the barn and locked the door behind her, the clouds opened and the rain dropped in a sudden torrent. The lightning stabbed through the clouds, and in its momentary brightness Jock could see the trees tossing wildly in the wind that howled through the river walls and roared across the highlands. He cringed in spite of himself at the exploding thunder as he ran toward the house. It sounded as if the earth were splitting behind him (Emery, 1965).

Or, an author might use language full of images:

> The sea became a wildcat now, and the galleon her prey. She stalked the ship and drove her off her course. She slapped at her, rolling her victim from side to side. She knocked the spars out of her and used them to ram holes in her sides. She clawed the rudder from its sternpost and threw it into the sea. She cracked the ship's ribs as if they were brittle bones. Then she hissed and spat through the seams (Henry, 1947).

The meaning of the story, both as intended and as perceived, is affected by the author's choice and use of words. Some of the ways to manipulate words are alliteration, personification, and metaphor and simile. In addition, an author can manipulate whole units of language to create moods.

Alliteration is the repetition of similar or near similar sounds in order to create an effect:

> And a noise that's a growl,
> and a roar,
> and a wheeze,
> and a whistle all stirred together (Alexander, 1960).

> "creepy-crawly caterpillar"

Personification is the suggestion of human traits in non-human animals, or animal traits in inanimate objects:

> The galleon shuddered. From bow to stern came an endless rasping sound! (Henry, 1947)

> Seashell, whisper in my ear
> All the secrets you hold dear (Fay et al., 1974).

> The wildcat sea yawned. She swallowed the men (Henry, 1947).

Metaphor and simile are comparisons that evoke mental images of sights, sounds, feelings, and tastes:

> The air was heavy, musky with an odor not unlike rotting fruit or aging garbage (Monteleone, 1974).

> It looked like a pile of broken twigs and oilcloth as it trembled and fluttered on the ground (Monteleone, 1974).

> The air about them quivered like a violin string. Then suddenly the string snapped, and the everyday world was all about once more (Henry, 1947).

Moods are suggested through the use of images and words that have strong connotations:

> For a while longer Tonka sat quietly on the mossy log in the sun, but the sun had little warmth even though it was late May. The last great Ice Age was gone, but its cold lingered on. He drew his fox skin more tightly around his shoulders and looked away through the forest. Perhaps, he thought, he might see one of the beasts that the hunters of the tribe often killed and brought back to the cave where they all lived. But the forest was dark and forbidding, and he dared not venture beyond the stream to see what was there (Hutchins, 1965).

Teachers should be careful not to inject their personalities into the story.

Theme Development. The theme of a piece of literature provides the reader with the significance of the action or experience (Cullinan, 1971). It is the message of the story, the purpose for which the author took pen in hand and placed words upon the page. The theme is a presence that transcends the characters, the plot, and the setting. The themes of greatest impact are generally implicit in the plot and characterizations. An explicit theme may tend to create an impression of moralizing or preaching.

The range of themes that is found in children's literature is immense. In order to fully appreciate an author's theme, however, pupils need to first understand that themes exist in literature. After realizing that, pupils need to have experiences with themes to which they can relate. Unless they "know" a theme before it is encountered, there is no way that it will be recognized within a story. Pupils, therefore, need exposure to various relevant themes so as to build a storehouse of universal ideas which they can relate to those found in their independent reading.

Uses of Literature

Children's literature can be categorized by the use to which it will be put (Cullinan, 1971). For example, the literature may be classified by an

When adults select children's books, they assume their view of relevance is shared by the children

educational use—say, by age groupings or reading levels. Or, it may be classified by the concepts that are to be developed—say, by cultures, occupations, or animal survival. Also, a work may be classified according to the influence it has on the reader. This use, called bibliotherapy, is discussed in greater length below.

Classifying children's literature by the manner it will be used is helpful only to the teacher. There is no real advantage to elementary pupils to understand this functional classification scheme because it provides them with no clear signals to the appreciation and understanding of an author's story and message. Therefore, although teachers will use this scheme for locating books, it is not one they would necessarily use for instructional purposes.

STRATEGIES FOR BRINGING CHILDREN AND LITERATURE TOGETHER

A successful literature program in the elementary school is contingent on the teacher's possessing two qualities: a knowledge of children's literature, and a positive attitude toward reading. Of the two, the second quality may be more important because a teacher can always receive assistance in selecting reading material for pupils. A positive attitude towards reading is something that teachers must develop before they can instill it in their pupils. It is quite difficult to develop an appreciation for the author's craft without being a habitual, appreciative, discriminating reader oneself. As was indicated in Chapter 1, teachers need to have an awareness of the world beyond their technical training—and one way in which this is accomplished is through the reading of literature.

Teachers must have a positive attitude toward reading

Using Library Resources

Wherever one teaches, the school library should function as an integral part of the classroom reading program. The teacher should be aware of what transpires in the library, and the librarian should know the activities taking place in the classroom. When the library is integrated with the classroom reading and literature programs, it provides effective service at varying levels. The library becomes an adjunct to the classroom, and the teacher becomes apprised of the availability of library materials and the librarian of the individual abilities of the pupils. This joint venture can lead

The library is an integral part of the reading program

to meaningful, effective, and valuable experiences for the pupils, the teachers, and the librarian.

Classroom libraries can be built up by borrowing books from the school library or the local public library. The librarian can assist in selecting the books and stories, or the teacher can refer to one of the resources indicated below. Classroom libraries can also be organized with books and other reading matter donated by the pupils. After permission has been obtained from parents, the pupils can lend the classroom library some of their books for the duration of the school year. Or, pupils can be encouraged to join book clubs and leave their selctions in the class library until the year ends.

Whatever means is used, the pupils must have a source from which they can select reading material that varies in topics, difficulty, and interests: books, short stories, magazines, plays, poems, and newspapers.

Selecting Children's Literature

Readings should have literary quality

The books, poems, plays, and stories chosen for use in the planned literature program should reflect some qualities of literary merit. A review of often-used texts on the use of children's literature in the elementary school revealed that

1. The factors that determine literary quality in children's literature are the same as those in adult literature: plot, content, theme, characterization, style, and form.
2. The choice of subject matter and its treatment differentiates children's literature from adult literature, not the quality of writing or the depth of emotion expressed (Ladevich, 1974).

Aside from selecting literature through established criteria, literature can be judged to be of some merit and quality when children themselves select the material for their independent reading. Children have a need to satisfy a basic desire to stretch beyond their surroundings and themselves (Fenwick, 1968). When they consistently choose from among the same core of books and stories, there is evidence that those materials have some measure of literary quality. Therefore, teachers should be sure to consider children's tastes when books are being labeled as fine literature (Darkatsh, 1974).

With the many books being published each year, teachers need some way to differentiate among them. In order to guide teachers, the following questions (from Huck and Kuhn, 1968) can be used to assist in judging children's fiction:

Plot

    Does the book tell a good story? Will children enjoy it?
    Is the plot original and fresh?
    Is it plausibile and credible? Do the events logically follow one another?
    Is there an identifiable climax?
    How do events build to a climax?
    Is the plot well constructed?

Setting

    Where does the story take place?
    How does the author indicate the time?
    How does the setting affect the action, characters, or theme?
    Does the story transcend the setting and have universal implications?

Theme

    Does the story have a theme?
    Is the theme worth imparting to children?
    Does the theme emerge naturally from the story or is it stated too obviously?
    Does the theme overpower the story?
    Does it avoid moralizing?

Characterization

    How does the author reveal characters? Through narration? In conversation? By the thoughts of others? By the thoughts of the character? Through action?
    Are the characters convincing and credible?
    Do we see their strengths and their weaknesses?
    Does the author avoid stereotyping?
    Is the behavior of the characters consistent with their age and background?
    Is there any character development or growth?
    Has the author shown the causes of character behavior or development?

Style

    Is the style of writing appropriate to the subject?
    Is the style straightforward or figurative?

Is the dialogue natural and suited to the characters?
Does the author balance narration and dialogue?
What are the main characteristics of the sentence patterns?
How did the author create a mood? Is the overall impression one of mystery, gloom, evil, joy, security?
What symbols or signs has the author used to communicate meaning?
Is the point of view from which the story is told appropriate to the purpose of the book?

Format

Do the illustrations enhance the story?
Are the illustrations consistent with the story?
How is the format of the book related to the text?
What is the quality of the paper?
How sturdy is the binding?

Other Considerations

How does the book compare with other books on the same subject?
How does the book compare with other books written by the same author?
How have other reviewers evaluated this book?

In order to guide teachers, the following questions (also from Huck and Kuhn, 1968) can be used to assist in judging informational books for children:

Accuracy and authenticity

What are the qualifications of the author?
Are facts accurate?
Is the book realistic?
Are facts and theories clearly distinguished?
Do text and illustrations avoid stereotypes?
Is the book up-to-date?
Are significant details omitted?
Do generalizations go beyond present knowledge?
Are differing viewpoints presented?
In geographic books, is diversity revealed?
In science books, is anthropomorphism omitted?
Are phenomena given teleological explanations?

Content
    Is this a general survey book or is this one of some specific interest?
    Is the coverage of the book adequate for its purpose?
    Is the book within the comprehension and interest range of the age for which it is intended?
    Do experiment books lead to understanding science?
    Are experiments and activities safe and feasible?
    Does the book present interrelationships of facts and principles?
    Do science books indicate related social problems?
    Is the book fresh and original?
    Does the book help the reader understand the methods of science and social science?

Style
    Is information given directly or in story form?
    Is the text interesting and appropriate for the age level intended?
    Do vivid language and appropriate metaphor engender interest and understanding?
    Is the language pattern clear and simple, or heavy and pedantic?
    Is there an appropriate amount of detail?
    Does the book encourage curiosity and further study?

Format and Illustrations
    Do illustrations clarify and add to the text?
    Do different types of media maintain clarity of concepts?
    Are illustrations explained by captions or labels?
    Are size relationships made clear?
    Do size of type and use of space contribute to clarity?
    Are endpapers used effectively?

Organization
    Are subheadings used effectively?
    Do the table of contents and index help the reader locate information quickly?
    Does the bibliography indicate sources used by the author, and sources for further reading by the children?
    Do appendixes extend information?

RESOURCES FOR THE TEACHER

When teachers do not have the time, the experience, or the interest to assess all the books that will be made available to their pupils, there are other means that may be used to assist them in selecting reading material of exemplary literary quality. They can refer to professional texts, book lists, professional journals, and instructional materials.

Professional Texts

Professional texts written to inform teachers of the entire field of children's literature usually contain references to books, stories, plays, and poems of exceptional quality. Two comprehensive references are:

> Arbuthnot, May Hill and Sutherland, Zena. 1972. *Children and Books.* 4th Edition. Glenview, Ill.: Scott, Foresman.
>
> Huck, Charlotte S. 1976. *Children's Literature in the Elementary School.* 3rd Edition. New York: Holt, Rinehart and Winston.

A good reference that is available in paperback is:

> Larrick, Nancy. 1975. *A Parent's Guide to Children's Reading.* 4th Edition. New York: Doubleday. Available in paperback from Bantam Books.

Book Lists

There are many books lists available for guiding teachers in the selection of children's literature. These can be considered "starter lists" to which other books of matching quality can be added. Some of the lists are general, others specific, depending upon the agency that compiled them. Two sources of general lists are:

> The Children's Services Division
> American Library Association
> 50 East Huron Street
> Chicago, Illinois 60611
>
> The Children's Book Council
> 175 Fifth Avenue
> New York, New York 10010

An annotated list of books arranged by age, compiled by teams of teachers representing the Children's Book Council and the International Reading Association, resulted from the field testing of books. The list contains those books that children either selected to read or asked to be read to them. The two organizations plan to compile and publish an annual list of children's choices.

> "Classroom Choices: Children's Trade Books, 1974," *The Reading Teacher* 29 (November 1975): 122-32.

Specialized lists are available that cover a wide range of topics. In developing literature programs for fostering an appreciation of the pluralistic nature of American society, the following lists may be useful. Others can be obtained from the ERIC Clearinghouse on Reading and Communication Skills, 111 Kenyon Road, Urbana, Illinois 61801.

> Arth, Alfred A., and Whittemore, Judith D. 1973. "Selecting Literature for Children That Relates to Life, the Way It Is." *Elementary English* 50: 726-28, 744.
>
> Reed, Linda. 1976. "Multi-Ethnic Literature and the Elementary School Curriculum." *Language Arts* 53: 256-61.

The following is intended for junior and senior high school students, but the material could be a source of materials for reading to elementary pupils.

> Stensland, Anna Lee. 1973. *Literature By and About the American Indian: An Annotated Bibliography.* Urbana, Ill.: National Council of Teachers of English.

There are many periodicals for children which can be located through Association for Childhood Education International. *Guide to Children's Magazines, Newspapers, Reference Books.* Washington, D.C.: Association for Childhood Education International.

> Martin, Laura K. *Magazines for School Libraries.* New York: R. R. Bowker Co.

Professional Journals

Various journals contain listings and reviews of current publications. The first two references are devoted entirely to children's literature. The others contain regular features in which current children's literature is reviewed.

> *Bulletin of the Center for Children's Books.* The University of Chicago Press, 5801 Ellis Avenue, Chicago, Illinois 60637.
>
> *The Horn Book Magazine.* Horn Book, Inc. 585 Boylston Street, Boston, Massachusetts 02116.

Language Arts. National Council of Teachers of English, 1111 Kenyon Road, Urbana, Illinois 61801.

The Reading Teacher. International Reading Association, 800 Barksdale Road, Newark, Delaware 19711.

The School Library Journal. R. R. Bowker Co. 1180 Avenue of the Americas, New York, New York 10036.

Instructional Materials

When teachers have the opportunity to select materials for their literature programs, there are a number of sources from which they can choose. Almost every major publisher has a children's book division which often makes books available in both hardcover and paperback. Also, some publishers deal entirely in reprinting books in paperback and then in making those selections available through book club plans to the schools:

Scholastic Book Services
50 West 44th Street
New York, New York 10017

Weekly Reader Paperback Book Club
Education Center
Columbus, Ohio 43216

Xerox Education Publications Book Clubs
245 Long Hill Road
Middletown, Connecticut 06457

When teachers feel insecure about making selections, there are ready-made sources on which they can rely. Some of the publishers of basal reading series provide literature anthology series. A good anthology series has selections with a wide range of topics, interests, styles, and forms.

One exemplary series is:
Sounds of Language Readers. 1974. Revised. New York: Holt, Rinehart and Winston.

Teachers who wish to develop their literature program as an individualized reading experience will find that some publishers also package books in what are infelicitously called "supplementary libraries." Each contains a variety of books and is accompanied by activity cards and lessons. Representative of such libraries are:

One-To-One: A Practical Individualized Reading Program. Tarrytown, N.Y.: Prentice-Hall Media. (Junior Edition for grades 1–4, and Senior Edition for grades 4–8.)

Individualized Reading. New York: Scholastic Book Service. (Units for each grade 1-6.)

Random House Individualized Skill Pacers. New York: Random House. (Kits for each grade 1-6.)

The following two guides provide teachers with extensive plans for selected children's books. Included are a wide range of activities and suggested further readings for each theme and book. Teachers can develop their own lessons for other books following the format set out in the guides.

Reasoner, Charles F. 1968. *Releasing Children to Literature.* New York: Dell.

Reasoner, Charles R. 1972. *Where the Readers Are.* New York: Dell.

ACTIVITIES FOR DEVELOPING AN UNDERSTANDING AND APPRECIATION OF LITERATURE

In order to foster the development of literature reading strategies, pupils should be engaged in activities designed to challenge their thinking. Pupils can be asked to undertake the following:

Activities should challenge pupils' thinking

☐ Construct a chart or "map" of the plot of a story. The pupils are to draw in the main plot and any subplots, indicating how the important events are produced as these meet or diverge. Also, the activity of the main and minor characters can be traced in relation to the movement of the main events of the story.

☐ Read or listen to a story up to a point near the climax. Have the pupils discuss possible endings of the story which would be logical with the flow of the events and the credibility of the characters. Complete the reading of the story and compare the pupils' endings with that of the author.

☐ Select vocabulary from some classic piece of children's literature and discuss whether the words are still used in the same manner today. Have pupils suggest what words might be used to "modernize" the story.

☐ Analyze the illustrations that accompany some work of literature.

Have the pupils decide whether the illustrations enhance the story or distract from it. Try to have the pupils determine whether the illustration is appropriate in topic, style, and color for the particular story or poem.

☐ Analyze television programs and movies by the same criteria for judging the quality of children's fiction. Have the pupils classify the program or movie by plot, theme, characterizations, and language style.

☐ Select a paragraph from a story and rewrite it by changing the vocabulary without changing the paragraph's meaning.

☐ Listen to two or more different recordings of the same story or poem. Have the pupils discuss the quality of the oral presentation in relation to the intended meaning of the author.

☐ Compose stories and poems based upon models that have been studied. Pupils can begin by making parodies of some classic fairy tales and by "extending" stories and poems that use repetitive elements. As the pupils gain familiarity with plot structures, themes, and characterizations, they should compose original stories and poems.

To extend the pupils' understanding of characterizations and plot development ask the pupils to:

☐ Prepare a situation in which two or more characters from different books meet. The meeting should be a logical outcome of incidents in both books, and the conversation that ensues should be credible and consistent with the portrayal of the characters.

☐ Construct plot, events, and theme for the character in a story. The pupils may be familiar with "spin-offs" that result from a minor character on a television series being highlighted in a new series. Have the pupils create a "spin-off" based upon some secondary character in a story.

☐ Select a plot from a familiar story and create a different theme. The pupils are to decide how the characters might be portrayed differently in order for that theme to be significant.

In order to encourage pupils' interest in a variety of literary forms and styles, have the pupils share their books through reports, art projects, and dramatizations. Ask the pupils to:

☐ Create collages, dioramas, "movie" boxes, posters, and book jackets that illustrate an important aspect of the story.

It may be the unfamiliar, not the familiar, that intrigues children

☐ Select an event and dramatize it through a puppet show. The pupils are to construct the puppets to represent the characters in the story. The dialogue may be taken from the story, or it can be fictionalized.

☐ Entice other pupils to read the book through written advertisements or book auctions in which succeeding portions of the story are revealed for "a price."

☐ Study in depth one particular author or illustrator. Have the pupils read as many works as possible of that individual as well as any available biographies. Then have the pupils write and/or illustrate their own stories in the style of the person studied.

STRATEGIES FOR USING BIBLIOTHERAPY

Bibliotherapy is based upon the premise that books are dynamic and have the potential to change the attitudes, habits, and skills of the individuals

Meaningful reading can lead to changed attitudes

who read them (Shepherd and Iles, 1976). When a pupil is engaged in appropriate and meaningful reading, the reader's personality is affected by that particular book, story, or poem. The result is that the reader may develop (1) an enlarged sphere of interest, (2) an increased social sensitivity, (3) the realization that others have a life struggle, and (4) the realization that there is more than one solution to a problem (Corman, 1975).

As a process, bibliotherapy takes the reader through the stages of

1. Identification. The reader, vicariously participating with a character in a book or story, realizes that there is some common trait or bond between them. The reader makes an identification with the story character and becomes ready to "live the other's life."
2. Catharsis. After identification with a character is established, the reader can experience a release of emotions as the character works through a problem.
3. Insight. When the experience results in a shaping and changing of an individual's manner of thinking, then bibliotherapy has been effective. The reader realizes that a transfer of the actions and/or attitudes of a story character can be made to a real life situation (Corman, 1975).

Bibliotherapy works best with individuals who are not severly maladjusted

The processes should not be viewed as a cure-all. There are no guarantees that a particular book will influence any particular pupil, or that the influence, if it does occur, will be in the desired direction (Corman, 1975). Bibliotherapy is not foolproof. It seems to work best with individuals who are not severely maladjusted. Therefore, the following guidelines should be followed whenever teachers attempt to effect a change in pupils' interests, attitudes, or behavior through the reading of books:

1. Aim towards helping the child with a minor problem or question. Any seriously disturbed child should be referred to the school psychologist, guidance counselor, or nurse.

2. Avoid directly mentioning the problem. The intent is not that teachers become the therapeutic agents but that they merely arrange a situation that may have beneficial effects.
3. Select books the content, characterizations and situations of which are believable. Unless the book is real to the individual, there can be no identification with a character.
4. Create situations in which the pupils will select books without coercion. The individual must "happen" upon the book or story. Since all people, children and adults, live with a romanticized vision of themselves, any direct threat on that vision is greatly resisted. The best results seem to occur serendipitously (Shepherd and Iles, 1976).

In order to undertake the use of bibliotherapy in the classroom, teachers need books that naturally portray the problems and conflicts pupils encounter in their lives. Sometimes a teacher will wish to affect the attitudes of an entire class; at other times, there will be an interest in attending to the needs of just one pupil. The following is a major resource for locating literature appropriate for use in working out problems of human relations.

Reid, Virginia. 1972. *Reading Ladders for Human Relations.* 5th Edition. Washington, D.C.: The American Council on Education. Available from: National Council of Teachers of English, 1111 Kenyon Road, Urbana, Illinois 61801.

A list of suggested books about bibliotherapy can be found in the following annotated bibliography.

Riggs, Corinne W. 1971. *Bibliotherapy: An Annotated Bibliography.* Newark, Del.: International Reading Association.

DISCUSSION QUESTIONS AND ACTIVITIES

1. Find out what children are reading. Visit a school and public library and interview children about their book selections. Find out why they are choosing the books they do. Then, interview teachers and librarians to find out what they think children *are* and *should be* reading. Compare the results of the two sets of interviews.

2. Investigate the criteria by which books are given awards. Information can be obtained from The Children's Book Council and the American

Library Association. Select one year's awards and compare the winner and the runner-ups. Would your decision have been the same as that of the judges?

3. Investigate the current movement in the media arts toward "visual literacy." In what ways do the criteria for quality and for understanding differ between the judging of a visual story and a written story?

4. Explain what Charlotte Huck (1968) may mean in the following:

> The ultimate experience of a story or a poem lies in the way it is told, not in just the facts or events it relates.

5. Is it true, as John Barrett (1968) says, that

> Only that book which helps the student to clarify and thus to define is going to be seen by him as relevant and will thus be for him an experience that has meaning; all other books will be irrelevant and meaningless.

6. Plan a topical unit for use with pupils in a particular grade level. Develop the theme of the unit through a variety of literary forms and styles. Be sure to include selections appropriate to a wide range of reading abilities.

7. Plan a bulletin board display to be used for introducing pupils in the primary grades to the different types of literary forms.

8. Plan a book fair, and contact local merchants or book suppliers about the availability of books. Then plan a campaign to encourage elementary pupils and their parents to attend. If possible, work with a local parents' or teachers' organization to actually hold the book fair.

9. Explain what this statement by Helen Koss (1972) means to you: "Relevance is a matter of applicability."

10. What is your definition of "literature"? Investigate how various authors define the term, then write your own definition.

FURTHER READINGS   The first reference discusses the place of literature in elementary education. The author presents a theory with practical instructional suggestions for unifying the language arts so literature is the center of language studies.

    Sloan, Glenna Davis. 1975. *The Child As Critic: Teaching Literature in the Elementary School.* New York: Teachers College Press, Columbia University.

Those who wish to delve more into the effects reading has upon the individual should read

    Russell, David H. 1970. *The Dynamics of Reading.* Edited by Robert B. Ruddell. Waltham, Massachusetts: Ginn and Co.

In addition to the general texts mentioned within the chapter, the following should provide teachers with a comprehensive perspective of a balanced literature program:

    Anderson, William, and Groff, Patrick. 1972. *A New Look At Children's Literature.* Belmont, Cal.: Wadsworth.

The following text organizes and discusses children's literature in terms of social issues.

    Rudman, Masha Kabakow. 1976. *Children's Literature: An Issues Approach.* Lexington, Mass.: D. C. Heath.

The following monograph, although it uses mostly examples from the secondary school level, contains ideas that can be made applicable at all grade levels.

    Weiss, M. Jerry, Brunner, Joseph, and Heis, Warren, eds. 1973. *New Perspectives on Paperbacks.* Monograph No. 1. The College Reading Association. (May be obtained from Strine Printing Co., 391 Greendale Road, York, Penn. 17403.)

The International Reading Association (Newark, Delaware) has published a number of collected articles on topics relating to the teaching of children's literature.

    Carlson, Ruth Kearney, ed. 1972. *Folklore and Folktales Around the World.*

    Catterson, Jane H., ed. 1970. *Children and Literature.*

    Huus, Helen, ed. 1968. *Evaluating Books for Children and Young People.*

    Painter, Helen W. 1970. *Poetry and Children.*

    Painter, Helen W., ed. 1971. *Reaching Children and Young People Through Literature.*

    Sebasta, Sam Leaton, ed. 1968. *Ivory, Apes, and Peacocks.*

    Tanyzer, Harold, and Karl, Jean, eds. 1972. *Reading Children's Books, and our Pluralistic Society.*

The following, also published by the International Reading Association, is an interpretive paper meant to help teachers deal with children having problems by building their self concept.

Quandt, Ivan. (Undated.) *Self Concept and Reading.*

Periodically, *Language Arts* (formerly *Elementary English*) focuses on various themes related to children's literature. The following issues may be of interest:

Volume 53, March, 1976: "Realism for Ethnic Groups" January, 1975: "Experiencing Poetry"

Volume 52, October, 1975: "Encouraging Students to Read" May, 1975: "Combating Stereotypes"

Volume 51, October, 1974: "Books and Children" September, 1974: "Editors Write About Authors" March, 1974: "Children, Books, and Literature"

Volume 50, November/December, 1973: "Poetry" October, 1973: "Women and Girls" May, 1973: "Children's Literature" February, 1973: "Special Needs of Ethnic Groups"

References

Alexander, Anne. 1960. *Noise in the Night.* Chicago: Rand McNally.

Arth, Alfred A., and Whittemore, Judith D. 1973. "Selecting Literature for Children That Relates to Life, The Way It Is." *Elementary English* 50: 726–28, 744.

Barret, John. 1968. "Relevancy of Content to Today's Students." In Helen Huus, ed. *Evaluating Books for Children and Young People.* Newark, Del.: International Reading Association.

Corman, Cheryl. 1975. "Bibliotherapy—Insight for the Learning Handicapped." *Language Arts* 52: 935–37.

Cullinan, Bernice E. 1971. *Literature for Children: Its Discipline and Content.* Dubuque, Iowa: William C. Brown Co.

Cullinan, Bernice E. 1974. "Teaching Literature to Children, 1966–1972." In H. Alan Robinson and Alvina Truet Burrows, eds. *Teacher Effectiveness in Elementary Language Arts: A Progress Report.* Urbana, Ill.: National Council on Research in English/ERIC-RCS, pp. 25–37.

Darkatsh, Manuel. 1974. "Who Should Decide on a Book's Merit?" *Elementary English* 51: 352–4.

Elkind, David. 1972. "Ethnicity and Reading: Three Avoidable Dangers." In Harold Tanyzer and Jean Karl, eds. *Reading Children's Books, and Our Pluralistic Society*. Newark, Del.: International Reading Association.

Emery, Anne. 1965. *A Spy in Old West Point*. Chicago: Rand McNally.

Fay, Leo, and Anderson, Paul S. 1974. *Young America Basic Reading Program*. Level 11, Teacher's Edition. Chicago: Rand McNally.

Fay, Leo, Ross, Ramon Royal, and LaPray, Margaret. 1974. *Young America Basic Reading Program*. Produced by Lyons & Carnahan. Chicago: Rand McNally.

Fenwick, Sara Innis. 1968. "Selecting and Evaluating Materials for Recreational Reading." In Sam Leaton Sebasta, ed. *Ivory, Apes, and Peacocks: The Literature Point of View*. Newark, Del.: International Reading Association.

Henry, Marguerite. 1947. *Misty of Chincoteague*. Chicago: Rand McNally.

Higgins, James E. 1970. *Beyond Words: Mystical Fancy in Children's Literature*. New York: Teachers College Press, Columbia University.

Huck, Charlotte. 1968. "Reading Literature Critically." In Sam Leaton Sebasta, ed. *Ivory, Apes, and Peacocks: The Literature Point of View*. Newark, Del.: International Reading Association.

Huck, Charlotte S. and Kuhn, Doris Y. 1968. *Children's Literature in the Elementary School*. 2nd Edition. New York: Holt, Rinehart and Winston.

Hutchins, Ross. 1973. *Tonka, the Cave Boy*. Chicago: Rand McNally.

Huus, Helen. 1975. "Approaches to the Use of Literature in the Reading Program." In Bonnie Smith Schulwitz, ed. *Teachers, Tangibles, Techniques: Comprehension of Content in Reading*. Newark, Del.: International Reading Association.

Jenkins, Esther C. 1973. "Multi-Ethnic Literature: Promise and Problems." *Elementary English* 50: 693–99.

Koss, Helen G. 1972. "Relevancy and Children's Literature." *Elementary English* 49: 991–2.

Ladevich, Laurel. 1974. "Determining Literary Quality in Children's Literature." *Elementary English* 51: 983–86.

Lear, Edward. 1966. *The Complete Nonsense Book*. New York: Dodd Mead & Co.

Lundsteen, Sara W. 1976. *Children Learn to Communicate: Language Arts Through Creative Problem Solving*. Englewood Cliffs, N.J.: Prentice-Hall.

Merla, Patrick. 1972. "'What Is *Real*?' Asked the Rabbit One Day." *Saturday Review* (November 4, 1972): 43–50.

Monteleone, Thomas F. 1974. "The Thing from Ennis Rock." In Roger Elwood, ed. *More Science Fiction Tales.* Chicago: Rand McNally.

Painter, Helen. 1975. "Literature Develops Reading Skills." In Bonnie Smith Schulwitz, ed. *Teachers, Tangibles, Techniques: Comprehension of Content in Reading.* Newark, Del.: International Reading Association.

Reed, Linda. 1976. "Multi-Ethnic Literature and the Elementary School Curriculum." *Language Arts* 53: 256-61.

Shepherd, Terry, and Iles, Lynn B. 1976. "What Is Bibliotherapy?" *Language Arts* 53: 569-71.

Sims, Rudine. 1976. "What Else Are Kids Reading?" Paper presented at the Preconvention Institute, "What Could/Should Kids Be Reading?" at the 21st Annual Convention of the International Reading Association, Anaheim, California, May 10.

Sloan, Glenna Davis. 1975. *The Child As Critic: Teaching Literature in the Elementary School.* New York: Teachers College Press, Columbia University.

Smith, Nila Banton. 1960. "Literature for Space-Age Children." *Education Magazine,* pp. 1-4.

Terry, Ann. 1972. *Children's Poetry Preferences: A National Survey of Upper Elementary Grades.* Urbana, Ill.: National Council of Teachers of English.

12

Strategies for Pupils with Special Needs

Focus Questions:

1. What problems in learning to read are faced by speakers of divergent dialects?
2. How can nonnative speakers of English become effective readers in English?
3. What are the characteristics of reading and learning disabilities?
4. How can pupils with special needs be instructed in the regular classroom?

A common idea can be found in the following discussions of pupils with special needs.[1] Basically, it is that their inability to function in school is due to an inability to effectively receive and transmit information. Since the vehicle for communication is language, an understanding of the nature of verbal and nonverbal communication (such as that given in Chapter 2) is essential to an understanding of pupils' lack of effectiveness in learning to read in school.

We will talk about three types of pupils with special needs—speakers of divergent dialects, pupils for whom English is a second language, and pupils with difficulties in learning to read.

An inability to function in school may be due to an inability to receive and transmit information

---

1. This chapter was written with Michele K. Heiman.

UNDERSTANDING THE NEEDS OF DIVERGENT DIALECT SPEAKERS

In every major language there can be found variations among its speakers in the pronunciation of sounds, in the formation of sentences, and in the use of meanings assigned to words. When these variations are consistently used by an identifiable group of speakers, it is called a dialect. American English speech is a family of dialects; each individual dialect is a legitimate form of communication for its speakers (Goodman, 1969). Within a language group, dialects seem to have two dimensions (Foerster, 1974). One is geographic and is observable in regional dialect variations such as those heard in Maine, New York, and Texas. The other is closely allied with the socioeconomic status of individuals. At one extreme is the speech of the poor and disenfranchised. At the other extreme is the speech of the affluent and the highly educated. Between them lie many other dialects. These two dimensions function simultaneously so that each regional grouping has its own socioeconomic variations.

Each English dialect is a legitimate form of communication

A dialect is not "slang," which is a deliberate word substitution within a dialect. All dialects can have expressions that are considered slang.

Standard American English is just one dialect that has been arbitrarily set by society as the language of business, government, and mass communication. Standard American English is that language most commonly used by announcers and newscasters and heard on most national radio and television news and informational programs. It is not sharply set off from most other main dialects, and there is no one region that solely possesses this variety of the English language. The reason for this seems to be the extreme regional and social mobility within the general society. The word "standard" in regard to this language variety is probably unfortunate and misleading. Just as a "standardized test" score is not something that represents an ideal toward which all instruction should aim, the "standard dialect" should not be so conceived either. Even the written form does not represent any extensively used spoken form and should not be used as the basis for oral language instruction.

The standard dialect is not an ideal

Black American Dialects

The largest group of divergent dialects within American society are those labeled Black American English. An understanding of how the Black dialects evolved should help to clarify the nature of the existing differences between Black American English and Standard American English. The history of Black American English can be summarized as follows (Stewart, 1966).

Africans made up some of the very first immigrants to colonial America when they were brought as slaves. As were all immigrants, they were faced with the problem of acquiring the language of the new nation. As a result of slave trade, a kind of pidgin was formed. (Pidgins are hybrid forms of language that are used by individuals who are native speakers of another language.) Many Africans who were brought to America were already speakers of an English pidgin, as were many of the Americans engaged in the slave trade. The policy of slave owners and slave buyers to mix the Africans of different language and cultural groups forced the Afro-American to rely on this means rather than their native tongue to maintain communication with others. The pidgin flourished, and seems to have affected the English spoken by both slaves and slave owners.

Today, communities in many urban and rural areas display a range of dialects. Much dialect blending occurs as members of the different linguistic communities become mobile.

Unquestionably, the term Black American English is stereotypical, but it does exist. Many features of pronunciation, grammar, and lexicon are shared by a large number of speakers (Labov, 1966). These features are acquired socially and perpetuated socially. Research into the forms of these features has indicated how Black American English and Standard American English differ (Baratz, 1968). Examples of these differences can be found in Table 12-1. It should be noted that not all researchers agree as to the form and frequency in which these features are found in Black American English. It might be best to look upon these features as those that are often used by a majority of the speakers in Black urban communities. No one individual would probably use them all, all of the time.

Barriers to Comprehension

Barriers to effective communication were discussed in Chapter 2. Two factors discussed then are relevant to the discussion here: Communication may be hindered because of the use of different linguistic codes or because of "emotional static." The first barrier occurs when two or more individuals are attempting to communicate in the belief that their utterances are mutually intelligible. The other may occur when attitudes about the back-

Communication may be hindered by emotional static or codes that are not shared

TABLE 12-1: Features of Black American English

Phonological Features

Certain sounds may be omitted from medial and/or final positions:
- /r/ from words such as *guard* (becoming /god/)
- /l/ from words such as *tall* and *help* (becoming /taw/ and /hep/)
- /t/, /d/, /s/, and /z/ in final clusters in words such as *past, bites, nest* (becoming /pass/, /bite/, and /nes/)
- Some final consonants may be lost in words such as *bat* and *hand* (becoming /bah/ and /han/)

Certain sounds may be similarly pronounced or interchanged:
- /m/ and /n/ may be indistinguishable in words such as *ram* (becoming /ran/)
- /th/ in initial position may become /d/ in words such as *them* (becoming /dem/)
- /sk/ in medial or final position may become /ks/ in words such as *ask* (becoming /aks/)
- /th/ in final position may become /v/ or /f/ in words such as *breathe* and *both* (becoming /breev/ and /bohf/)
- /sk/ may be substituted for /st/ in initial position in such words as *street* (becoming /skreet/)
- /e/ and /i/ may become indistinguishable in words such as *pen* and *pin* (becoming /pin/ and /pin/)

Syntactic Features

Certain transformations may occur in verb forms:
- The present tense, third person: *He walks* becomes *He walk*.
- The present progressive: *She is singing* becomes *She sing*.
- The past tense irregular: *He took it* becomes *He taken it*.
- Past perfect irregular: *He has taken it* becomes *He have took it*.
- Future: *I am going to do it* may become *I'm a do it*.
- Present habitual: *She is* (always) *doing it* may become *She be doing it*.
- Past habitual: *He used to do it* may become *He been doing it*.

Certain transformations may occur in sentence structure:
- Negation: *They don't have any* may become *They don't got none*.
- Questions
  - Indirect: *I asked if he fixed it* may become *I asked did he fix it?*
  - Direct: *How did you do that* may become *How you do that?*
- The subject: *My mother is there* may become *My mother, she there*.
- Plural nouns: *Those pencils* may become *Them pencils*.
- Possessive: *Phillip's book* may become *Phillip book*.

SOURCE: After Zintz (1975).

grounds of pupils with divergent dialects interfere with the acceptance of their ideas and contributions in school.

For many years, speakers of divergent dialects—which usually meant speakers of Black American English, but also may have included any minority members—were considered as "disadvantaged" learners. It was felt that their "disadvantagedness" resulted from their "substandard" speech and thinking. Sometimes the term "culturally disadvantaged" was applied to indicate that the pupils were not prepared by the pre-school environment to cope with school situations. Such, however, are definitely misnomers, since group members which society has so labeled learn to function as well as any other group members among their peers (Wheat, 1974). The label becomes the reality when individuals are taken from a familiar environment and placed in a system that seems alien.

Pupils who come from minority cultures and speak a divergent English dialect may come to school not having had some experiences that it might be presumed they had. Success in school is therefore hindered not because the pupils cannot do the school tasks, but because they bring different understandings to the task. This then works with the pupils' unfamiliarity with certain linguistic conventions used in school. The result is an apparent lack of understanding and an inability to perform school tasks.

There are a number of important learnings which are prerequisites to successful school achievement (see Chapter 6). The pupils who receive sensory and intellectual stimulation of the kind upon which school learnings are based generally possess these prerequisites. However, some pupils may be deprived of these learnings or may have received markedly different learnings which may interfere with their school achievement (Edwards, 1969). It is *not* that such pupils cannot speak and think; it is just that what they do think and speak about is different from what they may be asked to do in school. Their cognitive and linguistic backgrounds are different, not inferior.

Pupils come to school with the ability to communicate with others within their immediate social environment. It is when some pupils are confronted with the unfamiliarity of the school code and experiences that these pupils are presented with a barrier for communicating and comprehending. Researchers have discovered that when two communicators do not share considerable experiences or points of view, if they are to communicate they need to use an elaborated code—one that employs extensive language signals. The factor controlling the extent to which a message needs an elaborated code is the extent to which the communicators share attitudes and experiences, or "context" (Erickson, 1968). High shared context situations allow for the use of a restricted code since there is considerable overlap of experience and points of view between the communicators. Low shared context situations necessitate the use of the elaborated codes. "As context increases the volume of necessary communication signals decreases" (Erickson, 1968).

Developing Comprehension Across Dialects

Three alternative views have been offered by various authorities for developing literacy among speakers of different dialects. They are: (1)

teach standard American English before teaching the pupils to read, (2) create instructional materials using the dialect patterns, and (3) allow the pupils to retain their dialect patterns while reading standard patterns.

Those who advocate teaching Standard American English prior to formal reading instruction generally recommend that the standard dialect be taught as a "second language." Many instructional plans use the procedures of foreign language teachers. Others imply that standard forms should be learned because the dialects represent stunted language growth (Bereiter and Englemann, 1966; and Englemann, 1969). This is pure nonsense. Every language and dialect is a highly complex system capable of ordering and categorizing the world, though each might do it a little differently. The fact that some ideas are difficult to express in a dialect also holds true for the standard dialect. Thus, although no one disagrees on the advantage of being familiar with standard English patterns, there is little evidence that they must be spoken before learning to read.

The creation of basal series in dialect patterns is probably one of the most volatile issues in the Black literacy controversy. Some almost immediately reject their use because they are pictured as texts in the style of Harris' *Tales of Uncle Remus*. The fear that this will happen might be allayed by the knowledge that the dialect basals, when used, have been intended as transition texts—a step toward reading standard English.

However, the process of this transitional step may be unnecessary and prolong the time when pupils are able to function in "regular" school texts. Also, the use of a dialect text may be impractical. Black American English dialects may have certain common features, but they do vary. A text appropriate for use with Blacks in northern urban centers may be of little value for use with Blacks in southern rural areas.

The third alternative, allowing the pupils to retain their dialectal patterns but to receive instruction in standard language patterns, is what generally occurs in most schools with most pupils. The written dialect transcends all spoken dialects and permits effective communication between speakers of all dialects of American English. The use of standard written forms together with the dialectal spoken forms of the pupils becomes ineffective only when teachers and pupils do not share a common context—when teachers do not recognize, accept, and understand the language patterns used by the pupils, and the pupils are made to feel that their language patterns are inappropriate for academic success.

Pupils will need to know the structure of the language they will read

Instruction for speakers of divergent dialects should aim to teach them about the structure of the material they will be asked to read. They need to learn how to use their own knowledge of language to predict what will be found in the books they read. They must be taught that they can approach the printed page with confidence and that they have the "tools" for discovering the author's meaning (Lloyd, 1969). Learning to read for speakers of divergent dialects, then, should be no different than it is for speakers of standard dialect. When readers can predict a great deal of the meaning in the printed matter the result is "comprehension." Predictability is as crucial for divergent dialect speakers as it is to other speakers. If predictability is desirable, then it seems logical to suggest that any pupil who can speak a language, but who has no reading ability, can be best guided *in the initial acquisition of literacy* by the use of predictable written language—that is, by written language which at least comes close to matching the oral language patterns used. (See Chapter 7.)

The implications of the above discussion for teaching pupils with divergent dialects seem to be:

1. Regardless of which alternative teachers select for instructing speakers of Black American English, or any other divergent dialect, they should be prepared to meet some opposition. The choice as to what instructional procedures to undertake should be made after a complete analysis of the local school situation and an evaluation of each school's particular needs.
2. Whatever instructional approach is taken, teachers should improve their understanding of the English language and its many varieties. The language each pupil brings to school should be accepted as a legitimate means for communication.
3. If there is a difference between the pupils' normal speech patterns and that used in the school, then it seems incumbent upon the school personnel to determine which items of language require attention because communication is inhibited. Analyze, do not criticize!
4. The development of literacy among all the pupils should be accomplished through the mutual involvement of teachers and pupils. Together they should attempt to understand the alternatives available to them and to select those which seem comfortable and appropriate to the situation.

UNDERSTANDING THE NEEDS OF SPEAKERS OF ENGLISH AS A SECOND LANGUAGE

School programs for pupils for whom English is not a native language exist in a variety of forms and for a variety of purposes. Some programs are intended to teach pupils to speak English. These are generally known as "English as a Second Language" Programs (ESL). They are conducted much like the foreign language programs found in many high schools and in a few elementary schools. Other programs for nonnative speakers of English try to provide instruction in two languages. These bilingual programs conduct certain instructional periods in the native language and others in English. For instance, public school bilingual programs sometimes conduct instruction in mathematics, social studies, and science in the native language and language arts instruction in English. Some parochial school programs provide religious studies in one language and secular studies in English. A third form of program for nonnative English speakers is provided in English but takes into account the linguistic and cultural features of the native language. These programs are sometimes labeled "education of the bilingual."

It should be apparent that bilingual education and education of the bilingual as here used are two different things. The discussion here will focus on the latter: the education of pupils for whom English is not a native language but who have achieved a degree of proficiency in spoken English so they can receive reading instruction in English.

When an individual becomes bilingual, a language continuum is created (Ching, 1976). When proficiency in both languages is attained, it is possible for the speaker to "glide" at will from one end of the continuum to the other. What becomes evident to many teachers is the apparent "mixing" of the two languages by pupils who have not become totally bilingual. In some areas the pejorative terms *TexMex* and *Spanglish* are used to denote the language of individuals who intermix forms of Spanish and English. What teachers need to realize is that it may not be the language differences or the intermixing of language forms that interferes with reading. What may interfere with the pupils' learning is the influence the language of such speakers has on teachers and through them on the learning environments (Gumperz and Hernandez-Chavez, 1972).

There is evidence that code switching—alternately using forms of two languages—is persistent wherever a minority language group comes in contact with a majority language group under conditions of rapid social change (Gumperz and Hernandez-Chavez, 1972). Alternating between languages seems to serve definite and clearly understandable communicative ends. It does not represent "errors" on the part of the speaker; rather, it is the creative use of alternative language forms to convey specific meanings. At this time, there seems to be no way in which to predict when a switch in linguistic form will occur nor to predict its particular meaning. The use of alternative language forms of different languages seems to be akin to the process by which a speaker will choose certain words rather than their synonyms because of their connotations or because of the effect they will have upon the listener. It is a verbal strategy used much as one can adjust his or her speech to various degrees of formality or informality of a situation. Teachers, therefore, should accept speech varieties as potentially meaningful and should attempt to interpret them in relation to the context of the situation in which they occur.

To be able to interpret a message contained in a mixed code, speakers must share a cultural and linguistic context. They need to have had common experiences which may be functions of home background, peer group experiences, and education. For teachers who do not speak the native language of the pupils, communicating may be extremely difficult.

Speakers must share a cultural and linguistic context

What then can teachers do to effectively instruct bilingual pupils? One thing teachers can do is to learn as much as possible about the language and culture of the group.

When dealing with nonnative speakers of English, teachers should be acutely sensitive to the pupils' cultural values: their aspiration levels, their value orientations, and their process of socialization. Whenever there are differences between the cultural values of the schools and those of the local culture, a breakdown in the communication between teachers and pupils is likely. Effective communication is hindered when there is a failure on the teacher's part to consider these differences, since "the basis for using language for information, action, or emotion in educational content is the assumption that the child has already mastered the essentials" of language (Mackey, 1973).

Teachers should develop a learning situation in which nonnative speakers of English have many opportunities to develop a sense of security, acceptance, and recognition. Actually, this should not be a difficult task since all pupils need these for successful school experiences.

In dealing with the language of nonnative speakers, teachers should develop an awareness of the differences that exist in the way experiences and concepts are encoded, the similarity or lack of similarity in phonemes, the vocabulary, and the syntax. A contrastive analysis of the languages can reveal potential sources of confusion and barriers to effective communication. For example, some pupils may be reluctant to speak or write English because they are unsure of or confused by language forms that do not exist in their native language. Or, some pupils may be unfamiliar with the connotations of certain words or the appropriateness of certain words or phrases in a given situation. The result is embarrassment or frustration whenever they are required to use English in situations for which they do not possess adequate English language skills. Teachers can avoid potentially emotional situations only through an understanding of the language system of the pupils.

Strategies for Teaching

There are various approaches to working with pupils for whom English is a second language. Since the purpose here is to discuss the bilingual pupil who has not developed proficiency in English similar to that of a native, no attempt will be made to discuss ESL or bilingual programs. The focus of the discussion is how to provide instruction in reading for the bilingual pupil in typical classroom situations.

Teachers need to identify the English proficiency of the pupils

Before adequate instruction can be provided, teachers need some means for identifying the English proficiency of the pupils. After a discussion of assessment instruments and procedures, attention will be given to instructional strategies and then to resource materials.

Assessment. Teachers can use formal and informal means of assessing the pupils' English language proficiency. Formal means consist of standardized instruments that measure the pupils' skills in English and/or in the native language. Informal means consist of teacher-made tests and inventories for measuring the pupils' understanding and use of English forms.

The following are standardized tests that rate the pupils' bilingual skills. They use comparable forms in English and Spanish and measure similar skills in both languages. They can be used for assessing the pupils' strengths in using similar strategies in different linguistic contexts.

Bilingual Syntax Measure. New York: Test Department, Harcourt Brace Jovanovich.

Hoffman Bilingual Schedule. New York: Teachers College Press, Columbia University.

Cooperative Inter-American Tests. Princeton, N.J.: Educational Testing Service.

When standardized instruments are unavailable, teachers can construct their own means for determining pupils' readiness for reading instruction. The performance rating scale shown in Figure 12–1 is one means for localizing the aspects of language which may hinder pupils' progress in learning to read English.

The scale is used by observing the pupils in a variety of social and educational situations. Or, the teacher can set up a series of games in which the pupils are asked to perform tasks revealing their language proficiency. For example, games can be played that reveal whether the pupils can auditorily distinguish between similar English phonemes—/*shin*/ and

FIGURE 12-1: Performance Scale for Assessing Language Skills of Nonnative English Speakers

	Listening	Speaking	Reading	Writing
Pronunciation/ spelling		_____		_____
Vocabulary:				
Word meanings	_____	_____	_____	_____
Morphological units	_____	_____	_____	_____
Sentence patterns	_____	_____	_____	_____
Intonational patterns:				
Oral usage		_____		
Related to written form				_____

Ratings: The pupil, compared to age level peers, understands and/or uses Standard American English patterns:

1. Like a local native speaker.
2. With accent and some situationally inappropriate forms.
3. In most situations but must make conscious effort to avoid code switching with native language forms.
4. To a small degree, or haltingly.
5. Not at all.

/*ch*in/—or between contrastive elements in English and the native language—/hump/ and /jump/. Similarly, activities can be designed to reveal the pupils' proficiency in speaking, reading, and writing. In all cases, the standard against which the nonnative English speaker is judged is the performance of native English speakers of that person's age.

In addition, the exercises and activities in the following section on instructional strategies can be modified for use as informal testing procedures.

The mistakes pupils make during these activities undoubtedly should mean more to someone who knows the learner's native language than to someone unfamiliar with it. Just as native speakers pass through stages of development that can be identified through an analysis of their performance, so can the development of nonnative speakers be assessed. Consider their "errors" as miscues which may have resulted from the pupils' inability (1) to deal with contrastive forms of the two languages, (2) to understand a particular English language form, (3) to realize the ambiguity of a speech form, or (4) to use certain irregular English forms. Only through an awareness of the linguistic and cultural features of the pupils' native language can teachers effectively assess the importance and meaning of the pupils' language divergences.

Instructional Strategies. The activities and exercises in the ensuing discussion are not exhaustive. They are presented as representative of the type that can be developed to assist those pupils who have at least a rudimentary knowledge of English. Such pupils would receive scores of three and four on a performance scale like Figure 12-1. As pupils are taught the various structures and forms of English, they should be given an explanation as to how these differ from or parallel those in their native languages.

Teachers should explain how English differs from or parallels the pupils' native language

The first step in developing the bilingual pupil's reading proficiency is to link together their oral language with the reading act. This is accomplished by using the language experience approach. The ideas in Chapter 6 for developing readiness for reading instruction and those in Chapter 7 for using the language experience approach as a means for introducing pupils to literacy are applicable with pupils for whom English is a second language.

Oral and written language proficiency can be developed through activities that direct the pupils' attention to significant features of English. Bilingual pupils can become fluent in English through tasks that have them

☐ Practice through a series of pattern drills (Saville-Troike, 1973). The practices should include:

1. Mimicry. The pupils imitate a sentence attempting to use the same intonational pattern as the teacher. These sentences can be continually used until the pupils memorize them.
2. Chain drill. This activity is similar to a game of follow the leader. One pupil makes a statement which is then repeated by the other pupils.
3. Substitution. Pupils are asked to substitute a word or phrase for another of the same grammatical function.
4. Replacement. Pupils are to replace a word or phrase with a substitute word, in most cases, a pronoun.
5. Conversion. Pupils change the tense of the sentences in a predetermined manner.

Each pupil who experiences difficulty in learning to read may do so for a variety of reasons

    6. Expansion. A word or group of words is added to a sentence.
    7. Transformation. The word order of a sentence is changed so a sentence becomes a question, or an affirmative becomes a negative, or an active becomes a passive.

☐ Develop a sense of adjectival modification through the expansion of noun phrases. The pupils should develop a sense of the order of modifiers: nationality, color, shape, size, quality, cardinal, ordinal, defining, indefinite or inclusive.

☐ Develop a sense of adverbial modification through tasks requiring the placement of adverbs in sentences. A distinction should be made between adverbs that move without changing a sentences' meaning and those that qualify only a particular unit within the sentence.

☐ Develop an understanding of common, multiple use function words such as *have* and *do*. Pupils should become acquainted with constructions using *have*:

> **have** + **infinitive** (to show necessity)
>
> **have** + **to have** (to show necessity)
>
> **have** + **noun** (to show causative action)
>
> **have** + **noun** + **verb** (to show directives)

Resources. Cities and states that have populations containing a large number of pupils for whom English is a second language often develop instructional guides to meet the needs of these pupils. The following are series designed to introduce and develop English for nonnative speakers.
English Around the World. 1975. Glenview, Ill.: Scott, Foresman.
English Experiences. 1975. New York: Institute of Modern Languages.
English Series: *A Complete Course in English as a Second Language.* 1973. New York: Regents Publishing.

A single causal interpretation of reading difficulties does not seem possible

UNDERSTANDING THE NEEDS OF PUPILS WHO HAVE DIFFICULTY IN LEARNING TO READ

The reading act is quite complex and many characteristics of child growth and development have a bearing on reading success. A single causal interpretation of reading difficulty does not, therefore, seem to be possible. Each pupil who experiences difficulty in learning to read may do so for a wide variety of reasons. The assessment of each such case involves a study of the pupil within a particular social and educational setting.

There is a growing trend among school personnel to label pupils experiencing a variety of difficulties as "learning disabled." When the difficulty is specific to the learning of reading strategies, the term "dyslexia" is used. Other terms have been and are being used, but the one that seems to persist is dyslexia. Among its users, the term is often used in ways that may seem confusing. Depending upon the individual's conceptual background, the term can have several different meanings.

Historically, interest in dyslexia sprung from the various branches of preventive and rehabilitative medicine, from remedial reading, and from the study of learning disabilities in the area of special education. Now, those who study dyslexia include researchers in fields that are tangential to reading behavior, including those studying the sociological, psychological, political, and economic effects of reading failure. Basically, there are two separate approaches, the medical and the educational, to the study and instruction of dyslexia (Lerner, 1971). Medically, dyslexia is viewed as an inability to read due to brain damage or central nervous system dysfunction. Educationally, dyslexia is viewed as an inability to read when no specific causes are evident.

A review of the literature (Lerner, 1971) suggests dyslexia as the cause of reading problems when there is

1. Evidence of brain damage.
2. Behavioral manifestations of central nervous system dysfunctions.
3. Evidence that the problem is genetic or inherited.
4. Evidence of a general language disability.
5. The presence of the syndrome of maturational lag.
6. The presence of reading retardation.

Most educators at this writing define dyslexia to conform with the Education for All Handicapped Children Act, Public Law 94–142, which states that children with learning disabilities are

> children who have a disorder in one or more of the basic psychological processes involved in understanding or in using language, spoken or written, which disorder may manifest itself in imperfect ability to listen, think, speak, read, write, spell, or do mathematical calculations. Such disorders include such conditions as perceptual handicaps, brain injury, minimal brain dysfunction, dyslexia, and developmental aphasia. Such terms do not include children who have learning problems which are primarily the result of visual, hearing, or motor handicaps, of mental retardation, of emotional disturbance, or environmental, cultural, or economic disadvantage.

If one uses the above definition, dyslexia seems to become a learning disability for which no cause is known. What results is that the pupils become the victim of a blind label. A review of the literature reveals many inconsistencies in the definition of dyslexia (McCarthy and McCarthy, 1971). Defining it as a single "disease" is unacceptable because so many different manifestations of it seem to be possible. Also, educators are beginning to feel that a variety of factors are possible causes for pupils' learning difficulties—social problems, emotional maladjustments, general health status, and defective teaching (Ellingson, 1967). However, the definition as contained in Public Law 94–142 says that no such causes can be considered in defining a dyslexic child.

There are no clear criteria for determining a learning disability

Many myths seem to be developing about dyslexia because there is no clear set of criteria for determining who really has a "learning disability." In fact, the phenomenon identified as dyslexia may in actuality be that which educators for many years have labeled "reading disability." "There is little if any difference between learning by disabled children and many of the other children being seen by the reading specialist. A false dichotomy has been created because the two specialists imply different terms, different diagnostic approaches, and different remedial methods" (Hartman and Hartman, 1973).

Identification of the Reading Disabled

The most prevalent means for determining whether pupils are reading disabled is by establishing some relationship between their ability levels and their performance levels. Ability is determined by using a mental maturity or intelligence measure and reading ability by using standardized reading instruments. Through the use of an index or formula, a ratio between performance and ability is computed. When pupils' performance levels are more than two years below their potential or anticipated performance level, then they are considered reading disabled. When there is no direct evidence of a cause for their apparent inability to read, the pupils are labeled by many as dyslexic.

This labeling procedure is not as simple as it appears. From the discussion in Chapter 4 it should be evident that standardized intelligence and reading tests have serious limitations. It may not always be factors associated with the pupils that cause low scores. Also, the use of various indexes can produce varying results (Samuels, 1970; Reed, 1970). First, there is a large discrepancy among the results different formulas and indexes yield. Whatever index is used to establish reading retardation not only influences the pattern of the relationship between verbal and nonverbal intelligence scores which will be found among retarded readers, but it also affects the incidence of retarded readers for any given population. There is disagreement as to how great a discrepancy between actual and potential achievement should be used as an index of disability. The cutoff figure of two years is an arbitrary point, but no empirical evidence exists that this identifies the instance of disability.

The prevalence of learning disability in school settings is not at all clear

(Bruininks, Glaman, and Clark, 1971). It seems that the learning problems found among different general school populations have a wide variation in the proportion and characteristics of the pupils so labeled. The reviewers of the literature ascribe the cause of these variations to the influence of differences in (1) the defining criteria, (2) the instrumentation used for measurement, (3) the methods used to analyze the data, (4) the characteristics of the sample drawn from school populations, and (5) the quality and extent of the instructional history of the subjects. Their conclusion is that few current estimates of the prevalence of pupils with school learning problems are supported by findings from empirical studies.

For those adhering to a medically influenced model of reading disability, an inability to achieve intersensory transfer or intersensory perceptual shifting is advocated as a possible cause. Intersensory transfer is the translation of information from the terms of one sensory channel to those of another. Perceptual shifting is the changing of attention from one sensory channel to another. A review of the research literature in these areas points out some limitations in applying the conclusions of research findings to reading achievement (Jones, 1972). In regard to intersensory transfer and reading achievement, the evidence suggests that it is highly probable that ability to associate intersensory stimuli is significantly related to the ability to read. However, the research investigating the relationship of cross-modal transfer skills and intelligence has been conflicting. There is a general softness in the studies. They lack control of visual clues during presentation of auditory stimuli, and possible variation in stimulus patterns due to human error. Also, many of the sample populations are unrepresentative of normal school populations. In regard to intersensory perceptual shifting and reading achievement the research is insufficient to allow for the drawing of conclusions. In regard to modal preference and reading achievement the conclusions of the research indicate that the presentation of information through printed or oral channels under various conditions is pertinent for learning in general, but not for learning to read. One major problem is the identification of a preferred modality through a valid test of modal preference.

In conclusion, it seems that the modality deficiencies, the cognitive deficits, the aptitude weaknesses, and the relation of verbal to nonverbal performance abilities will vary according to the method of identifying the retarded reader. The fact that different criterion measures will yield different results makes it clear that the final truths about retarded readers may be difficult to discover. The particular pattern of deficits may only represent an artifact of the investigator's decision to use one measure of potential in-

Final truths about retarded readers may be difficult to discover

stead of another (Reed, 1970). Finally, in no way do most of the studies take into account the possibility or the assumption of the adequacy of the instruction given to those pupils (Samuels, 1970).

A Developmental Concept of Disability

Two concepts of reading disability are the deficiency concept and the developmental concept

There seem to be two common frameworks within which reading and/or learning disabilities are placed. One may be termed the deficiency concept and the other the developmental concept. The deficiency concept starts with the idea that pupils who are lacking certain vital skills cannot function. The adherents to this concept postulate one or more traumas occurring in the pupils' lives which have interfered with their ability to perform some educational tasks. Taking their cue mainly from the medical profession, the proponents of a deficiency model suggest that once the causative factors have been identified, correction procedures can be instituted. This thinking is, of course, very much like that which was prevalent at the onset of the compensatory programs for the educationally disadvantaged. It is notable that these programs seemed to have failed whenever they were built on an erroneous concept of "disadvantagedness."

The developmental concept posits that pupils may not achieve because they are not ready

The developmental concept of learning disability posits that pupils may not achieve in school because they are not ready to perform certain tasks. This concept demands that any single performance be evaluated in relation to preceding or subsequent performances. Since human behavior is a function of structure, individuals seem to behave largely because of the way they have developed (Ames, 1968). Behavior, therefore, is patterned, predictable, and ordered, as is the physical organism.

The pupils who exhibit learning disabilities are usually considered different, yet they may not be as different from other pupils as is usually thought. It may just be more a matter of timing than of actual difference in potential (Ames, 1968). To understand the pupils (and to be able to work toward preventing disruptions in learning), each pupil's developmental history should be known. It is important to measure and identify the stage of development that the pupils have reached. The pupils lacking the appropriate readiness will appear to be learning disabled, yet all that might be missing is the prerequisite conceptual background in thinking and motor abilities. For those pupils who seem to be having a great deal of difficulty with learning, their problem may be "rooted in some aspect of the child's basic individuality or learning ability" (Ames, 1968).

The maturational process is linked to age. A maturational lag, the slow or delayed development of those brain areas which mediate the acquisition of age-linked development skills, may be the cause of apparent disability for some pupils. The pattern of deficits observed in dyslexic pupils, rather than representing a unique syndrome or disturbance, often resembles the behavior patterns of chronologically younger pupils who have not yet developed certain skills. In such cases, the patterns of deficits would vary as a function of the age at which certain skills are undergoing primary development (Satz and Sparrow, 1970).

In addition to differing developmental growth patterns, pupils may also differ in their approaches to problem solving (Wagner and Wilde, 1973). Pupils' cognitive styles and/or conceptual tempos may influence their problem solving strategies, and this may result from a blending of perceptual, cognitive, and personality factors. Individual problem solving strategies may range along a psychologically differentiated continuum. Where on the continuum the pupils' strategies are located may explain their attempts to organize their environment in meaningful ways. Pupils might differ in their cognitive styles depending on where they lie on the following continuums:

Locus of Control (approach to the environment)
External————Internal

Field Articulation (organization of experiences)
Dependence————Independence

Mode of Conceptual Tempo (problem solving reaction time)
Impulsivity————Reflective

Preferential Mode of Perceptual Organization and Conceptual Categorization (processing of stimuli)
Relational————Analytic

If further research reveals that there are differences in the manner in which pupils undertake problem solving, the teachers might be able to understand that all pupils can be "disabled" when expected to perform tasks in a manner which might not be consistent with their particular approach to processing information. For an extended discussion of the development of human thinking, refer to Chapter 3.

Assessment of Disability

When problems exist, individuals are prone to seek out a cause. Chapter 4 contains a full discussion of the nature and uses of analytical teaching. Here, discussion will focus on two types of assessment, or diagnosis, for pupils exhibiting reading disabilities (Brown and Botel, 1972).

Status assessment is like inventorying: it may be used to find the range and content of pupils' repertoire of responses. It is usually undertaken with one or more standardized "diagnostic" instruments designed to categorize tasks or items pupils know from those they do not know.

In regard to identifying or "diagnosing" pupils with learning disabilities associated with reading, the instruments most commonly used are those of a predictive nature. Norm referenced instruments attempt to predict those pupils who will not succeed on the assumption that a severe disability already exists and that intervention is necessary. Two examples of instruments commonly used are the *Developmental Test of Visual Perception* (Frostig, 1964) and the *Illinois Test of Psycholinguistic Abilities* (ITPA) (Kirk, McCarthy, and Kirk, 1968). The *Developmental Test of Visual Perception* contains five subscores and a total that are used to identify the pupils who may have a high chance of failure. It is then implied that those five so-called "perceptual skills" are the prerequisites for learning to read. So far, there is no empirical evidence that those five subtests have anything to do with the learning to read process. The test is a predictive instrument that explains nothing about why or how the pupils are not performing. (Refer to Chapter 4 for a discussion about the use of predictive tests for determining causality.)

The ITPA is a popular diagnostic instrument which is used extensively in schools with pupils who experience various learning difficulties. The test writers say that it measures abilities which underlie language development. Yet, the reliability and validity of the various subtests have not been clearly established. No specific information exists concerning the relationship between poor performance on the subtest and reading disability; therefore, its use might be rather limited (Ekwall, 1976). Two researchers who reviewed studies in which the ITPA was employed concluded that its use for individual diagnosis is not supported and recommended that the test should not be used for the purposes of

1. Determining the cause of academic failure.
2. Devising strategies for the remediation of academic problems.
3. Selecting instructional programs that are psycholinguistically appropriate.
4. Screening individual pupils to locate those who might have a high probability of failing basic school subjects (Newcomer and Hammill, 1975).

The second type of assessment, *process analysis,* is related more closely to the natural behavior of children. Using it, one attempts to analyze the sequence of steps or structures the individual learner uses to produce any given response (Brown and Botel, 1972). Unlike status assessment, in which pupils might provide the "right" answer for the wrong reason, the process framework seeks to evaluate any single performance in relation to preceding or subsequent functioning. The key to understanding process analysis may be found in the ability to understand functional relationships.

Process analysis is undertaken when teachers attempt to determine *how* pupils perform the reading act and why they might not be proficient at it. The psycholinguistic perspective set forth in this text should provide the framework in which to undertake this assessment. Process oriented assessment techniques, such as those explained in Chapter 5, should provide teachers with a starting place.

In conclusion, learning disabilities should not be viewed as strange phenomena that have to be approached with reverence and awe. The teacher's task is not to require pupils to meet any shortsighted, rigid requirements for which they may not be ready. The task is to adjust instructional expectations to fit the developmental pattern of the pupils and to provide alternative learning procedures which are appropriate for their stage of development and cognitive style.

DISCUSSION QUESTIONS AND ACTIVITIES

1. Someone proposes to you that the pupils who speak Black American English should be placed in a "special" class because they lack the normal conceptual background, an adequate vocabulary, and the experiences in handling written verbal symbols to remain in a heterogeneously grouped class. How would you answer?

2. Examine reading materials that have been prepared in a Black American English dialect. In what ways do these materials meet or fail to meet the criteria for acceptability according to the critical questions to be answered about reading materials set forth in Chapter 3 on pages 76 to 79?

3. The following statement about reading readiness is from Chapter 6. How can it be rewritten to replace "reading readiness" with "learning disability" so that the basic intent and meaning of the statement is retained?

> In a Piagetian sense, readiness means possessing those skills and abilities of a preceding stage of development.

4. What factors need to be taken into consideration when administering, scoring, and interpreting the informal language assessment procedures (including the miscue analysis) to bilingual and bidialectal speakers? How could features of their language patterns be misconstrued as "errors"?

5. Locate and examine at least three definitions of dyslexia from current texts or journal articles. Do they contain common aspects? Prepare a statement for possible use at a parents' meeting that interprets these definitions in light of the information presented in this chapter and Chapters 2 and 3.

FURTHER READINGS

Much of the recent literature concerning teaching speakers of divergent dialects also concerns teaching speakers of English as a second language. The references below should be helpful to teachers who are seeking additional information about either of these topics.

 Baratz, Joan C. and Shuy, Roger W., eds. 1969. *Teaching Black Children To Read.* Washington, D.C.: Center for Applied Linguistics.

 Cazden, Courtney B. 1972. *Child Language and Education.* Chapter 7: "Dialect Differences and Bilingualism." New York: Holt Rinehart and Winston.

 Ching, Doris C. 1976. *Reading and the Bilingual Child.* Newark, Del.: International Reading Association.

 Figurel, J. Allen, ed. 1970. *Reading Goals for the Disadvantaged.* Newark, Del.: International Reading Association.

 Fox, Robert P., ed. 1973. *Essays on Teaching English As A Second Language & As A Second Dialect.* Urbana, Ill.: National Council of Teachers of English.

 Hall, Vernon C. and Turner, Ralph R. 1974. "The Validity of the 'Different Language Explanation' for Poor Scholastic Performance by Black Students." *Review of Educational Research* 44: 69–82.

 Horn, Thomas D., ed. 1971. *Research Bases for Oral Language Instruction.* Urbana, Ill.: National Conference on Research in English.

Johns, Jerry L., ed. 1974. *Literacy for Diverse Learners: Promoting Reading Growth at All Levels.* Newark, Del.: International Reading Association.

Kleinfeld, J. S. 1973. "Intellectual Strengths in Culturally Different Groups: An Eskimo Illustration." *Review of Educational Research* 43: 341–60.

Laffey, James L. and Shuy, Roger W., eds. 1973. *Language Differences: Do They Interfere?* Newark, Del.: International Reading Association.

Somervill, Mary Ann. 1975. "Dialect and Reading: A Review of Alternative Solutions." *Review of Educational Research* 45: 247.

There is much material available about learning and reading disabilities. However, much of it contains the unfounded assumptions discussed in this chapter. The text below is a good general reference that surveys the field and provides the reader with a background in the various diagnostic procedures and teaching strategies.

Lerner, Janet W. 1971. *Children with Learning Disabilities: Theories, Diagnosis, and Teaching Strategies.* Boston: Houghton Mifflin.

The following is a critical examination of some programs used for children with learning disabilities and contains a good template for evaluating other programs.

Kaufman, Maurice. 1973. *Perceptual and Language Readiness Programs: Critical Reviews.* Newark, Del.: International Reading Association.

For additional readings in the area of reading and learning disabilities, reference should be made to current issues of the *Journal of Learning Disabilities* and the studies below.

Case, Robbie. 1975. "Gearing the Demands of Instruction To The Developmental Capacities of the Learner." *Review of Educational Research* 45: 59–88.

Samuels, S. Jay. 1973. "Success and Failure in Learning To Read: A Critique of the Research." *Reading Research Quarterly* 8: 200–39.

Silverston, Randall A. and Deichmann, John W. 1975. "Sense Modality Research and the Acquisition of Reading Skills." *Review of Educational Research* 45: 149–72.

References

Ames, Louise B. 1968. "Learning Disability: The Developmental Point of View." In Helmer R. Myklebust, ed. *Progress in Learning Disabilities.* New York: Bunne and Stratton.

Baratz, Joan C. 1968. "Linguistic and Cultural Factors in Teaching Reading to Ghetto Children." *Elementary English* 45: 199–203.

Bereiter, C. and Englemann, S. 1966. *Teaching Disadvantaged Children in the Preschool.* New York: Prentice Hall.

Brown, Virginia, and Botel, Morton. 1972. *Dyslexia: Definition or Treatment?* ERIC/CRIER Reading Review Series.

Bruininks, Robert H., Glaman, Gertrude M., and Clark, Charlotte R. 1971. *Prevalence of Learning Disabilities: Findings, Issues, and Recommendations.* Project No. 332185, Grant No. OE-09-332189-4533(032). Washington, D.C.: DHEW/OE Bureau of Education for the Handicapped.

Ching, Doris C. 1976. *Reading and the Bilingual Child.* Newark, Del.: International Reading Association.

Edwards, Thomas J. 1969. "Learning Problems in Cultural Deprivation." In Althea Beery, Thomas C. Barrett, and William R. Powell, eds. *Elementary Reading Instruction—Selected Materials.* Boston: Allyn and Bacon.

Ekwall, Eldon E. 1976. *Diagnosis and Remediation of the Disabled Reader.* Boston: Allyn and Bacon.

Ellingson, Careth. 1967. *The Shadow Children.* Chicago: Topaz.

Englemann, Siegreid. 1969. *Preventing Failure in the Primary Grades.* New York: Simon and Schuster.

Erikson, Frederick D. 1968. "'F'get You Honkey!' A New Look At Black Dialect and the School." *Elementary English* 45:495–99, 517.

Foerster, Leona M. 1974. "Language Experiences for Dialectally Different Black Learners." *Elementary English* 51:193–97.

Frostig, Marrianne. 1964. *Developmental Test of Visual Perception.* Chicago: Follett.

Goodman, Kenneth S. 1969. "Let's Dump the Uptight Model in English." *Elementary School Journal* 70:1–13.

Gumperz, John J., and Hernandez-Chavez, Eduardo. 1972. "Bilingualism, Bidialectalism, and Classroom Interaction." In Courtney B. Cazden, Vera P. John, and Dell Hymes, eds. *Functions of Language in the Classroom.* New York: Teachers College Press, Columbia University.

Hartman, Nancy C., and Hartman, Robert K. 1973. "Perceptual Handicap or Reading Disability?" *The Reading Teacher* 26:684–95.

Jones, John Paul. 1972. *Intersensory Transfer, Perceptual Shifting, Modal Preference and Reading.* Newark, Del.: International Reading Association.

Kirk, Samuel A., McCarthy, J. J., and Kirk, Winifred D. 1968. *The Illinois Test of Psycholinguistic Abilities.* Revised Edition. Urbana, Ill.: University of Illinois Press.

Labov, William. 1966. "Some Sources of Reading Problems for Negro Speakers of Non-standard English." Unpublished paper, Columbia University. ERIC ED 010688.

Lerner, Janet W. 1971. *Children and Learning Disabilities: Theories, Diagnosis, and Teaching Strategies.* Boston: Houghton Mifflin.

Lloyd, Helen M. 1969. "Progress in Developmental Reading for Today's Disadvantaged." In Althea Beery, Thomas C. Barrett, and William R. Powell, eds. *Elementary Reading Instruction—Selected Materials.* Boston: Allyn and Bacon.

Mackey, William F. 1973. "Language and Acculturation." In Robert P. Fox, ed. *Essays on Teaching English as a Second Language & as a Second Dialect.* Urbana, Ill.: National Council of Teachers of English.

McCarthy, James J., and McCarthy, Joan F. 1971. *Learning Disabilities.* Boston: Allyn and Bacon.

Newcomer, Phyllis L., and Hammill, Donald D. 1975. "ITPA and Academic Achievement: A Survey," *The Reading Teacher* 28:731–42.

Reed, James C. 1970. "The Deficits of Retarded Readers—Fact or Artifact?" *The Reading Teacher* 23:247–52.

Samuels, S. Jay. 1970. "Reading Disability?" *The Reading Teacher* 24:267, 271, 283.

Satz, Paul, and Sparrow, Sara S. 1970. "Specific Developmental Dyslexia: A Theoretical Formulation." In Dirk J. Bakkar and Paul Satz, eds. *Specific Reading Disability—Advances in Theory and Method.* Rotterdam: University of Rotterdam Press.

Saville-Troike, Muriel R. 1973. "TESOL: Methods and Materials in Early Childhood Education." In Robert P. Fox, ed. *Essays on Teaching English as a Second Language & as a Second Dialect.* Urbana, Ill.: National Council of Teachers of English.

Stewart, William A. 1966. "Nonstandard Speech Patterns." *Baltimore Bulletin of Education,* pp. 52–66.

Strickland, Dorothy S. 1972. "Black Is Beautiful, White Is Right." *Elementary English* 49:200–23.

Wagner, Steven R. and Wilde, John. 1973. "Learning Styles: Can We Grease the Cogs in Cognition?" *Proceedings of the Claremont Reading Conference,* pp. 135–41.

Wheat, Thomas. 1974. "Reading and the Culturally Diverse." *Elementary English* 51:251–56.

Zintz, Miles V. 1975. *The Reading Process: The Teacher and the Learner.* 2nd Edition. Dubuque, Iowa: William C. Brown.

NAME INDEX

Aiken, Lewis R., Jr., 338, 358
Albert, Burton, Jr., 327, 358
Alexander, Anne, 370, 388
Allen, Claryce, 191, 211
Allen, Roach Van, 191, 196, 211, 212
Ames, Louise B., 410, 416
Anastasiow, Nickolas, 151, 179
Anderson, Paul S., 206, 212, 367, 389
Andresen, Oliver, 359
Armentrout, William, 17, 21
Arth, Alfred A., 363, 388
Aulls, Mark, 286, 312

Baratz, Joan C., 395, 417
Barnhart, Clarence L., 304
Batine, Patricia, 217
Bell, Wendell, 4, 21
Bellugi, Ursula, 64, 81
Bercari, Joan, 193, 211
Bereiter, C., 398, 416
Bickely, A. C., 98, 107
Blanton, William E., 144, 148, 149, 179
Blitz, Barbara, 13, 21
Bloom, Benjamin S., 101, 107
Bormuth, John, 136–137, 139, 140, 226, 235, 236, 273
Botel, Morton, 411, 413, 416
Brewer, A. C., 323, 324, 351, 352, 353, 358
Broman, Betty L., 171, 279, 281, 312
Brown, Roger, 64, 81
Brown, Virginia, 411, 413, 416
Bruininks, Robert H., 409, 416
Bruner, Jerome, 6
Burke, Carolyn L., 72–73, 82, 113, 117, 124, 141
Burns, Paul C., 171, 279, 281, 312
Burrows, Alvina T., 200, 211

Burton, Elizabeth H., 297, 313
Byers, Happie, 27, 30, 49
Byers, Paul, 27, 30, 49

Carroll, John B., 51–52, 81
Chester, Robert, 212
Ching, Doris C., 401, 416
Christapherson, Steven L., 235, 273
Chomsky, Carol, 297, 312
Chomsky, Noam, 33, 49
Church, Marilyn, 148, 179
Clark, Charlotte R., 409, 416
Cohen, Alice, 296, 312
Cohen, Elizabeth G., 15, 22
Combs, Arthur, 185, 212
Congreve, Willard J., 11, 22
Cramer, Ronald L., 187, 211, 228, 273
Crist, Barbara I., 285, 312
Cullinan, Bernice, 162, 179, 364, 369, 371–372, 388

Davis, O. L., 319, 321, 323, 353, 358
Deese, James, 52, 81
Deighton, Lee C., 285–287, 299, 312
Donlan, Dan, 281, 312
Downing, John, 162, 179, 296, 301, 312
Duchastel, Philippe, 185, 212
Durkin, Dolores, 145, 149, 179, 293, 313

Edwards, Thomas J., 397, 416
Ekwall, Eldon E., 412, 416
Elkind, David, 56, 81, 144, 179, 364, 389
Ellingson, Careth, 408, 416
Emery, Anne, 370, 389
Englemann, S., 398, 416
Erickson, Frederick D., 397, 416
Esposito, Dominick, 14, 22

Fairbanks, Grant, 39, 49
Fay, Leo, 135, 201, 205-206, 212, 233, 241, 274, 367, 371, 389
Feininger, Andreas, 79, 81
Foerster, Leona, 150, 159, 179, 283, 310, 313, 394, 416
Friend, J., 47, 49
Frostig, Marrianne, 412, 416
Fu, Lewis L., 15, 23
Furth, Hans G., 53, 54, 81

Gardner, Eric F., 91, 106
Garland, Neil, 324
Gelb, Larry, 188, 212
Gephart, William J., 5, 22
Geyer, John J., 69, 71, 81
Glaman, Gertrude M., 409, 416
Glass, Gerald, 297-298, 313
Gombrich, E. H., 3, 22
Goodlad, John, 18, 22
Goodman, Kenneth S., 6, 22, 72-73, 77, 81-82, 113, 117, 141, 146, 180, 310, 313, 394, 416
Goodman, Yetta, 72, 82
Gorman, Alfred H., 172, 179
Greet, W., 305
Guilford, John P., 56, 58, 59, 82
Gumperz, John J., 400, 416

Hall, Mary Anne, 188, 211, 212
Hammill, Donald D., 412, 417
Harker, W. John, 226, 272, 274
Hartman, Nancy C., 408, 417
Hartman, Robert K., 408, 417
Havighurst, Robert J., 10, 22
Heiman, Michele K., 393
Hernandez-Chavez, Eduardo, 400, 416
Henderson, Edmund H., 294, 313
Henry, George H., 240, 274
Henry, Marguerite, 370-371, 389
Herber, Harold L., 337, 355, 358
Higgins, James E., 366, 389
Horton, Raymond Joseph, 136, 141
Howell, K. W., 294-295, 313
Hutchins, Ross, 371, 389
Huus, Helen, 358, 361, 365, 389

Jacobs, Leland, 2, 17, 22
Jenkins, Esther C., 362, 389
Jenkins, William A., 304, 305
Johnson, Ronald E., 271, 273
Jones, John Paul, 409, 417
Jones, Margaret B., 137, 141

Karlin, Robert, 357-358
Karlsen, Bjorn, 91, 106
Kavanagh, James F., 146, 180
Kelly, Truman L., 91, 97, 106
King, Frederick, 328, 333, 358
Kingston, Albert J., 14, 22
Kirk, Samuel A., 412, 417
Kirk, Winifred D., 412, 417
Kumar, V. D., 59, 62, 69, 82

Labov, William, 395, 417
Lacey, Patricia A., 338, 358
Lapp, Diane, 184, 212
LaPray, Margaret, 135, 201, 205, 212, 241, 274
Lear, Edward, 368, 389
Lee, Doris, 196, 212
Lerner, Janet W., 407, 417
Lindsay, Peter H., 59, 60, 62, 63, 82
Lloyd, Helen M., 398, 417
Lohmann, Idella, 210, 212
Lundsteen, Sara W., 145, 180, 231, 274, 362, 367, 389

McCarthy, Joan F., 407, 417
McCarthy, James J., 407, 412, 417
McDonell, Gloria, 145, 146, 162, 180
MacGinitie, Walter H., 98-99, 107, 145, 168, 180
McLuhan, Marshall, 1, 22
McNeil, John, 212
Mackey, William F., 401, 417
Madden, Richard, 91, 106
Maffei, Anthony C., 335, 359
Manzo, Anthony V., 278, 313
Marksheffel, Ned D., 356, 359
Marquardt, William F., 32, 49
May, Frank B., 177, 180
Mayer, Jeri E., 148, 180
Menyuk, Paula, 64, 82
Meridith, Robert, 146, 180
Merla, Patrick, 363, 389
Merrill, Paul F., 185, 212
Michaelis, John O., 316, 359

Mickish, Virginia, 295, 313
Miller, George, 48, 49
Miller, John W., 271, 274
Mishler, Elliot G., 146, 157, 180
Monson, Dionne L., 211
Monteleone, Thomas F., 371, 390
Morine, Greta, 9, 22
Morine, Harold, 9, 22
Myers, R. E., 207, 208
Myers, Shirley, 212

Nelson, Joan B., 337, 358
Newcomer, Phyllis L., 412, 417
Norman, Donald A., 59–60, 62, 63, 82
Notkin, Jerome J., 324
Nuthall, Graham, 8, 22

Okrent, Marilyn, 213
Oliver, Marvin E., 14, 23
Oliver, Peter, 162, 179
Olmo, Barbara G., 234, 274
Otto, Wayne, 184, 212

Pace, Judy, 137, 141
Painter, Helen, 362, 390
Paulk, Walter, 334, 359
Pehrsson, Robert, 233, 274
Peltz, Fillmore K., 266, 273
Piaget, Jean, 52–56
Pikulski, John J., 101, 107, 137, 141, 168, 180, 189, 212
Postman, Neil, 1, 23
Pyrczak, Fred, 98, 107

Randhawa, Bikkar, 15, 23
Raven, Ronald, 67, 71, 82
Reed, James C., 408–409, 417
Reed, Linda, 362, 390
Rinehart, George J., 11, 22
Robinson, H. Alan, 18, 23, 242–243, 247, 274, 321, 359
Robinson, Helen M., 138
Ross, Ramon Royal, 135, 201, 205, 212, 241, 274
Rude, Robert T., 168, 180
Rudman, Herbert, 106
Ryan, Ellen, 71–72, 82

Salzer, Richard, 67, 71, 82
Samuels, S. Jay, 408, 410, 417
Sapir, Edward, 26–28, 49
Sargent, Eileen E., 330, 359
Satz, Paul, 411, 417
Sawyer, Diane J., 162, 168, 180
Sceats, John, 301, 312
Schaff, Adam, 32, 49
Schell, Leo M., 287, 312
Schiller, Andrew, 304, 305
Schwartz, Elaine, 296, 312
Schwartz, Judy I., **188**, 212
Semmel, Melvyn L., 71–72, 83
Shepherd, David L., 356, 359
Sherk, J. K., 278, 313
Simons, Herbert D., 226, 274
Sims, Rudine, 363–364, 390
Sloan, Glenna Davis, 369, 390
Slobin, Dan, 64, 82
Smith, E. Brooks, 146, 180
Smith, Frank, 111, 141, 228, 271, 274, 293–294, 296, 313
Smith, James A., 150, 180
Smith, Nila Banton, 316, 359, 362, 390
Snook, Ivan, 8, 22
Spache, George, 17
Sparrow, Sara S., 411, 417
Stauffer, Russell G., 71, 83, 189, 200, 211, 212
Stewart, William A., 395, 417
Strang, Ruth, 97, 103–104, 107
Sund, Robert B., 357

Terry, Ann, 367, 390
Thompson, William Irving, 2, 16, 23
Thorndike, E. L., 304
Toffler, Alvin, 2, 23
Toothaker, Ray, 281, 313
Torrence, E. Paul, 207–208
Tuinman, J. Jaap, 98, 107

Vendig, Anne, 149, 180
Vargas, Julie S., 184–185, 212
Vilscek, Elaine C., **188**, 212
Vogel, Susan A., 168, 180

Wagner, Steven R., 411, 418
Wardhaugh, R., 32, 49
Waugh, R. P., 294–295

Weaver, Wendell W., 72, 83, 98, 107
Wehmeyer, Lillian M., 342, 359
Weil, Philip E., 338, 358
Weiner, Roberta, 13, 23
Wheat, Thomas, 397, 418
Whittemore, Judith D., 363, 388
Wilde, John, 411, 418
Winkley, Carol K., 99, 107
Williams, Joanna P., 71, 83
Williamson, Leon E., 279, 313
Winsch, Jane L., 137, 141

Zintz, Miles V., 396, 418
Zuck, L. V., 294–295, 313

SUBJECT INDEX

Academic potential, 102, 111
Accommodation, 54
Activities grouping, 13
Achievement tests, interpretation of results, 99–100
Advance organizers, 68
Affective language, 281
Affective readiness for reading, 157
Alphabetic writing, 293
American English. *See* English language
Analysis of series questions, 207
Analysis questions, 207
Analytic teaching, 85, 87, 109, 206
Assessment, 187
    formative, 85
    objectives of, 86–88
    oral reading, 113–127
    process, 412
    profiles, 127, 130
    reading disabled, 408
    silent reading, 132
    status, 412
    summative, 85
Assimilation, 54
Attention, 61
Author–idea map, 256
Author's craft, 369–372
Author's message, 225
    activities for reconstructing, 262–268

Background information, 110
Base (syntactic component), 34
Basic sight vocabulary, 292
Behavioral objectives. *See* Instructional objectives
Behavior modification, 8
Bilingual education, 400
    cultural values, 401
Bilingual Syntax Measure, 402

Bilingualism, 400
Black English, 394
Boehm Test of Basic Concepts, 169

California Reading Test, 95
California Test of Academic Aptitude, 103
Characterization, 261, 369
Charts, 196
Classification, 322
Classifying and patterning, 151–155
Classroom organizational patterns, 8
    research into, 14–16
Cloze procedure, 135–138, 232
    oral, 164
Code switching, 400
Coefficient of reliability, 93
Cognition, 52–56
Cognitive strategies, 146
Cognitive style, 231, 411
Cognitive readiness for reading, 151
Communication, 3, 25–31, 397
Comparison-contrast, 245, 321
Comprehension, 6, 25, 126, 132
    assessment, 117–124, 132–135
    confirmation strategies, 232
    dialect barriers to, 395
    failures in, 28–31
    human, 26
    instructional activities, 256–268
    instructional resources, 268
    in reading, 6, 44
    levels, 27
    listening, 111–112
    nonverbal, 27
    prediction strategies, 227
    retelling, 117, 132
    silent reading, 132–136
    subtest, achievement, 95
Concepts, 51, 150, 279, 281

Concluding paragraphs, 250
Concrete operations, 55
Confirmation strategies, 232
Connotations, 280
Consonants, 37
Content area reading, 328
  activities, 335
  instructional resources, 354
  vocabulary, 316
Content words, 45
Context clues, 286–288
Contract learning, 13
Convergent thinking questions, 207
Conversation, 47
Cooperative InterAmerican Tests, 402
Criterion referenced tests, 92–93
Cross-grade grouping, 11

Decoding, 72, 292, 297. *See*
  Graphophonological information;
  Word recognition
Deep structure, 34
Definitional paragraphs, 249
Denotations, 280
Departmentalization, 11
Descriptive paragraphs, 249
Details, 226
Developmental Test of Visual Perception, The, 412
Dewey Classification System, 341
Diagnostic-prescriptive instruction, 13
Diagnostic teaching, 86. *See also* Analytic teaching
Dialect
  comprehension barriers to, 395
  divergent speakers, 31, 125, 394
  effects of bilingualism, 400
  instruction in, 397–400
  shared context, 397
Dictionary usage, 301
  activities, 305
Differentiated staffing, 11
Diphthongs, 39
Directed reading lesson, 203. *See also*
  Guided reading-thinking lesson
Disadvantaged learners, 396
Divergent thinking questions, 207
Durrell Listen-Read Series, 112
Dyslexia, 406

Education for All Handicapped Children Act, 407
Effect-cause, 246
Embedding, 43–44. *See also* Transformations
Encoding, 62, 72. *See also* Spelling
Encyclopedias, 342
English language
  history of, 35–36
  phonemic elements, 39–40
  phonological features, 36
  second language speakers, 31, 399
  structure, 35
  syntactic features, 40
  written, 46
English as a second language, 399
  assessment, 402
  instruction, 404
  resources, 406
  teaching of, 402
Enumeration, 243
Environment for learning, 8, 10
Equilibration, 54
ERIC, 21
Euphemisms, 280
Evaluation questions, 208
Expectancies, 146
Explanatory paragraphs, 248

Figurative language, 283, 319
Flexible learning environment, 8, 10
Formal operations, 56
Functional shift, 280
Function words, 40, 45–46. *See also* Structure words

Gates-MacGinitie Reading Tests, 95
Generalizations, 244
Goodman Model of Reading, 71–76
Grade Equivalents, 88–90
Grade level classes, 11
Grammatical acceptability, 125, 131
Grammatical function, 124, 132
Graphics
  content area, 325
  effective use, 327
  in vocabulary development, 289
  reading problems, 327
  types, 325

Graphophonological information, 35, 124, 292–301
Groups
   forming, 174–175
   functions, 172–173
   organizing, 171
Guided reading-thinking lesson, 183, 200, 231, 251
   in content areas, 328
   lesson format, 251–256
Guilford's structure-of-intellect model, 56–59

Heterogeneous grouping, 14
Hoffman Bilingual Schedule, 402
Homogeneous grouping, 12, 14
Hypothesis formation questions, 207

Illustrations. *See* Graphics
Independent reading, 183
Indexes, 340
Individualized reading, 12, 15
Inferences, 226
Instructional objectives, 184–187
   criticisms of, 185–187
Instructional program, 6–16
Instructional techniques, selection, 6
Intellectual abilities, 56–59
Intellectual development. *See* Cognition
Intelligence, 102
International Reading Association, 19
Intraclass plans, 12–13
Introductory paragraphs, 247
Iowa Silent Reading Test, 95
ITPA, 412

Juncture, 39, 46

Kernal sentences, 41–44, 163
Kindergarten, 148
Knowing, 8
Knowledge of language questions, 125–127

Language
   development, 146
   development in children, 64–66
   function, 32
   generalizations about, 31–32
   knowledge of, 125
   learning, 64, 146
   mastery, 67
   primary system, 5
   secondary system, 5
   sentence formation, 65–66
   signals to meaning, 235–251
   structure, 32
   study of, 235
   variability, 29–30
Language experience approach
   activities, 189
   basic framework, 191–192
   defined, 187
   implementing, 192
   instructional resources, 198
   resources units, 198
   thematic units, 197
Learner's needs, 10
Learning, 10, 63, 67–68
   classroom environment for, 14–16
Learning Disability
   assessment, 411
   cognitive style, 411
   deficiency concept, 410
   developmental concept, 410
   intersensory transfer, 409
   maturational lag, 410
   prevalence, 408
Learning disabled, 406
Learning models
   Behavior-Control, 8
   Discovery-Learning, 8
   Rational, 8
Learning stations, 189
Lesson format, 251–156, 300–301
Letter clusters, 297
Library of Congress Classification System, 341
Library usage, 340
Linguistic readiness for reading, 161
Linguistics, 77
Listening, 4, 111–112
Literacy, 2
Literature
   author's craft, 369–372
   balanced program, 364
   classic, 365

Literature *(continued)*
  current trends, 363
  definition, 362
  fiction, types of, 366
  new, 365
  nonfiction, 367
  objectives, 361
  plays, 368
  pluralistic nature, 362
  poetry, types of, 367–368
  uses of, 372
Literature program
  activities, 381
  library usage, 323
  selecting books, 372
Locating information, 339
Long term memory, 62, 73–74, 147
Lorge-Thorndike Intelligence Tests, 103

Main Idea, 226, 242
Map reading, 344
Memory, 59–63, 112
  long term, 62, 73–74, 147
  sensoriregister, 60
  short term, 61, 74
Metacommunication, 27
Metropolitan Achievement Tests: Reading, 95
Minority cultures, 397, 400
Miscue analysis, 113–132
  profiles, 127, 130
Miscues, 76, 113
  analyzing, 124–132
Morphemes, 45, 299

Narrative paragraphs, 248
National Council of Teachers of English, 19
Needs grouping, 13
Newspapers, 345–346
  activities, 346
Nongraded classes, 11, 14
Nonverbal communication, 25–28
Norm referenced tests, 88–91

Open classroom, 13
Organizational patterns, 11
Organizing information, 349

Otis-Lennon Mental Ability Test, 103
Outlining, 349–352
  activities, 352–353

Paragraph
  functions, 247–251
  patterns, 243–247
  reading strategies, 241–251
  vocabulary development, 289
Paralinguistic sytem, 27
Percentiles, 90
Phonemes, 36
Phonics, 293. *See also*
    Graphophonological information:
    Word recognition
Phonological component, 34, 35
Piaget's developmental theory, 52–56
Pintner General Ability Tests, 103
Pitch, 39, 46
Pivot constructions, 65
Plot, 261, 369
Predictions, 73, 201, 328
Prediction strategies, 227–235, 398
  cloze, 231
  guided reading-thinking lesson, 200–201
  inquiry lesson, 234
Prefixes, 299, 300
Preoperational stage, 55, 64
Prescriptive Reading Inventory, 97
Problem-solution, 323
Problem solving, 6, 51–52, 63, 145
  implications for education, 67–68
Proficient readers, 72
Propaganda, 323
Psycholinguistics, 32
Psychomotor readiness for reading, 159
Pupil pairs, 13
Purposes, setting of, 228, 232

Questions, 117, 207–209, 328, 330–331
  guiding, 231
  limitations to use, 208
Question-answer, 246

Readiness
  affective factors, 157

cognitive factors, 151
defined, 143
development of, 145
formal instruction, 148
instructional resources, 175
kindergarten, 148
linguistic factors, 161
misconception about, 148
psychomotor factors, 159
skill sequence, 144
tests, 168
traditional programs, 162
Readiness programs, 148
Reading
comprehension, 44
content area, 315–334
defined, 5, 72
developing strategies for, 256
disability, 408
graphics, 325–328
guided reading-thinking lesson, 200–206, 328
instructional program, 6
limitations, 3
maps, 344
miscues, 113
newspapers, 339
oral assessment, 113–132
organizing the classroom, 8
paragraph strategies, 241–251
process, 4, 69, 71, 73
professional journals, 19, 20, 21
programs, 4, 5–6
psycholinguistic model, 69–76
readiness, 143–150
reference material, 339
research, 72–73
role in society, 2
sentence strategies, 235–241
silent assessment, 132–138
teaching of, 5
tests, 94–97
textbooks, 315
uses, 3
using effective strategies, 130
Reading difficulty, 406
Reading materials, selection, 77–79
Reciting, 333
Recognition questions, 207
Referents, 279. *See also* Words
Regressions, 72–73

Rehearsal, 62
Reliability, 92
Resource units, 198
Retelling. *See* Assessment; Comprehension
Reviewing, 334

Semantic component, 35
Semantics, 33, 44, 279
Sensorimotor stage, 54
Sensory register, 60
Sentence production, 34
Sentence reading strategies, 235, 237
in vocabulary development, 289
Sequence, 226, 245, 321
Sequential Tests of Educational Progress (STEP): Reading, 95
Sight Vocabulary, 165, 296
Sign language, 27
Silent reading, 132–138
Silent Reading Comprehension: Iowa Every Pupil Test of Basic Skills, 95
Slang, 280
Socialization, 52
Speech
development, 64
production, 29
Spelling, 46, 295, 297
Spoken prose, 47
SQ3R, 330–335
SRA Achievement Series: Reading, 95
Staccato reading, 327
Standard American English, 394
Standardized tests, 88–105
Standard error of measurement, 93
Stanford Achievement Test: Reading, 95
Stanines, 91
Story organization, 257
Strategy learning lessons, 251–256, 300–301
Stress, 39, 46
Structure-of-intellect model, 56–63
Structure words, 40, 45–46
Style
characterization, 369
figurative language, 370
plot development, 369
theme development, 371
Suffixes, 300
Subject area. *See* Content area
Surface structure, 34

Surveying, 331
Syllabication, 294, 297
Symbols, 279
Syntactic component, 34
Syntax, 33

Teacher
    as resource person, 189
    being informed, 16
    human qualities, 17
    roles, 9
Team teaching, 11
Tests
    academic potential, 103
    criterion referenced, 92–97, 100
    effective use of, 101–103
    limitations, 97–101
    norm referenced, 88–89, 94
    reading, 94–97
    standardized, 88
Textbook reading, 315
    vocabulary load, 316
Thematic units, 196
Theme, 262, 371
Thesaurus, 302
Thinking, 189. *See also* Problem solving
    children's, 56
Topic, 243
Topic development, 243
Transformational grammar, 33
    and memory, 62
Transformations, 40–44, 66
Transformation subcomponent, 34
Transitional paragraphs, 249

Understanding, 155–157. *See also* Comprehension

Validity, 92, 99
Verbal communication, 25–28

Vocabulary, 277–286
    activities, 282–286
    development, 281
    difficulties, 318
    mathematics, 318, 338
    referents, 280. *See also* Words
    science, 318
    specialized, 317
    subtest, achievement, 95
    successful programs, 279
    textbook, 316
    word recognition, 286
Vocabulary development, 281–292
    instructional resources, 307
Vowels, 37
    categories of, 38
    confusion about, 39
    in word recognition, 298

Word knowledge, 278. *See also* Vocabulary
Word Order, 40–41
Word recognition, 124, 132
    dictionary usage, 301
    effective instruction, 295
    graphophonological information, 292–301
    immediate, 296
    letter clusters, 297
    mediated, 297
    morphological units, 299
    thesaurus usage, 302
    using context, 286
Words
    referents, 166, 236
    in context, 203
Writing
    nature of, 46–47
    paragraph patterns, 243–251, 317–320
    sentence patterns, 40–44

47397

Hittleman, Daniel R.

LB 1050.53 H57

Developmental reading

DATE DUE

JUL 26 '83			
AUG 15 '83			
APR 21 '86			
JUL 25 '86			
JA 1 5 '90			
FE 26 '90			
AP 11 '00			

HIEBERT LIBRARY
Fresno Pacific College - M. B. Seminary
Fresno, Calif. 93702